# INTERNATIONAL RELATIONS – THE PATH NOT TAKEN

This book is a comprehensive analysis of the relevance of international law to the conduct of international relations and foreign policy. Written by a distinguished international lawyer and academic with over 35 years of experience, this book contains a systematic treatment of both fields of study. The work serves as an introduction to contemporary theories of international relations and as a primer on international law, especially for the nonlawyer. Focusing on contemporary problems of terrorism, nuclear nonproliferation, war and peace, economic development, protection of the global environment, reform of the United Nations, democracy, and protection of human rights, this work develops the thesis that international law is a neglected tool of foreign policy that can be used to address many of today's difficult and unresolved problems. It concludes by advocating a new global order in the form of the rule of law and multilateral solidarity in addressing world problems.

Thomas J. Schoenbaum received his J.D. in law from the University of Michigan and a Ph.D. in law from the University of Cambridge. He has practiced and taught international law since 1966 and is the author of numerous books and articles on legal matters. He has held academic appointments at the University of Cambridge and the University of Warwick in the United Kingdom, and from 1983 to 2003, he was Professor and Director of the Dean Rusk Center of the University of Georgia. He is now visiting Research Professor at George Washington University Law School in Washington, D.C., and Graduate Professor at International Christian University (Tokyo). He lives in both Tokyo and Washington, D.C.

# International Relations – The Path Not Taken

## Using International Law to Promote World Peace and Security

THOMAS J. SCHOENBAUM

George Washington University (U.S.A.)

International Christian University (Japan)

CAMBRIDGE UNIVERSITY PRESS
Cambridge, New York, Melbourne, Madrid, Cape Town, Singapore, São Paulo

Cambridge University Press
40 West 20th Street, New York, NY 10011-4211, USA

www.cambridge.org
Information on this title: www.cambridge.org/9780521862806

© Thomas J. Schoenbaum 2006

First published 2006

Printed in the United States of America

A catalog record for this publication is available from the British Library.

Library of Congress Cataloging in Publication Data

Schoenbaum, Thomas J.
International relations : the path not taken : using international law
to promote world peace and security / Thomas J. Schoenbaum.
    p.   cm.
Includes bibliographical references and index.
ISBN-13   978-0-521-86280-6 (hardback)
ISBN-10   0-521-86280-9 (hardback)
ISBN-13   978-0-521-68150-6 (pbk.)
ISBN-10   0-521-68150-2 (pbk.)
1. International law.   2. International relations.
3.   Security, International.   I. Title.
KZ1250.S36   2006
341 – dc22        2006000763

ISBN-13   978-0-521-86280-6 (hardback)
ISBN-10   0-521-86280-9 (hardback)

ISBN-13   978-0-521-68150-6 (pbk.)
ISBN-10   0-521-68150-2 (pbk.)

# Contents

# Preface and Overview

This book advances a simple but highly controversial thesis: International law and international institutions must be the focal points of foreign policy and international relations for all countries. Indeed, they should now be consciously employed to create a new global order in international relations. This thesis, termed "liberal internationalism" by specialists, is controversial because international law and institutions are regarded as having failed badly in the twentieth century after World War I and both are regarded by many as weak and of marginal significance today.

In the chapters that follow, my task is to convince readers that international law and institutions have matured over the past half-century to the point where they now have a proven record of usefulness and accomplishment. Both are also admittedly far from perfect and have obvious flaws. But the question is, What to do about these flaws and failings? My argument is that the way forward is not to ignore and deprecate international law and institutions but to reform and improve them. In other words, the glass is half full, rather than half empty.

My argument assumes that states, which are still central to international society, are rational actors that have interests and seek to further those interests. But I argue that there has been a paradigm shift in how states view their interests. The traditional approach to state-interests theory is to assume that individual interests predominate. Thus, international society is composed of atomistic, self-seeking states that will only cooperate in those relatively rare cases in which there is a coincidence of interests. This view is no longer adequate to explain the world of the twenty-first century.

This new view of international relations is evident in the pronouncements of world leaders. For example, on May 12, 2005, at a gathering of African and Asian leaders in Indonesia, Prime Minister Manmohan Singh of India stated: "Peace has been said to be indivisible [quoting independent India's first leader,

Jawaharlal Nehru]. So is freedom, so is prosperity now, and so is disaster in this world that can no longer be split into isolated fragments."

State interests today generally can be grouped into three categories: (1) individual state interests, (2) state interests rooted in cooperation with closely associated and allied states, and (3) state interests held in common with all of international society.

The presence and at times the dominance of categories two and three create a new paradigm that calls for new thinking about international relations. In the pages that follow, I make the case for the predominance of these categories of interests, but some examples are in order here. Interest category two was the reason why so many states allied or associated with the United States gave their support and even sent troops to participate in the Iraq War of 2003. The pull of their relationship with the United States was strong enough to overcome their national self-interest and even to defy national public opinion.

Interest category three is also self-evident: What else explains, for example, the worldwide concern and help in the aftermath of the Indian Ocean tsunami of 2004? In the not so distant past the death or suffering of thousands of people in some remote area was simply ignored. But in the twenty-first century the world is small, and people and their well-being are interconnected as never before. Not only did virtually all states come together to contribute aid coordinated by the United Nations (UN), but individuals, companies, and nongovernmental organizations (NGOs) pitched in as never before. In the United States alone, over 130 companies contributed at least $1 million each, as well as needed products and services, and individual contributions totaled $1.2 billion (one 10-year-old elementary-school student raised $17,000 from residents of his town).

Recognition of this third category of state interests has led to a broadened vision and definition of the concept of security. Until the early 1990s, security in international relations was narrowly defined as protection from external aggression. After the end of the Cold War a new definition emerged – security may now be subdivided into at least three dimensions: state security, human security, and environmental security because international security is threatened today not only by external threats, but also by disease, hunger, chronic proverty, and environmental and ecological disasters. For example, on January 31, 1992 the U.N. Security Council adopted the following understanding of security:

The absence of war and military conflicts amongst states does not in itself ensure international peace and security. The non-military sources of instability in the economic, social, humanitarian, and ecological fields have become threats to peace and security. The United Nations membership as a whole, working through appropriate bodies, needs to give the highest priority to the solution of these matters.[1]

Thus, every state in the world has an interest in preserving peace and security, and this includes dealing with problems of world poverty, disease, deprivation of human rights, and environmental degradation. These considerations increasingly have the power to cause even powerful states to submerge individual interests to achieve larger common goals. Some recent examples of this tendency include, the U.N.'s Millennium Development Goals established in the year 2000 combating poverty; the 2005 G-8 agreement for massive debt relief for poor countries; the ongoing Doha Development trade negotiations at the World Trade Organization, and the Global Fund to Fight HIV/AIDS.

This book shows how international law and institutions are indispensable to furthering state interests in categories two and three. The power of legal rules creates legitimacy as well as order and predictability in international relations. International institutions can give rise to multilateral action that multiplies the force of policy. This multiplier effect is indispensable to the solution of world problems. International institutions and law are more stable than, say, *ad hoc* "coalitions of the willing," which tend to be fragile mirages. A prime example is what happened in Iraq in 2003–5, when the coalition of the willing assembled by the United States melted away and both the U.N. and NATO were called upon to play essential roles.

But my thesis is not only that international law and institutions are essential to interest categories two and three; they are also essential even to realize traditional state interests, category one. This is because of the interconnectedness of international society and the fact that law and institutions form a worldwide network that must be viewed as a whole. This interconnectedness raises dramatically the cost of noncooperation with international legal and institutional norms. A state that follows its own individual interest in, say, controlling the emission of greenhouse gases that contribute to climate change, will pay a price in generating a lack of cooperation and sympathy when it comes to completely different issues of policy. U.K. Prime Minister Tony Blair summarized this point nicely when he stated in January 2005: "If America wants the

---

[1] Statement adopted by the U.N. Security Council 31 January 1992, quoted from Tatsuro Kunugi, "Redressing Security Deficits in our Fragmented World: U.N. Perspectives and Beyond," in *Toward a Peaceable Future* 13, 14 *(Thomas S. Foley Institute for Public Policy, Yoichiro Murakami, Noriko Kawamura, and Shin Chiba, eds. 2005).*

rest of the world to be part of the agenda it has set, it must be part of their agenda too."[2]

The events of September 11, 2001 made international relations a central concern for Americans. In the race for president in 2004, 41 percent of voters said they based their vote on foreign policy or national security.[3] This is an historic high matched only during the years of World War II. The reelection of President George W. Bush was generally considered a confirmation of his conduct of foreign policy since 9/11. Among voters who considered terrorism the critical issue – and there were many – President Bush won by 86 percent to 14 percent.

I have timed this work to follow closely and fit in with two important recent works: (1) *The 9/11 Commission Report* (2004), a best seller, the final report of the National Commission on Terrorist Attacks upon the United States, and (2) the *Final Report of the United Nations High Level Panel on Threats, Challenges and Change* (Dec. 2004), which calls for fundamental reforms of the United Nations.

This book is a critical assessment of international relations and America's role in the world. At the end of the Cold War, the United States found itself in an unparalleled position of global power and leadership. It seemed like a dream come true: The "evil empire" of communism disintegrated like an evil monster turned into dust. The United States stood tall – the good fight was over – as the last of the totalitarian "isms" of the twentieth century was finished for good.

With the end of the Cold War, the United States was free to choose a new basis for its relationship with the rest of the world. Briefly, under the first President George Bush (Bush 41) and his Secretary of State, James Baker, a new world order was proclaimed: America would rely on cooperation with the rest of the world. The touchstone of foreign policy would be international law and international institutions like the United Nations. Because the United States no longer had to worry about "enemies" (apart from a few, rather impotent "rogue nations"), international problems could be addressed cooperatively.

Alas, this did not come to pass. Frustration with the weaknesses and limits of international law and institutions and a consciousness of the overwhelming superiority of American power have led to ever-greater unilateral action in foreign policy and what is perceived by the rest of the world as arrogance on the

---

[2] Tony Blair, Speech at the Meeting of the G-7, Davos, Switzerland, January 27, 2005.
[3] Ian Bremmer, President of the Eurasia Group, "Sept. 11 Changed How U.S. Voters Pick a President," *Financial Times*, Nov. 15, 2004.

part of the United States. For example, the administration of George W. Bush repudiated or rejected six key international agreements, including the Kyoto Protocol to curb global warming and the International Criminal Court. International institutions and new multilateral initiatives like the 2004 Framework Convention on Tobacco Control, which combats tobacco consumption and cigarette smuggling on a global scale, are treated with benign neglect. In every field of foreign affairs the United States has made important decisions alone and overridden long-established rules and institutions. Cooperation has been reduced to "he who is not with us is against us" and the formation of "coalitions of the willing." John Bolton, the Bush Administration's Ambassador to the United Nations, appointed in 2005, has written: "We should be unashamed, unapologetic, uncompromising American constitutional hegemonists."[4]

This emphasis on power and confrontation is merely a twenty-first century version of the old game of balance of power in international relations. We know from history where this game leads. There are now glimmers of the old realities on the horizon. For example, Robert Kaplan, an author close to the Bush administration, has written an article, "How We would Fight China,"[5] an account of a predicted military confrontation in the Pacific over U.S. navigation rights in the seas off the Chinese coast. In contrast, this book demonstrates that international law can be used to resolve this dispute; ironically, the United States refuses to strengthen its hand by remaining one of the only countries in the world not to accept the U.N. Convention on the Law of the Sea.

The administration of George W. Bush casts its policies in highly moralistic terms, focusing on "the war against terrorism with a global reach," as a fight against pure evil by the forces of good and of human freedom. This good versus evil dichotomy has the advantage of justifying whatever measures the side of the "good" wishes to employ. Such a policy is in reality, however, *Realpolitik* of the kind that gave us the wars and disruptions of the nineteenth and twentieth centuries. American foreign policy, particularly since 9/11, is based on narrow conceptions of U.S. power and interests. The all-out effort to protect the American people against another Al Qaeda attack has endangered broader aspects of national security – the political and economic standing of the United States.[6] American unilateralism has called into question the very

---

[4] John E. Bolton, "Is There Really Law in International Affairs?," *Transnational Law & Contemporary Problems* 1 (2000): 98.
[5] Robert Kaplan, "How We would Fight China," *Atlantic Monthly* (June 2005): 49.
[6] During the 2004 campaign for president, Republican Senator Chuck Hegel of Nebraska said: "I think both these campaigns have let down this country. The most important issue

foundation of U.S. foreign policy since the end of World War II: the Atlantic Alliance and NATO. Many formerly close allies of the United States now suggest a parting of the ways; nations that cooperate with U.S. initiatives do so reluctantly and in token fashion.

U.S. foreign policy at the beginning of the twenty-first century is in crisis. The Bush administration team appointed in 2005 includes Condoleezza Rice, Secretary of State, an architect of the policy of disassociation and dismantling of international treaties, organizations, and laws, and Alberto Gonzales, Attorney General, the source of the legally flawed and misguided policy of executive power that led to the abuses of prisoners in Afghanistan, Iraq, and Guantanamo. Diplomacy is eschewed in favor of confrontation and war with disastrous results. Of the three nations President Bush singled out in 2001 as "an axis of evil," one, Iraq, has been attacked in a war that has become a debacle, and at this writing no clear policy other than possible attack has been established to deal with the other two – North Korea and Iran, which have become more defiant than ever.

Unilateralism is married to moral relativity, the idea that because America represents "the good guys" there are no standards of conduct: Dissembling to lead the nation into war, destroying cities to save them, and disregarding international norms forbidding torture and the inhumane treatment of prisoners are all permissible. The end justifies the means, and might is right.

As a result, U.S. standing in the world has taken an enormous hit. The widespread sympathy for America after 9/11 has been replaced by aversion. Opinion polls in European NATO-allied countries show a majority hold a negative opinion of the United States. In the Arab world this reaches 90 percent even in countries like Egypt that receive billions in U.S. aid. Among formerly sympathetic people there is a mixture of anger and apprehension and talk of an "American empire."[7]

The U.S. response to homeland security has been narrowly militaristic. This was the correct response in the case of Afghanistan in 2001 – targeting the elimination of Al Qaeda training camps and Taliban collaboration with terrorists. However, the 2003 war in Iraq was clearly an overreaction, as demonstrated by the 9/11 Commission Report of 2004, which found no link between Iraq and Al Qaeda. The Iraq War has been counterproductive to the war on

to address is how to put back together America's standing in the world." In James Bennet, "Foreign Policy Split: Wide Gulf or Not?," Washington Post, Nov. 1, 2004.

[7] John B. Judis, The Folly of Empire (2004).

terror, diverting American resources and power and serving as a recruiting tool for Al Qaeda. Unfortunately, the United States is now mired in a quagmire with no foreseeable escape.[8]

The narrow-minded homeland security policy of the United States, which is based on military action abroad and a fortress mentality at home, risks creating war without end and a "clash of civilizations"[9] with Islam. Current policy neglects the need for a fundamental reassessment of U.S. policies toward the Muslim world. It is common to say that the terrorists have "hijacked" an otherwise benign religion. This is only partially correct; it ignores the many passages in the Qur'an exhorting the faithful to "slay the infidals." It also ignores the widespread political oppression and denials of human rights in countries with a majority Muslim population, especially in the Arab world. The respected NGO, Freedom House, in its 2003 report, *Freedom in the World*, discloses that of forty-one predominantly Muslim countries in the world, not one is assessed as genuinely "free" or fundamentally respectful of political rights and civil liberties. The United States, with other like-minded states, especially in Europe, should engage the Muslim world in a broad policy dialogue to instill democracy, tolerance, and liberal principles in Islam. At the same time the United States should reevaluate its own policies toward Islamic countries, especially in the Middle East, to reduce its reliance on those policies that provoke anger and to install positively beneficial policies. For example, Deputy Secretary of State Robert Zoellick has proposed the creation of a Middle East Free Trade Area with the United States by 2013.

As Pakistan's President Pervez Musharraf warned in October 2004, "Action must be taken before an iron curtain finally descends between the West and the Islamic world."[10] Al Qaeda is not a state, does not have an army, and is not even an organization in the conventional sense. It can flourish only through the continuing recruitment of people motivated by anger and hatred. The pool it can draw upon is immense: Islam is the world's fastest-growing religion, and the Middle East leads the world in the rate of population growth. Al Qaeda and its allies can only be eliminated through political change.

This book argues that there are better, more effective values upon which foreign policy may be based – the path not taken: international law and

---

[8] The CIA warned in a confidential report in December 2004 that the situation in Iraq was deteriorating and would not rebound any time soon. Douglas Jehl, "CIA Reports a Bleak Outlook in Iraq," *Washington Post*, Dec. 8, 2004.

[9] The phrase comes from Samuel Huntington's 1996 book with this title.

[10] BBC News, International Version, http://news.bbc.co.uk/2/hi/south_asia/3681290.stm

international institutions, including the United Nations. These were once important forces in U.S. international relations, and in fact the United States played an essential role in creating much of the existing structure of law and international institutions. At present, however, they are dismissed as hopelessly out of date, too constrictive, or just plain irrelevant. No U.S. political figure dares to embrace these structures because they are considered political poison. The news media in the United States, with rare exceptions, commonly ridicule or ignore them.

As a result the U.S. public is largely unaware that much of the rest of the world, including most importantly the European Union, affirms that international law and institutions are the touchstones of foreign policy and international relations. Laila Freivalds and Jack Straw, the Foreign Ministers of Sweden and the United Kingdom, respectively, put it this way:

International law is a common baseline for all international relations, and central to our efforts to build a safer and more prosperous world. The postwar multilateral system, centered on the United Nations, has helped to prevent major world conflict for 60 years. . . . International law is also a framework for constructive collective action.[11]

This book is an exploration of the implications of this idea. It concludes that, although international law and institutions are no magic bullets, or panaceas – they are rather fragile and imperfect – yet they constitute the best hope for the construction of a better world. The American embrace of these structures would reduce the dangerous split with the rest of the world and foster the gradual emergence of a "global community of shared interest."[12]

International law and the United Nations are also in crisis. Certain aspects are clearly out of date, and their relevance is under attack. As the Secretary-General of the United Nations, Kofi Annan puts it, "We have come to a fork in the road." The United States and the rest of the world face a choice: either embrace reforms or allow the whole enterprise to slip away, much as did the League of Nations after World War I.

This book argues that international law and the United Nations are indispensable to human welfare in the twenty-first century. It will be a disaster if we allow this opportunity for reform to vanish. Reform will be difficult, and it may be that the international rule of law is doomed always to imperfections. But, as a former U.N. Secretary-General put it, "The U.N. was created not to take humanity to heaven but to save it from hell." International law and

[11] "A Global Order Based on Justice," *International Herald Tribune*, Sept. 15, 2003.
[12] This is also the vision of Zbibniew Brzezinski in *The Choice* (2004), p. vii.

institutions are much like Winston Churchill's view of democracy as "the worst form of government – except for all the others that have been tried." As former Secretary of State Henry Kissinger has stated,[13] "America's special responsibility is to work toward an international system that rests on more than military power – indeed that strives to translate that power into cooperation. Any other attitude will gradually isolate us and exhaust us."

[13] Quoted in the New York Post, August 11, 2002, p. 24.

# 1 Introduction: Two Very Different Wars in Iraq

"Because of the scope of the problems we face, understanding International Law is no longer a legal specialty, it is becoming a duty."
Sandra Day O'Connor, Associate Justice of the U.S. Supreme Court,
October 27, 2004

## OPERATION DESERT STORM

On January 17, 1991, in the early morning before dawn, two U.S. Air Force Special Operations helicopters lifted off from a base in Saudi Arabia, leading a squadron of Apache gunships. As the aircraft flew low over the dark expanse of desert in southern Iraq, two radar sites came into view; they were instantly obliterated along with their unfortunate personnel.

This began *Operation Desert Storm*, a massive air campaign followed by a ground assault that chased the forces of Saddam Hussein out of Kuwait. Despite threats by the Iraqi leader that "the mother of all battles" would be a bloodbath for opposition forces and similar fears expressed by some highly placed U.S. civilian and military officials, the Gulf War of 1991 proved to be a cakewalk. The poorly trained, poorly equipped, and demoralized Iraqi army collapsed and surrendered en masse.

The result was an unalloyed success for the United States and the international community. Saddam Hussein was humiliated, and international aggression was turned back. The U.S. military performed in awesome fashion, overcoming the degradation of the war in Vietnam. Under U.N. Resolution 687, adopted by the U.N. Security Council in April 1991, Iraq was compelled to renounce in a verifiable manner all weapons of mass destruction (chemical, biological, and nuclear) and to pay billions of dollars in compensation for the damage caused by the invasion, including reparations for environmental damage.

There was widespread and enthusiastic approval of American conduct of the Gulf War both at home and abroad. U.S. prestige in the world soared to heights not reached since 1945. Domestic critics of the war, such as conservative commentator Pat Buchanan, simply admitted they were wrong. In New York City, returning U.S. troops were greeted as heroes by a confetti-showered victory parade attended by more than a million applauding admirers.

## OPERATION IRAQI FREEDOM

On March 20, 2003, at 5:30 A.M. two U.S. F-117 stealth fighter planes dropped four 2,000-pound bombs on a house in a quiet Baghdad neighborhood. Almost simultaneously, Tomahawk cruise missiles launched from U.S. ships in the Persian Gulf scored direct hits on the same site.

These were the opening shots of *Operation Iraqi Freedom*, the second Iraq war, waged for the purpose of regime change, the removal of Saddam Hussein. The first strikes of the war were a (failed) attempt to assassinate Saddam, who was reportedly meeting in the house along with his sons, Uday and Qusay. At first there was guarded jubilation among U.S. war planners that they had gotten their man, but after a few weeks, it was clear this was a Central Intelligence Agency (CIA) miscue (one of many as it turned out).

On that same day began the main offensive as a huge U.S. armored force crossed the Iraq-Kuwait border heading for Baghdad and a British column charged toward Basra, the second largest Iraqi city. Air power and over 600 cruise missiles rained death on preselected targets; U.S. and British Special Forces secured Iraqi oil fields to prevent sabotage.

The conquest of Iraq in 2003 was even easier than ousting Iraq from Kuwait in 1991. In 2003, the Iraqi Army, having learned its lesson, simply melted away. The American and British invaders mainly encountered only light opposition from paramilitary forces in pick-up trucks and from civilians. By April 9, American troops were in control of Baghdad, and, symbolically, a giant statue of Saddam was toppled by a contingent of U.S. marines in Firdos Square. Although attended by a "crowd" of only about 150 people, the TV coverage and news photos beamed around the world made this appear to be a major event. On May 1, President George W. Bush donned a flight suit and landed in an Air Force jet on the returning aircraft carrier, *Abraham Lincoln*. (The carrier, which was anchored off San Diego, was compelled to delay its return for a day in order to accommodate the president's schedule). As the president landed, a huge banner (the work of the White House Press Office) was unfurled, proclaiming "Mission Accomplished."

Two victorious wars against the same brutal dictator and his government were fought by the United States in the space of thirteen years. In both, the American commander-in-chief was a president named George Bush, the father (George H. W.) in 1991 and his son (George W.) in 2003. But the 2003 Iraq War did not achieve the rosy outcome of the 1991 Gulf War.

After the 2003 war, the United States – virtually alone – became an occupying power in a faraway land fighting a brutal insurgency consisting of Saddam Hussein loyalists, religious fundamentalists, and foreign terrorists. Although the formal end to U.S. occupation came through naming a hand-picked interim Iraqi government followed by elections in January 2005, the ultimate outcome in Iraq remains unclear. Some have described Iraq as a quagmire; General Tommy Franks, who led the invasion, called it a "catastrophic success."

**THE COSTS OF WAR**

In contrast to the 1991 Gulf War, in which casualties and collateral damage were minimized, the costs of the 2003 invasion of Iraq continue to mount. The human cost can be tallied, at least on an interim basis. American casualties (as of January 2006) stand at more than 2,100 dead and 16,000 wounded, coalition forces (chiefly British) have suffered more than 300 dead and over 1,000 wounded, and Iraqi casualties – overwhelmingly civilian – are estimated to be well over 100,000. The insurgency continues against the coalition and the new Iraqi government with no end in sight.[1]

The economic burden on the United States continues to be huge. In contrast to the 1991 Gulf War, which was paid for largely by U.S. allies, America must shoulder the cost of the 2003 war and its aftermath virtually alone. (It appears to have come as a surprise to Bush administration officials, as well as to Congress, that invading and conquering an entire country make the victor responsible for its economic future.[2]) The United States must not only pay the cost of its continuing military operations in Iraq but it must also rebuild a shattered country of 26 million people. A Rand Corporation study commissioned by the Pentagon found in April 2005 that stabilization and reconstruction

---

[1] A leaked secret CIA report on December 8, 2004 warned that the situation in Iraq was deteriorating. *Washington Post*, Dec. 9, 2004, p. A1.
[2] International humanitarian law and the Hague Regulations of 1907, to which the United States is a party, require an occupying power after a conflict to "take all measures…to insure public order and life" in the occupied territory.

issues "were addressed only very generally" and that "no planning was undertaken to ensure the security of the Iraqi people" by the Bush administration
in advance of the invasion.[3] No one knows the true cost of Iraqi reconstruction, but this item represents a significant portion of the $413 billion budget
deficit of the United States in 2004 and will continue to be a drag on the U.S.
economy far into the future.

Equally serious was the political cost of the 2003 Iraq War. The decision to
go to war produced an unprecedented upsurge in anti-American sentiment
around the world and the deepest split in history between the United States and
many traditional friends and allies. France and Germany in particular antagonized Bush administration officials by their vocal opposition, but the debates at
the United Nations in early 2003 clearly showed that a vast majority of states –
including most pro-Western democracies – joined them in urging patience
and restraint. The French Foreign Minister, Dominique de Villepin, received
a rare standing ovation from fellow U.N. Security Council delegates on February 6, 2003, when he spoke out against a precipitous American invasion.

George W. Bush, in defense of the war, continually referred to a "coalition"
of forces in Iraq and the "widespread" support his war policy received from
"thirty or forty" governments. Indeed, some thirty-five nations sent troops to
Iraq, and other nations, such as Japan, contributed humanitarian aid and personnel. All but five of these nations, however, contributed only a few hundred
troops to the coalition; these were without exception small states that desired
to show solidarity with the United States in return for past or future favors.
The weakness of their commitment made them vulnerable to terrorist threats.
Spain withdrew its support after terrorist bombings occurred aboard com-
muter trains near Madrid's Atocha Station in March 2004. Italy announced
its withdrawal plans in March 2005 after an Italian security guard was mistakenly killed by American troops. Many states, such as Poland, Thailand,
the Philippines, and South Korea, reduced or withdrew their forces in the
face of terrorist threats. Commitments such as these are worse than no support at all because the action of withdrawal under pressure only serves to
encourage future terrorism and hostage taking. Even governments that had
associated themselves with the Iraqi invasion and occupation – Britain, Italy,
and Poland – did so against the wishes of the vast majority of their population. Consequently, their support of the United States carried adverse political
consequences for their leaders. For all practical purposes, the United States
stands alone in Iraq.

[3] "Pentagon Blamed for Lack of Postwar Planning in Iraq," *Washington Post*, April 1, 2005,
p. A3.

Why such different consequences and reactions with regard to the two Iraq wars? There is no gainsaying that Saddam Hussein was a brutal, cruel ruler; that he desired to acquire weapons of mass destruction; that he attacked his neighbors, Iran and Kuwait; and that he used poison gas against the Iraqi Kurds and killed and tortured thousands. Why did the 2003 Iraq War inspire widespread international opprobrium for America?

## CONTRASTING STATECRAFT

The 1991 Gulf War was preceded by scrupulous adherence to legal and institutional norms of behavior. On August 2, 1990, the very day of Saddam's invasion of Kuwait, the United States convened an emergency session of the U.N. Security Council and obtained a resolution establishing a violation of international law by Iraq and a condemnation of the Iraqi action. Working closely with allies and diplomats from member states of the United Nations, the Bush administration obtained eleven additional U.N. Security Council resolutions condemning Iraqi actions in Kuwait, including Resolution 678 of November 29, 1990, which set a deadline for Iraqi withdrawal from Kuwait and unequivocally authorized military force, if necessary.

By contrast, the George W. Bush administration first resolved in secret to go to war in Iraq and then went to the United Nations – primarily because of the urging of Prime Minister Tony Blair – only as an afterthought. Published memos from the U.K. Foreign Office show that Bush's National Security Advisor (now Secretary of State) Condoleezza Rice solicited U.K. participation in the war as early as March 2002. Foreign Office lawyers warned almost a year before the war started that the war would be illegal under international law. In a secret March 2002 memo, Foreign Office Political Director Peter Ricketts expressed doubts about the Bush administration's war rationale: "US scrambling to establish a link between Iraq and al Qaeda is so far frankly unconvincing," he wrote. "For Iraq, regime change does not stack up. It sounds like a grudge between Bush and Saddam."[4]

Instead of negotiating at the United Nations, Bush simply presented demands with undisguised arrogance in a speech to the U.N. General Assembly on September 12, 2002. As preparations for war proceeded, the Congress in October 2002 passed a joint resolution authorizing the use of armed force in Iraq, but calling on President Bush "to obtain prompt and decisive action

---

[4] This information is contained in eight U.K. Foreign Office memos all labeled "secret" or "confidential" that were obtained by British reporter Michael Smith and published in the *Daily Telegraph* and the *Sunday Times*. *Japan Times*, June 20, 2005, p. 5.

through the United Nations Security Council." A principal purpose of this joint resolution was to strengthen the president's diplomatic efforts at the United Nations.

The support in Congress and a belated diplomatic offensive – again at the urging of the British – bore fruit when the U.N. Security Council adopted Resolution 1441 (2002), which found unanimously (both France and Germany voted in favor) that Iraq was in "material breach" of U.N. Security Council resolutions, called for verifiable disarmament, and warned that enforcement action was inevitable if Iraq did not immediately come into compliance.

As a result, by January 2003, the situation in Iraq was fully under control. U.N. Resolution 1441 and the American and British show of force had induced full, if grudging, compliance by Saddam. U.N. weapons inspection teams headed by Hans Blix were able to go everywhere they desired without restriction. Over 70 percent of Iraq was a "no fly" zone, patrolled by American and allied planes. It was checkmate.

But Washington was intent on going to war. As we now know from several memoirs, the Bush Administration had secretly determined to go to war as early as November 2001.[5] This decision had long been advocated by a group of foreign policy experts known as neo-conservatives or "neo-cons" for short. These men believed that it had been a mistake to leave Saddam Hussein in power in Iraq in 1991. They lobbied for regime change. When the Bush administration came to power in 2001, these neo-cons gained key policy positions.

So the Bush administration ridiculed the U.N. inspection teams and proceeded with its war plans. On February 5, 2003, Secretary of State Colin Powell, to his later regret, put before the assembled U.N. Security Council what he described as specific evidence of Iraqi chemical and biological weapons facilities, as well as links with Al Qaeda terrorists. Not only was this information false (the product of CIA errors), but it was also effectively rebutted at the time by France's Foreign Minister, Dominique de Villepin. (CIA mistakes should not be a surprise; this is the agency that failed to foresee such events as the collapse of the Soviet Union and the terrorist attacks of 9/11). So in March 2003, the invasion of Iraq went forward. In a clear demonstration of its contempt for the United Nations, on March 20 the Bush administration simply sent a one-page letter to the president of the U.N. Security Council informing him that "military operations had begun in Iraq to secure compliance" with Security Council resolutions and that "these operations are necessary."

---

[5] The sequence of events is summarized in the book by Stefan Halper and Jonathan Clarke, *America Alone* (2004), and in Bob Woodward's book, *Plan of Attack* (2004).

## REASONS FOR GOING TO WAR

The two wars in Iraq were conducted for very different reasons. The reason for going to war in 1991 was clear from the beginning: to expel the Iraqi army from Kuwait after the illegal invasion of that country on the orders of Saddam Hussein. When this mission was accomplished by the international coalition, President George H. W. Bush ceased military operations. Although U.S. forces alone could have easily taken Baghdad and ended the tyranny of Saddam, President Bush refused, saying that this action was beyond the mandate of the U.N. Security Council.

In contrast, the reasons for the 2003 Iraq War are somewhat unclear. The reason given at the time of the invasion was the necessity to eliminate Iraqi weapons of mass destruction (WMD) – Saddam's chemical and biological arms and his suspected nuclear weapons program. However, we now know that U.S. intelligence agencies were – in the words of President Bush's own investigative commission – "dead wrong"[6] in their prewar assessments of Iraq's WMD programs. It has also come out that, before the 2003 war, the Bush administration routinely brushed aside or ignored what turned out to be the correct assessments of the U.N. arms inspectors and the International Atomic Energy Agency that Saddam's WMD programs had been dismantled.[7]

A second reason for the war that was equally without foundation was that Saddam was connected with Al Qaeda and Islamist terrorism. But Congressional studies have turned up no evidence of any prewar connection between Saddam and Al Qaeda, and paradoxically, the American-led invasion in 2003 opened the way for associates of Osama Bin Laden, such as the cruel and infamous Abu Musab Al Zarqawi, to operate in Iraq. Bin Laden was reportedly surprised by the success of the Iraqi insurgency and offered his support.

Faced with the necessity to justify the 2003 war after the fact, the Bush administration cites Saddam's brutality and tyranny. This is certainly correct, but the question remains whether the United States has a right to invade any country that is ruled by a brutal tyrant. And much of Saddam's brutality – such as his chemical weapons attack on the town of Halabja in 1988, which killed 5,000 Iraqi Kurds – occurred in the 1980s when the U.S. government was secretly helping Saddam.

---

[6] "Data on Iraqi Arms Flawed, Panel Says," *Washington Post*, April 1, 2005, p. A1. The Presidential Commission further called the intelligence data on Iraq "either worthless or misleading" and "riddled with errors." This resulted in "one of the most damaging intelligence failures in recent American history" in the words of the Commission.

[7] "Work of U.N. Arms Inspectors Was Ignored by U.S. before Iraq War," *Washington Post*, April 4, 2005, p. A3.

A final reason advanced for the 2003 Iraq War was the need to introduce democracy into the Middle East – part of President Bush's effort to shake up the undemocratic regimes in the region and to free up the democratic impulses of the Muslim world. Certainly the spread of democracy and freedom is a noble cause, but the question remains whether invasion is the proper or even the most effective method.

## INTERNATIONAL LAW AND INSTITUTIONS

Should international law play any role in important foreign policy decisions, such as the resort to war? In 1990–1 President George H. W. Bush scrupulously adhered to international law in his decision to use force. From the beginning, the U.N. Security Council was engaged, and legal norms were considered and kept.

By contrast, international law and institutions were largely bypassed in the Iraq War of 2003. The U.N. Security Council was ultimately brushed aside, and as reported in the British press, when Lord Goldsmith, the U.K. Attorney General, raised legal objections to the war, the head of British intelligence, Sir Richard Dearlove, told him that war was "inevitable" and that the legal case for war was being "fixed 'round the policy'" by the Americans. In other words, the legal case for war was assembled after the decision to invade had been taken.[8]

Many people, including the vast majority of international lawyers as well as U.N. Secretary-General Kofi Annan, judged the 2003 Iraq War to be contrary to international law.[9] The U.N. Charter states the basic rule that the international use of force is illegal except in self-defense (broadly defined and including collective self-defense) or under Security Council authorization. Should that make any difference?

President Bush does not believe so. On October 9, 2004, the President said:

We did not find the [weapons of mass destruction] stockpiles we thought were there. But . . . Saddam Hussein was gaming the oil-for-food program to get rid of sanctions. And why? Because he had the capability and knowledge to rebuild his weapon programs. And the great danger we face in the world today is that a terrorist organization could end up with weapons of mass destruction. Knowing what I know today, I would have made the same decision. The world is safer with Saddam in a prison cell.

---

[8]  Prime Minister Tony Blair reportedly agreed to go to war as early as April 2002. "MI6 Chief Told PM: Americans 'Fixed' Case for War," *Sunday Times*, March 20, 2005, p. 5.

[9]  See the articles cited in Further Readings at the end of this chapter.

Is the President's logic persuasive? Is it necessary at times to disregard law? The decision to go to war is the most important, most fateful decision that can be made by any nation or political leader. From even a cursory study of history, it is evident that warfare has existed since earliest times and can be said to be endemic to the human condition. In an attempt to place some limit on war, Christian writers, such as Augustine and Thomas Aquinas, influenced by the Roman lawyer Cicero, developed the theory of *just war* – that every war must have a just cause, a wrong suffered that must be corrected. This theory of just war was developed into a rule of what was considered "natural law" by European thinkers, such as Francisco de Vitoria (1557), Alberico Gentile (1598), and Hugo Grotius (1624). According to their formulations, warfare is just only in response to a "culpable offense" that endangers social values to an extreme degree.

The imprecision of this rule of just warfare is obvious, and it accomplished little. In the eighteenth and nineteenth centuries, war was considered to be outside the boundaries of law and totally in the domain of politics. The most famous expression of this is Clausewitz's (1832) famous dictum that war is simply "politics by other means." In its extreme form this was the idea that war is the natural function of a state and a prerogative of sovereignty. Recourse to war was accordingly the way for a powerful state to enforce its will and a preferred method of settling international disputes.

Only in the twentieth century were serious attempts again made to surround the decision to go to war with legal constraints. The first two major attempts were the League of Nations (1919) and the General Treaty of the Renunciation of War (1928), also known as the Kellogg-Briand Pact. Although both were spectacular failures, another attempt was made at the end of World War II with the founding of the United Nations. This time the attempt was made not only to establish norms of conduct but also to create institutional structures for peace enforcement and for the peaceful resolution of international disputes. We still live with these legal rules and institutions. Obviously they are far from perfect, but should they be abandoned or reformed?

## MULTILATERALISM VERSUS UNILATERALISM

The 1991 Gulf War is a case study in multilateral cooperation, the observance of international law, and the constructive use of international institutions. By contrast, the 2003 Iraq War is an example of unilateral statecraft by the United States as superpower to lay down the law, declare that "anyone who not with us is against us," and assemble "coalitions of the willing" – allies that agree to go along with a predetermined U.S. policy.

The statecraft of the two Iraq wars presents contrasting paradigms that vividly depict the fundamental choice the United States must make when it comes to many key policy questions: Should the United States in the conduct of international relations observe international law and work through international institutions, such as the United Nations? Or should the United States decide the best course of action (or inaction), inform the international community, and assemble "coalitions of the willing"? The first of these options is usually termed multilateralism, whereas the second is unilateralism. Although all nations in theory have this option, only the United States, by reason of its sole superpower status, is in the position of having the luxury of consistently ignoring the international community on important questions without suffering serious consequences.

## THE PATH NOT TAKEN

In the conduct of international relations there is no generally accepted authority or criteria by which to judge whether a decision or action is right or wrong. Comparing the decisions to use force in Iraq in 1991 and 2003 raises difficult and puzzling questions. Which decision was correct – the decision against regime change in 1991 or the decision in favor in 2003, the decision to respect international law and the United Nations in 1991 or to override them in 2003?

These paradigm cases show, however, that despite the many complexities of international politics, there is consistently one broad choice to be made in virtually every case: whether to follow the path of international law, international institutions, and multilateralism or whether to ignore or dismiss this path in favor of unilateral action. Of course this is not always a stark either-or choice. Especially for the United States, unilateral action cannot be totally excluded. What matters, however, is the presumption employed and the effort expended. Should there be a broad consensus that unilateralism should be highly exceptional? Or should the United States as the sole superpower rely on unilateralism that uses multilateral institutions only when convenient?

Since the end of the Cold War, American foreign policy has increasingly taken the unilateralist path. International law and institutions are viewed either as obstacles or as follow-on conveniences to be addressed as aids to a predetermined policy. As a result many important international initiatives are proceeding without U.S. participation or are seriously impeded by U.S. policies. Some important examples include the International Convention on the Law of the Sea, the International Criminal Court, the Kyoto Protocol for the control of global warming, many international human rights agreements, and programs for the reduction of international poverty and disease. American policymakers show increasing distrust and contempt for the United Nations. Disregard of international regimes is even considered a badge of honor. For example, U.N. Ambassador John Bolton was quoted as saying that his signing of a document formally notifying U.N. Secretary-General Kofi Annan of the U.S. decision to withdraw from the International Criminal Court was "the happiest moment of my government service."

This book analyzes *the path not taken*: how adherence to international law, international institutions, and multilateralism offers a more effective way to deal with international problems in the globalized world of the twenty-first century. President George W. Bush has called for the establishment of democracy and liberty all over the world; this is a noble goal, but is by itself not enough. States that love and respect democracy and freedom must join to establish the rule of law in international relations. This involves respect for international institutions even without any formal surrender of sovereignty.

The rule of law and respect for international institutions can become the touchstone of international relations in the twenty-first century because, for the first time in human history, people and nations all over the world have shared goals and interests: an end to violence and war, economic prosperity, environmental protection, reduction of poverty and disease, and protection of human rights. This is not to deny the separate interests of states as well, but in our time shared interests increasingly dominate as never before in human history.

Of course, international law and institutions are far from perfect, but it is important to reform, rather than ignore or simply criticize them. This book offers suggestions for reform as well.

The chapters that follow make the case for *liberal internationalism* as the basis for the conduct of international relations. The pedigree for liberal internationalism hearkens back to Woodrow Wilson and the years following the First World War. Despite this association, it has long had a bad name among diplomats and international relations experts. Derided as utopianism and hopelessly naïve, liberal internationalism did not survive the cataclysm of the 1930s and World War II.

The premise of this work is that liberal internationalism represents the best way forward in the twenty-first century and that international law and international institutions, preeminently including the United Nations, should be the touchstones of foreign policy decision making. The case for liberal internationalism rests upon the idea that international law and institutions have attained a certain maturity so that, although they are far from perfect, they can be improved and are better than any alternative. The chapters that follow advance the following three broad ideas:

1. International law is a comprehensive body of rules, standards, and procedures that, if followed, is capable of establishing order in international affairs. International law is a comprehensive normative system, and legal principles now govern every important international issue; this law is derived from long experience and the consent of the international community of states. International law is capable of bringing the rule of law to the international order without world government and is consistent with the preservation of national sovereignty.

2. International institutions are functioning in virtually every area of international relations and provide a basis for enhanced cooperation among states. Even when flawed, international institutions are capable of constructive action that in most cases will be superior to unilateral action. An objection frequently advanced for using international institutions is that member states always vote their own interests. This is a simplistic view that assumes states have no common interests or that individual state interests are always dominant. To the contrary, in the twenty-first century, there is increasingly a core of interests – peace and security, alleviation of poverty, human rights, protection of the environment, and economic growth – that is common to all states and that outweighs separate state interests. This core of common interests is growing as a result of the phenomenon of globalization. The threats we face today are also interconnected. No state is immune from the impact of disease, war, poverty, terrorism, or environmental degradation anywhere in the world. As a result, members of international institutions have growing incentives to follow these common interests or to compromise.

3. There is a growing sense of responsibility among members of the U.N. Security Council with respect to peace and security. We must not assume that the U.N. Security Council and other international institutions are incapable of correcting past errors; lessons have been learned. This is reflected in the actions of the Security Council since the terrorist attacks of 9/11. Crucial resolutions have been passed dealing with such matters as terrorism, nuclear proliferation and weapons of mass destruction, the withdrawal of Syrian troops from Lebanon, Iraq, Afghanistan, human rights and armed conflict in Africa, and peacekeeping missions around the world. The Security Council is increasingly active: An average of sixty resolutions have been passed each year since 2002, and vetoes are now extremely rare. All resolutions are legally binding and must be respected by all states.

America has rightly adopted as a goal for the twenty-first century the end to tyranny and the spread of democracy and freedom. But an international order based on justice and liberty is impossible without the rule of law. And the rule of law will not arise spontaneously and cannot be imposed. It can only come about through respect for and participation in appropriate international institutions.

**FURTHER READINGS**

Bob Woodward, *Plan of Attack* (2004).

Stephen Tanner, *The Wars of the Bushes* (2004).

Philippe Sands, *America and the Breach of Legal Rules* (2005).

William Shawcross, *Allies, the United States, Britain, Europe in the War in Iraq* (2003).

For a detailed analysis of international law and the Iraq wars, see Sean Murphy, "Assessing the Legality of Invading Iraq," 92 *Georgetown Law Journal* 173 (2004); A. V. Lowe, "The Iraq Crisis: What Now? 52 *International and Comparative Law Quarterly* 859 (2003); and the contributions to Agora, "Future Implications of the Iraq Conflict," 97 *American Journal of International Law* (2003): 553–642.

*Report to the President: Commission on the Intelligence Capabilities of the United States Regarding Weapons of Mass Destruction*, co-chaired by Laurence Silberman and Charles Robb (2005).

F. de Vitoria, *De Indis et De Jure belli relectiones*, E. Nys, ed.; J. P. Bate, trans. *Classics of International Law* (Washington DC, Carnegie Institution 1917).

Alberico Gentile, *De Jure Belli* 1612 (1933).

H. Grotius, *De Jure Belli ac Pacis Libri Tres* (Kelsey trans. 1913).

Carl von Clausewitz, *On War* (Graham trans. 1908).

Onuma Yasuaki, *A Normative Approach to War: Peace, War, and Justice in Hugo Grotius* (1993).

# 2 The Twenty-First Century – The End of History or a New Beginning?

## AFTER THE "END OF HISTORY"

In the waning years of the twentieth century, Francis Fukuyama famously argued that the end of the Cold War and the collapse of the Soviet Union amounted to "the end of history."[1] After the collapse of the Soviet Union in 1991, only one superpower remained – the United States of America – and one international system was indisputably on top: liberal (free-market) democracy. According to this idea, the twenty-first century would be a mopping-up operation: Politics would consist of dealing with largely technical problems of satisfying consumer demands, advancing technology to better the human condition, and dealing with environmental concerns. Americans in particular would have no cause to worry about nasty international problems. After all, the mightiest government the world had ever known protected us.

Such cozy security lasted through the decade of the 1990s, when we wallowed in the irrational exuberance of the stock markets and President Clinton's sexual indiscretions. We celebrated the end of the century one year early, the night of December 31, 1999, so we could breathe a sigh of relief when our computer-driven society did not crash under the weight of the leap to the year 2000 and the world did not come to an end. The true beginning of the new millennium, January 1, 2001, was an anticlimax that did not disrupt our *fin de siecle* partying mood.

Then came the real end of the century and a new beginning: September 11, 2001. We knew immediately that the world had changed and that frightening

---

[1] Francis Fukuyama, *The End of History and the Last Man* (1992). Apologies to Professor Fukuyama for this overly simplistic characterization of his book, which is a subtle and profound study of the significance of the end of the Cold War. The reader is urged to seriously peruse this book, a blend of political and historical analysis.

14

new realities were afoot. The terrorist attacks of that day, additional terrorist attacks all over the world, wars in Afghanistan and Iraq, and continuing strife in the Middle East and elsewhere made clear that we had had our heads in the sand. The new world after the fall of communism was not any safer. The United States, for all its power and might, is not capable alone of combating or even managing the threats to human well-being that hang over us. Even the government of George W. Bush, which at first acted unilaterally and simply made demands on the international community, learned the hard way that solving world problems is simply beyond the capacity of any one nation, even the most powerful.

Global terrorism, for all its horrors, is only one of the difficult problems in the world of the twenty-first century. World peace and security are also threatened by hundreds of actual and potential violent conflicts on every continent and their underlying ethnic, social, or economic causes. Globalization means that the economic well-being of every nation, including the United States, is inextricably tied to events and policies in other parts of the globe. Environmental problems, for the first time on human history, are truly global in scope and magnitude. Poverty in developing countries and the enormous divide between rich and poor nations threaten world stability. Ensuring the worldwide observance of human rights is a global undertaking of great importance. Combating hunger and diseases such as HIV/AIDS will take a global effort. Finally, we must manage an unprecedented increase in population. During the twentieth century, global population went from 1.6 billion in 1900 to almost 6.1 billion in 2000. During the twenty-first century – barring catastrophe – human population growth will continue to reach about 9 to 10 billion by mid-century, and virtually all of the increase will occur in developing countries where poverty is endemic.

This enumeration, which merely scratches the surface of what faces humankind in the new century, is daunting. What is new about the times in which we find ourselves is that, although domestic and regional concerns have not gone away, a new and terrifying set of global problems confront us. All are beyond the capacity of any one nation, even the most powerful. Our world, which for political action is organized around approximately 193 nation-states, has no real success or even experience in dealing with problems of this scope.

The key questions that we face as a human community in this era of globalization are: How can we deal with these unprecedented problems? Are we prepared? If not, what should we be doing to prepare ourselves? One thing is clear: We must not bury our heads in the sand and hope for the best. This is what made 9/11 unavoidable. In retrospect there were plenty of warning signs

that were missed. We know in our hearts that the events of September 11 need
not have happened. We must prepare now the strategies and the institutions
we need to deal with such problems before they overwhelm us.

## LESSONS FROM THE PAST: THE TWENTIETH CENTURY

The twentieth century was bloody and brutal beyond all imagining. But at
its beginning this was not at all apparent; the dominant chord was instead an
absolute faith in human progress. This faith in science and technology was
particularly evident: A popular collection of essays published in 1901, *Progress
of the Century*, detailed advances in physics, chemistry, and biology; technical
advances in photography, cinematography, transportation, and communication; and revolutions in medicine, agriculture, and food sciences. New social
sciences, such as economics, sociology, and politics, held out the promise of
progress in human relations that would match the sciences. The "civilized"
areas of the globe were at peace, and the newly created states of Italy and
Germany had brought a new stability to Europe. Great cities, such as New
York, London, Paris, Vienna, and Berlin, had developed and were thriving.
Through "colonialism," the progress of civilization would be brought to the
impoverished and backward masses in other parts of the world. To be sure,
there were voices of dissent, such as Friedrich Nietzsche and Karl Marx, but
most people were convinced that the future was bright (see "Prelude to the
Twentieth Century").

### The First World War

The relative stability and peace of the early twentieth century in Europe
were a mirage. International relations were premised on a balance of power
system, which broke apart in the hot summer of 1914. The spark that set off
the crisis was the assassination of the heir to the Hapsburg throne as ruler of
Austria-Hungary, Archduke Franz Ferdinand, by a Bosnian Serb nationalist.
The European alliances quickly swung into action, and on August 1, Germany
declared war against Russia. The Triple Alliance fought the Triple Entente
(each with its African and Asian colonies), and other states took sides. Before
it was over most European states – as well as Turkey, Japan, China, Siam
(Thailand), Australia, New Zealand, Canada, the United States, and various
Latin American states – joined the carnage.

This was the First World War, also known as the Great War. At the outset
there was popular enthusiasm and jingoistic patriotism as millions of men

## PRELUDE TO THE TWENTIETH CENTURY: AN EXPLOSIVE MIX OF BAD IDEAS

The tragic wars of the twentieth century took place against a background of evil ideologies that were rampant 100 years ago. Some of these were as follows:

■ Nationalism – belief in the inherent superiority of one's nation or ethnic group

■ Racism – belief in the inherent superiority of people of a certain race

■ Imperialism – the idea that certain nations or peoples may properly dominate or control other nations or peoples

■ Statism – the idea that the state is the highest and supreme manifestation of human destiny

■ Social Darwinism – the idea that biological evolution has a socioeconomic counterpart and that "survival of the fittest" (a phrase not used by Charles Darwin) characterizes the evolution of international society

■ Class struggle – the idea that conflict between different classes of people is inevitable and endemic in human society

■ *Realpolitik* – the aggressive assertion of the state and national interests in international relations

*The Manifesto of Futurism*, published in Paris in 1909 by Filippo Tommaso Marinetti, assembled these ideas and declared: "We will glorify war – the world's only hygiene – militarism, patriotism, the destructive gesture of freedom-bringers, beautiful ideas worth dying for."

(and for the first time significant numbers of women) mobilized for the fight. All were convinced that (1) their side would win and (2) it would be over quickly. For the first time in history battles were fought on land, sea, and in the air. Modern weapons of conflict included airplanes, tanks, submarines, machine guns, and terrible devices, such as flamethrowers, trench mortars, and poisonous gas. Incredibly, these coexisted with cavalry on horseback, transport by donkey cart, and, for the French, their traditional blue coats, red kepi, and trousers. By December 1914, it was clear that neither side could prevail, but there was no way out. Futile and senseless killing by soldiers facing each other in trenches went on for years – in the battle of the Marne, at Ypres, at Verdun, and the battle of the Somme and Passchendaele, all on the infamous Western front. In places less well known the killing was just as real. Political leaders were helpless to stop the fighting. Only the entry of Americans into the war in 1917 on the side of the Allies turned the tide. The end finally came on November 11, 1918, a date still known as Armistice or Remembrance Day in many countries.

The human and material tolls of the war were horrendous. Between 9.4 and 11 million people were killed, most of them soldiers, but almost a million civilians died. Probably three times those numbers were wounded. Towns and cities in northern France, Belgium, Poland, and western Russia were in ruins. European economies were in shambles. The war was financed on borrowed funds, mainly from abroad. Every European family and every aspect of life were adversely affected. Technology, which before the war was associated with human progress, was now linked with death and destruction.

Yet even this does not begin to tell the true costs. The First World War had a malignant effect on the world for the entire century, and it affects us still. Four European empires – the Ottoman (the Balkans), Hapsburg (Austria-Hungary), Romanov (Russia), and Hohenzollern (Germany) – passed into history, bringing not only a host of new nations into existence but also many dark forces. Ensuing political violence created the Soviet Union and paved the way for fascism, communism, totalitarianism, and anti-Semitism. War weariness did not prevent widespread hatred and cries for vengeance. With the Treaty of Versailles (1919) Germany lost its colonies and was saddled with huge reparation payments. The European economies could not recover from the burdens of death, devastation, and debts. Europe lost its role as the leader of Western civilization, probably forever.

Even today we wonder how the First World War could have happened. The contesting states were the most advanced, most civilized, and richest on earth. They had willingly assumed the burden of teaching the "brown, black, and yellow races" of the world the wonders of science and civilization. Yet this advancement was the instrument of their own destruction. Historians are still debating whether the war was purely accidental, deliberate, or inevitable. Those who believe the war to be accidental focus on the miscalculations: Germany and Austria did not believe France and especially Britain would enter the war, and Austria was expecting only a local conflict in the Balkans. Other historians say the war was deliberate, blaming Germany. A third school of thought is that the war was the inevitable product of the military and economic competition and the colonial rivalries of the European system.

Why was not war prevented? Surely, leaders and even ordinary people were aware of the growing destructiveness of modern weapons. Were international relations and institutions so rudimentary that, whatever the cause or causes, such a tragedy could happen? The answer is yes, but this requires explanation.

## The Balance of Power System

The basic international system of order 100 years ago was known as *balance of power*. In this system, the nation-state was supreme and sovereign. Sovereignty means that there is not and cannot be any higher power. Thus, in 1905 international law meant only that a state might consent to a limit on its powers of action, but this consent could also be revoked at any time. The only real constraint on a state under this system was the opposing power of other states. Order was maintained only if opposing powers or blocs of alliances were roughly equal, economically and militarily. If and when inequalities developed, there was the danger of collapse, friction, or war.

This leads to a great paradox of the international balance of power system – it is sometimes necessary to make war to prevent war! The idea here is that in no event can the balance of power be allowed to go out of alignment. But the only remedy for misalignment is warfare. The truth of this paradox was clearly expressed by world leaders of the time. William Gladstone, the great liberal British prime minister of the nineteenth century, said, "However deplorable wars may be, they are among the necessities of our condition. And there are times when justice, when faith, when the welfare of mankind, require a man not to shrink from the responsibility of undertaking them. And if you undertake war, so also you are often obliged to undertake measures which may tend to war."[2] From this idea it is a small step indeed to espouse the famous dictum of Carl von Clausewitz (1832) that war is simply "a continuation of policy by other means." An academic writer of the time, Oxford don Geoffrey Woolsey, wrote in 1899:

To states, by the divine constitution of society, belong the obligations of protecting themselves and their people, as well as the right of redress, and even perhaps of punishment. To resist injury, to obtain justice, to give wholesome lessons to wrongdoers for the future, are prerogatives deputed by the Divine King of the world to organized society, which, when exercised aright, cultivate the moral character and raise the tone of judging throughout mankind. (Woolsey, Introduction to International Law 184 (5th ed. 1899)).

This is a statement of a divine right of warfare accorded to the state.

A second paradox of the balance of power system showed itself during the prosecution of the First World War. The German sociologist, Max Weber, pointed out in an essay published in 1915 that war, once begun, produces a fear of the consequences of a subsequent peace. "The prolongation of the war,"

---

[2] Quotation from Mr. Gladstone's Midlothian speech (no date given) in F. E. Smith, *International Law* 13, n. 2 (London, 1900).

he wrote, "is entirely the result... of a fear of peace.... To a far greater extent
still... people are afraid of the domestic political consequences of the disillusionment that will inevitably set in, given the foolish expectations that have
now run riot."[3]

Opposing the balance of power system before the war were only an incipient
system of international law and a mechanism for the peaceful resolution of
international disputes. In 1899 and again in 1907, diplomatic representatives
of the major powers met at The Hague, in Holland, to conclude international
agreements known as The Hague Peace Conference. The idea behind these
initiatives was the prevention of war and the creation of an "age of peace."
To this end there were proposals and agreements to reduce weaponry and to
submit international controversies to binding arbitration. A Permanent Court
of Arbitration was set up at The Hague in 1899. But most people at the time
were skeptical. Oxford Professor F. E. Smith wrote in his book, *International
Law*, published in 1900, " I do not think that accurate observers will dispute
the gloomy conclusion that the prospects of universal peace have seldom been
less encouraging."[4] Unfortunately, he was correct. The international system
of the time placed no real limits on a sovereign state's freedom to wage war.

## The Interwar Period

The cultural impact of the First World War was enormous. The unquestion-
ing faith in human reason and scientific progress that had been ascendant
since the period of the eighteenth century known as the Enlightenment was
no longer possible. The German historian Oswald Spengler published a book
aptly titled, *The Decline of the West* (1918). The greatest poets of the age, T. S.
Eliot and W. B. Yeats, wrote, respectively, about "The Wasteland" and "the
center cannot hold." Strange new artistic movements flourished – dadaism,
surrealism, and the "fauves" (wild ones). Pessimism was in vogue: The English
writer Robert Graves wrote a classic account of his experiences in the army,
*Goodbye to All That*. Sigmund Freud's theories of irrational and uncontrol-
lable drives in the unconscious mind captured and expressed the new disillusionment. Searing novels about the irrationality and horror of war appeared –
for example, Ernest Hemingway's *A Farewell to Arms* (1929) and Erich Marie
Remarque's *All Quiet on the Western Front* (1932).

The economic situation all over the world in the interwar period went
from bad to worse. Unemployment and inflation were rampant and beyond

---

[3]  Max Weber, *Gesammelte Politische Schriften*, page 48, essay entitled "Zur Frage des Frieden-
schliessens" (1920). [translation by the author].
[4]  F. E. Smith, International Law 13 (1900).

the control of governments. Even the United States, which produced the only booming economy in the world in the 1920s, fell into the Great Depression. As the stock market crashed and American workers lost their jobs, the Federal Reserve Bank of New York raised interest rates – exactly the wrong medicine – and the situation worsened. Desperate to do something, the United States led the way in restricting international trade, which made things even worse. In Germany, for example, there was a glimmer of hope in 1929, but by 1931 4.4 million people were unemployed, and this number increased to over 6 million by 1933. In the Far East, Japan was cut off from needed sources of raw materials.

The disillusionment, economic chaos, and *revanchism** created political upheavals. Italy was the first democratic state to dissolve into fascism when Benito Mussolini gained absolute power in 1924. Dictatorships also came to power in Spain and Portugal. In 1933 Adolph Hitler and the Nazis took over in Germany. In the Soviet Union, Josef Stalin consolidated totalitarian communist power in the 1930s through bloody purges. In 1936, Spain slid into civil war followed by dictatorship. In East Asia, Japan offered proof of its big power status by moving into Manchuria and China. By 1938 when Nazis operatives engineered the annexation (*Anschluss*) of Austria by Germany, the stage was set for a new war. In a classic book published in 1939, the specialist in international relations, E. H. Carr, characterized the interwar period as *The Twenty Years' Crisis.*

Once again attempts to create international institutions and an international order to forestall war were weak and inadequate. U.S. President Woodrow Wilson's idealistic vision of "Fourteen Points" and the creation of a League of Nations to keep the peace were rejected by the U.S. Senate, and the League, which set up shop in Geneva, Switzerland, lacked all credibility. And the League did not *prohibit* resorting to war, but only required that certain procedures be undertaken by a state before declaring war. The only major effort to restrain war was the Kellogg-Briand Pact of 1928, signed by twenty-six states and still in force; it was the first international instrument to prohibit war as an instrument of foreign policy. Of course these structures were far from adequate to prevent the outbreak of the Second World War in 1939.

## The Second World War and Postwar Developments

The horrors of the Second World War outstripped all imagination. As many as sixty million people may have perished throughout the world – we will never know the true toll. Millions of Jews and other minorities were systematically eliminated in the Holocaust. Much more even than in the First World War,

---

* A term derived from the French word *revanche*, "revenge," meaning a political campaign to regain lost territories or lost prestige.

## THE RISE AND FALL OF EUROPEAN HEGEMONY

Beginning about the year 1000, Europe began to emerge from the centuries of invasions and unrest that marked the end of the Roman Empire. Building upon its heritage of Christianity and classical culture, and blessed by a warming climate and freedom from outside invasion, the European population roughly doubled by the year 1250, and new technologies created a vibrant new economic life. Urban life, commerce, art and architecture revived and flourished. The greatest minds of the age produced a magnificent synthesis of belief in the Christian God and classical Greco-Roman cultural values. This was the view that human reason and revealed religion lead to the same fundamental truths. Thomas Aquinas (1223–74) penned still unsurpassed systematic accounts (appropriately entitled *Summas*) of the consistency of human and divine knowledge. The *Divine Comedy* of Dante Alighieri (1265–1321) provided a comprehensive guide to the universe and precise instruction on the purpose of human life. The age produced the idea of the rule of law (which was developed in two forms: the common law of England and the civil law derived from the law of ancient Greece and Rome) and the idea of the university as an indispensable institution for the discovery, preservation and purveyance of knowledge.

Increased study of classical culture helped produce the European Renaissance, which not only created new forms of art and literature but also a new spirit of scientific inquiry. The resulting discoveries transformed our conception of the world. Europe led the way in the physical exploration of the planet and in making new scientific findings such as the discoveries of Copernicus, Galileo and Newton. These were matched in the political realm by the invention of the modern state and the concept of sovereignty.

The new scientific methods and discoveries culminated in the European Enlightenment, a new faith in the ability of human reason to produce progress in all aspects of human life – especially the political, social and economic spheres. The Enlightenment in turn produced the French Revolution with its new emphasis on liberty equality and human rights. France, the superpower of the age, violently overthrew the old order; but the revolution was captured by excesses, the Reign of Terror (1792–94) and the wars of Napoleon (1795–1815).

After the defeat of Napoleon, the five great powers, Great Britain, Prussia, Russia, France, and Austria, created a new order, the Concert of Europe, in 1815, a loose alliance to restore the old order and to maintain a balance of power among European states. This effort was soon undermined by the continuing influence of the liberal ideas of the French Revolution and the economic liberalism of the first Industrial Revolution. Socioeconomic grievances produced popular uprisings in European capitals in 1830 and especially 1848. But, disgruntled revolutionaries were no match for the governments, liberalism was suppressed, and the old order emerged largely intact.

The last half of the nineteenth century witnessed both the apogee of European hegemony and the birth of ideas and events that would cause Europe's downfall. The benign national pride of the early nineteenth century gave way to an expansive belief in nationalistic superiority; the Darwinian idea of survival of the fittest became justification for scientific racism and the superiority of the white race. The collaborative diplomacy of the Concert of Europe yielded to *realpolitik*, the aggressive assertion of national power and superiority. War became a moral duty of statecraft: the Crimean War (1853–56), the Austro-Prussian War (1866), and Franco-Prussian War (1870–71) led to the defeat of Russia, Austria and France, and the creation of the modern states of Germany and Italy. Great Britain and Germany emerged as the new superpowers.

By the beginning of the twentieth century, the remarkable economic prosperity of the second Industrial Revolution masked an explosive mixture of unresolved social, ethnic and class conflicts within, and nationalism, imperialism and *realpolitik* in the foreign policies of European states. The stage was set for the conflagrations of 1914 and 1939, which ended European hegemony.

Nevertheless, Europe in the twenty-first century has emerged as a "softpower" leader through emphasizing the neccessity of international relations rooted in the rule of law, justice and international institutions. The European Union and other common European institutions have remarkably ended past internecine conflict and knitted together diverse peoples and cultures. The European Union has proved its worth as the correct political formula for a diverse and dynamic continent. But the EU is not destined to evolve into a super state. Rather the EU will continue to evolve into an umbrella organization that requires and promotes deep and positive political and economic changes in its member states, but provides shifting coalitions and options. For example, the single currency and the Schengen zone of passport-free travel are options taken up by some but not all members. With the failure of the proposed European Constitution, an EU of minimum requirements and optional functional coalitions of states appears to be the European future.

civilians shared the carnage with soldiers. The notion of battlefields of war dissolved into the concept of total war, which targeted civilians and cities and towns. The last year of the war, 1945, was especially brutal as bombing campaigns pounded defenseless civilians in such cities as Hamburg and Dresden and Tokyo, and hundreds of thousands of Japanese people (as well as some Koreans and others, even including a few Americans) were vaporized – or worse – by the nuclear bombs dropped on Hiroshima and Nagasaki. By the end of the war, hundreds of cities in Europe and Asia were totally devastated, there were over 50 million refugees, and once again, economic chaos reigned. This time the two principal losers of the war, Germany and Japan, were occupied by the victorious powers, and their new constitutions were written carefully under the tutelage of the United States, the principal victorious nation and now a budding superpower. In both cases, the rehabilitation was successful, and both nations soon took their places among the leading democracies of the world.

Again the victorious allies had the task of setting up a postwar international order. This time lasting institutions were created that are still key today. Foremost was the United Nations, created in 1945 to be the foundation of a new world order. For the first time in world history an international organization was created as universal, open to all states, and with a comprehensive mandate. The Security Council of the United Nations has the task of dealing with threats to world peace, and it has enforcement power by military means, if necessary. The General Assembly has important, although not law-making powers. The International Court of Justice can hear and settle disputes, but is without mandatory jurisdiction. Additional specialized agencies of the United Nations deal with a wide range of matters, such as refugees, health, culture, human rights, and the oceans.

The United States, now clearly acting as a hegemonic power, took the lead in setting up and implementing postwar economic institutions, such as the World Bank, the International Monetary Fund, and the GATT (General Agreement on International Tariffs and Trade), which became the World Trade Organization (WTO) in 1995. The United States, through the Marshall Plan and a successful seven-year occupation of Japan, acted both unilaterally and as a multilateral hegemon to spearhead a successful postwar economic recovery. With enthusiastic U.S. backing, six Western European states formed new international economic and human rights organizations to create a new European political order that would overcome past warfare. This effort – the European Communities and then the European Union – has been spectacularly successful, perhaps the single most important political development of the twentieth century. At least in Europe, the balance of power system was overcome.

### The Cold War

From 1946 to 1990 there raged a new kind of war, the Cold War between the United States and the Soviet Union as principals. This war was cold in the sense that the principals avoided direct conflict – only because each had massive nuclear arms capable of totally annihilating the other – yet there were plenty of hot or real wars between "proxy" and allied states on each side. The Cold War divided Europe most importantly, but divisions (that occasionally shifted) occurred all over the world. Superpower tensions, confrontations, small and medium-sized wars, and potentially deadly crises – events such as the Korean War, the Cuban Missile Crisis of 1962, and the Vietnam War – characterize this period. Yet, the unremitting hostility between both camps was punctuated by *détente;** agreement on smaller issues; exchanges of scholars, culture, and technology, and larger matters, such as the Nuclear Nonprolif- eration Agreement (1968), still the cornerstone of control of nuclear weapons in the world, and the Limited Nuclear Test Ban Treaty (1963).

The Cold War fostered estrangement and bizarre ideas on both sides of the Iron Curtain. At the height of the Cuban Missile Crisis in 1962, I attended a concert performance of the touring Moscow Symphony Orchestra in Ann Arbor, Michigan. It was a magical evening, filled with marvelous Russian music of Tchaikovsky, Borodin, and Stravinsky, and the audience responded with repeated emotional applause. Soon a palpable bond, the like of which I have never felt before or since, arose between the musicians and the audience, expressed by smiles and tears of genuine friendship. But when it was over, all of us knew that there was a real chance that we would awake, if at all, to a world literally in flames. Yet, we had received sparkling entertainment from these Russian men and women, all characterized in the media of the time as a cold, heartless people bent on world domination. But I saw them as we were ourselves, filled with terror at what our leaders might do to the world either by accident or misguided purpose.

The Cold War was a bitter competition between two political, social, and economic systems. The free world, led by the United States, was based on values derived from the eighteenth-century Enlightenment and from mod- ernism: individual liberty, human dignity, and equality. The Soviet Union was based on the Marxist nineteenth-century critique of those values, the inevitability of class conflict; and government planning, control, and repres- sion. The competition was won in the realms of economics and ideas, thank- fully not military conflict. Simply put, the Soviet system could not provide the essential framework necessary for human flourishing; it lost out on everything from creative ideas and culture to consumer satisfaction.

In retrospect, multilateral solidarity was the key to winning the Cold War; America did not try to pursue it alone. Despite some major missteps

---

* A diplomatic term used at the time to refer to a general relaxation of tensions.

(in southeast Asia for example), American presidents exercised wise leadership. Military power was necessary but not sufficient. The West had to show that freedom, democracy, and respect for human rights offered a better life to ordinary people.

That the Soviet system collapsed in 1988–90 was not as remarkable as the way it was handled by the three key leaders of the time: Mikhail Gorbachev, Ronald Reagan, and George H. W. Bush. These three men, their aides, and other world leaders magnificently altered the political configuration of a huge area of the world, not only without significant bloodshed but also in a spirit of goodwill and peace. This was one of the great accomplishments of the century for which future historians will give increasing credit.

Although high praise for the United States is out of fashion in most quarters, future historians must give America its due for the role it played during most of the twentieth century. Repeatedly, justice, freedom, and the spirit of humanity were preserved through American action and resolve. The First World War was ended by America; in the Second World War America saved the world from fascism, racism, and militarism. The post-1945 world was rehabilitated according to American ideals and under American leadership. Finally, American strength and resolve defeated communist totalitarianism and repression.

Although we should give the United States its due for the role it has played, much of this book is critical of current American foreign policy. Of course, a similar critique or worse could be offered for most countries, but the United States is simply more important than any other country and must play a central role if international solutions are to be found.

The reason for the unique and central role of the United States is not only its sole superpower status. We forget that 100 years ago democracy was not the dominant form of government in the world. The European-centered world of 1905 was based on Western dominion and imperialism; there were few true democracies even in Europe. Now in 2005 an overwhelming majority of states are democratic, and those that are not clearly are moving in that direction. Democracy has become the system of government of choice in the world. The model for this was and is the United States. Even the Europeans who ruled the world 100 years ago are now fashioning a European Union that is heavily influenced by the American experience. This is why America is a lightning rod and is singled out both for praise and for criticism.

### The State of the World Today

What is the state of the world at the beginning of the twenty-first century? The worrisome headlines and breathless media reports of terrorism, genocides and devastation belie the fact that, compared to the past, there is significant progress in reducing political violence and the other ills that have plagued mankind throughout history. The 2005 Human Security Report compiled by Andrew Mack of the University of British Columbia[5] at the request of the governments of Canada, Norway, Sweden, Switzerland and the United Kingdom, presents a comprehensive survey of world crises, wars and human rights abuses in the context of a broad vision of human security concerns.

The Report finds that all forms of political violence except terrorism have declined substantially since the end of World War II, and particularly since the end of the Cold War. The number of armed conflicts in the world has declined by 40 percent since 1992. Wars between countries, for centuries the most common and deadly type of conflict, are now rare, constituting only 5 percent of armed conflicts. The number of military coups – another once common occurrence – has dramatically declined: there were 25 such coups in 1963; only 10 were recorded in 2004. Most armed conflicts are now in Africa, but even here the number has dropped from 41 in 2002 to 35 today. The number of international crises that may lead to war is down by 70 percent last year compared to 1981. Wars are also much less deadly today than in former times.

Moreover, despite the horrors of recent killings in Darfur, Sudan, Rwanda and Srebrenica, Bosnia, and the events of 9/11, the number of genocides and mass killings is also down compared to their scale in the first part of the twentieth century. Such killings declined by more than 80 percent after 1989, the end of the Cold War. Human rights abuses declined in 5 out of 6 regions of the developing world since 1990. The number of authoritarian regimes has also declined from 90 in 1978 to 30 in 2005.

The Human Security Report credits these declines to three factors: (1) the end of colonialism, which was involved in over 60 to 100 percent of all armed conflicts, depending on the year, until the 1980s; (2) the end of the Cold War, which fueled various "proxy wars" in the third world; and (3) the unprecedented effort to create legal and institutional constraints in order to stop ongoing violence and to prevent new wars from breaking out. This latter point bears emphasis: the United Nations has spearheaded this multilateral effort. Since 1989 there has been a six-fold increase in U.N. preventive diplomacy and conflict resolution; a four-fold increase in U.N. peacekeeping missions; and an eleven-fold increase in the number of states subject to U.N. Security Council mandated sanctions to pressure warring parties. The Report cites a Rand Corporation study that finds that two-thirds of recent peacebuilding and

---

[5] The Human Security Report (Oxford University Press, 2005) available also at www.humansecurityreport.info.

peacekeeping missions have succeeded. The total cost of these U.N. operations was less than 1 percent of annual world military spending.

This hopeful news is not, of course, grounds for complacency. There are today 60 armed conflicts raging in the world. Terrorism is a continuing threat, and human rights abuses and genocides affect many areas of the globe. But there has been undeniable progress.

## China: The "Enemy" of the Twenty-First Century?

The rise of China as a "great power" of the twenty-first century is now a universal prediction. What should be our reaction to this China's dramatic rise? Should it inspire apprehension and even fear? What should or can be done to prepare for it?

Already key elements of the American government and U.S. allies are preparing for what they assume will be an inevitable and growing conflict with China. The unabashed expectation is of a new cold war that may turn hot at some point in the future. A glimpse of this thinking is provided by the June 2005 issue of the *Atlantic Monthly*, which features articles by Washington insiders about China. One article, entitled "Managing China's Rise",[6] assumes that the right mix of military and economic power can somehow intimidate and defang the Chinese dragon. A second article, "How We Would Fight China",[7] confidently predicts that China will be a "more formidable adversary than Russia (sic – it was the Soviet Union, remember?) ever was." Even more darkly, the author predicts, "The American contest with China will define the twenty-first century." The theater of this coming hot or cold war is said to be the Pacific region where "the Chinese military challenge is already a reality." As a solution the author recommends increased military preparedness and the "correct calibration of power relationships," which means, more crudely put, that we should make sure our power is greater than theirs.

Japan too is preparing for the worst, no doubt with American encouragement. In December 2004 the Japanese government released a Defense White Paper that designated China a potential security threat. The Japan Defense Agency revealed an internal planning document detailing Japan's "island defense strategy" against China. It involves new force deployments and bases in southern Japan and in the Southern Ryukyu Islands.

Certainly the rise of China in the new century poses many important challenges (see China Rising). The meteoric rise of the Chinese economy

[6] Benjamin Schwarz, "Managing China's Rise," 295 *Atlantic Monthly* 5(2005): 27.
[7] Robert D. Kaplan, "How We Would Fight China," 295 *Atlantic Monthly* 5(2005): 49.

## CHINA RISING

China, by reason of its history, culture, population, and geographical position, has a claim to being classed among the great world powers. China's history as the Middle (or Central) Kingdom goes back over 5,000 years; it is the natural cultural leader of East Asia and has always played that role with respect to such other states as Japan and Korea. During much of the brilliant Tang Dynasty (618–906 CE), Chinese civilization led the world in sophistication and subtle beauty. China's population has always been relatively large; now its 1.2 billion people comprise about one-fifth of humankind. Geographically too, China extends over the entire heartland of East Asia; it is the natural continental power of the region.

China's bright star was eclipsed for almost 200 years due to a combination of factors, both its own internal failings and onslaughts from abroad. Now at the beginning of the twenty-first century, China seems poised to resume its ancient role as a political, economic, and cultural great power.

China's rise should be welcomed, not feared or impeded in any way. China's economic growth has lifted millions out of poverty and has brought prosperity to its neighbors. China's destiny cannot be denied; the question both for the Chinese leadership and the rest of the world is how to manage China's rise to great power status.

Accommodating the rise of China is one of the greatest challenges of the twenty-first century. The stakes are high for both Asia and the rest of the world. Without China's positive influence, peace and prosperity will be elusive. No other Asian country is capable of anchoring the stability of the region.

The great danger is that the United States and its allies will attempt to manage the rise of China the same way that the European powers tried to manage the rise of Germany in the late nineteenth and early twentieth centuries – through *Realpolitik* and balance of power decisions and alliances. Such a policy would likely have the same unhappy result as the world experienced in 1914.

Rather the rise of China should be accompanied at every turn by welcoming and embedding it in the system of international law and institutions of the modern world. An excellent start has been made along this path: China plays a key role in such institutions as the United Nations and the WTO. China must also live up to its new-found responsibilities for world peace and stability.

The challenge of accommodating China is bound up with additional difficult problems in East Asia:

■ The legacy of World War II still hangs over East Asia. In contrast to Europe, which has put this war to rest, great antagonism, policy disputes, and differences still exist between Japan and other Asian countries, especially China.

■ The Cold War also lingers in East Asia. North Korea is still an outpost of oppression and a potential flashpoint for war.

■ A solution must be found to the problem of Taiwan that is acceptable both to China and to the people of Taiwan.

■ China's political future as a one-party state is doubtful at best. Social, political, and economic tensions within China must be resolved peacefully; the Chinese leadership must accommodate and encourage peaceful political change, democracy, and human rights.

■ Asia must institute pan-Asian institutions analogous to the pan-European institutions that have knitted the peoples of Europe together. As a beginning, an Asian Economic Community – a free trade area – should be created to include China, Japan, South Korea, and the ten ASEAN (Association of Southeast Asian Nations) countries. In addition, there should be an Asian version of the Organization for Security and Cooperation in Europe, a forum for security and conflict resolution addressing military, economic, and human rights issues.

All of these issues are complex and difficult. All are also soluble with patience and good will. The mandate to world leaders is to prevent them from flaring into war and to manage them so as to make possible a solution at some future time.

has already caused dislocations and trade frictions with Europe and the United States. China's military spending has greatly increased, and its new emphasis on projecting naval power is certainly important and worrisome. There are increased tensions over Taiwan, as well as a nasty dispute with Japan over conflicting sovereign claims to the Senkaku (Chinese name, Daioyu) Islands in the East China Sea. As a one-party state, China does not observe global norms of human rights as well as it should, as demonstrated most egregiously by the brutal crackdown of the democracy demonstrations in Tiananmen Square in 1989. China's environmental record is already bleak, and by 2020 it will surpass the United States as the world's greatest emitter of greenhouse gases that contribute to the problem of global climate change.

Yet, China's rise has undeniable positive effects as well. The increasing economic power of China has been key to making Asia the world's fastest-growing economic region, lifting millions of people out of poverty and spurring the economies of China's trading partners, including Japan. China and the United States, China and Japan, and China and the European Union enjoy trade and investment relationships totaling billions of dollars annually. Present and future world prosperity depends upon the continuity of these relationships.

The best and primary means of "managing" the rise of China is through international law and international institutions.[8] Firmly embedding China in this existing web of worldwide legal relationships will avoid war and ensure the dominance of the positive aspects of China's rise to great power status. In every important potential area of conflict with China – regional security, military, economic, maritime affairs, the environment, and human rights – there are existing rules and institutions that China purports to accept as legally binding. These serve two important functions: (1) as systems of rules of behavior and (2) as forums for discussing and solving problems and disputes in a peaceful manner. Of course, power relationships will still be important, but law and institutions are essential in order to use power in subtle and creative ways, rather than merely as a blunt instrument.

For example, in April 2001 a Chinese F-8 fighter jet engaged a U.S. EP-3E reconnaissance plane in harassment maneuvers over the South China Sea, resulting in an accidental collision that downed the Chinese jet and forced the EP-3E to make an emergency landing on China's Hainan Island. With the 24-member EP-3E crew in Chinese hands, the U.S. power tactic – harsh denunciations and demands – was totally ineffective. After fruitless tough rhetoric, the United States was forced to apologize in order to gain the return of the crew and the plane, which conservative voices in the United States (with some justification) denounced as "a national humiliation."[9]

A far better tactic would have been to emphasize international legal norms that China has explicitly accepted that permit even military surveillance flights over ocean waters to within twelve nautical miles of a country's coastline.[10] By emphasizing power and not law, the United States put itself at a disadvantage, and the U.S. position elicited little sympathy around the world. The United States was also at a disadvantage even in asserting its legal rights because unlike China, America does not accept the U.N. Convention on the Law of the Sea, which expressly sorts these matters out. The United States accepts these rules, but only as "customary" law, which is much weaker than treaty law in a U.N. convention. In 2005 the United States still refuses to ratify the U.N. Convention on the Law of the Sea, although this document will be crucial in any future conflict with China over maritime rights in the Pacific area. It

---

[8] Of course, as the late Zhao Ziyang, former prime minister and secretary-general of the Communist Party is reported to have said, "China's development must be on the path of democracy and the rule of law. If not, China will be a corrupt society" (quoted by an associate, Zong Fengming). *International Herald Tribune*, June 3, 2005, p. 1.

[9] Robert Kagan and William Kristol, *The Weekly Standard*, April 16, 2001, pp. 12–14.

[10] Article 58 of the U.N. Convention on the Law of the Sea posits freedom of overflight and navigation by all states in ocean areas beyond the twelve-mile territorial sea.

is a supreme irony that the United States is one of the only states in the world not to ratify this Convention, which is a kind of constitution for the use and protection of the oceans of the world. This document guarantees the right of the U.S. Navy to navigate the seas of the world, including the East and South China Seas.

Even a cold war with China would be catastrophic for the world in the twenty-first century. Reliance upon international legal norms and regimes and multilateral solidarity are keys to the peaceful solution of the difficult political problems in East Asia.


## SUMMING UP: AVOIDING "BACK TO THE FUTURE"

The terrible events of the twentieth century took or ruined tens of millions of lives and profoundly affected those who were physically spared. Consider the impact on culture and on humanity's place in the world. The Enlightenment faith in progress and liberal ideas was shaken to the core. Political, social, and economic liberalism gave way to dark forces, and three key figures emerged as the dominant thinkers of the new order: Friedrich Nietzsche, Sigmund Freud, and Karl Marx. These three men, justly termed by the French Philosopher Paul Ricoeur as "masters of suspicion," undermined optimistic thinking and raised problems of false consciousness, the ideas that human beliefs and certainties are merely products of our hidden cultural, psychological, and economic drives. For Nietzsche moral values were simply a mechanism of power and deceit, and Freud told us we are controlled by irrational and repressed sexual drives. For Marx modernity was merely a mask for vested economic interests. The events of the twentieth century made these men seem like prophets. People lost faith or questioned all traditional systems of belief.

The impact of this loss of faith is vividly present in the ideas of two of the most famous and influential philosophers of the century, Martin Heidegger and Jean-Paul Sartre, the proponents of existentialism – the idea that human beings choose their mode of life in a world devoid of meaning. Heidegger was the elder of the two, born in 1889. In his major work, *Being and Time*, he investigated the meaning of *Dasein* or being in the world and concluded that human beings have little control over their lives – we are born into a preexisting culture and circumstances, and we seek to make our way by formulating plans and projects. But our dominant condition is anxiety, and the best we can do is choose to live "authentically." For Heidegger this meant alliance with Nazi fascism, which he never renounced before his death in 1976. Sartre, who was born in 1905, accepted Heidegger's idea of radical freedom of choice because there is no God or compulsory system of belief. But Sartre chose to be a resistance fighter against the Germans who were occupying France, and after the war he became a committed Marxist until his death in 1980. In his major work, *Being and Nothingness*, Sartre argued that as humans condemned to freedom in a world without God, the best we can do is to make our own life and world the best we can.

How will the events of the twenty-first century shape the human spirit? To be sure the threats and international problems have changed in the past century. But there are almost four times as many people in the world today as in 1900, the world is more chaotic, and, if anything, the risks are greater, ranging from nuclear weapons to environmental disasters. The crucial question is, have we created an international system that is capable of dealing with the international problems we face – problems that are beyond solution by any one state: global security and terrorism, poverty, hunger and disease, abuse and neglect of human rights, and environmental degradation? If the answer is "no," as I think it is, then the question becomes: What are the elements of a new world order, and how do we create a better world, a new international system that will protect us? The answers to these questions are what this book is about.

One last point is crucial. Some may say that the solution to creating a new world order is simple – leave it to the United States. After all, America took care of business in the last century; why not depend on her benevolent action again?

Simply put, this would be bad policy even if it were possible, given our belief in inclusiveness of all the peoples of the world. And contemporary problems are beyond the capacity of any one nation, even the most powerful. Witness the fight against terrorism and weapons of mass destruction and the miscalculations of the Bush administration in Iraq.

Just as in the twentieth century, America can lead, but the question is how to exercise that leadership.

**FURTHER READINGS**

Mia Bloom, *Dying to Kill: The Allure of Suicide Terror* (2005).

Francis Fukuyama, *The End of History and Last Man* (1993).

Eric Hobsbawm, *Age of Extremes: A History of the World, 1914–1991* (1995).

Samuel Huntington, *The Clash of Civilization and the Remaking of World Order* (1996).

Michael Howard and William Roger Lewis, *The Oxford History of the 20th Century* (2000).

John Merriman, *A History of Modern Europe* (1996).

Robert Pape, *Dying to Win: The Strategic Logic of Suicide Terrorism* (2005).

Peter Watson, *The Modern Mind: An Intellectual History of the 20th Century* (2000).

# 3  International Power Politics

## THE STATE SYSTEM

The world of the twenty-first century is a world of sovereign states. We take for granted that the state system is the basis of political order on the planet, the primary organizing principle of world politics. The territory of the earth is divided among 193 states having the attribute we call sovereignty. (The precise number of states is, of course arbitrary: In 1945 there were 53, and in 1700 there were about 2,000). In principle, all lands, inland waters as well as islands, and large expanses of ocean waters are included in this political system. Only the so-called high seas and the continent of Antarctica, to which a special regime applies, are outside national jurisdictions. The territorial and maritime frontiers among states are the products of both history and agreement.

The state is so dominant today that we tend to forget this was not always the case and that the state system is not an immutable feature of the world. There are in theory manifold ways of organizing civil society; history is littered with the wreckage of all sorts of political entities that have existed, many with great success: empires, commonwealths, city-states, colonies, and various feudal structures that have come and gone on the world stage.

The contemporary state system was not decreed or invented – it evolved over hundreds of years. Its origin was in Europe in the early modern period. Historians and political scientists, who like to assign dates for everything, mark the beginning of the state system in Europe as 1648, the date of the Treaty of Westphalia, which ended the religious conflict known as the Thirty Years War. In reality there were states before 1648, so that it may be more accurate to say that on this date the state became the dominant political form of organization in Europe, and from there it spread to the rest of the world. At the end of the twentieth century, the process of globalization of the state system appears to be complete – the last phase was the break-up of the Soviet Union and former Yugoslavia, which created many new states. The future will no doubt see changes in boundaries and split-ups or mergers of states, but no alterations as dramatic as in the past. The state system appears to be here to stay, affecting everyone on earth.

The intellectual justification of the state is the subject of debate. Political theorists, such as Hobbes, Locke, and Rousseau, advanced the social contract theory for the origin or at least the justification of the state.[1] According to this theory, the state is the product of agreement by free individuals, and therefore, the state must serve their interests and recognize their rights. The German philosopher Hegel, on the other hand, found the justification of the state in the "way of God in the world, the manifestation of the divine on earth," the inevitable product of the spirit of history in the world. (The philosopher Karl Popper famously criticized this deification of the state in his classic study, *The Open Society and Its Enemies* [1945]). Many contemporary thinkers see the state system as simply a human convenience, the product of impersonal historical forces and political trial and error. In this view the state exists to provide its citizens and residents security, freedom, order, justice, and welfare. Its ability to provide these elements can serve as criteria for judging the merit of any contemporary state.[2]

What are the characteristics of the modern state? The diversity of the states that currently make up the global system is so great that lawyers and political scientists identify only a few minimal but important requirements. First, a state must have a defined territory. This is not to say that its frontiers must be undisputed, but it must claim a geographical area. Second, a state must have a permanent population, but there is no minimum necessary number. Third, a state must have a government; again the type of government – democracy, monarchy, or oligarchy – is not important. Fourth, a state must have political independence so that it is capable of entering into legitimate international relations with other states. This characteristic may be qualified as well; for

---

[1]  This modern view of the state contrasts with the earlier theory derived from Aristotle (*Politics*, Book 1, Ch. 1–2) and Thomas Aquinas (*Summa Theologiae, Prima Secundae*) that political organization is part of the natural order of things. From this theory lesser thinkers derived the divine right of kings and the subjection of men and women to state authority. A contrasting idea of the social contract theory of the state was advanced by the eighteenth century conservative thinker Edmund Burke, who believed that society is a social contract between the dead, the living and those yet to be born. Edmund Burke, *Reflections on the Revolution in France* (1790).

[2]  So-called critical theory urges the analysis of the underlying social structures of the state and the elimination of built-in pathologies and forms of domination and exploitation. M. Horkheimer, *Critical Theory* (1972).

example, Monaco has ceded its foreign policymaking powers to France, but Monaco is still regarded as a state. Statehood should be distinguished from the related concept of recognition of the government of a state. As a practical matter, recognition means only that diplomatic relations are desired with the state. Recognition is a political and legal act of legitimacy, but recognition by other states is not a constitutional requirement of statehood. For example, the People's Republic of China was a state from its inception in 1949, although the United States and many other countries refused recognition of its government for many years.

The concept of the state is different from the concept of nation. A nation is a community of people considered to have a common identity based on ethnicity, culture, language, or history. Sometimes the state and nation closely coincide, for example Italy, where almost all people consider themselves ethnically Italian. In this case it is proper to speak of the nation-state – the state is also a nation. However, many states today are multinational or multicultural; for example, India, China, and the United States. Moreover, there are some states that are devoid of nations – the Vatican, for example, does not involve any national group. In addition, there are cases of stateless nations, such as the Palestinians and the Kurds. This is frequently a source of international tension.

A further characteristic of states is that they are formally equal because they all enjoy the attribute of sovereignty, defined as independence and legal autonomy. This formal equality is limited, however, because in reality states have widely different economic, political, military, social, and cultural characteristics.

## Sovereignty

The meaning and importance of the key term *sovereignty*[3] has changed radically over the past 100 years and continues to change today. In its traditional and pristine form, sovereignty was regarded as a concept unique to states and the very essence of statehood and membership in the international system. In its traditional formulation, sovereignty means that the state is subject to no higher power, and this implies a dual claim. First, within its territory and with respect to its own citizens the state has absolute and exclusive authority. This is the source of the idea (happily disputed today) that the state can do whatever it wants to the population within its territory. Second, the state has

---

3  The term "sovereignty" was first coined and defined by the French political philosopher Jean Boudin in his essay, "De Republica" (1576).

a right to exercise unrestrained power internationally. This is the origin of the (equally pernicious) doctrine that any state has a right to go to war to assert its interests.

These bold ideas came out of the formative period of the state system in Europe, and they are attributed to the Renaissance French thinker, Jean Boudin, and the English political philosopher, Thomas Hobbes. These men posit a system of anarchy in international relations. The theoretical independence of states makes them judges in their own cause, and they may do anything they can get away with to pursue their interests. As a legal and political idea, this notion of sovereignty has always been incorrect, but like many wrong ideas, it has had tremendous influence that continues today.

Historically, the high-water mark of sovereignty was the nineteenth century in Europe when, beginning in 1815 after the defeat of Napoleon, the so-called Concert of Europe tried to maintain international order through consultations and negotiation. This was the balance of power system that ultimately came crashing down in 1914. Since the First World War the concept of sovereignty has been down but not out, as we shall see. The doctrine of sovereignty keeps popping up, often in new guises. In the twenty-first century sovereignty has a new and simple meaning – the right of the citizens of a state to determine their own destiny.

## The State Today

What is the status of the doctrine of sovereignty today? In formal terms, there is still no higher authority than the state, and we still speak of sovereign concerns. But the classical view of sovereignty is discredited, and international relations experts debate how far the doctrine of sovereignty has eroded and what it means today. In this debate there tend to be political differences of opinion, with conservatives generally defending sovereignty, whereas liberals downplay its current significance.

Objectively speaking, a certain erosion of the doctrine of sovereignty is undeniable. First, in the twentieth century, many international actors emerged that share power with states.

■ Intergovernmental organizations, such as the United Nations, NATO, and the International Monetary Fund, have the authority to take actions independent of states. Ironically, the European political order today in dominated by such an intergovernmental organization, the European Union, which in most ways is the antithesis of the nineteenth-century Concert of Europe.

■ Multinational and transnational corporations are also major international actors today; many of these are richer, more powerful, and independent of all but the major sovereign states.

■ Nongovernmental organizations (NGOs), ranging from the Red Cross to the Catholic Church to Greenpeace, have unprecedented influence and often a certain moral authority.

These international actors counterbalance the power of states.

Second, it is no longer accepted today that the state can exercise unrestrained power either internally or externally. Accepted international legal norms constrain state power. For example, states no longer enjoy absolute immunity in domestic courts of law. Under the U.S. Foreign Sovereign Immunity Act and its analogue in other states, a foreign state may now be sued and will be liable in contract and in tort. Foreign states that foster terrorism may be sued for damages. The International Law Commission (an organ of the United Nations) has formulated broad rules for "international state responsibility" as well. States bear international responsibility and may have to pay damages for conduct that is in breach of international law.

Third, in the second half of the twentieth century important standards for the protection of human rights were formulated that must be observed by all states. A state that mistreats its population may be subject to enforcement action under the U.N. Charter, and there may be a right of "humanitarian intervention" even apart from the Charter. Moreover, a head of state as well as state officials who perpetrate violations of human rights may be prosecuted criminally for their actions. In the Pinochet case (2000)[4], for example, the U.K. House of Lords ruled that a former head of state is not immune from prosecution for international crimes. New international criminal tribunals, including a permanent International Criminal Court, have been constituted.

Fourth, in the twenty-first century it is widely conceded that interdependence has replaced independence as a characteristic of the global order of states. Globalization, the disputed characteristic that in any case defines our times, means that every state and its citizens are affected by events that may occur in far-flung places – because, simply put, there really are no far-flung places any more. Moreover, the international problems that we face – peace and security, protection of the environment, and economic development – are beyond the capability of any one state. There is no choice but to cooperate.

---

4  Ex Parte Pinochet, [2000] 1 AC 147 (House of Lords).

Fifth, it is accepted today that states have international responsibility as well as rights. *State responsibility* arises from the violation by a state of an international obligation. This obligation can be derived from either customary law or treaty law. International responsibility means that a state must desist from breaching the obligation and must make reparation for any damages caused. International law contains what are referred to as both primary and secondary rules concerning state responsibility. The primary rules define what is substantively a wrongful act over a broad spectrum of areas, such as human rights, protection of the environment, breach of a treaty obligation, violation of the laws of war, and mistreatment of foreign nationals. The secondary law of state responsibility covers general and technical matters, such as the manner of attributing wrongful acts to a state, the mechanics of enforcement, and various defenses to state culpability.[5] This international regime of state responsibility is still embryonic and controversial (in some ways it is the antithesis of the doctrine of sovereignty), but there is a growing movement among legal and political scholars and practitioners to implement it widely in coming years. State responsibility is essential to the international rule of law.

In sum, the state and its concomitant, sovereignty, are not metaphysical in origin or divinely ordained; they are human institutions devised to serve instrumental ends – to provide the necessary framework for human flourishing. Scholars may debate the extent and necessity of the erosion of sovereignty, but a premise of this book is that sovereignty in the twenty-first century must be exercised within a framework of law and international institutions.

## INTERNATIONAL RELATIONS

International relations (IR) is the term commonly used to encompass the relationships and interactions among international actors, chiefly governments and states. This broad concept includes international politics – the policy relationships among states in widely diverse fields, ranging from nuclear nonproliferation to the protocol of receiving diplomatic visitors. Areas covered typically include security and military concerns, economics and trade, resources, environment, culture, and social and ethnic concerns – anything and everything a state may find of interest. IR also includes international law, the legal norms that are supposed to govern state behavior. For the purpose of interacting with other states and asserting their perceived interests, every state has established mechanisms of foreign policy formulation. States also have

---

[5] James Crawford, *The International Law Commission Articles on State Responsibility* (2002).

## INTERNATIONAL RELATIONS AND FOREIGN POLICY

International relations deals with transactions and relationships among the international actors of the world. States are the focal points of these relationships, but nonstate actors also play important roles. The chief categories of nonstate actors involved in international relations are (1) intergovernmental organizations, such as the United Nations; (2) multinational corporations, some of which exceed many states in yearly financial turnover; and (3) international NGOs.

Foreign policy is uniquely the province of states and consists of the sets of attitudes, transactions, and relations adopted with respect to external problems, situations, and conditions. Domestic actors and influences typically influence foreign policy, to a greater or lesser degree.

a variety of methods and instruments to assert their interests, but here states differ – powerful states have more ways to assert interests than weaker ones (see "International Relations and Foreign Policy").

An essential assumption of IR is that states, like individuals, have interests to promote that will enhance their well-being. The way to promote these interests in the arena of international politics is to possess power, which may be derived from many sources – military, economic, social, or diplomatic; even cultural power can be influential. As one of the most famous IR experts of the twentieth century, Hans Morgenthau (1965), put it, "[International] politics is a struggle for power over men, and whatever its ultimate aim may be, power is its immediate goal and the modes of acquiring, maintaining, and demonstrating it determine ... political action."[6]

Although IR is a relatively recent field of study,[7] the underpinnings of this view of power can be found in history. One of the most famous instances is the account by the Greek historian Thucydides (404 BCE) of the relations between Athens and Melos during the Peloponnesian War waged between Athens and Sparta in the fifth century BCE. The inhabitants of Melos, a small island city-state in the Aegean Sea, were Dorian Greeks, who were closely related to the Spartans, but they chose neutrality during the war. In 416 Athens decided to enlist Melos as an ally and for this purpose mounted

---

[6]  Hans Morgenthau, *Politics among Nations* 15 (1965).
[7]  Interntional relations was not recognized as a field of study separate from political philosophy and international law until after World War I. The first holder of a university professorship in international relations was A. E. Zimmern at the University of Wales, Aberystwyth, in 1919.

an expeditionary force of 38 ships, 320 archers, and 2,700 hoplites (infantry soldiers). Before attacking, the Athenian general held a parley with his Melian counterpart. Thucydides recounts verbatim the dialogue between the two men. The Athenian general explains his desire to preserve the Melian city "to our mutual advantage" and demands Melian submission and alliance: "Your subjection would give us security and an extension of empire," he explains. The Melian general demurs, arguing that subjugation of neutral Melos is not in Athens' interest: "Will you not be making enemies of all who are now neutral?" But the Athenian general is adamant: "You are weak, and a single turn of the scale may be your ruin," he warns. "We are not doing anything that goes beyond what men . . . desire in human relationships. For we believe . . . of men, that by a necessity of nature, wherever they have the power, they will rule. We did not make this law, and we are not the first to act upon it. . . . We obey it in the knowledge that . . . if you had our strength, you would do the same."

The Melians call their leaders together to determine what to do. They decide to reject the demand for submission and give the following answer: "Our resolution is unchanged – we will not . . . surrender that liberty which our city, founded seven hundred years ago, still enjoys . . . We are ready to be your friends and enemies neither of you nor the [Spartans], and we ask you to leave our country when you have made such a peace as appears to be in the interest of both parties."

The Athenians do not leave, but lay siege to Melos, which is soon forced to capitulate. The Athenians then "put to death all men of military age, and sold the women and children as slaves. They took over Melos itself, establishing later a colony of 500 people." This incident shocked even many Athenians. The treatment of the Melians is thought to have inspired Euripides' antiwar drama, *The Trojan Women* (411 BCE), as well as Aristophanes' play, *Lysistrata* (407 BCE), which is about the women of Athens deciding to withhold sexual favors until war is ended.

The viewpoint of the Athenian general was echoed during the Italian Renaissance by the influential Florentine courtier, Niccolò Machiavelli (*The Prince*, 1507). Machiavelli counseled that men are more prone to evil than to good and that politics is essentially a struggle for power, not a pursuit of ideals, although the struggle will be concealed by pious sentiments. Therefore, conflict and competition are natural components of international politics, and a cruel but strong leader – Machiavelli admired the way Caesare Borgia brought unity and order to the Italian province of Romagna – is better than a benevolent weakling. A century later, the English philosopher Thomas Hobbes agreed in his famous work, *Leviathan* (1641), that nations are perpetually at odds because there exists no acknowledged sovereign to pronounce judgments that put an end to their disagreements.[8]

## REALISM

Realism is the modern label for this view of international society as anarchical and emphasizing the necessity of power arrangements to advance state interests. The "founding fathers" of realism – Thucydides, Machiavelli, and Hobbes[9] – are known as *classical realists*. Although realists today do not advocate enslavement or mass murder, they do continue to emphasize the dichotomy of good and evil in the world and the necessity for the unilateral assertion of power – or, as it is put in contemporary language, firmness, toughness, and a willingness to take preemptive measures in the face of challenges. This is *power politics* in the international arena (see "Theories of International Relations").

Power politics emphasizes, especially, military and economic power, which provides the leverage to make demands and the ability to devise strategies, policies, and plans to achieve goals. A state playing power politics will look upon alliances only as a means of increasing power. Increasing power may lead to hegemony or overwhelming dominance. Bargains can sometimes be struck through positive actions that are designed to induce the other side to cooperate. For example, President Nixon's strategy to reduce China's support for North Vietnam and the Soviet Union during the Cold War was to relax the U.S. economic embargo of China. This led to reciprocal actions that culminated in Nixon's historic visit to China in 1972. Frequently, however, strategic leverage of a negative sort must be employed against others through deterrence or a threat or show of force to demonstrate to the other side the potentially great negative consequences of its actions.

Many believe that this is how the international system works and will always work. Note the differences between this system and what most people would consider good or right in private ethics and morality. In the sphere of international politics, moral considerations must frequently be ignored. This was

[8] The classical realist tradition is commonly said to include also such political thinkers as Spinoza, Hume, Rousseau, Hegel, Marx, and Weber.
[9] For an excellent account of Hobbes and his views on international law, see Charles Covell, *Hobbes: Realism and the Tradition of International Law* (2004).

## THEORIES OF INTERNATIONAL RELATIONS

Specialists often devise theories of international relations to show how various patterns of conduct of international actors explain, influence, and determine policy and decisions. Many influential international relations theories exist, but two polar opposite theories are realism and liberal internationalism.

Realism assumes the following:

■ States are the dominant actors of international society.

■ States act rationally to pursue their interests and to maintain and increase their power.

■ State interactions are dependent on power relationships.

■ Cooperation is relatively rare and depends on the coincidence of state interests.

Liberal internationalism emphasizes the following:

■ the role of international law in modulating state interactions

■ the role of nonstate actors, such as intergovernmental organizations

■ multilateralism and the collective benefits of cooperation

■ the predominance of long-term common interests over narrow self-interests

These two theories are not mutually exclusive; the key question is how to balance them and which should predominate.

exactly the point made by Thucydides, Machiavelli, and Hobbes. "We" have to be strong so that the "bad guys" never get the upper hand.

But hold on a minute. The realist system just described is virtually identical to the world system described in Chapter Two, the nineteenth-century balance of power system that collapsed in disaster in World War I. Have we learned nothing in the last 100 years? Perhaps the answer is no, the world is unprepared and has not changed and cannot change – we just have to muddle through as best we can. Or we can say that the difference between 1905 and 2005 is that now the United States is the sole superpower – *hegemon*, as the political scientists would put it – and the United States is always right (well, almost always anyway), so we do not have to worry about something like 1914 happening again.

But we do have to worry about a future 1914 – of course in an updated, twenty-first-century form – something that we cannot predict in advance, just as no one in 1914 conceived of even the possibility of the horrors and the course of history of the twentieth century. Who predicted the 9/11 terrorist attacks on the United States? In retrospect we know there were warnings that were ignored. We have to establish new systems to safeguard the world against future catastrophes that may be widely ignored by the news media and may be outside present public consciousness.

Nor can we put complete trust in the United States as the sole superpower. As a hegemon, the United States can do many things, and many things well. A brutal dictator, Saddam Hussein, was toppled in 2003 by a military campaign lasting just three weeks. But American hegemony also has many limitations. The United States found that it could not handle the aftermath of the Iraq War alone and sought help from NATO, allies around the world such as Japan, and even the United Nations. This is just one example; in fact, resolving most of the problems of the twenty-first century is beyond the capability of any one state. In addition, we cannot depend on the leaders of the U.S. government to make the right decisions. Despite the best intentions, they may get it wrong. It used to be said that U.S. leaders were "the best and the brightest." This phrase was turned into irony by David Halberstam's book, which employed it as a title and minutely dissected the misguided decision making of the Vietnam War. It is remarkable that no one describes U.S. leaders this way anymore, even in jest.

## LIBERAL INTERNATIONALISM

Why did realism become the dominant way of thinking in international relations after the disasters following 1914? Why did the world not turn away in revulsion from the failed thought of the past? Is there any alternative to power politics?

In fact, there was an alternative and a champion well placed to put it through, none other than the president of the United States, Woodrow Wilson. In 1918, with American prestige at a high point, Wilson dramatically called for changing the very basis of international relations in the world. What he termed "material interests" of states should not be determinative; foreign policy should instead be based upon morality, not expediency: "We will never condone iniquity because it is the most convenient thing to do," Wilson declared. He proposed "Fourteen Points" upon which international relations should be conducted to "make the world safe for democracy." His goal was permanent peace. His key proposal was the League of Nations, which was in fact established by the Paris Peace Conference in 1919. This new world order was called *liberal internationalism*.

This effort regrettably came to naught. Wilson was incapacitated by illness, and the U.S. Senate rejected the League of Nations. Wilson's allies fought for acceptance of the ideas of liberal internationalism, but it was a losing battle. The high point of the new movement was the Kellogg-Briand Pact of 1928, which outlawed war as an instrument of policy. In retrospect, liberal internationalism was never really given a chance. The League of Nations was never taken seriously, and the Kellogg-Briand Pact was a "one-off" pronouncement, a momentous step with little preparation and no follow-up. Wilson's premature demise also removed the most eloquent advocate of political change.

Liberal internationalism also was defeated by the history and culture of the interwar period. As explained in Chapter 2, the impact of the First World War on culture was to throw into question the Enlightenment project – the orthodoxy held since the eighteenth century that through rationality and scientific principles human life will progress to new stages of peace and prosperity. Liberal internationalism as proposed by Wilson was drawn from the Enlightenment belief in reason and progress. The League of Nations was an idea similar to a proposal by the German philosopher Immanuel Kant in 1795 in his essay, *Perpetual Peace* – that the nations of the world must establish a League of Peace (*foedus pacificum*), a united international system to prevent war.[10]

## BACK TO REALISM

World War I and its aftermath caused many people to lose faith in reason and rationality. The two most influential cultural figures of the time were Nietzsche and Freud, both iconoclastic thinkers. Freud applied his psychological theories to society in his book, *Civilization and Its Discontents* (1933). His analysis of human nature was that our intellect is only a weak plaything of our subconscious desires and emotions. Our divided selves are torn between rationality and our irrational urges, which we can deal with only by repression and

---

[10] An opponent of Kant's *Perpetual Peace* was the nineteenth-century German philosopher Hegel, who maintained that war is necessary to the "dialectic of history" in order to prevent stagnation. War for Hegel was the principal means by which the "spirit of the people" can acquire renewed vigor and sweep aside decay. *Sammtliche Werke* (G. Lasson and J. Hoffmeister), Vol. VI, pp. 185 and 209.

sublimation. So too we live in a sick society potentially dominated by cruelty and animal instincts that cannot be easily denied. Nietzsche too emphasized the irrational side of human nature and questioned the moral order of the universe. He argued for a new morality based upon a "will to power," which would involve both cruelty and creativity for humankind. In this new world the rule of force would replace the rule of law, and the strong must naturally dominate the weak. The analyses of Nietzsche and Freud became dominant; all rational values and the very possibility of objective truth were thrown into question.

The foremost authorities in IR of interwar period mirrored these cultural trends. The British scholar E. H. Carr, writing in his 1939 book, *The Twenty Years' Crisis*, labeled Wilson's vision "utopian," accusing him of misunderstanding the fundamental facts of history and human nature. According to Carr, International relations is a never-ending struggle between conflicting interests and desires. A second influential voice was Hans Morgenthau, who, echoing Nietzsche, spoke of the human "lust" for power. Universal moral principles cannot be applied to statecraft without endangering national interests. Liberal internationalists were "utopian idealists" who ignore "reality." The realist view seemed vindicated with the failure of appeasement of Hitler in Munich in 1938. These men and other IR specialists, known as *neo-classical realists*, ridiculed the liberal internationalist idea of "law, not war" as hopelessly naive.

This power-politics approach was based upon the determination to avoid another Munich and to reject anything that smacked of appeasement. The focus on Munich downplayed the failures in the international system that led to World War I, and neo-classical realists continued to regard Wilsonian ideas as utopian folly. When the realist paradigm led to mistakes, as in Vietnam, it was regarded mainly as a cost of doing business, not a fundamental error.

Experts in IR and academicians largely concurred in the realist approach, but in the second half of the century new ideas and nuances developed. With the onset of the Cold War and the possibility of nuclear annihilation, it was realized that realist thinking had to incorporate methods to facilitate cooperation or at least ways to avoid disaster. Thomas Schelling[11] (winner of the Nobel Prize in Economics in 2005) was a leader in developing what is termed *strategic realism* through a careful analysis of various stratagems and mechanisms by which states engaging in confrontation in a nuclear-armed world could generate collaboration or prevent conflict. One of his insights,

---

[11] Thomas Schelling, *The Strategy of Conflict* (1980).

for example, is that in a confrontation between nuclear powers it is important for each side to leave open to the other side an honorable way out and not force a choice between extremes that may lead to a first strike.

Another seminal thinker is Kenneth Waltz,[12] who tried to put realist thinking into context by emphasizing the underlying political, social, and economic structures that necessarily shape foreign policy decisions. This approach, called *neo-realism* or *structural realism*,[13] recognizes that states have greatly varying capabilities for action and that these capabilities differ over time, as well as across different units of government. Waltz is at pains to show that these structural characteristics constrain actions and even may compel actions in a certain way. This view, for example, would explain the dissolution of the Soviet Union as dictated less by conscious free choice as by the structural position – in economic and military terms – of the Soviet bloc vis-a-vis the Western bloc in the 1980s. Structural realism thus purports to facilitate future strategy and to explain international political outcomes.

Neo-realism also provides an explanation and a scenario for collaborative bargains among states. Neo-realists accept that states are capable of cooperation, but only for absolute political or economic gains. Economic theory and rational choice analysis are therefore useful in determining conditions for state cooperation. A bargain will be struck and kept if a state's gains are not only greater than what it gives up but also if its absolute gains are greater or at least equal to the gains of all other parties to the bargain. This is a pessimistic theory of state cooperation that explains why true agreement must be rare; its premise is that cooperation is always a zero-sum game, which in today's world is often not the case.

## BEHAVIORISM, EMPIRICISM, AND GAME THEORY

Many neo-realists, especially in the United States, have moved away from the anecdotal approach of Carr and Morgenthau and have tried to put realism on a more scientific basis. Three related methods have been used: behavior analysis, empirical research, and game theory. Behavioralists focus on actual state behavior and try to discover patterns, causes, and effects that are both predictive and explanatory. The empirical approach formulates testable hypotheses of IR conduct. For example, a recent study exhaustively analyzed all multinational peacekeeping operations to determine the optimum conditions

---

[12] Kenneth Waltz, *Theory of International Politics* (1979).
[13] Structuralists generally emphasize the influence of international organizations and structures on decision making.

for their effectiveness.[14] Finally, game theory analogizes IR to various games involving a conflict between collective welfare, on the one hand, and individual benefit, on the other. Game theory assumes that IR bargaining involves this same conflict and that, through the analysis of game moves and outcomes, we can discover and predict certain IR outcomes.

Game theory, then, employs the mathematical modeling of rational choice in competitive or cooperative situations. Three games are especially popular with IR game theorists to demonstrate the difficulties and conditions of international cooperation. One is the "prisoners' dilemma," which posits two men in police custody for a crime they both may have committed. The two are questioned separately so they cannot communicate with each other, and each is told that he will receive lenient treatment if he confesses. The best possible outcome is cooperation and silence because in that case both will go free. However, each man will have a great incentive to "defect" from cooperation and confess to save his own skin. This game may both explain why international cooperation is so difficult to achieve and reveal how the game should be changed to achieve cooperation. A similar game is "stag hunt," which posits a band of hunters chasing a large stag; all must cooperate to take down the prize. But suddenly a hare appears that will also provide food, albeit a lesser amount. How can we keep one or more of the hunters from quitting the stag hunt to chase the hare? Another analogy to IR is the game of "chicken" where two contestants try to face each other down in a confrontation. Who will give way first? If both refuse to break off, thinking the other will surely yield, disaster may occur. This game became frighteningly real during the Cuban Missile Crisis of 1962. Luckily for the world, as Dean Rusk put it at the time, "the other fellow blinked first," and there was a cooperative outcome in the sense that the world survived a possible nuclear holocaust.

Such games demonstrate the realists' idea that international confrontation is the norm and cooperation is exceedingly rare and difficult to achieve.

## THE NEO-CONSERVATIVES: UNILATERAL AMERICAN NATIONALISTS

A group of neo-conservatives (commonly termed "neo-cons" for short) dominate U.S. foreign policy at the beginning of the twenty-first century. Two big

---

[14] Virginia Page Fortna, "Does Peacekeeping Keep Peace?" 48 International Studies Quarterly 269 (2004). There are also many empirical studies of war and the causes of war. One area of research purports to show that democratic states tend not to start wars. See Michael Nicholson, International Relations 148 (1998).

ideas anchor their thinking and policies: (1) American nationalism, aggressive assertion of what is perceived as being in the national interest of the United States, and (2) unilateralism, the idea that international institutions are hopeless, discussions with allies are useless, and only America knows best. Thus, international problems are best handled on a unilateral basis[15] with an attempt to attract followers – "coalitions of the willing," as they are called. Even long-standing and traditional allies of the United States are castigated if they do not cooperate with perceived U.S. interests, and any state that does not follow U.S. policy interests is considered in the enemy camp. Multilateral institutions are dictated to and are derided or undermined if they do not serve U.S. policy interests. The neo-cons are convinced that, as the world's only superpower, the United States is uniquely free to project its military, economic, and political power to enhance its values and interests, which they assume are (or should be) shared by the rest of the world.

Neo-conservatives are disdainful of conventional diplomacy and antagonistic to international treaties and laws. They emphasize confrontation[16] – military and economic challenges to every regime hostile to U.S. values and interests. *Global unilateralism* is their watchword – asserting U.S. power to effect change. The neo-con creed emphasizes hard power – military force – rather than the soft power of diplomacy and persuasion.[17] After the events of 9/11, the neo-con network in Washington gained dominance with a president inexperienced in foreign policy, who found that playing sheriff in a ten-gallon hat resonated with the American public.

This neo-conservative foreign policy has produced a crisis of unparalleled proportions in relations between the United States and the rest of the world. American moral authority is questioned as never before. Opinion polls in Europe, Japan, and Canada show that large majorities condemn U.S. policies and distrust American leadership.[18] This rising anti-Americanism abroad is

---

[15]  For example, Secretary of State Condoleezza Rice, while she was National Security Advisor to President Bush, publicly derided "the belief that the support of many states – or even better the United Nations – is essential to the legitimate exercise of power," quoted in Robert Kagan, *Of Paradise and Power: America and Europe in the New World Order* (2003).

[16]  For example, military action against Iraq was a long-standing neo-conservative objective that was implemented once neo-cons gained power. Stefan Halper and Jonathan Clarke, *America Alone: The Neo-Conservatives and the Global Order* (2004), pp. 147, 306.

[17]  The term "soft power" was invented and extensively analyzed by Joseph S. Nye, Jr., *The Paradox of American Power* (2002).

[18]  Stefan Halper and Jonathan Clarke, *America Alone: the Neo-conservatives and* the Global Order (2004), pp. 311–2; John Sperling, Suzanne Helburn, Samuel George, and Carl Hunt, *The Great Divide* (2004); Sam Roberts, *Who We are Now – The Changing Face of America* (2004); David Lebedoff, *The Uncivil War* (2004).

matched by a deep split over foreign policy among U.S. citizens, as symbol-ized by the red state and blue state divide, which is a split over foreign policy as much as domestic issues. Neo-conservative policies of one-sided support of Israel and confrontation with Islam have inadvertently focused and acceler-ated terrorist activity all over the world. Neo-conservatives have appropriated belief in American "exceptionalism" – the idea that American values, insti-tutions, and leadership are indispensable to global progress – to characterize differing cultural and social values as potential security threats. As a result, Islamic radicalism is becoming the dominant voice of the Muslim world, creating the danger of a clash of civilizations, which would mean unending warfare and disaster for the entire world.

## SUMMING UP

When we consider the history of the twentieth century from an IR perspec-tive, we see an undercurrent of liberal internationalism dominated almost continuously by other perspectives – realism in its many guises, imperialism, totalitarianism, and unilateralism. Only on three brief occasions did liberal internationalism – deference to international law and multilateral institu-tions – become the norm. The first occasion was, as we have seen, the early interwar period of 1919–28. This was the time of the League of Nations and the Kellogg-Briand Pact, which not only failed but also were derided by the realist camp. The second internationalist period came at the end of World War II. In this period of transition, important multilateral institutions were created that are still with us today – the United Nations, the International Monetary Fund, the World Bank, and the GATT (General Agreement on Tariffs and Trade), predecessor of the World Trade Organization – all products of the mid- to late 1940s. Even in today's globalized world, it would be difficult or impossible to create such organizations now. The mood of the times can be gleaned from a statement made by President Harry Truman at the conclusion of the 1945 San Francisco Conference that established the United Nations: "Americans must recognize that no matter how great our strength, we must deny ourselves the license to do always what we please. This is the price each nation will have to pay for world peace." The third period of internationalism occurred at the end of the Cold War when, briefly, Presidents Bush of the United States and Yeltsin of Russia proclaimed a new world order, and coop-eration with the United Nations and other multilateral organizations seemed to be the wave of the future. The diplomacy and primacy of international insti-tutions that typified the Gulf War in 1990–1, however, were short lived. They did not prevent tragedies and genocides in the Balkans, Rwanda, and else-where. September 11, 2001, seemingly sounded the death knell of the new world order.

This book poses the question whether the rejection of liberal internation-alism has been premature. Certainly, international law and institutions have manifest defects. But is there anything better or more reliable – is there any alternative? Despite the narrow Republican victory in the presidential election of 2004, there is a sense even among charter members of the neo-conservatives that international laws and institutions have been dismissed too quickly. This realization has come from bitter experience. For example, when a Chinese F-8 fighter jet intercepted a U.S. EP-3 reconnaissance plane over the South China Sea, forcing it to land on China's Hainan Island in 2001, the foreign policy team of the Bush administration at first took a hard-line stance demand-ing the immediate return of the plane and its crew. This stance turned out to be counterproductive, and the administration was forced to back down, make a statement of regret, and undertake patient negotiations. Some in the neo-con camp called this "a national humiliation," but the crew and the plane were returned. Similarly, in Iraq the Bush administration, after point-edly brushing aside the United Nations and other international bodies, now find these institutions indispensable to American goals. Condoleezza Rice, who as National Security Advisor to the President in 2002 urged a lack of concern for the opinions of an "ephemeral" international community, as Sec-retary of State in 2005 said that "no nation can build a safer, better world alone."

Neo-conservatives are committed to high ideals in their foreign policy goals. For example, President Bush in his second inaugural address in 2005 announced, "It is the policy of the United States to support the growth of democratic movements in every nation, with the ultimate goal of ending tyranny in our world." The wellspring of this ideal is a highly moralistic vision of bringing freedom and democracy to all peoples and bringing an end to what U.S. Secretary of State Rice terms "outposts of tyranny." These high ideals are redolent of Wilsonian liberal internationalism. The danger is that, despite the nobility of the ideals, this vision will founder on the methods employed, just as President Wilson's vision foundered on the partisan interests of the European powers and on the reluctance of the U.S. Congress and the American people to undertake his agenda.

The way forward in the twenty-first century is to marry the ideals of the neo-conservatives to reforms in international law and international institutions that will allow the implementation of these goals.

## FURTHER READINGS

Neil Walker (ed.), *Sovereignty in Transition* (2003).

Thomas Hobbes, *Leviathan* (1641).

For a sampling of older IR theories, see *Classical Theories of International Relations* (Ian Clark and Iver B. Newmann, eds. 1996).

A voice of criticism of realism and advocate of liberal internationalism before World War I was Norman Angell, *The Great Illusion* (1909).

Chalmers Johnson, *The Sorrows of Empire* (2004).

Samuel P. Huntington, *The Clash of Civilizations and the Remaking of World Order* (1996).

Stefan Halper and Jonathan Clarke, *America Alone: The Neo-Conservatives and the Global Order* (2004). This book is a severe criticism of the neo-conservative network from the point of view of traditional Republican principles of the conduct of foreign policy.

Irwin Stelzer, *The Neocon Reader* (2004).

Anne Norton, *Leo Strauss and the Politics of American Empire* (2004).

Joseph S. Nye, Jr., *Soft Power* (2004).

Joshua S. Goldstein, *International Relations* (3d ed. 1999)

Robert Jackson and Georg Sorensen, *Introduction to International Relations* (1999)

K. J. Holsti, *International Politics* (1995).

David Boucher, *Political Theories of International Politics* (1998).

Andreas Hasenclever, Peter Mayer, and Volker Rittberger (eds.), *Theories of International Regimes* (1997).

# 4 A New Global Order Based on International Law and Multinationalism

## A NEW GLOBAL ORDER

The realist idea that each state has only isolated, individual interests has reduced validity today. In our world of the twenty-first century there is growing interest convergence – a growing harmony of interests – among states. States all over the world now have shared interests in peace, security, economic well-being, environmental quality, and even human rights. Therefore, international cooperation cannot be exceptional, as the realist model would have it; we need a system in which cooperation is the norm. In addition, states today are not the only international actors. International organizations, transnational companies, and international NGOs are as important or more important than many states.

The United States in particular should not take a narrow view of its national interest. As the preeminent global power the United States cannot appear to be acting as if its own self-interest is all that matters. The United States must act and be perceived as acting to benefit all humanity. U.S. policies uniquely affect all nations and peoples. If America exercises its power for narrow, partisan reasons, it inspires only resentment and condemnation. The global interests of the United States demand this broad view of its national interest. Taking a global approach instead of a narrow partisan view is not "international social work"[1]; it is rational self-interest. The United States more than any nation is threatened by disorder anywhere in the world and benefits from a stable world order based on the rule of law.

In his Second Inaugural Address in January 2005, President Bush proclaimed on behalf of the United States that tyranny and oppression anywhere

---

[1] This charge was frequently made by critics of the first Clinton administration.

in the world cannot be allowed to stand and that democracy and freedom must become universal. This is an explicit affirmation of the dominance of common values in the twenty-first century. But democracy and freedom are important not only in themselves but also for their relevance to other concerns. By implication there is a common interest among all the nations of the world in such matters as peace and security, human rights, alleviating poverty and disease, and protecting the global environment.

The spread of democracy and freedom alone will not produce world order and solve world problems. There must also be a new order in international relations – a *new global order* based upon international law and multinational institutions. What does this mean? Fundamentally it is a simple idea: Political leaders of all countries including the United States must agree to observe international legal norms of behavior and must carry out their international policies through established transnational institutions. This would be a new paradigm for international cooperation – not world government but rather respect for international legal norms and international institutions. The realism paradigm for international relations would not be overthrown so much as it would be incorporated into the new framework. Power politics would not disappear, but instead of unilateralism, powerful states would have the opportunity to use their power to shape international law and institutions. Moreover, there would still be areas of international intercourse for which legal norms and institutions do not exist. Unilateral freedom of action would still be appropriate for such cases. But with respect to important areas of international policy for which we have established institutions and standards of behavior, these standards would have to be obeyed. The rule of law must replace the rule of force in the world.

A key to establishing this new internationalism is the concept of *global governance* as a supplement to the state system of political organization. Global governance recognizes the legitimacy and essential need for international institutions and regimes and their role in reconciling and accommodating diverse interests and organizing cooperative action to deal with international problems. There is no single model or form of global governance; it is a broad, dynamic, complex process of interactive decision making that varies according to the circumstances and issues being addressed.

Under this new internationalism and global governance system, international law will become a primary basis for international relations. The postwar multilateral system, centered on the United Nations and its specialized agencies, will be strengthened and reinvigorated. International law will not only be the foundation of the system for the maintenance of peace and security in the world but it will also provide the framework for collective action to solve the problems of the twenty-first century – diseases such as AIDS, poverty, lack of resources, violations of human rights, and environmental degradation. (See "The State and Human Security – A History.")

The new internationalism will be based on the important recognition that state sovereignty is not absolute. Sovereignty is not outmoded, but its meaning changes with the times. The notion that each state is a single, all-powerful sovereign is obsolete. There are in fact overlapping spheres of sovereignty with respect to international problems that are beyond the competence of any one state. Such areas may be few but are important; they are discussed in later chapters of this book.

Why is international law necessary as a basis for international relations? The realist paradigm for the conduct of international relations simply does not fit the factual context of the twenty-first century. In our world of accelerating globalization, people all over the world are more interconnected than ever before. State interdependence has metamorphosed into a genuine interdependence of peoples. State boundaries are growing ever more meaningless. In our time, perhaps for the first time in human history, we are all citizens of the world. More and more people feel at home in many different areas of the world. We are closer than ever before to realizing the eighteenth-century Enlightenment ideals of world citizenry and *cosmopolitan right*.[2] This was the vision of Immanuel Kant in 1787 of a universal community in which all members are entitled "to present themselves in the society of others by virtue of their right to the communal possession of the earth's surface."[3] Philosophers call this a right of hospitality.

## NEW THEORIES OF INTERNATIONAL RELATIONS

New theories of international relations emphasize broad incentives toward cooperation and the necessity to observe international rules. In some respects, this is an evolution not a revolution. The U.S. Supreme Court recognized as long ago as 1900 in the *Paquete Habana* case[4] that "international law is the law of the United States." International relations specialists have also developed ideas that accorded international law more respect. Beginning in the 1950s new paradigms to explain interstate cooperation were developed that differ from

---

[2]  This was first expressed by the German political philosopher Christian Wolff in his treatise, *Jus Gentium* (The Law of Nations), p. 25 (1749).
[3]  Immanuel Kant, *Essay on Perpetual Peace* (1787).
[4]  The Paquete Habana, 175 U.S. 677 (1900).

## THE STATE AND HUMAN SECURITY – A HISTORY

Because violence appears to be endemic to the human species, mankind throughout history (and doubtless before) has sought ways to enhance order and security. In the ancient world this led to the creation of various forms of **city-states**, most strikingly in the Near East, China, and Greece. The city-state system, however, did not end violence, but rather moved it to a new level. Warfare and shifting power alliances tended to culminate in a new political order, the **hegemon**, as weaker entities were conquered or dominated by stronger ones. Examples of hegemons include ancient Pharaonic Egypt, the League of Corinth organized by Philip II of Macedon after the Battle of Chaeronea (338 bce), the Zhou conquest in China (about 1050 bce), and the later rise of various empires, most notably the Roman Empire and the Chinese imperial system.

Although the hegemon system supplied a modicum of human security, periodic breakdowns resulted in various forms of **feudalism** in such widely disparate places as Europe and Japan. The modern **state system** in turn is the result of the consolidation of past city-states, hegemons and feudal orders into approximately 193 entities shaped and determined by both political will and historical accident.

In the past many political thinkers saw no alternative to the domination of the weak by the strong. Dante Alighieri (*De Monarchia*, 1310) advocated the idea of a benevolent universal hegemon, whereas Niccolò Machiavelli (*The Prince*, 1507) believed the hegemon must be prepared to use cruelty to assert its power.

In contrast, Hugo Grotius (On *the Law of War and Peace*, 1625) argued in favor of an international system based on law, and Immanuel Kant (*Perpetual Peace*, 1787) advocated international institutions. Since 1945 the world has moved toward embracing the ideals of Grotius and Kant as keys to human security. In the age of globalization human security means more than peace and order; it also includes meeting a modicum of other needs as well as protection of the global environment.

realist assumptions. After World War II many countries developed a high level of transnational relations in many fields, particularly in defense, trade, and investment. Scholars realized that these relations created interdependence that fed on itself, producing even closer relations. This process was termed *functionalism*[5] – the idea that greater economic interdependence could lead to peace. Ernst Haas developed a theory of *neo-functionalism*[6] to explain the

[5] David Mitrany, *The Functional Theory of Politics* (1943).
[6] Ernst B. Haas, *Beyond the Nation-State: Functionalism and International Organization* (1958).

process of European integration that began in the 1950s. Haas recognized that international cooperation is a process, not a one-off, isolated phenomenon.

After the 1950s, specialists in international relations developed a general theory to explain cooperation among states. Robert Keohane and Joseph Nye in their 1977 book, *Power and Interdependence: World Politics in Transition*, suggested that there exists a "complex interdependence" among states that is qualitatively different from earlier and simpler kinds of interdependence. Although previously interdependence had been achieved only with respect to security and defense, in the second half of the twentieth century interdependence concern economic, social, and cultural matters as well. Moreover, relations among states involve not only national leaders but also transactions on many levels of government and increasingly among nonstate actors. Military concerns often fade into the background, and social and economic welfare issues come to the fore. Complex interdependence means that international politics is more like domestic politics: There are a wide variety of issue areas and shifting coalitions of actors (termed "pluralism") involving NGOs and transnational corporations, as well as governments. This leads to a world of more cooperative international relations.

A further development of the ideas of complex interdependence is known as *regime theory* or *institutionalism*.[7] An international regime is a set of rules, norms, principles, decisions, and procedures around which the expectations of state and nonstate actors revolve and converge. Regimes involve many different issues from arms control to climate change to Antarctica. Each regime comprises many like-minded states that agree and expect others to live up to certain standards of behavior. NGOs, transnational corporations, and other nonstate actors and interest groups participate in regimes vicariously through states or as nonvoting observers. Regimes typically involve the creation of international organizations that operate independently to some degree from their member states.

In the latter half of the twentieth century, international regimes became an important and widespread phenomenon, dominating many issue areas, such as climate change, international trade, and international monetary policy. At the beginning of the twenty-first century not only do these regimes now cover virtually every conceivable international field, but many have universal state membership or nearly so. For example, the United Nations with its many specialized agencies that deal with everything from health to the oceans has 191 members. The International Monetary Fund and World Bank have this many members as well; the World Trade Organization has 149, and more

---

[7] See Fred Kratochwil and Edward D. Mansfield, *International Organizations* (1994).

members join each year. Thirty or forty additional regimes have members that number about 100 states. In addition to multilateral global regimes, regional and bilateral regimes are also very important and common.

As a result, the international relations of most states today is mostly conducted through regimes and international institutions. States increasingly must formulate their foreign policies across a web of interconnected past actions taken by themselves and their regime partners. A president or prime minister will inevitably seek to justify a policy in terms of accepted behavioral norms and institutions. Even when governments change there is continuity of policy because of membership and commitments made in these international regimes. These commitments constrain state sovereignty and independence in international relations. Scholars taking note of this development go so far as to say that, in today's world, state interests and identities are profoundly affected and even forged by the international regimes in which they participate. This idea – which is called *constructivism* – stands the realist paradigm on its head.[8] Thus, realism is not an adequate explanation of international relations in the twenty-first century.

Closely allied with these new approaches are specialists in international relations who posit an international society of states bound together by common interests and values. States then seek to formulate a common set of rules and institutions to guide their relations. This process is creative of an international society[9] governed by law, diplomacy, and institutions, as well as by power relationships. This international society is neither prone to unending discord and warfare nor is it a developing world community of unlimited progress. Rather, international society must be guided as a specialized branch of human relations for the management of world problems. The leading proponent of this view, Hedley Bull,[10] recognizes the role of overlapping and segmented international authorities and nonstate actors, such as NGOs, companies, and institutions, but regards states as of central importance.

All of these new theories have in common an emphasis on international law. What must occur is nothing less than a revolution in the way international relations is conducted. As Philip Allott has written:

International Society . . . chose to be an unsocial society creating itself separately from the development of its subordinate societies, ignoring the ideal of democracy,

---

[8] See especially, J. G. Ruggie, *Constructing the World Polity: Essays on International Institutionalism* (1998), and Alexander Wendt, *Social Theory of International Politics* (1999).

[9] This approach to international relations is also known as rationalism and the English School because it is dominated by British academics.

[10] Hedley Bull, The Anarchical Society: A Study of Order in World Politics (2d ed. 1995).

depriving itself of the possibility of using social power, especially legal relations, to bring about the survival and prospering of the whole human race.

There is no reason why international society should not reconceive itself as a society, using social power, and especially legal relations, to bring about the survival and prospering of the whole human race.[11]

## INTERNATIONAL LAW: ECLIPSE AND REVIVAL

The close connection between international law and the new thinking in international relations appears to be obvious.[12] Take regime theory, for example. What are rules, norms, principles, and decisions, if not law? Do not functionalism, neo-functionalism, institutionalism, constructivism, and all the other "isms" of IR scholarship and thinking presume old-fashioned law?

Somewhat surprisingly, however, until recently neither IR academics nor practitioners had much regard for international law. Even now, pick up any book about international relations, and international law will be presented if at all as an arcane area of study that is not important (along with, frequently, international organizations) and anyway can be left to the strange specialists who are interested in this kind of thing.

For many IR specialists international law is merely another tool of the trade – to be used when convenient and to be ignored when demanded by circumstances or overriding concerns. This view also colors how political leaders view international organizations: They are considered to be only convenient meeting and discussion forums, not separate and important entities capable of taking action in their own right.

The eclipse of international law's relevance to dealing with world problems reflects the dominance of the realist paradigm in international affairs. Traditional realism, as we have seen, emphasizes what Hans Morgenthau famously declared to be the "iron law of international politics, that legal obligations must yield to the national interest."[13] Realist practitioners of international relations regard international law as a potential trap: Law is incapable of creating order on the international plane, and it is naive to think that all that is required for world order is the right kind of law. Furthermore, international law presumes international cooperation and international organizations established to pursue the common interests of humankind. For the realist, however,

[11]  Phillip Allott, *Eunomia: A New Order for a New World* (1990), pp. 416–7.
[12]  See Robert J. Beck, Anthony Clark Arend, and Robert D. Vander Lugt, *International Rules* (1996).
[13]  Hans Morgenthau, *In Defense of the National Interest*, p. 144 (1951).

national policy interests are paramount, and cooperation is a will of the wisp, difficult to achieve and illusory in the end.

This disdain for international law among realists was famously displayed by former U.S. Secretary of State Dean Acheson in his comments on the 1962 Cuban Missile Crisis, which was triggered by the emplacement of Soviet missiles in Cuba that brought the United States and the Soviet Union to the verge of nuclear war. "I must conclude," he said, "the propriety of the Cuban quarantine [the successful U.S. blockade of Cuba] is not a legal issue."

This view that international law is not important or can be manipulated is prevalent even today. Disregard of international law is illustrated by the U.S. government's handling of the 2003 invasion of Iraq and the abusive treatment of prisoners in Iraq, Afghanistan, and Guantanamo Bay, Cuba. The U.S. government, we know now, simply went shopping for the "right" legal opinions. In the case of the Iraq War, recognized experts were ignored, whereas the advice of an obscure law professor at the University of California was found to be authoritative. In the prison abuse cases, standards of treatment based on international legal norms advocated by U.S. State Department attorneys were ignored in favor of memoranda written by lawyers at the Pentagon and the Justice Department. Is it any wonder that, if the way to treat legal constraints is to shop for an answer you like, the administration got into so much hot water? It is as if taxpayers could pay any amount of taxes that was convenient as long as they could find a lawyer willing to agree with their position.

Although international law was always more relevant than the realists liked to admit, even during the Cold War, beginning in the 1990s leading academics in both international relations and international law engaged in a cooperative dialogue and programs of joint research.[14] International relations experts now readily admit the relevance of legal rules and processes in the construction and operation of international regimes and international problem solving. International law also offers IR new and useful models of cooperation; game theory is no longer the only explanation for international cooperation.[15] International law is a means for both asserting individual interests while arriving at a common position that serves all participants.

---

[14]  See especially, Kenneth W. Abbott, "Modern International Relations Theory: A Prospectus for International Lawyers," 14 *Yale International Law Journal* 335 (1989); Anne-Marie Slaughter, "International Law and International Relations Theory: A Dual Agenda," 87 *American Journal Of International Law* 205 (1993).

[15]  Martti Koskienniemi, drawing on his experiences as a Finnish diplomat, argues that normative discourse during a crisis has the capacity to focus and transform the interests of states and can create the conditions for cooperation. "The Place of Law in Collective Security," 17 *Michigan Journal of International Law* 455 (1996).

But not everyone is convinced; in fact, doubters are probably in the majority.[16] There are five principal reasons for disdain for international law:

1. International law is a variety of discredited "natural law."

2. The concept of law, a system of common rules, is out of step with the pluralism of the state system.

3. There is no way to enforce law against sovereign states.

4. International law is an impractical system of morality.

5. International law is antithetical to democratic values because it pays need to norms generated by undemocratic countries and nondemocratic processes.

Let us consider these objections in turn.

## Natural Law Origins

The historical roots of international law derive from the ancient Romans, who posited a theory of natural law. The clearest statement of natural law comes from the Roman lawyer and statesman Marcus Tullius Cicero (100–43 BCE), who stated,

True Law is Reason, natural justice, commanding people to fulfill their obligations and forbidding them from doing wrong. Its validity is universal; it is immutable and eternal. All good men keep its commands and prohibitions; those not influenced by such law are bad. Any attempt to supersede this law is wrong.[17]

This is a concept of a good and perfect law that exists in the realm of ideas. Lawyers like Cicero believed that this *lex naturalis* (natural law) had its source in innate ideas naturally present in all human beings and was discoverable by a priori (deductive) reasoning.

During the Christian Middle Ages in Europe, this overriding natural law was considered a reflection of the mind of God. Thomas Aquinas (1224/25–1274), the most influential medieval Christian theologian, writing in the thirteenth century, stated that law is a creation of human reason that participates in the eternal law of God.[18]

Lawyers and scholars put international law to practical use in the sixteenth century. The most famous example is the exploration undertaken by the

---

[16] See Jack L. Goldsmith and Eric A. Posner, *The Limits of International Law* (2005).
[17] Marcus Tullius Cicero, *De Republica* (On the State, 46 BCE).
[18] Thomas Aquinas, *Summa Theolgiae, Prima Secundae*, 90–1.

Spanish Dominican priest and professor of theology, Francisco de Vitoria (1480–1546), of the conquest and colonization of the Americas in his book, *De Indis* (On the Indians), and its sequel, *De Jure Belli* (On the Laws of War).[19] Taking his cue from Aquinas, Vitoria argued that there is a *jus gentium* (literally "law of peoples," but always rendered in English as "law of nations") binding on all nations that have achieved a modicum of social organization; it is a universal order of right to which rulers must conform their actions. The norms of *jus gentium* derive their authority from the natural law, and because they are known naturally (*naturaliter*), they are knowable by all human beings regardless of culture. Although ultimately justifying the Spanish conquests on what we would today consider dubious grounds (various acts of misconduct by the Indians), Vitoria nevertheless articulated standards that must be observed in warfare (no killing of noncombatants or prisoners).

The title of "father of international law" is accorded to the Dutch lawyer, Hugo de Groot (1583–1645), known as Grotius, because he clearly differentiated natural law from the law of nations. In his book, *De Jure Belli ac Pacis* (On the Law of War and Peace, 1625), Grotius classified two different forms of law: (1) natural law, which is a universal law of reason, and (2) a voluntary law of nations created by the will and agreement of rulers and states. Grotius did not deny the natural law, but he maintained that the law of nature would be the same even if God did not exist. Grotius argued that treaties are binding not only on the rulers who conclude them but on their states as well. This principle of justice and morality makes it possible for states and rulers to create by their will and agreement a body of positive, voluntary law. States must adhere to both types of law, as Grotius wrote: "The state which transgresses the laws of nature and of nations cuts away the bulwarks which safeguard its own future peace."[20] This was a reaction to the ongoing slaughter of the Thirty Years War.

Grotius thus began a tradition that would grow into the international law that we know today: a set of rules based on will and not innate ideas derived from some metaphysical "universal reason." This tradition is known as *positivism* – the idea that law is created by conscious, voluntary acts of will, and that state practice and treaties create international law to govern relations among states. This idea fit in nicely with the emergent state system that arose out of the Peace of Westphalia (1648).

[19] Both were first given as lectures in 1537 at the University of Salamanca, and later published in 1557. They are available in English translation as *De Indis et de Jure Belli Reflectiones* in J. P. Bate, ed., *Classics of International Law* (1917).
[20] Grotius, *On the Law of War and Peace* (1625).

Grotius's ideas were more fully developed by the seventeenth century German scholar Samuel Pufendorf (1632–94) in his book, *De Jure Naturae et Gentium* (1688), formulated three categories of natural law principles binding on states: (1) respect for mutual rights and the duty to refrain from harming others; (2) the duty of good faith, and (3) the duty to keep agreements and promises. Yet, Pufendorf posited an idea of sovereignty that meant that states were supreme and unaccountable to higher authority. This highlighted two fundamental defects in the law of nations – the absence of centralized institutions of law making, adjudication, and executive enforcement of laws and the impossibility of sanctions in the case of breach of obligations.

These defects led the lawyer and philosopher Christian Wolff (1679–1754)[21] to invent the idea of a world civil society (*civitas gentium maxima*), a kind of supreme world state of which all states are presumed to be members. Through this *civitas gentium maxima* voluntary law was embedded in the natural law of reason, which he termed "necessary law." Wolff's *civitas gentium maxima* was a device to explain how the law of nations could be binding on all states.

Despite the appeal of these ideas, the metaphysical and theological origins of international law cast doubt on its legitimacy. W. W. Bishop makes this point as follows:

Building upon what seems to us a curious hodgepodge of recorded practice, ideas of ethics and morals, accounts in imaginative literature, legal doctrines of Roman law and of the Canon law, theological speculations, and whatever else came to hand, these writers formulated the principles and rules of international law.[22]

Men influenced by the new science of the Enlightenment and the empiricism of the philosopher John Locke repudiated this early conception of natural law and the law of nations. Empiricism denied the existence of innate rational ideas and stressed that all ideas ultimately derive from experience. Scholars such as Richard Zouche (1590–1660) in England and Cornelius van Bynkershoek (1673–1743) in Holland enhanced the new approach to international law we term *positivism*.[23] International law is created not from innate ideas or deductively from reason, but rather from the actual practices and agreements of states. This positivist conception of international law triumphed in the nineteenth and twentieth century. Today, as we shall see, international

---

[21] Christian Wolff, *Jus Gentium Methodo Scientifica Pertractatum* (1749).

[22] W. W. Bishop, *International Law* 17 (1971).

[23] The term "positivism" was popularized by the French philosopher and sociologist Auguste Comte (1798–1857). See Auguste Comte, *Early Political Writings* (trans. H. S. Jones, 1998). The key idea is distrust of any claim that cannot be objectively observed, explained, or measured. When applied to law, positivism demanded that the sources of law be objectively verifiable and empirical, not a priori and based only on reason and innate ideas.

law is fully positivist. As a result, the natural law objection to international law is without foundation.

## Pluralism

The idea of an international society of states did not appear historically until the mid-eighteenth century in Europe. The person most responsible for this conception was the Swiss jurist, Emerich de Vattel (1714–67), whose fame rests on his book, *Droit de Gens* (Law of Nations), published in 1758. Vattel's work was positivist in orientation, with elements drawn from the older natural law tradition. He rejected Grotius's understanding of international law as a unitary law of nature binding upon all states; but he also rejected Christian Wolff's conception of a great world community, the *civitas gentium maxima*. Instead Vattel posited a universal society of all nations founded on the notion of sovereign equality. Vattel's universal society differed from that of Wolff in being a society of free, independent, and equal states that constituted the foundations of the voluntary, positive law of nations. This is a doctrine of pluralism and a conception of an international law "which proceeds from the will and consent of nations." Vattel recognized the primacy of the will of states, rather than of human reason, in law making. He placed great store in the equality and independence of states and the duty of nonintervention. His ideas laid the groundwork for the pluralist idea that because every state has its own separate interests, law can play only a very limited role in international relations. In Vattel's view the balance of power among states had primacy over any legal restraints.

Nevertheless, Vattel maintained that pluralism is not unlimited and that natural law has a role to play in international relations.[24] Even in a pluralistic system there are what he called "offices of humanity," a strong duty to assist, for example, a nation if it is unjustly attacked by a powerful enemy. Vattel even posited the necessity of what we would call today humanitarian intervention; he wrote that international society should unite "to repress . . . outrageous fanatics" – states that violate treaties and promises or that oppress their own people. Thus, pluralism and the existence of separate state interests were not incompatible with law even in the eighteenth century. In the twenty-first century, although our conception of international society has not yet reached the point of Wolff's *civitas gentium maxima*, we can identify many more common interests than existed among states in Vattel's time. Thus, correspondingly, there is more need for and more scope for international law.

---

[24] Andrew Hurrell, "Vattel: Pluralism and its Limits," in *Classical Theories of International Relations*, eds., Ian Clarke and Iver B. Neumann, 1996, p. 233.

## Lack of Coercive Enforcement

Vattel's universal society of free, equal, and independent nations highlights an old difficulty: the lack of coercive enforcement. How can there be law among states that are subject to no external higher authority? Two answers were provided to this problem.

First, the philosopher Immanuel Kant (1724–1804) put forth a solution in his book, *Perpetual Peace* (1795). He proposed that the way to overcome the natural tendency of states to wage war was to create a constitutional foundation for the law of nations in the form of a federation of free states. This federation should be created by treaty in which the parties commit to the rule of international law. This idea presages the creation of the United Nations; Kant was more than 150 years ahead of his time.

Second, the doctrines of positivism and pluralism led to a new and more fundamental objection to international law. Nineteenth century legal philosophers, such as Jeremy Bentham (1748–1832)[25] and John Austin (1790–1859), attacked the claim that international law is really law. After all, they reasoned, What is law but the product of some recognized, positive law-making process undertaken by a sovereign state? Furthermore, to be law, a rule must be backed by coercion in the form of sanctions. When tested against these criteria, international law is not law: There is no sovereign and no recognized law-making body. Most important, there is no centralized system of sanctions or coercion. International law is a system that allows all states discretion about what the law is and how it should be interpreted, so it cannot be law in the true sense of the word. International law is really only a system of international morality. This viewpoint is still very persuasive to many people.

This objection raises the question, What is law? If the essence of law is sovereign command and coercion, Bentham and Austin are correct. But, as argued in the next section of this chapter, if law is possible without a sovereign command and coercion is not the essence of law, international law is really law.

## International Law as Morality

Reducing international law to morality accounts for the objection that the legalistic-moralistic approach cannot provide practical answers to international problems. George Kennan, diplomat and author of the famous memorandum on containment, which from 1946 provided the central tenet of U.S.

---

[25] Jeremy Bentham is responsible for the term "international law" replacing the older term "law of nations." In his book, *Introduction to Principles of Morals and Legislation* (1789), he argued that international law was a more meaningful term. His idea caught on.

policy toward the Soviet Union, attacked international law on this ground, and said that "there are no accepted standards of morality to which the U.S. government could appeal if it wished to act in the name of moral (meaning international legal) principles." He decried moralistic (synonymously, legalistic) thinking as "the most serious fault" of American foreign policy. Law should be kept out of foreign policy, Kennan believed, because "[international] law is too abstract, too inflexible, too hard to adjust to the demands of the unpredictable and the unexpected."[26]

Kennan mistakenly equated international law with morality, as many people do even today. This is a legacy of the criticisms of the positivist critics, such as John Austin. International law has responded to this criticism, as detailed below, by developing distinctly positivist foundations that are no longer dependent on natural law ideas and theories. There is no moral compulsion to comply with international law not only because states are not moral actors but also and more fundamentally because law and morality are distinct. Both law and morality are normative systems, but they stand on independent foundations. Moral norms are founded on a system of religious or humanistic belief or authority; legal norms rest on a *sui generis*, positivistic foundation that has been termed the *Grundnorm* (Basic Norm or first constitution)[27] or "rule of recognition."[28] Of course, the two normative systems of law and morality are closely related and frequently coincide, but this does not destroy their distinctness. Legal norms are frequently either less demanding or more demanding than moral codes. International law, like law generally, is not rooted in any general or particular system of morality.

The separation between law and morality is poorly understood, because the *Grundnorm* or rule of recognition that is the basis of law has never been clearly defined.[29] I attempt to do so in the next section. Briefly put, this *Grundnorm* is *community* and *justice*.

## Democratic Values

There is an argument that international law is antithetical to democracy because it is made by unrepresentative institutions and by states that are

---

[26] George Kennan, *American Diplomacy 1900–1950* (1951), p. 82.
[27] Hans Kelsen, *General Theory of Law and State* (1946).
[28] H. L. A. Hart, "Positivism and the Separation of Law and Morals," 71 *Harvard Law Review* 593 (1958).
[29] Some legal theorists, such as H. L. A. Hart, would by-pass the necessity of grounding legal rules in some basic norm that gives the rest their legitimacy. Hart states in his Concept of Law (Oxford, 1961), pp. 223–4, "The rules of a simple structure are, like the basic rule of more advanced systems, binding if they are accepted and function as such."

undemocratic and even abusive to their people. Why should the United
States be bound by treaties or courts staffed by people from such states and by
unelected international bureaucrats? This objection raises a further question –
what is the basis of obligation under international law? Many theories of
the foundation of obligation have been advanced, but there is one common
thread – no state is bound under international law, whether to a treaty or even
customary law, without its participation and consent. Thus, the foundation of
international law, unlike domestic law, is consent. This means that, when
the law binds the United States or any other state, it has participated in the
making of the law and has chosen to be bound. A converse proposition is
that the United States or any other state can choose not to accept specific
rules or regimes. But once consent has been given, repudiation of the obligation must be done according to accepted legal norms. Thus, the process
of accepting obligation under international law is consistent with democratic
values because the only way that international law can bind the United States
is through consent expressed by a decision (or decisions) taken pursuant to
established constitutional norms; in other words, through regular democratic
constitutional processes.

   With this introduction, we can now proceed to defining what we mean by
law and international law.


## UNDERSTANDING INTERNATIONAL LAW: A PRIMER

### The Function of Law in Society

What is the function of law in society? This is not well understood, even,
or I should say especially, by lawyers. Most people think of law as a system
of rules, most of them negative or unpleasant. Do not drive over the speed
limit, file your tax return with a postmark of April 15, and so on. But this is
an erroneous oversimplification. Law is not a set of rules. Rather, *law is a
system of legal relations between people and all other components of society.*[30]
Law creates and maintains an invisible web of connections between you
and the members of your family, your employer, your government, and any
other governments, companies, and organizations with whom you choose to
deal. Law does this through a complex web of rights, liberties, powers, and
immunities and corresponding duties, nonrights, liabilities, and disabilities.

---

[30]  This insight I owe to Charles de Montesquieu (1689–1755). The Baron de Montesquieu's
    most famous political work is *The Spirit of the Laws* (1748). For him laws "are the necessary
    relations deriving from the nature of things."

For example, the law gives me a copyright in the book I am writing. This creates a right to the product of my work and a duty on the part of other people to recognize my right. I have a liberty to do what I wish to my work and a power to sell it. I have immunity if I destroy or alter it.

Law has a creative function – what it has the power to create is society. Politics cannot perform this creative function. Political relationships are not firm or binding. Political relationships and processes create and alter legal relationships, but the legal relationships are crucial because they alone carry the weight of obligation, which is essential to the creation of society. *Law and society are co-terminous; each is an integral part of the structure of society.*

This society-creating function of law is the reason why law is indispensable for international society as well. This is the point that is overlooked by international relations specialists who adhere to the centrality of the realist paradigm: Law performs the same function in international society as it does in domestic societies and is just as essential. Law creates relations among international actors and thereby creates international society. It is law that ties all actors together in a vast infinite web of relations and thereby conditions individual actors' behavior, as well as the common interests of that society as a whole. *International society could not exist without law.*

How does law accomplish this function? Political scientists who formulate institutionalism and regime theories of international relations sometimes overlook the *transforming power* of law. Modern IR theories define regimes as sets of rules, principles, norms, and decisions, and these "sets" are considered political in nature because political processes create them. But in fact, although political processes create these sets, after their creation they change character: they become law.

How does this transformation occur? The key concept of this transformation is *obligation*, the idea that international actors are legally bound to comply with their commitments. Obligation creates law and legalization. Legalization is different in kind from politics or morality because it creates relationships in the form of rights and duties. Whereas power and interests are all important in political discourse, legalization transforms this discourse into nonpower terms, the terms of rights and duties. Legalization therefore transforms a power-oriented society into a rule-oriented society. Power obviously is still important, but its impact is diminished.

Legalization opens a whole new world of concepts that are essential but are generally overlooked. First, international law obligations that are undertaken must be implemented, which usually means through the passage of appropriate domestic legislation and administrative regulations. Second, there is a duty of compliance, the duty to observe domestic norms and to fulfill international commitments. Third, a dispute may arise concerning the international obligations undertaken; it is therefore necessary to make provision for dispute resolution or to refer a matter to a duly authorized tribunal. This involves the creation of systems for adjudication of international disputes. Fourth, transnational and international organizations and the United Nations may play a central role, particularly in evaluating the effectiveness of an international regime in attaining its purpose. It may be the case that, even with perfect implementation and compliance, more should be undertaken to achieve the intended result. For example, the Kyoto Protocol on Climate Change will achieve only a minimal reduction of greenhouse gas emissions; additional actions will be necessary to ameliorate climate change. In short, legalization on the international plane means the creation and operation of an international legal system.

The international legal system creates and maintains the rule of law in international society. This is why international law is so important. Only law is capable of transforming the power relationships of realism into the non-power relationships of community. The power of international actors is not eliminated, but it is transformed. This is the power and role of international law, which, along with international organizations, is now central to international relations.

## INTERNATIONAL SOCIETY

What is international society? Does such a thing really exist? To understand this term, it is necessary to refer to the origin of society itself. According to modern political theory, the origin of human society is founded on the principle of necessity: As Thomas Hobbes (1588–1679) stated in his work, *Leviathan*, the natural state of mankind is a "condition of war" in which "the notions of right and wrong, justice and injustice have no place." As a consequence the life of men is "nasty, brutish and short." Civil society for Hobbes is a social contract to establish justice and the basic principles of social order. John Locke (1632–1704) echoed Hobbes' views in his *Two Treatises on Civil Government* (1690). Jean-Jacques Rousseau (1712–78) added the crucial insight that, rather than an historical event, the social contract is an ongoing enterprise, a shared commitment, which he termed "la volonté generale."[31] Of course, this social contract is reflected in the constitutions and laws that are its positive embodiments.

---

[31] Jean-Jacques Rousseau, *The Social Contract* (Maurice Cranston, trans. 1968)

## INTERNATIONAL SOCIETY

What is international society? Three conceptions may be distinguished:

1. International society is limited to states.

2. International society includes all international actors – in addition to states, it includes intergovernmental organizations, NGOs, multinational corporations, and even individuals. This view is sometimes called pluralism or cosmopolitanism.

3. There is no international society; the term is a convenient fiction. This is the view of classical realists who posit that that the rules of the international system create anarchy, in which power is the only effective restraining force.

International society must be understood in the same way. Without international society, international relations can be based only upon power. International society does not eliminate power, but it interjects additional values based upon justice and the rule of law. International society then is also an ongoing "volonté generale," and the creative force behind it is international law.

International society includes all international actors and subjects that are affected, in the sense that they derive rights and duties from the international legal system. As we shall see, this includes individual and institutional actors as well as states (see "International Society").

## The International Legal System

As might be expected, the international legal system is very different from the legal system of any sovereign state. This should not be surprising or off-putting. After all, there is no mandatory pattern to which legal systems must conform, and the national legal systems of the world differ widely. It is commonplace to hear people – even international lawyers who should know better – say that the international legal system is "primitive." This pejorative label is to be vigorously denied. The international legal system is far from primitive; on the contrary, it is extremely sophisticated and complex, as I show here.

The complexity of the international legal system is such that the reader will have to persist to the end of this book to obtain a grasp of the details. Even this entire book provides only an introduction to the topic. But here I sketch the bare outlines of the international legal system in order to provide a frame of reference for what is to come.

International law has changed and progressed dramatically in the past 100 years, probably more so than any other field of law. To the lawyer of 1914, the year of the outbreak of the First World War and the beginning of the travails of the twentieth century, the international law system of today would be unrecognizable. Our system of international law is what is essentially different about the international system of today compared to that of 1914. This international legal system is what will spare us, one hopes, from reliving something akin to the horrible events of the past.

International law has now departed its natural law roots in response to the positivist challenge. In fact, the positivist and realist challenges have been extremely useful in stimulating new thinking and reforms. In this introduction, I summarize the essential aspects of the international law system.

## Sources of International Law

Because there is no world government or legislative body, the international legal system has had to elaborate a complex system of sources of law and law making. On this point positivist critics have been heard. Natural law is no longer considered a legitimate source, though occasionally even respected scholars lapse into this fallacy. An elaborate doctrine of sources of international law has been formulated to replace natural law and to meet the objections of positivist critics, such as John Austin.

**Treaty Law.** There is now a recognized hierarchy of positive sources of international law. The most important source is *treaty law*. A treaty is an international agreement usually between states, but sometimes with or between international organizations. The term "treaty" covers all kinds of international agreements – conventions, covenants, protocols, pacts, accords, and so forth.

Treaties are essentially contracts between the parties who agree to them because nonparties' rights are unaffected. Treaties cover every conceivable topic and international operation from peacemaking to the transfer of territory. They may be bilateral (two-party) or multilateral. Many treaties, such as the Charter of the United Nations, are virtually universal in that almost all states are parties. The treaty form was the main method used to create the European Union (EU) and the process of European integration. Thus, the treaty is the principal method for creating international regimes and institutions. More than 400,000 bilateral and multilateral treaties have been registered with the U.N. Office of Legal Affairs.

Most treaties are registered with the United Nations and published in the U.N. Treaty Series, which runs to hundreds of volumes. The law pertaining to treaties was codified and adopted in 1969 as the Vienna Convention on Treaties. So we even have a "treaty on treaties" as our guide in this field. Treaty law is framed to make treaties binding obligations once they are agreed upon and go into force, but accepting a treaty obligation is voluntary, and there are legal ways to withdraw from or terminate a treaty. A treaty is analogous to legislation in domestic law: It is a formal method of defining international legal obligations and relationships. The Vienna Convention on Treaties is very important because it sets out clear rules as to what is a treaty and how treaties operate and are to be interpreted. Three factors are important in interpretation: (1) the literal meaning of the words used, (2) the context, and (3) the purpose. Supplementary means of interpretation, such as the debates and documents leading up to the treaty, cannot be used in interpretation unless employing the aforementioned factors "leaves the meaning ambiguous or obscure" or "leads to a result which is manifestly absurd or unreasonable" (Articles 31–2).

**Customary Law.** *Custom* is a second, much less important but still valid source of international law. Custom as a source of law has an ancient pedigree going back to the ancient world. In English common law, custom was important, and this importance was carried over to American law. Custom is still used by American courts to create law. An important instance was in 1970 when the Oregon Supreme Court declared a customary law right for the public use of beaches on the Oregon coast.[32]

How does custom create law? The fundamental idea is that a state practice vis-a-vis other states that is carried on over a sufficient period of time may ripen into law. There are two separate requirements that must be present for this change to occur. First, the state practice must be widespread on a global or at least regional basis for a certain length of time, usually a long period. Second, the state practice in question must be carried on not for convenience or out of good will, but out of a sense of legal obligation. In other words the state officials must say to themselves, "Well, we have always done x and we expect x from other states, so there is no choice in the matter." Custom recognizes that a right/duty relationship has been created through state practice. For example, diplomatic immunity was long recognized as a customary law right before there were treaties on the subject.

It is easy to criticize the doctrine of customary international law – it is a very vague and indeterminate doctrine. How many years and how universal must a practice be? There is no firm answer. How can we infer that a practice is done out of a sense of legal obligation when there is almost never an explicit announcement that this is the case – states do not like to assume obligations unnecessarily.

---

[32]  State ex rel. Thornton v. Hay, 254 Or. 584, 462 P. 2d 50 (1970).

But the doctrine of custom is real lawyers' law. Every lawyer worth his or her salt gets a warm feeling at the idea of handling a custom case. Determining each of the two elements of custom is simply a matter of finding proof on a case-by-case basis. On both sides of the issue this is lawyers' work – gathering and presenting the evidence and making legal arguments. Although not every case of custom is a close one – most are fairly clear – the cases on the margin are extremely interesting and often quite important. For example, in 1900 the U.S. Supreme Court considered the case of the *Paquete Habana*,[33] concerning two Cuban fishing boats that were seized by U.S. warships while fishing on the open seas. Because the seizures occurred just after the Spanish-American War had broken out (Spain was the colonial master of Cuba), the vessels were seized as prizes of war. The Cuban owners won their case by providing meticulous proof that for centuries coastal fishermen were allowed to ply their trade even in times of war, and this was the customary law rule. Reading the opinion of the Supreme Court, one gets a sense that the Justices had great fun poring over the evidence and debating the issues.[34]

Another famous custom debate occurred in the *North Sea Continental Shelf* cases (1969)[35] between Germany on the one hand and Denmark and the Netherlands on the other in connection with drawing (the technical term is "delimiting") the maritime boundaries between the three countries. At stake were billions of dollars worth of offshore oil and gas in the North Sea. In litigation before the International Court of Justice, a key issue was whether a principle of law for delimiting maritime boundaries known as the "equidistance principle" was customary law. Under the equidistance principle Germany would get very little oil and gas because of the concave character of the coastline in the frontier areas in question. The International Court, after carefully considering the evidence, concluded that the equidistance principle had not been accepted by a sufficient number of states for enough time to be a customary law rule. This opened the way for Germany to claim and obtain a much greater share of the offshore riches.

Despite the indeterminacy of customary international law, vast areas of international relations are regulated – with remarkable success for the most part – by custom considered as legally binding. For example, the United States has been content to allow the entire law governing the oceans of the world – the

---

[33]   175 U.S. 677 (1900).
[34]   As an aside the rule of law in this case is now completely different. Under the U.N. Convention on the Law of the Sea each coastal state has an exclusive economic zone (EEZ) over which it exercises control over coastal fishing in war and in peace.
[35]   169 ICJ Rep. 3.

law of the sea – to be governed by custom because it has declined to be a party to the U.N. Convention on the Law of the Sea. Other important areas of law are also left to custom: for example, the law relating to territory and state sovereignty and jurisdiction. Custom even supplements treaty law in certain areas, such as the law relating to the use of force.

**General Principles.** A third source of international law is called *general principles of law*. These are rules of general applicability that are features of a great number of the legal systems of the world and include due process of law, the right to certain procedural standards in any legal proceeding, and the rule that no party should be the judge of its own case. This source of law relies upon the method of comparative law to derive a legal rule. The search for a general principle of law involves surveying the law of many and various national jurisdictions to determine the existence of common doctrines. General principles of law are not allowed to displace either treaty law or customary law and so are relegated to filling the gaps in international law. Nevertheless, a general principle can be determinative. In the 1937 *River Meuse*[36] case between Belgium and the Netherlands, the International Court applied the general principle, "where two parties have assumed an identical or a reciprocal obligation, one party which is engaged in continuing non-performance of that obligation should not be permitted to take advantage of a similar non-performance of that obligation by the other party." The court accordingly ruled that the Netherlands could not complain in court against Belgian diversion of the Meuse River shared by the parties, where the Netherlands was also making unauthorized use of the river waters.

A very useful general principle employed in certain cases is the rule of equity. Equity as a general principle of law is the idea that in certain cases the inflexibility of a rule of law must be modified to some degree in order to come to a just result. Sometimes a rule of law must be particularized or fit into the unique circumstances of an individual situation; equity is based on the concept that one size does not fit all. Equity also can be used to supplement legal rules. In this way it functions to fill gaps and to prevent what is called a *non liquet*, a refusal by a court to decide a case because of the lack of any applicable legal principle. Equity as a general principle of law must be distinguished from the idea of a judge deciding a case without regard to any rule of law, totally on the basis of what is "fair and good" (*ex aequo et bono*). In applying equity as a general principle, the judge will use the framework of existing law as far as possible. A good example is the aforementioned *North Sea Continental*

---

[36]  1937 PCIJ Rep. series A/B, 70.

*Shelf cases*, where the court ruled that equitable considerations applied to the boundary delimitation and formulated certain equitable principles, but left it to the parties to actually apply them to the case at hand.

**Subsidiary Sources.** Finally, there are two sources of international law that are termed "subsidiary" (secondary) by international lawyers, but are often very important in practice: *decisions of international courts and tribunals* and *writings of legal experts*. Decisions of international courts and tribunals are important for the basic reason that consistency is regarded very highly as a virtue in the law. Therefore, international lawyers pay attention to precedents, not because they are controlling strictly speaking, but because they are clear examples of applications of a rule and often provide interpretations of what a rule means. International judges are not supposed to formulate rules of law on their own, but interpretations, often of great importance, are common in individual litigated cases. Judges also strive to be consistent in the sense that they apply the same rule of law to factually similar cases, or they will find a rule of exception if the general rule does not apply.

The writings of legal scholars and other experts are also useful, not for speculation about what the law should be but for clear statements and interpretations of existing law. This is a second subsidiary source of international law.

## REPLIES TO CRITICS

The doctrine of sources was developed in international law to reply to the positivist critics who expressed doubt whether international law was really law. It sets out positive law-making processes based upon the wills and actions of states. International law is not a system of innate or inborn ideas based on reason or morality. It is the result of an international legislative "will."

But many critics today, although not denying that international law is really law, maintain that it is of minimal significance because, although states purport to follow law when they enter into treaties or comply with customary rules, they are really only following their own self-interest. By implication, therefore, they will always break the rules of law when it is in their interest to do so. In this view, international law can never play an important role in international relations.[37]

---

[37] This view, which still is dominant among international relations specialists and political scientists, is set out in detail in Jack L. Goldsmith and Eric A. Posner, *The Limits of International Law* (2005).

Certainly there is no doubt that states use international law instrumentally to promote their self-interests. The real question, which is addressed especially in the following chapters, is whether law in conjunction with international institutions has a positive role to play in solving problems and attaining objectives that are in the interests of humankind as a whole.

The view that international law is simply self-interested behavior ignores the complexity and the positive, dynamic function of law in society. This approach considers legal rules in splendid isolation. For example, older rules of customary international law, such as the rule of the *Paquete Habana* case (noted above) that enemy coastal fishing vessels are exempt from the right of capture during war, may reflect simple coincidence of interest, rather than international law. By implication the case could (or should) have been decided the other way, and it would not have made much difference if it had been. This may have been true concerning nineteenth- and even early twentieth-century rules, but international customary law plays a much different role today. Customary law is almost never an isolated occurrence, but rather is intimately entangled with treaty law, general principles, and decisional law. When a coastal fishing vessel is seized today, it calls into play not only custom but also the provisions of the U.N. Convention on the Law of the Sea, general principles of fair trial and due process, relevant human rights standards, and, more likely than not, the dispute resolution procedures of the International Tribunal for the Law of the Sea.[38] Customary law still plays an essential role, but it is nested in a complex mixture of closely related legal doctrines. Any one component of the rule regime may be explainable in terms of the interests of one or a few states, but the whole is the product of complex legal interactions that go beyond simple state interest. Rather, what is reflected is the mutual interest of international society as a whole.

A similar approach with respect to treaty obligations is also erroneous. A state self-interest, rational choice perspective, presumes that each treaty obligation may be considered in isolation by the state concerned. Confronted with the choice whether to adhere to or break a rule, the state will simply weigh in the balance the consequences, which are assumed to be only two: reputation loss and retaliation. From that perspective, the pull of compliance with legal rules again amounts to self-interest, after weighing the positive and adverse consequences involved.

---

[38] See, for example, The "Juno Trader" Case (*Saint Vincent and the Grenadines v. Guinea-Bissau*), Application for Prompt Release, Judgment, 18 December 2004, *International Tribunal for the Law of the Sea*, 44 ILM 498 (2005).

This book argues that this view of treaties and international law is an over-simplification that ignores the following crucial considerations.

■ Treaties are not simply reflective of self-interest; they often shape the self-interest of the states accepting them so that adherence to a regime reflects a positive commitment to work together to solve a problem or to create an ongoing institutional capability.

■ Multilateral and even bilateral treaties frequently employ a package approach to obligations so that some obligations may be accepted by a state against its interest in order to obtain certain other advantages that are in its interest.

■ Multilateral treaties create regimes that have a dynamic, multiplier effect that is valuable both in problem solving and inducing compliance with legal and institutional norms.

■ International relations increasingly forms a seamless web so that breaking the law in one area has repercussions throughout the system. Similarly, adherence to legal rules fosters greater world order as a whole.

The rational choice perspective of international law is very similar to the realist perspective that posits that state cooperation and coordination can occur only rarely and with great difficulty. This explanation is too simplistic to explain the over 400,000 international agreements now in operation. No doubt, rational choice is a very important explanation for state cooperation, but this book argues that there is a core of important values and issues shared in common by all international actors, and here international law and institutions can play the central role.

## VARIETIES OF LEGAL OBLIGATION

The international legal system, like domestic legal systems, exhibits many different varieties of legal obligation. These varieties reflect the unique character of the system, however, in the case of international law.

First, there is a division between what are called primary rules and secondary rules. Primary rules are legal rules that constrain the behavior of states and other international actors in particular ways, typically by requiring either some action or restraining or forbidding some action. For example, a treaty might require a 50 percent reduction in emissions of sulfur dioxide or an agreement requiring the freezing of assets of groups supporting terrorist activities. In the modern international law system, primary rules have been adopted on an astonishing array of topics.

Secondary rules, on the other hand, are rules about rules – they do not impose obligations, but concern how the primary rules should be applied and the procedures for recognizing their legitimacy, for their modification, and for their adjudication. International law developed these secondary rules largely in response to positivist critics, such as H. L. A. Hart,[39] an Oxford jurist. Thus, for example, we now have rules that tell us how treaties are negotiated, ratified, modified, and terminated. We also have rules on state responsibility that define the circumstances under which an action can be attributed to a state and the circumstances giving rise to a duty to pay compensation. These secondary rules are essential to the proper functioning of the international system.

There are also hierarchies of obligation. Many rules are quite precise, requiring little or no interpretation, but rather a technical determination. An example is the degree of reduction of greenhouse gas emissions by developed countries that are parties to the Kyoto Protocol to the U.N. Climate Change Convention. Other rules are precise, but they contain terms that are subject to interpretation. An example is the term "self-defense" in Article 51 of the U.N. Charter. A third type of rule is expressed in very general terms so that the nature of the obligation cannot be determined except in extreme or obvious cases. An example of this is the rule of customary law that forbids significant environmental transboundary harm.[40] Often this type of rule must be supplemented by more precise rules for it to become operative. Such rules are nevertheless useful, because they establish the need for more work and further agreement. A fourth type of rule is the qualified obligation. An example is the U.N. Convention on Biological Diversity (1992), which qualifies most of its obligations with the phrase, "to the extent feasible and appropriate." This qualification gives the parties great discretion over the means, the timing, and the substance of the action required.

The international legal system also recognizes what is called "soft law." These are nonbinding injunctions or propositions that may become law in the future, but have not yet reached that status. Soft law also refers to general principles of conduct, such as the principle of sustainable development and the principle of special and differential treatment for developing countries, that are elaborated in many agreements and will find application in the specifics of future treaty law. Resolutions of the U.N. General Assembly

---

[39] H. L. A. Hart, *The Concept of Law* (1961).    [40] This is discussed in detail in Chapter 7.

and international bodies also fall into the category of soft law because they are nonbinding but authoritative and may become legally binding in the future.[41]

A most interesting category of legal rule is known as *jus cogens*, a Latin phrase meaning "compelling law." This term, usually translated as "peremptory norm," is used to refer to legal rules that are regarded as so fundamental that no derogation is permitted, even if validly passed under one of the accepted source rules. Examples are the rules prohibiting slavery, piracy, and terrorism. In 1992, the Ninth Circuit Court of Appeals ruled in the *Siderman* case[42] that freedom from torture was also a *jus cogens* right. International jurists disagree, however, on the extent of other *jus cogens* rules and on the source of this idea. Some say it is an example of a natural law rule that is still operational today; others maintain it is a customary law rule.

## INTERNATIONAL ACTORS

It is no longer true to say that states are the only international actors. States are still the most important features of the international law system, but international organizations, business entities, nongovernmental organizations (NGOs), and individuals have increasing rights and duties under international law. Individuals and companies can be civilly liable for damages and even subject to criminal prosecution. Individuals and companies also can derive rights under international law. For example, many export-import contracts concluded today are subject to the U.N. Convention on the International Sale of Goods. Individual investors are protected directly under international law norms.

Thus, international society is not limited to the international society of states. Individuals and companies participate and benefit both directly and indirectly. International law not only provides a framework for state interactions but it also supplies the rules and legal foundations for the burgeoning international economy, encompassing annually more than $7 trillion in trade in goods, almost $2 trillion in trade in services, and $600 billion in foreign direct investment. Without international law, international business transactions on this scale would not be possible.

---

[41] For an example of a U.N. General Assembly resolution creating law (the right of self-determination), see the *Western Sahara* case decided by the International Court of Justice, 1975 I. C. J. Rep. 12, 31–37.

[42] Siderman de Blake v. Republic of Argentina, 965 F. 2d 699, 717 (9th Cir. 1992).

The topic of international law is commonly divided into public international law, which focuses on states, and private international law, which concerns individuals and business transactions. This division assumes that private international law, which concerns such arcane matters as conflicts of laws and international enforcement of judgments, is really about how domestic laws interact on the international level and that nonstate actors cannot be directly affected by international law.

But in the last fifty years, this division has broken down to the point where it is now virtually meaningless. Whereas formerly companies and individuals had access to the international system only under the rubric of diplomatic protection in which their interests were represented by the states to which they belonged, today they are free to file lawsuits directly against states in the international legal system over such matters as investment disputes and denials of human rights.

Moreover, international business today draws its legal rules overwhelmingly from true international law sources, not domestic law. This is sometimes termed "the new *lex mercatoria* (law merchant), in comparison to international commercial codes that were current in Europe in the Middle Ages. Such sources of international business law are the following:

- Multilateral conventions,
- Uniform laws promulgated by international organizations,
- Bilateral treaties,
- Codifications of custom and usage promulgated by NGOs,
- International trade terms promulgated by NGOs,
- Model contracts,
- Model laws, and
- Restatements of the law by scholars and organizations.

In addition, international business today largely bypasses national court systems to settle disputes, preferring to use international dispute settlement systems, such as binding arbitration.

## INTERNATIONAL ORGANIZATIONS

In the international legal system, international organizations perform key functions. Although their activities are constrained by their members, some exercise executive powers, and their technical expertise gives them some degree of political power. International agencies can maintain full-time staff and can hire consultants. In many respects they operate as the ministries of the international system, exercising power delegated by states. Like national ministries and administrative agencies, they oversee implementation of policies. Some, such as the World Bank, have the power to draft rules and regulations. Sometimes too, as with the World Trade Organization, they maintain systems for the resolution of disputes. Thus, they actively participate in law making, executive action, and adjudication.

A key type of international regime of growing importance is the *framework treaty organization*. Frequently, states will agree on the fact that an international problem has arisen, but they are unable to agree on specific action. A solution is to agree on a framework treaty to study the matter and to create an organization with a full-time staff to recommend actions. Then at periodic conferences of the parties to the treaty, progressive steps can be approved by the state-parties to deal with the problem. Many international issues, such as climate change and protection of biological diversity, are being handled in this way.

The United Nations and its specialized and affiliated agencies are the key multilateral participants in this important system. U.N. agencies have responsibility for every important international problem from peace and security to culture. They are a remarkable force with great potential if they receive cooperation and backing from key member states. The great range of organizations that are part of the United Nations System is shown in the following chart.

The specialized agencies of the United Nations perform essential humanitarian and technical work that benefits people all over the world. There is a popular impression that the U.N. agencies waste a lot of money, but this is an exaggeration. The entire U.N. budget for its worldwide humanitarian work is less than $1 billion annually. By comparison, the annual governmental spending of the state of Maryland, a rather small U.S. state, is about $3 billion. Of course, no large organization is flawless, but the U.N. agencies deliver essential services that cannot be provided by anyone else:

■ The World Health Organization (WHO) monitors the spread of infectious diseases and has the expertise to take action to combat disease and to prevent epidemics. WHO is credited with quick action to stop the SARS epidemic that broke out in Asia in 2003. WHO also plays a crucial role in the fight against HIV/AIDS.

■ The world food supply is monitored by the Food and Agriculture Organization (FAO), which sponsors research to improve agricultural productivity and food relief programs to relieve famine.

# The United Nations system

## PRINCIPAL ORGANS

| Trusteeship Council | Security Council | General Assembly | Economic and Social Council | International Court of Justice | Secretariat |
|---|---|---|---|---|---|

**Subsidiary Bodies**
Military Staff Committee
Standing Committee and ad hoc bodies
International Criminal Tribunal for the Former Yugoslavia
International Criminal Tribunal for Rwanda
UN Monitoring, Verification and Inspection Commission (Iraq)
United Nations Compensation Commission
Peacekeeping Operations and Missions

**Subsidiary Bodies**
Main committees
Other sessional Committees
Standing committees and ad hoc bodies
Other subsidiary organs

UNHCR Office of the United Nations High Commissioner for Refugees
WFP World Food Programme
UNRWA[2] United Nations Relief and Works Agency for Palestine Refugees in the Near East
UN-HABITAT United Nations Human Settlements Programme (UNHSP)

INSTRAW International Research and Training Institute for the Advancement of Women

**Programmes and Funds**
UNCTAD United Nations Conference on Trade and Development
ITC International Trade Centre (UNCTAD/WTO)
UNDCP United Nations Drug Control Programme[1]
UNEP United Nations Environment Programme
UNICEF United Nations Children's Fund

UNDP United Nations Development Programme
UNIFEM United Nations Development Fund for Women
UNV United Nations Volunteers
UNCDF United Nations Capital Development Fund
UNFPA United Nations Population Fund

**Research and Training Institutes**
UNICRI United Nations Interregional Crime and Justice Research Institute
UNITAR United Nations Institute for Training and Research

UNRISD United Nations Research Institute for Social Development
UNIDIR[3] United Nations Institute for Disarmament Research

UNU United Nations University
UNSSC United Nations System Staff College

UNAIDS Joint United Nations Programme on HIV/AIDS

**Other UN Entities**
OHCHR Office of the United Nations High Commissioner for Human Rights

UNOPS United Nations Office for Project Services

### Functional Commissions
Commissions on:
Human Rights
Narcotic Drugs
Crime Prevention and Criminal Justice
Science and Technology for Development
Sustainable Development
Status of Women
Population and Development
Commission for social Development
Statistical Commission

### Regional Commissions
Economic Commission for Africa (ECA)
Economic Commission for Europe (ECE)
Economic Commission for Latin America and the Caribbean (ECLAC)
Economic and Social Commission for Asia and the Pacific (ESCAP)
Economic and Social Commission for Western Asia (ESCWA)

### Other Bodies
Permanent Forum on Indigenous Issues (PFII)
United Nations Forum on Forests
Sessional and standing committees
Expert, ad hoc and related bodies

### Related Organizations
WTO[3] World Trade Organization
IAEA[4] International Atomic Energy Agency
CTBTO Prep.Com[5] PrepCom for the Nuclear-Test-Ban-Treaty Organization
OPCW[5] Organization for the Prohibition of Chemical Weapons

### Specialized Agencies[6]
ILO International Labour Organization
FAO Food and Agriculture Organization of the United Nations
UNESCO United Nations Educational, Scientific and Cultural Organization
WHO World Health Organization

WORLD BANK GROUP
IBRD International Bank for Reconstruction and Development
IDA International Development Association
IFC International Finance Corporation
MIGA Multilateral Investment Guarantee Agency
ICSID International Centre for Settlement of Investment Disputes

IMF International Monetary Fund
ICAD International civil Aviation Organization
IMO International Maritime Organization
ITU International Tele-communication Union
UPU Universal Postal Union
WMO World Meterological Organization
WIPO World Intellectual Property Organization
IFAD International Fund for Agriculture Development
UNIDO United Nations Industrial Development Organization
WTO[3] World Tourism Organization

### Departments and Offices
OSG Office of the Secretary-General
OIOS Office of Internal Oversight Services
OLA Office of Legal Affairs
DPA Department of Political Affairs
DDA Department for Disarmament Affairs
DPKO Department of Peace-keeping Operations
OCHA Office for the Coordination of Humanitarian Affairs
DESA Department of Economic and Social Affairs
DGACM Department for General Assembly and Conference Management
DPI Department of public Information
DM Department of Management
OHRLLS Office of the High Representative for the Least Developed Countries, Landlocked Developing Countries and Small Island Developing States
UNSECOORD Office of the United Nations Security Coordinator
UNODC United Nations Office on Drugs and Crime

UNOG UN Office at Geneva
UNOV UN Office at Vienna
UNON UN Office at Nairobi

**NOTES:** Solid lines from a Principal Organ indicate a direct reporting relationship; dashes indicate a non-subsidiary relationship. [1]The UN Drug Control Programme is part of the UN Office on Drugs and Crime. [2]UNRWA and UNIDIR report only to the GA. [3]The World Trade Organization and World Tourism Organization use the same acronym. [4]IAEA reports to the Security Council and the General Assembly (GA). [5]The CTBTO Prep.Com and OPCW report to the GA. [6]Specialized agencies are autonomous organizations working with the UN and each other through the coordinating machinery of the ECOSOC on the intergovernmental level, and through the Chief Executives Board for coordination (CEB) at inter-secretariat level.

Published by the UN Department of Public Information
DPI/2342—March 2004

■ The United Nations (through various committees) plays an essential role in overseeing the international law pertaining to human rights.

■ The U.N. Environment Program (UNEP) administers many of the global treaties on environmental protection.

■ International communications are facilitated by the work of the International Telecommunications Union (ITU) and the International Postal Union (IPU).

■ The International Labor Organization (ILO) administers an extensive network of treaties protecting the health, safety, and rights of workers

■ The office of the U.N. High Commissioner for Refugees administers programs to care for millions of people displaced by warfare and violence.

■ Cultural affairs are the province of the U.N. Educational, Scientific, and Cultural Organization (UNESCO). This organization plays a leading role in preserving "world heritage" sites, natural and man-made places that have value as "the common heritage of humanity." There are currently 788 sites on the World Heritage List, ranging from the Galapagos Islands to the temples of Kyoto, Japan.

■ The International Civil Aviation Organization (ICAO) is responsible for coordination of international air travel and safety.

■ The International Maritime Organization (IMO) deals with ocean and port safety, navigation, and the control of maritime pollution.

■ The World Meteorological Organization (WMO) coordinates global weather information and research.

■ Numerous associated U.N. agencies administer or coordinate aspects of the world economy: the International Monetary Fund, the World Bank, the World Trade Organization, the International Finance Corporation, the U.N. Industrial Development Organization, the Multilateral Investment Guarantee Agency, the World Intellectual Property Organization, the U.N. Conference on Trade and Development, and the U.N. Development Program.

■ The U.N. is involved in the fight against illicit drugs through the U.N. Drug Control Program.

■ The U.N. deals with the problems of cities through the U.N. Committee on Human Settlements.

## ADJUDICATION AND DISPUTE SETTLEMENT

Legalization carries with it the idea that there must be a system both for the authoritative interpretation of norms and rules and the adjudication of disputes. International law has responded to this need. The U.N. Charter (Article 33) requires the peaceful resolution of international disputes:

The parties to any dispute, the continuance of which is likely to endanger the maintenance of international peace and security, shall, first of all, seek a solution by negotiation, enquiry, mediation, conciliation, arbitration, judicial settlement, resort to regional agencies or arrangements, or other peaceful means of their own choice.

To facilitate dispute settlement, the Vienna Convention on Treaties (Article 31) sets out a common standard as a guide for interpretation of treaties. The language of a treaty provision can be interpreted from three points of view. The plain sense of the language is the most important way to obtain meaning. But it may also help to consider the purpose of the provision – what was the intent of the parties? This may provide helpful guidance for interpreting meaning. In addition, the context of the provision is important. How does the provision fit into the overall agreement? It may also be necessary to consider additional agreements between the parties on the same or similar subject matters.

International law does not provide a unitary system of dispute settlement in the manner of national court systems administered by states. Instead, the international system provides multiple methods and multiple forums for adjudication. Individual regimes typically provide tribunals or other dispute settlement mechanisms. For example, the World Trade Organization operates a dispute settlement in trade matters, the International Tribunal for the Law of the Sea (ITLOS) deals with certain maritime disputes, and the International Commission for the Settlement of Investment Disputes (ICSID) deals with investment matters. There are, of course, centralized, general systems of dispute resolution; for example, the International Court of Justice and the Permanent Court of Arbitration, both of which are located in The Hague. In addition, ad hoc, one-off dispute settlement – usually in the form of arbitration – is very important. Although, as a general rule, a state must consent in advance for it to be summoned before one of these tribunals, international litigation is well established, and most states are regularly engaged in international adjudications.

The international legal system also provides a menu of options of different methods of dispute settlement, ranging from diplomatic negotiations to traditional litigation to such informal methods as arbitration and mediation. The weakness of this system is, however, that none of these methods is compulsory – a state does not have to submit a dispute for adjudication or resolution unless it wants to do so. This is a major reason for the fragility of international law.

The charge is frequently made that international dispute settlement is little used and awards and decisions are impossible to enforce. This is untrue. Since the end of the Cold War, state versus state international litigation has dramatically increased not only in the International Court of Justice but also in such new forums as the World Trade Organization. In addition, at the present time hundreds of investor/state proceedings are ongoing, as well as hundreds of human rights cases. At all times as well, there are thousands of private business arbitrations all over the world based on international law. Compliance with judgments rendered by international tribunals is also substantially equivalent to compliance with domestic court orders and judgments.

## ENFORCEMENT AND SANCTIONS

Realist and positivist critics of international law always focus on the lack of sanctions and enforcement. But the prevalence of international litigation of all types belies this charge. The international legal system allows aggrieved parties – usually states, but in some cases private individuals and companies – to complain in an appropriate legal forum. In most cases only a specifically affected party has standing to complain, but the International Court of Justice has recognized that some claims such as apartheid are so serious that any state may complain (this is known as an *erga omnes* claim).

Enforcement is admittedly a problem on the international level, but enforcement mechanisms have become more sophisticated in recent years. Enforcement differs for each international regime, but there are generally three categories of enforcement strategies: (1) coercion or retaliation, (2) incentives, and (3) reporting, inspections, and disclosure obligations.

In some cases, international tribunals have the authority to assess compensation to be paid by states that are guilty of violating an international obligation and to fashion provisional and permanent remedies. When this is possible, the record of compliance with the decisions of international tribunals is good, even when the states involved do not enjoy friendly relations. In the event of noncompliance, international law authorizes various nonviolent self-help remedies called reprisals and countermeasures. These are generally economic and diplomatic sanctions; they vary in effectiveness.

Individual treaty regimes may employ compliance and enforcement mechanisms, often very innovative in nature. For example, the Montreal Protocol regime for the protection of the earth's ozone layer uses an innovative system for implementation review that monitors compliance and provides assistance if needed. Interest groups and NGOs also assist international compliance by evaluating and publicizing violations.

The international system does provide a centralized system of enforcement of international norms that is in the hands of the U.N. Security Council, which can pass resolutions that are binding on all states. These resolutions can involve economic sanctions and even military force. Of course, Security Council resolutions are subject to veto by any one of the five permanent members (China, France, Russia, the United States, and the United Kingdom).

## A REDUCTIONIST FALLACY: INTERNATIONAL LAW AS A TOOL TO ASSERT STATE INTERESTS

What is the function of international law in international society? A new generation of skeptics admits the reality of international law, but holds that it is a vague and ambiguous set of rules that is simply manipulated by states to assert their self-interest in international relations.[43] They arrive at this conclusion by making a critical initial assumption: that rational choice theory provides an authoritative and comprehensive way to define the way international law functions in international society.

Rational choice theory is derived from a fundamental principle of microeconomics that explains human decisions about resources, goods, and services. Economists argue that human behavior – being selfish, inconsistent, or altruistic – is predictably based on a person's weighing the costs and benefits of decisions. Carried over to states and international relations, this theory holds that law is simply one of the costs or benefits of international decision making. So when a state makes a decision about security, the use of force, economics, or human rights, law plays no special role; it is one (probably minor) factor in deciding what to do. Furthermore, international law often plays a pernicious role because states may use legal rhetoric to mask their true intentions.

Rational choice theory also leads to additional conclusions that further deprecate the role of international law: (1) International law is merely instrumental; it is only a means to an end, and that end is self-interest;

---

[43] This is the thesis of Jack L. Goldsmith and Eric A. Posner, *The Limits of International Law* (2005).

(2) international law is incapable of restraining state behavior; and (3) states are not moral agents so there is no moral or "cosmopolitan" duty to comply with international law when it does not accord with self-interest. This leads to the inevitable conclusion of the neo-conservatives: that international law can be brushed aside or "fixed 'round the policy"[44] where necessary.

This conclusion is an example of reductionism: the belief in one explanation for complex realities and then reducing the complexities to explain all data in terms of the theory. Like Freud's theory of human psychology and Marx's theory of the proletarian revolution, rational choice theory is difficult to refute because inconsistencies can be explained as mistakes or dissembling and all compliance with international law can be explained as masking or rationalizing self-interest.

Furthermore, it is undeniably true that rational choice analysis is a useful tool that explains how and why most international law comes into being. Treaties and customary legal norms are instances of coordination and cooperation based upon a coincidence of state interests. The question is not whether to accept this theory – it is clearly valid. Rather, the key consideration is whether rational choice is a complete explanation for all of international law. Examination shows that this theory is important, but not all encompassing in scope.

The assumptions of rational choice are too narrow. Drawn from microeconomics are three assumptions: (1) States are assumed to be essentially atomistic, self-interested, and rational, with very individual ideas of what is good; (2) their interests are completely exogenous to social interactions; and (3) international society is merely a strategic realm in which states come together to pursue their preconceived self-interests. All these assumptions are questionable at best. The atomistic, presocial assumptions of state interest formation ignore two salient realities. First, there is increasingly a convergence of interests in the globalized world of the twenty-first century in that every state has an interest in peace and security in every part of the world, as well as in ameliorating global problems – disease, poverty, environmental degradation, and deprivations of human rights. For example, when a powerful tsunami killed over 200,000 people in South and Southeast Asia in 2004, there was an outpouring of aid from all over the world. No state, however far removed from the effects of the disaster, could take the view that its self-interest was not affected. Second, states seldom see their self-interest in atomistic terms; self-interest is often constructed through the necessity to preserve preexisting alliances, relationships and institutions. For example, why did over

---

44  See the instance of this in Chapter 1.

thirty-five nations initially support the United States in the 2003 invasion of Iraq in the face of overwhelmingly negative public opinion? Clearly the answer is because of their preexisting relationships and alliances with the United States. States also alter their idea of self-interest depending upon the international institutions to which they adhere. For example, in 1995 the United States unilaterally slapped 100 percent tariffs on Japanese autos and auto parts because of domestic pressures and a perception of unfair trade by Japan. When bilateral diplomacy proved fruitless, Japan brought a complaint to the newly formed World Trade Organization (WTO) in Geneva. Because the tariffs were clearly in violation of WTO rules and defiance of the WTO would have disrupted the fledgling organization and relations with other trading partners, the United States withdrew the unilateral measures.

Rational choice theory, which is based on microeconomic theory, also overlooks the positive macroeffects of international law. International law is primarily responsible for the very creation of international society, as we have seen, through creating a web of relationships based on obligation. Furthermore, there is no alternative to the rule of law in creating an orderly international society; power is insufficient for this purpose. Overwhelming military superiority did not protect the United States from the terrorism attacks of 2001, and the United States found it necessary to invoke the aid of international law and international institutions, such as the United Nations and NATO, in prosecuting its War on Terrorism. The rational choice model in which political actors decide their atomistic self-interests and cooperate only upon a fortuitous identity of views also does not adequately describe the wide range of functions played by law in international society. International law provides a common set of normative rules that at a minimum play a modulating or intermediary function with regard to differences of views and interests. States may conform their behavior to their interests in order to preserve the integrity of the entire system. For example, this was clearly the reason why many states, such as Japan, joined the Kyoto regime on the control of greenhouse gases; the United States, which rejected participation, thought otherwise. International law also plays a problem-solving role in international relations: Many controversies, such as territorial, boundary, maritime, and trade disputes, are handled very much like domestic legal cases and are settled on the basis of applicable legal norms. Finally, international law has a multiplier effect through the phenomenon of multilateralism. Only through this multiplier effect are problems able to be confronted and solved. For example, the depletion of the earth's protective layer of ozone gases is being successfully addressed in this manner.

Rational choice theory also assumes a simplistic theory of compliance with international legal norms. This view holds that state cooperation or coordination that appears to accord with international law is only rational self-interested behavior. This must be so, it is stated, because there is no evidence of states complying with international legal norms against their interests. Therefore, international law is incapable of constraining state self-interest.

This formulation obviously begs the question: By definition every instance of compliance will be out of self-interest because, of course, no state ever announces, "We are going to comply with the law even though it goes against our national interest." A further difficulty is that this theory assumes a coercion idea of law – that law only plays a coercive role in society. As I have argued, this is false; law both creates and facilitates social relations and interactions. Increasingly in the present century, state rational self-interest is shaped by the forces of globalization and by international society. Although there are still independent state interests, there is an emerging international agenda of overriding common issues and problems that can best be addressed by international law.

Reducing international law to the self-interested behavior of states does not adequately cover how law functions in international society.

## COMMUNITY AND JUSTICE: THE TWIN BASES FOR INTERNATIONAL OBLIGATIONS

Much has been made of the fact that there is no international police force or other system of coercion on which international obligations can be based. This has led positivists and realists to conclude that international law is not really law. From the foregoing it can be seen that international law has met this claim head on; real systems of enforcement and even coercion have been developed. It is no longer true to say that there is no possibility of enforcing international law. Nevertheless, it is worth considering the validity of the premise of the positivist claim that coercion and sanctions are the basis for law and for legal obligation. Is this correct?

Why do most people choose to obey the law? Empirical and sociological analysis and plain common sense suggest that coercion is not the principal reason why people obey laws. Most people obey the law without being coerced to do so; if coercion were the only way to stimulate law-abiding behavior, society would be impossible because there is no way to back up every conceivable law with coercion. Furthermore, even in the domestic context, there is no way to coerce compliance with most laws. We deal with each other without threats of sanctions and even with the knowledge that if we had to go to court to make our case, it would be difficult or impossible to get relief. We also deal with governmental entities on many matters knowing that the government, which after all is sovereign, could simply declare a moratorium on all its obligations. The overwhelming majority of people obey laws out of a sense of justice, a conviction that it is right and necessary to live in society.

Another basic reason why we obey laws is out of a sense of community. Plato made this point eloquently early in the fourth century BCE in his dialogue, *Crito*. This work describes the death of Socrates, who was unjustly condemned to die by the Athens Assembly for corrupting the youth of Athens by his teaching that undermined belief in the gods. The friends of Socrates arrange for his escape. All is set, and Socrates can easily choose to flee execution, go into exile, and wait for the matter to blow over. But he refuses and elects to comply with the law, including his sentence of death. Why? He cites community values that mean more to him even than his own life. He refuses to defy the will of the community in which he was born and flourished during his lifetime. To uphold these values, he will obey even an unjust legal rule. Probably most of us would not go as far as Socrates in our devotion to community, but the point here is a universal one. We obey laws fundamentally out of a sense of community.

International law is no different. More than ever in this age of globalization, we live in an international community, which includes not only states but also other essential actors. In fact, as we have seen, law and legalization help constitute that community. And this is the basic reason why international law is obeyed and why it should be obeyed – out of a sense of the primacy and necessity of community and societal values.

Additional reasons are no doubt important as well. Legal experts have cited a great number of reasons for obeying international law. Most of these theories are replete with jargon and hence incomprehensible to all except fellow experts. One leading scholar has, however, captured the essence of the reason why the international system exerts what he calls "compliance pull"; that is *fairness*.[45] For this scholar, Thomas Franck, the legitimacy of international law depends upon its fairness, in the sense that states and international actors will obey law that satisfies criteria of fairness. This is another way of saying that for most of us, the law must be just. Most of us would not be willing to go along with Socrates' view that even an unjust legal order must be obeyed. We demand justice. So too on the international level, the international system must fulfill criteria of correlative and distributive justice to function properly and as a basis for compliance. Correlative (also called commutative and corrective) justice means that there must be a sense of substantive and procedural equivalence

[45]   Thomas M. Franck, *Fairness in International Law and Institutions* (1995).

and impartiality with regard to all kinds of transactions and exchanges. Distributive justice means that there must be a fair and proportional sharing of benefits and burdens.

If justice has to be a central feature of the international system of the twenty-first century, then the view of the realists that morality interferes with international relations is incorrect. Rather, morality is a central concern, as most of us would agree it must be. Furthermore, the legalization process captures and tames the power relationships so dear to the realists. The power of rules and relationships modulates military and other less benign international forces.

### SUMMING UP

In the twenty-first century we must develop a new paradigm for the conduct of international relations, one based not on power and individual state interests but rather on international law and institutions, justice, and fairness. Of course, critics – often quite rightly – point out the limitations and imperfections of the international law system. But the solution is not therefore to disregard the system or to undermine it: rather, it must be corrected, improved, and strengthened in order to deal with the international problems we face.

Some may also say that international legal norms are too convoluted and complex; we cannot expect our leaders to be legal scholars. I answer this objection by showing in the following chapters that most international legal rules are actually quite simple and understandable. They also make eminent sense if our governmental leaders would take them seriously and explain them properly to the public. Of course, some situations involve technical legal issues and do require special help from legally trained advisors. But is this so unusual? We all expect our government to faithfully observe complex legal rules in such important matters as education, Social Security, Medicare, welfare, and taxation. Why not in international relations? And we all have the experience each year of observing tax laws and regulations in the tax code that is thicker than the Manhattan telephone book. Believe me, international law is a lot simpler than the U.S. tax code.

### FURTHER READINGS

Louis Henkin, *International Law: Politics and Values* (1995).

Rosalyn Higgins, *Problems and Process: International Law and How We Use It* (1994).

Oscar Schachter, *International Law in Theory and Practice* (1991).

Ian Brownlie, *Principles of Public International Law* (6th ed., 2004).

Eyal Benvenisti and Moshe Hirsch (eds.), *The Impact of International Law on International Cooperation* (2003).

Jonathan Charney, "Universal International Law," 87 *American Journal of International Law* 529 (1993).

For the debate over neo-realism, see Robert O. Keohane (ed.), *Neorealism and Its Critics* (1986), and David A. Baldwin (ed.), *Neorealism and Neoliberalism: The Contemporary Debate* (1993).

Kennan's views may be found in George Kennan, *Realities of Amending Foreign Policy* (1954).

The first path-breaking book challenging realist assumptions was R.O. Keohane and Joseph Nye, *Transnational Relations and World Politics* (1971).

Martin Wight, a partisan of the English international society approach, sets out a theory that there are basically three traditions in IR: realism, rationalism, and revolutionism. See M. Wight, *International Theory: The Three Traditions* (1991).

There is controversy over whether the origin of international law is the work of Hugo Grotius, *On the Law of War and Peace* (De Jure Belli ac Pacis) published in 1625, or the sixteenth-century writings of two Spanish authors, Francesco Suarez and Francesco de Vitoria. See James Brown Scott, *The Spanish Origin of International Law* (1934).

The writings of the most important historical figures of international law/law of nations are available in the multivolume work, *The Classics of International Law*, edited by James Brown Scott (1933). This work features the writings of Alberico Gentile, E. Vattel, H. Grotius, C. Zouche, S. Pufendorf, F. Suarez, F. de Vitoria, Christian Wolff, John Selden, and Frederic de Martens.

See Hedley Bull, *The Anarchical Society: A Study of Order in World Politics* (2d ed., 1995).

Harold Hongu Koh, "Why do Nations Obey International Law?" 106 Yale Law Journal 2599 (1997). This puts forth a theory of participation as the basic reason why states observe international law.

For the classic argument against coercion as the essence of law, see Louis Henkin, *How Nations Behave* (2d ed., 1979).

Immanuel Kant, *Perpetual Peace* (Lewis White Beck, ed, 1957, originally published in 1795).

Christian Wolff, *Jus Gentium* (1749) is available in German in Wolff, *Gesammelte Werke* (Marcel Thomman ed. 1972).

For regime theory, see Stephen. D. Krasner, *International Regimes* (1983); Andrease Hassenclever, Peter Mayer, and Volker Rittberger, *Theories of*

*International Regimes* (1997); Robert O. Keohane, *After Hegemony: Cooperation and Discord in the World Political Economy* (1984); and R. O. Keohane, *International Institutions: Two Approaches* (1988).

H. Lauterpacht, *The Function of Law in the International Community* (1933).

A. P. Sereni, *The Italian Conception of International Law* (1943).

The best-known contemporary work on justice is *A Theory of Justice* by John Rawls (1971). His distributive justice argument is what he calls the "difference principle" that social and economic inequalities are permissible if and only if the arrangements generating them work out better for the most disadvantaged person (the worst-off person) than any more equal structure. This is certainly a debatable proposition and in any case is not intended to apply to the international context.

Philip Allott, "The True Function of Law in the International Community," *Indiana Journal of Global Legal Studies* 5 (1998) develops the idea that relations constitutes the true function of law.

Thomas M. Franck, *The Power of Legitimacy Among Nations* (1990); *Fairness in International Law and Institutions* (1995).

For morality and international relations, see Mervyn Frost, *Ethics in International Relations: A Constitutive Theory* (1992).

Some legal scholars and IR specialists are collaborating on joint research. *Legalization in World Politics* (Judith L. Goldstein, Miles Kahler, Robert O. Keohane, and Anne Marie Slaughter, eds., 2001). See also "International Law and International Relations Theory: A New Generation of Interdisciplinary Scholarship," by Anne Marie Slaughter, Andrew S. Tulnells, and Stepan Wood, 92 American Journal of International Law 367 (1998).

A landmark of constructivist political thought is Anthony Clark Arend, *International Legal Rules* (1996).

The basic book on neo-realism is Kenneth Waltz, *Theory of International Politics* (1979).

For a discussion of game theory, see Kenneth W. Abbott, "Modern International Relations Theory: A Prospectus for International Lawyers," 14 *Yale Journal of International Law* 335 (1989).

See R. O. Keohane and J. S. Nye, *Power and Interdependence: World Politics in Transition* (1977) for the complex interdependence theory.

The most influential traditional realist text is Hans Morgenthau, *Politics among Nations: The Struggle for Power and Peace* (1948).

Henry Kissinger, *Diplomacy* (1994).

For a constructivist view of international relations, see Alexander Wendt, *Social Theory of International Politics* (1999).

Rosemary Foote, John Lewis Gaddis, and Andrew Hurrell, eds., *Order and Justice in International Relations* (2003).

J. Craig Barker, *International Law and International Relations* (2000).

Michael Byers, *Custom, Power and the Power of Rules: International Relations and Customary International Law* (1999).

Ian Clarke, *Globalization and International Relations Theory* (1999).

Martti Koskenniemi, *From Apology to Utopia: The Structure of International Legal Argument* (1989).

H. Lauterpacht, *The Function of Law in the International Community* (1933).

Phillip Allott, *Eunomia: A New World Order for a New World* (1990).

Knud Haakonssen, *Natural Law and Moral Philosophy from Grotius to the Scottish Enlightenment* (1996).

John F. Murphy, *The United States and the Rule of Law in International Affairs* (2004).

# 5 Peace and Security: Reinventing the United Nations

"We are led by events and common sense to one conclusion: The survival of liberty in our land increasingly depends on the success of liberty in other lands. So it is the policy of the United States to seek and support the growth of democratic movements and institutions in every nation and culture, with the ultimate goal of ending tyranny in our world."

> President George W. Bush, Second Inaugural Address, January 22, 2005

"The stark reality is that the United States does not have the right structural capacity to stabilize and rebuild nations.... The United States needs an effective United Nations."

> Samuel R. Berger and Brent Scowcroft, National Security Advisors to Presidents William Clinton and George H. W. Bush, respectively, July 27, 2005

## THE OPPORTUNITY FOR A NEW BEGINNING

The present generation of world leaders has an opportunity that comes exceedingly seldom in historical terms: They are being called upon to restructure the global architecture that is responsible for world peace and security. To grasp the importance of this opportunity, consider this: The last time this opportunity was possible was in 1945 (the end of World War II); before that it was in 1918 (the end of the First World War) and before that it was in 1815 (after the wars against Napoleon).

The task presented is to thoroughly reform and update all aspects of the United Nations. If this work is properly carried out, the world may enjoy an unparalleled period of peace and prosperity in the twenty-first century.

The opportunity for fundamental reform of the United Nations is presented now because of a coincidence of factors. Many believed that the end of the

Cold War would give the security architecture of the U.N. system a chance to work as was intended in 1945. But events of the last fifteen years have conclusively demonstrated that the United Nations is fundamentally flawed and is not up to the task of preserving peace and security in the new century. The litany of failures and difficulties is well known: peacekeeping missions gone awry in places like Somalia, the former Yugoslavia, and the Republic of the Congo; the expulsion of U.N. weapons inspectors from Iraq in 1998; the failures of the U.N. Security Council to deal expeditiously with breaches of the peace in many places, including Rwanda, Kosovo, Darfur in western Sudan, and Iraq; and the corruption scandal concerning the Iraq oil-for-food program, to mention only the most egregious instances.

The necessity of reform is admitted even by the United Nations' most ardent supporters, and in 2003 U.N. Secretary-General Kofi Annan, stating that the United Nations had come to a "fork in the road," set up a High Level Panel on Threats, Challenges, and Change to examine the institution and to come up with a new vision of how it should operate. This special panel comprised sixteen "eminent" persons from as many different countries drawn from all the regions of the world including all five permanent members of the U.N. Security Council (the U.S. member was Brent Scowcroft, U.S. National Security Advisor under the first President Bush).

On December 2, 2004 the panel transmitted its final report, entitled *A More Secure World: Our Shared Responsibility*.[1] The report was generally favorably received, but the splash of publicity quickly faded away in the holiday season. Most news accounts mentioned only one aspect of the panel's work – reform of the U.N. Security Council, a topic that has been discussed for several years. So most people other than the experts greeted the report with a kind of "ho-hum – so what else is new" attitude. This is very unfortunate, because the panel's report contains a thorough discussion and recommendations for complete revamping of the security architecture, in particular the entire U.N. system. U.N. Secretary-General Kofi Annan has endorsed the report and has put forth a specific reform plan of his own.[2]

Ironically, during this period of intense criticism, the United Nations is exhibiting a new spirit. Reform has breathed new life into the U.N. Charter. The Security Council especially is taking its responsibilities seriously. In the period from 2003–5 the Council passed over 100 resolutions taking action with respect to threats to peace all over the globe. Peacebuilding missions

---

[1] The report and supporting documents are available on the U.N. web site, www.un.org.
[2] Report of the Secretary General, *In Larger Freedom: Toward Development, Security and Human Rights for All*, March 21, 2005.

were created in Iraq and Afghanistan, and peacekeeping missions were established and expanded all over the globe. The Council has also acted to combat terrorism and the proliferation of weapons of mass destruction. Particularly important in this regard is Resolution 1540, which requires all states to enact, implement, and enforce controls on weapons of mass destruction and prohibiting any form of support for terrorist nonstate actors. This resolution establishes a "1540 Committee" of the Council to monitor compliance by all states. Belatedly, the Council addressed the Sudan, authorizing peacekeeping forces (regretfully too small in number) in the south and the west of the country, imposing sanctions on those responsible, and referring them to the International Criminal Court.

U.N. peacekeeping is also changing in character to correct past failures. Peace missions all have their own rules of engagement, but no longer is it assumed that the mere presence of blue-helmeted soldiers on the ground will bring peace. In the Congo, for example, U.N. peacekeepers have gotten tough – they are surrounding villages and searching hut by hut for guns in the effort to quell tribal violence. "It may look like war," the Congo force commander Lieutenant General Babacar Gaye said recently, "but it's peacekeeping."

A further irony is that it is the memory of genocide in Rwanda in 1994, arguably the United Nations' worst failure, as well as the failures of Bosnia and Somalia in the 1990s, that has inspired these changes. "The ghost of Rwanda lies very heavily over the U.N. and the Security Council," said David Harland, a top official of the U.N. Department of Peacekeeping Operations in New York.[3]

## "AMERICA ALONE"

The U.S. Central Command (Centcom) is perhaps the most potent military force in history. Its theater of operations is the entire Middle East, from Egypt to Pakistan. From its headquarters in Qatar, Centcom's military might includes the U.S. Navy's Fifth Fleet in Bahrain to the west; the aircraft carrier *Harry S. Truman* and its task force on patrol in the Persian Gulf to the north; over 7,000 U.S. troops in Afghanistan to the east; about 1,000 troops in the Horn of Africa in the south; and to the northwest almost 160,000 U.S. troops fighting the insurgency in Iraq. The commander of this force, General John Abizaid calls this war against Islamic extremism the "Long War." It is a war that the United States is fighting virtually alone.

[3] *New York Times*, May 23, 2005.

"*America Alone*" is in fact the title of a remarkable book written by two conservative commentators, Stefan Halper, a former Republican government official, and Jonathan Clarke of the Cato Institute.[4] In minute detail the authors dissect the neo-conservative foreign policy of unilateralism and confrontation and the resulting damage to American interests around the world. Their thesis is that as the result of the repudiation of international institutions and the narrow focus of American foreign policy, which after 9/11 has been transfixed upon the War on Terror, the invasions of Afghanistan and Iraq, and the transformation of Islam and the Middle East, the United States is isolating itself from the rest of the world; others are shaping the international agenda.

Another important book is *The Folly of Empire*[5] by John B. Judis, senior editor of *The New Republic*. He argues that the foreign policy of the United States has drifted badly off course from the emphasis on international cooperation of Presidents Wilson, Franklin Roosevelt, and Truman and hearkened back to the imperialist policies of Presidents McKinley and Theodore Roosevelt, who sought American domination. Neo-conservatives themselves see the essence of American foreign policy as "actively promoting American principles of governance abroad – democracy, free markets, respect for liberty."[6] Some openly state, "American imperialism can bring with it new hopes of liberty, security, and prosperity."[7] Most use code phrases, such as "hegemony" or "America is the sole world superpower."[8] *The Economist* defines the essence of American foreign policy under the neo-conservatives as "a mixture of hawkishness and idealism: hawkishness on projecting American power abroad, but idealism when it comes to using that power to spread good things like freedom and democracy."[9]

These realities make it very unlikely that the United States will place a high priority on reform of the United Nations and the international security system. Rather, there is the danger that U.S. policymakers consider the United Nations, as President George W. Bush said in his September 2003 address to the U.N. General Assembly, as "fading into history as an irrelevant debating society." The U.S. Secretary of State Condoleeza Rice is on record saying that

---

4  Stefan Halper and Jonathan Clarke, *America Alone: The Neo-Conservatives and the Global Order* (2004).
5  John B. Judis, *The Folly of Empire: What George W. Bush Could Learn from Theodore Roosevelt and Woodrow Wilson* (2004).
6  William Kristol and Robert Kagan, "Reject the Global Buddy System," *New York Times*, Oct. 25, 1999.
7  Thomas Donnelly, "The Past as Prologue: An Imperial Manual," *Foreign Affairs* (July 2002).
8  Thomas Ricks, "Empire or Not," *Washington Post*, Aug. 21, 2001.
9  *The Economist*, March 19, 2005, p. 31.

U.S. policy will "proceed from the firm ground of the national interest, not from the interests from an illusory international community."[10] One former U.N. ambassador has derided the High Level Panel as merely "relics trying to reform a relic."[11] This attitude is unfortunate; reform of the United Nations should be a matter of the highest priority.

## A DANGEROUS DIVIDE

The narrow focus of U.S. foreign policy has created a dangerous split with the rest of the world. The U.S. preoccupation with homeland security and the war in Iraq has relegated much of the rest of the world to the back burner. As a result the United States is losing influence on all fronts, and traditional allies are openly discussing a parting of ways. Consider the following developments.

■ The European Union is using the United States as a foil to create its own common foreign policy and defense structure.[12] Distinct EU policies that diverge from those of the United States are now in place with respect to a wide range of issues from Iran to global warming to lifting the Western arms embargo on China. Despite the apparent failure of the proposed EU constitution, the EU is emerging as a strategic competitor to the United States, which endangers the Western alliance.

■ In Asia, flawed U.S. diplomacy has allowed the problem of North Korean nuclear arms to remain unchecked. China has emerged as a strategic competitor to the United States and the leader of an possible future East Asian Economic Community. Japan remains a firm U.S. ally only because of the threat from North Korea and unresolved territorial disputes with its neighbors – China, South Korea, and Russia.

■ The 2005 report of the U.S. National Intelligence Council entitled, "Mapping the Global Future Out to 2020," predicts the emergence of China and India as global superpowers, transforming the world economic and political landscape.

---

[10] Condoleezza Rice, "Promoting the National Interest," *Foreign Affairs* (Jan–Feb. 2000).

[11] *The Economist*, Nov. 16–26, 2004.

[12] There is an interesting difference of opinion among conservative U.S. policymakers about Europe and the Atlantic Alliance. During his February 2005 trip to Europe, President Bush stated, "America supports a strong Europe." But Gerard Baker, in an article in *The Weekly Standard*, a neo-conservative journal, warned that Europe is seeking to become a "counterweight to the U.S. in world affairs." Robert Kuttner, "A Neocon No to Europe," *Boston Globe*, Feb. 24, 2005.

■ In the Muslim world an arc of instability runs across North Africa, the Middle East, to Southeast Asia; there is the danger that Islamist terrorist movements will merge with local Muslim protest and separatist movements active in many parts of the world.

■ In Latin America Brazil is an incipient great power and a strategic competitor to the United States. In 2004, Brazil frustrated U.S. plans for a Free Trade Area of the Americas. Brazil is the leader of a coalition of developing countries attacking U.S. trade policies. U.S. relations and influence in Latin America are at their lowest point in decades.

Paradoxically, the U.S. policy of unilaterally promoting U.S. values abroad is having the opposite effect. Public opinion polls in all countries show a remarkable decline in respect for the United States. Over 60 percent of people oppose U.S. policies in the world, and this is in traditionally *friendly* countries. In most of the developing world and in Muslim nations, opposition to the United States registers at from 50 to 95 percent.[13] The rhetoric of American leaders that the United States is "the greatest force for good on this earth" (George W. Bush), and "when America was created, the stars must have danced in the sky" (Vice President Cheney) may play well in Peoria, but is greeted with derision in the rest of the world.

The United States is playing a power game, pursuing its own narrow interests and largely ignoring the needs and wants of the rest of the world. Military and economic confrontation has become the principal tool of U.S. foreign policy. This stance is out of step with much of the world, especially America's traditional allies and friends. This power-politics stance has hurt the very values the United States tries to achieve and entails heavy political, economic, and security costs and risks. U.S. influence in the world is at a post-World War II low despite its status as sole superpower and Cold War victor.

**THE WAY FORWARD**

To regain its footing the United States must espouse a new foreign policy based on law, justice, and international institutions. Rather than acting as *hegemon* – bullying and dictating to the rest of the world – it must exercise leadership. As the respected political scientist Joseph Nye has pointed out,

---

[13] A public opinion survey in March, 2005 found that even in Australia, people are evenly divided over whether the greatest threat to the world today comes from American foreign policy or Islamic fundamentalism. Lowy Institute for International Policy, www.lowyinstitute.org.

a key to America's preeminence has been its willingness to work through international regimes: "Multilateralism . . . is . . . key because it reduces the incentives for constructing alliances against us."[14]

Justice means that international law must become the basis of international politics. Law in the sense of binding norms of behavior can be an empowering framework for constructive, collective action for peace and security in the world. International institutions are instruments for what political scientists call multilateralism, the coordination of policies and efforts among many different states. Multilateralism is a different dynamic than bilateralism, a deal between two states based on reciprocal, usually short-term advantage. Multilateralism is a long-term arrangement in which it is assumed that the costs and benefits of interaction will balance out over time. In multilateralism there is a multiplier effect from the adoption of any policy. Every member of a coalition gets the benefit of all the others' actions in such a coordinated system.

Of course, multilateralism is not a magic bullet, and multinational institutions such as the United Nations have glaring flaws. But many of the defects of international institutions flow from a lack of leadership. If the United States were to take a leadership role, these institutions would operate more effectively. Such a turnabout would be welcomed by much of the world. The U.S. approach to international institutions and multilateralism at present may be characterized as opportunistic and *ad hoc* multilateralism. The United States tries to be multilateral as a last resort and on a purely opportunistic basis – putting together "coalitions of the willing."

The "coalitions of the willing" strategy is wrong for three reasons. First, there is no continuity – such coalitions shift with time and events. Second, there is no stability – in Iraq, for example, several key coalition partners soon bailed out. Third, such partners usually provide only token support.

This change in U.S. policy toward multilateralism hearkens to the years after World War II when, before the rise of the Soviet threat, U.S. leaders exercised leadership in creating major multinational organizations, such as the United Nations and the Bretton Woods international economic institutions, the International Monetary Fund and the World Bank, as well as the Marshall Plan and NATO. In creating these institutions, U.S. leaders emphasized the long-term interests not only of the United States, but also of the rest of the world. The United States made clear it would play by the rules it expected other states to follow. U.S. leaders must again follow this path.

Peace and security are the most important and fundamental values that a government must provide for its people. At the beginning of the twenty-first

---

[14] Joseph Nye, *The Paradox of American Power* (2002), p. 159.

century security concerns are common to all peoples. In our globalized world, violence everywhere is a concern; no state, especially the United States, can afford to ignore violence or the conditions that lead to violence – poverty, disease, and environmental degradation – until it hits home. This is one of the lessons of 9/11. A threat anywhere in the world is a threat to all. There is need for a common collective security system that commits all to act cooperatively against dangers.

## THREATS TO PEACE AND SECURITY

What are the threats to peace and security in the early twenty-first century? In traditional terms security is related to the danger of interstate war. A nation must be strong militarily to defeat its adversaries. But this is not the principal danger we face in the twenty-first century. Rather we face these broader threats to human security:

- *Terrorism,* and to be more precise Islamist terrorism. The response to Islamist terrorism is no mystery. As *The 9/11 Commission Report* puts it, "What is needed is a tripod of policies to (1) attack terrorists and their organizations; (2) prevent the continued growth of Islamist terrorism; and (3) protect against and prepare for terrorist attacks."

- *Weapons of mass destruction* (nuclear, chemical, or biological weapons), whether in the hands of rogue states or terrorist organizations. Two states in particular stand out: North Korea has declared that it has nuclear weapons, and Iran may have a clandestine nuclear weapons program. The danger of weapons of mass destruction is magnified by terrorism. Al Qaeda in particular has tried to make or acquire weapons of mass destruction for at least ten years.

- *Regional conflicts and civil wars* in many parts of the world. These are local but often bloody confrontations centering on ethnic, religious, and political rivalries. These conflicts occur in many different guises, from civil unrest or war within a single country to a conflict that spills over international borders. The most severe is the ever-present Israeli-Palestinian conflict, but actual or potential regional wars exist in dozens of hot spots around the world, such as Chechnya, Colombia, the Congo, Liberia, Sri Lanka, the Balkans, and the Caucasus. Two dangerous situations are in Asia: the dispute between India and Pakistan over Kashmir and the Chinese desire to regain sovereignty over Taiwan. Terrorism is a feature of many of these regional disputes, and the use of nuclear weapons is a possibility in a regional dispute as well, especially in the case of India/Pakistan and in the Middle East.

■ *Poverty, infectious disease, and environmental degradation.* As the report of the U.N. High Level Panel (2004) points out, "Poverty, infectious disease, environmental degradation and war feed upon one another in a deadly cycle. Poverty... is strongly associated with the outbreak of civil war... Diseases such as malaria and HIV/AIDS... cause large numbers of deaths and reinforce poverty. Disease and poverty in turn are connected to environmental degradation."

A common thread runs through all these security threats – the overwhelming power of the U.S. military can play only a limited role in meeting them. None of these threats can be stamped out by force alone. Similarly, the power politics of the past can play only a limited role. This means the United States must seek the cooperation of other countries. As *The 9/11 Commission Report* (2004) says, "We should reach out, listen to, and work with other countries that can help." We are in a new era of international relations – the touchstones of this new era are the rule of law, justice, and multilateralism.


## COLLECTIVE SECURITY

The United Nations was founded upon the concept of collective security, the idea first proposed over 200 years ago by Immanuel Kant that there should be a broad alliance of states to oppose threats to international peace and security. Although the threats to peace and security are different today, the United Nations is still central to this task. Only the United Nations has the universal membership, the agreed system of rules, the collective security institutions, and the wide-ranging mandate – including both traditional threats to the peace and humanitarian concerns of social, economic, and environmental problems – that are an integral part of peace and security in the twenty-first century.

Although the flaws of the United Nations are well known, its successes are underpublicized. For example, the number of interstate wars has dramatically decreases since the United Nations was founded, and the number of civil wars has also decreased in direct proportion to the UN's peacekeeping efforts.[15] The 1991 Gulf War and the 1999 East Timor intervention are examples of prompt and effective Security Council action. On the day after

[15]   U.N. High Level Panel Report, p. 17 (2004).

the terrorist attacks of 9/11, the U.N. Security Council took action to impose uniform, mandatory counterterrorist obligations on all states and established a Counter-Terrorism Committee to monitor compliance. That same day, September 12, 2001, France introduced and the Security Council unanimously passed Resolution 1368, which condemned the attacks and opened the way for the U.S.-led military action against the Taliban regime in Afghanistan. After the Afghanistan War, the United Nations presided over the Bonn Agreement, which created an interim government, and U.N. officials helped draft the country's new constitution and assisted in the organization of the 2004 election. In Iraq the United Nations has also been quietly active in humanitarian work and in helping organize the 2005 election.

As stated by the U.N. High Level Panel: "In its first sixty years, the United Nations has made crucial contributions to reducing or mitigating . . . threats to international security. While there have been major failures and shortcomings, the record of successes and contributions is underappreciated. This gives hope that the organization can adapt to successfully confront the challenges of the twenty-first century."[16]

## INSTITUTIONAL REFORMS

The U.N. High Level Panel offers a new vision of collective security for the twenty-first century. In the main its recommendations are sound. Central to the proposed reform is updating and restructuring the institutions through which the United Nations operates. U.N. Secretary-General Kofi Annan has followed up the High Level Panel Report with his own proposal that follows most of the Panel's recommendations.[17] The High Level Panel recommends changes in all the principal U.N. institutions:

■ The General Assembly would be strengthened by focusing, shortening, and restructuring its agenda and adding new mechanisms for input by civil society organizations, such as NGOs. Smaller, more focused committees would be created.

■ The Security Council would be expanded to twenty-four members, but there would be no expansion of the veto, which would remain confined to the five permanent members: China, France, Russia, the United Kingdom, and the United States. New procedures would be added to improve the Security Council's accountability and responsibility.

[16] Ibid., p. 25.
[17] Report of the Secretary-General, supra note 2.

■ A new Peacebuilding Commision would be created that would have the task of dealing with "failing states," nations that for any number of reasons may be sliding into collapse. The Peacebuilding Commission would identify such states and provide proactive assistance, peacekeeping, and conflict resolution services.

■ The Economic and Social Council would be restructured and refocused to deal with the social and economic aspects of security threats and to achieve greater policy coherence with other international institutions.

■ The Commission on Human Rights would be reformed to reduce its politicization and the scandalous influence of countries with the worst human rights records. The Commission would be expanded to universal membership, all members would be required to designate prominent and experienced heads of delegations, and an independent advisory committee would be created to guide its work. The Secretary-General's Report proposes instead that the Commission on Human Rights be replaced by a smaller Human Rights Council that would specifically undertake to abide by the highest human rights standards.

■ The Secretariat and the Office of the Secretary-General would be reformed and made more accountable. This would involve major changes in the UN's admittedly stultifying bureaucracy. The High Level Panel did not mention the Iraq oil-for food corruption scandal,[18] but it would be ⁻addressed as well.[19]

■ Cooperation between the United Nations and regional peace organizations would be strengthened. Such organizations as NATO, the EU, and the African Union that have a capacity for conflict prevention or peacekeeping would work cooperatively with the Security Council to make available a rapid-reaction force to deal with a crisis. This would greatly improve the Security Council's effectiveness.

## THE U.N. SECURITY COUNCIL

Although all of these institutional reforms are important, the most crucial aspect of the High Level Panel report concerns restructuring the Security

[18] Jim Hoagland, "Lack of Nerve Undermines U.N. Reform," *Washington Post*, Dec. 8, 2004.
[19] Both the U.S. Congress and a special U.N. commission headed by the former head of the U.S. Federal Reserve, Paul Volcker, have addressed this problem. Volcker has made the point that, although the oil-for food program was corrupt, the "big money" corruption concerned smuggling Iraqi oil into Jordan and this was fully known to U.N. Security Council members at the time it occurred.

Council, the main decision-making body of the United Nations in matters concerning peace and security. Under the U.N. Charter, the Security Council must take the lead in addressing any situation that may endanger international peace or security. The Council may investigate any such dispute or situation and may make nonbinding recommendations to the parties involved.[20]

If this action does not resolve the crisis, added powers come into play. If the Council "determines the existence of [a] threat to the peace, breach of the peace or act of aggression,"[21] enforcement action under U.N. Charter Chapter VII may be taken or authorized. This may take the form of economic sanctions[22] and, if these are inadequate, armed force – "action by air, sea, or land forces as may be necessary to maintain and restore international peace and security."[23]

Under the current arrangement, the Security Council has two tiers: (1) the five permanent members – China, France, Russia, the United Kingdom, and the United States – enjoy a right to veto any nonprocedural matter, and (2) ten rotating members without veto-power are elected (five each year) by the General Assembly to serve two-year terms.

There is general agreement that this arrangement is out of date and ill suited to the challenges of the twenty-first century. The five permanent members are the states that were on the winning side in World War II; the number of states in the world has more than tripled since 1945, and important states and regions of the world are left out or underrepresented. Yet, reform is difficult and controversial because none of the permanent members is willing to give up its place, and many states can make a case for joining this elite body.

The U.N. High Level Panel's proposal for reform starts from the idea that there is "no practical way of changing the existing [permanent members'] veto power," but there should be "no expansion of the veto." The Panel then recommends consideration of two alternative approaches to expanding the membership of the Council to twenty-four states: (1) Add three new rotating two-year members and six new permanent members (most likely Japan, Germany, Brazil, India, Egypt, and either Nigeria or South Africa) that would not have veto power or (2) add eight new semi-permanent members with renewable four-year terms (no veto) and one additional rotating member with a two-year term (see Tables 5.1 and 5.2).

The Panel's recommendation, which was echoed by the Secretary-General, was made in the hope that it would provide a starting point for negotiations

<hr>

[20] U.N. Charter, Chapter VI.
[22] Ibid., Article 41.
[21] Ibid., Chapter VII, Article 39
[23] Ibid., Article 42.

**TABLE 5.1. SECURITY COUNCIL REFORM: MODEL A**

| Regional area | No. of states | Premanent seats (continuing) | Proposed new permanent seats | Proposed two year seats (nonrenewable) | Total |
|---|---|---|---|---|---|
| Africa | 53 | 0 | 2 | 4 | 6 |
| Asia and Pacific | 56 | 1 | 2 | 3 | 6 |
| Europe | 47 | 3 | 1 | 2 | 6 |
| Americas | 35 | 1 | 1 | 4 | 6 |
| Total Model A | 191 | 5 | 6 | 13 | 24 |

Model A provides for six new permanent seats, with no veto being created, and three new two-year term nonpermanent seats, divided among the major regional areas.

among U.N. members, who will have to approve any reform.[24] Both alternatives are superior to the present arrangement and should receive urgent consideration.

Just as important as making the Security Council more representative is increasing its accountability and responsibility. The U.N. Charter confers great and extraordinary powers, but does nothing to ensure that they are fulfilled. Too often in the past, members of the Council simply voted their own narrow interests. If Council members are to have responsibility for the peace and security of the entire world, they should be prepared and pledge to act out of collective concern. There should be objective mechanisms to ensure this occurs as far as possible. For example, there should be specific criteria that members of the Council must meet to be eligible for membership, all members should pledge to uphold these criteria, and an outside advisory body should issue periodic reports on the fulfillment of each member's responsibility. India, for example, should not be permitted to join without ratifying the Nuclear Non-Proliferation Treaty. Eligibility for continued membership or reelection should depend on the performance of responsibilities for the maintenance of peace and security.

Mechanisms should be adopted to encourage greater accountability in the exercise of the veto as well. One idea advanced by the U.N. High Level Panel is "indicative voting," an initial nonbinding vote of public positions on

---

[24] Reform of the Security Council requires amendment of the U.N. Charter, which requires approval in the General Assembly by two-thirds of the 191 member states, including all five permanent members of the Security Council, and ratification by the legislatures of their governments.

**TABLE 5.2. SECURITY COUNCIL REFORM: MODEL B**

| Regional area | No. of states | Premanent seats (continuing) | Proposed four year renewable seats | Proposed two year seats (nonrenewable) | Total |
|---|---|---|---|---|---|
| Africa | 53 | 0 | 2 | 4 | 6 |
| Asia and Pacific | 56 | 1 | 2 | 3 | 6 |
| Europe | 47 | 3 | 2 | 1 | 6 |
| Americas | 35 | 1 | 2 | 3 | 6 |
| Total Model B | 191 | 5 | 8 | 11 | 24 |

Model B provides for no new permanent seats, but creates a new category of eight four-year renewable-term seats and one two-year nonpermanent (and nonrenewable) seat, divided among the major regional areas.

a proposed action. This would be followed by a second formal vote under current procedures. Such indicative voting would expose a state's position to public scrutiny (and criticism) in advance of any action and would discourage use of the veto for narrow political reasons.


## USE OF FORCE

One of the great accomplishments of the twentieth century in the long history of international relations was to impose legal constraints on the organized violence we call war. Until this recent time, states and their predecessor political entities looked upon war as a prerogative of political power. Continuous warfare has plagued humankind throughout history. After the Second World War, in full recognition of the costs and horrors of war, came an effort to make war universally illegal.

The U.N. Charter, intended in 1945 to be a kind of fundamental law for the world, addresses this goal by stating in the famous Article 2(4) that all members

[S]hall refrain in their international relations from the threat or use of force against the territorial integrity or political independence of any state, or in any manner inconsistent with the purposes of the United Nations.

This provision is authoritatively interpreted to outlaw wars of aggression; to preclude the use of force to alter existing frontiers, including armistice and provisional lines of demarcation; to ban forcible reprisals; and to outlaw assisting or fomenting civil strife in another state through terrorism or training armed bands of guerillas.[25] Although this principle has been violated hundreds of times even by states that have accepted it, we must work to make it a reality in the twenty-first century. The alternative would be to return to the free-for-all of the past when war was considered "politics by other means."

The U.N. Charter admits only two exceptions to the rule outlawing the use of force: (1) individual and collective self-defense and (2) enforcement action authorized by the U.N. Security Council under Chapter VII. A key question is whether the realities of the twenty-first century require updating these legal restrictions. To answer this, we must explore the existing rules in more detail.

## Self-Defense

The U.N. Charter (Article 51) explicitly affirms a broad and flexible right of self-defense. Of course, this is a customary law right that predates the Charter and one that can be exercised unilaterally, without prior authorization. The trigger for the exercise of the right of self-defense is armed attack. An armed attack includes not only aggression by an organized force but also more limited incursions, such as covert operations by armed guerillas and terrorism. An attack need not be on the homeland; it includes violence against citizens or facilities located outside the state itself. Self-defense also includes the right to take preemptive action against an attack on the brink of launch, as well as the right to take offensive action to prevent future attack if one attack has already occurred and the victim learns that more attacks are planned. The right of self-defense is limited by the principles of *necessity* and *proportionality* – this means that defensive force must be limited to measures that are necessary to respond to an attack and are proportionate in scope.[26] In other words, a massive invasion is not a lawful defensive response to a minor border shoot-out.

---

[25] The judgment of the International Court of Justice in *Nicaragua v. US*, 1986 ICJ Rep. 14, stated that an armed attack includes "the sending by or on behalf of a State of armed bands, groups, irregulars or mercenaries, which carry out acts of armed force against another State of such gravity as to amount to an actual armed attack, or its substantial involvement therein." But a controversial aspect of the court's judgment was that "armed attack" did not include assistance to rebels in the form of the provision of weapons or logistical or other support, although this was a violation of the principle of nonintervention in international law.

[26] These requirements were reaffirmed by the International Court of Justice in the *Nicaragua case (Nicaragua v. US)*, 1986 ICJ Rep. 14; the *Nuclear Weapons Advisory Opinion*, 1996 ICJ Rep. 226; and the *Iran Oil Platforms case (Iran v. US)*, 2003 ICJ Rep. 78.

The United States and other nations have exercised this right of self-defense many times without international controversy or objection. For example, after the U.S. Embassies in Kenya and Tanzania were bombed in August 1998, the U.S. cruise missile attacks upon installations in Afghanistan and Sudan were deemed acts of self-defense. Another example of the exercise of self-defense is the right of a state to use force to rescue or to protect its nationals abroad; this has been done many times by the United States, United Kingdom, France, and Israel.[27]

After the terrorist attacks of 9/11, the United States again invoked the right of self-defense when it invaded Afghanistan. This was fully accepted at the United Nations, and the Security Council adopted Resolutions 1368 and 1373 (2001) implicitly affirming the right of self-defense in this situation. Thus, it is clear that a terrorist attack triggers the right of self-defense under international law and, just as important, that a state that provides a haven or a base for terrorists may be subjected to acts of armed self-defense even if it did not itself mount the attack. Thus, the United States was within its rights in taking action in Afghanistan against Al Qaeda and against the Taliban regime.

### Collective Self-Defense

The U.N. Charter recognizes not only a right of individual self-defense but also a broad, corresponding right of collective self-defense. This right is not just a compilation or collection of individual rights of self defense, but a right that permits a state suffering attack to receive military or civil assistance from allied states, even those not under any attack themselves. This right of collective self-defense validates security organizations such as NATO, which contain the provision that an attack upon *one* party-member of the alliance is treated as an attack upon *all*.

The United States took the lead after World War II in creating the principle of collective self-defense, organizing NATO and other collective security arrangements around the "free" world. Collective self-defense was one of the keys to victory in the Cold War. In 1991, to justify the invasion of Iraq to repel Saddam Hussein's aggression against Kuwait, the United States and its allies invoked the principle of collective self-defense.

Curiously, U.S. policymakers overlooked and even rejected collective self-defense during the War on Terrorism. Immediately after the tragic events of

---

[27] Examples include the United States in the Dominican Republic (1965), Grenada (1983), Panama (1989); the United Kingdom in Suez (1956); France in Ivory Coast (2004); and Israel at Entebbe (1976). It is frequently charged that the United States violated the requirement of proportionality particularly in Panama and Grenada.

9/11, NATO, the Organization of American States, and the United Nations met and passed formal resolutions specifically invoking the right expressed in the Charter to collective self-defense and offering assistance to the United States. Many European allies offered to participate in the Afghanistan War in 2001. The United States rejected all offers by security alliances, preferring to work with the British on a bilateral basis. The United States did not wish to go to the trouble of gaining approval of allies and did not need any military help – it could do the job alone, thank you. Of course, this was a correct judgment as far as military operations were concerned – U.S. forces were quickly victorious. But this was the easy part; U.S. policymakers did not plan ahead. The aftermath of the military victory was far more complex than the subjugation of the Taliban. U.S. forces were not trained for occupation, reconstruction, and rehabilitation work. Belatedly, after first snubbing them, NATO and the U.N. were asked for help, but the United States refused to share control. NATO was invited in to assist with troops, but even now, years later the NATO force is not well integrated into U.S. operations.

Unlike the Afghanistan War, which was justified (though this point is not without controversy) under the principle of self-defense under the U.N. Charter, because the Taliban in Afghanistan were training and harboring the terrorist organization that had attacked the United States, the 2003 invasion of Iraq could not be justified on this basis. By defying the U.N. Security Council as well as the U.N. Charter, the United States embarked on a war without a legal basis. It also broke openly with Germany and France – two of its three main NATO allies (the United Kingdom being the third) over the war. European reservations about U.S. policy, which is widely regarded as nationalistic and imperialistic, are now seriously affecting the role of NATO and the whole Atlantic alliance. Many people now wonder if the right of collective self-defense was a casualty of the War on Terrorism.

## Preventive War

Legal experts debated all during the Cold War and after whether Article 2(4) of the U.N. Charter outlawing international war was viable or whether it was just a dead letter. This debate became a matter of crucial international importance after the terrorist attacks of 9/11. In May 2002, in a speech at West Point, President Bush announced a new American doctrine that would partially overrule the U.N. Charter's prohibition against the use of force – the doctrine of *preventive war*. This new policy says that the United States intends to strike militarily against dangerous regimes before they become imminent threats and even without clear evidence of their intent to attack.

The first exercise of this new doctrine was the Iraq War of 2003.[28] The principal reasons given by the United States and United Kingdom for attacking Saddam Hussein's regime were the danger of weapons of mass destruction and the possible link with Islamist terrorists, including Al Qaeda. Neither assumption turned out to be true – the error is now blamed on faulty intelligence. Yet, no prominent American political leader, least of all President Bush, is willing to repudiate the invasion or the doctrine of preventive war. The 2004 Republican Party platform boldly stated, "We do not equivocate. . . . The best intelligence available at the time indicated that Saddam Hussein was a threat. . . . President Bush . . . chose defending America." The 2004 Democratic Party Platform equivocated, stating, "People of good will disagree about whether America should have gone to war in Iraq."

This is a serious matter. The United States for the first time since World War II promulgated a major change in the rules governing the use of force. What will be the consequences if the doctrine of preventive war is adopted by other states? Is it in the interest of the United States to have this rule? When combined with the idea that preventive war is justified even if it later turns out to be based upon false assumptions, what kind of world will have in the future? Some may argue, as does Strobe Talbott, Deputy Secretary of State under President Clinton, "The sheer preeminence of American power could, in itself, be the ordering and taming principle of a disorderly and dangerous world." But this makes the United States the self-appointed world policeman. Is this what we want or need?

The new doctrine of preventive war is neither desirable nor necessary; rather it is a recipe for present and future difficulty. What is sauce for the goose is also sauce for the gander, and the world will be in tremendous danger if preventive war becomes a universal principle available to every nation. The United States will not prosper in an anarchic world in which every state is free to launch a preventive strike against its enemies.

Nevertheless, there is force in President Bush's argument that, in a world of massively lethal weapons that can be delivered with devastating effect without

---

[28] The United States also sought to justify the Iraq invasion in a letter dated March 20, 2003 on the basis of existing Security Council resolutions, including Resolutions 678 (1990) and 687 (1991). For the text of this letter see 97 *American Journal of International Law* 427 (2003). This was a spurious legal argument not accepted by most international lawyers. In their view, no reading of the 1990–1 U.N. Security Council resolutions yields authorization to use force twelve years later in 2003. Furthermore, Security Council Resolution 1441 in 2002 was passed on the premise that the 1990–1 resolutions did *not* authorize force in the crisis of 2002–3. For detailed analysis see Sean D. Murphy, "Assessing the Legality of Invading Iraq," 92 Georgetown Law Journal, No. 4 (2004).

warning, it is unreasonable to require a nation to wait until an attack occurs before taking action. There are several solutions to this problem:

■ A right of anticipatory or preemptive self-defense, presently an open question under international law, should be admitted as necessary to peace and security in the twenty-first century. The law of self-defense that requires an attack to be imminent was developed in the nineteenth century[29] when "imminence" and "attack" had different meanings than they do today. The test of imminence must be broadened to comport with realities of the twenty-first century. The right of self-defense should be interpreted to allow a state to take proportional military action against a proven threat being prepared against it by another nation. An example is the preemptive military action taken by Israel in 1967 after Egypt mobilized its military forces on Israel's border and evicted U.N. peacekeepers. Another more controversial example is the Israeli bombing of an Iraqi nuclear reactor in 1981.

■ A Security Council enforcement action can authorize preventive war under Article 42 of the U.N. Charter. This presumes, however, that at least nine of the fifteen members vote in favor and that none of the permanent members decides to exercise veto power.

■ If the Security Council is deadlocked and cannot act, there must be an alternative remedy. Two options may be considered in such a case. First, the General Assembly may authorize force under the Uniting for Peace Resolution passed in 1950. This would appear impractical, however, unless and until the General Assembly is substantially reformed. Second, a right of military intervention on the part of regional alliances and regional security organizations could be recognized. Examples of this intervention in the past include (1) the NATO intervention in Kosovo in 1999, undertaken after the Security Council refused to act, and (2) the Cuban Missile Crisis in 1962, in which the Security Council was blocked by a potential Soviet veto, but both NATO and the Organization of American States unanimously approved the U.S. "quarantine" (a blockade under international law) that led to the successful resolution of the crisis. Recognition of this right would require an amendment to the U.N. Charter (Article 53), which allows regional organizations to intervene with force only with the approval of the Security Council.

---

[29] The law of-self defense is derived form the case of the *Caroline* (1841), an American ship used by Canadian rebels to harass authorities in Canada. While the ship was moored in an American port near the Canadian border, the *Caroline* was attacked by the British and destroyed. The U.S. government (Daniel Webster) protested the attack as not within the right of self-defense.

Recognition of these latter two rights, both of which admittedly are highly controversial (and hopefully would not have to be used), would both deter aggression and spur the Security Council to act, by holding its feet to the fire.[30]

## Security Council Enforcement Actions

The U.N. Security Council's operates under broader rules than individual states when it comes to the use of force. After determining the existence of a threat to the peace, breach of the peace, or act of aggression, the Council can make recommendations as it sees fit. In addition, the Council can order members of the United Nations to apply sanctions, which "may include complete or partial interruption of economic relations and of rail, sea, air, postal, telegraphic, radio and other means of communication, and the severance of diplomatic relations."[31] If sanctions are considered inadequate, the Council may use or authorize armed force.[32]

## A Mixed Picture

How has the system that puts so much faith and trust in the U.N. Security Council worked? This must be admitted – not as well as it should. During the period of the Cold War, the Security Council was deadlocked by superpower rivalry and could not function as it was intended. At certain times, however, the Council did play a crucial role – in 1950 at the beginning of the Korean War when the Soviet Union's absence allowed enforcement action to be taken against North Korean aggression; and in 1962, during the Cuban Missile Crisis, when the U.S. representative, Adlai Stevenson, forcefully laid out evidence of Soviet missiles in Cuba. Another high point during the Cold War was reaching agreement on how to settle the Israeli-Palestinian conflict. Resolution 242 (1967) outlines the solution that all subsequent agreements and "road maps" have tried to implement without success: mutual recognition of the rights of both sides, renunciation of violence, and withdrawal by the Israelis from the Occupied Territories.

After the end of the Cold War, the Security Council briefly functioned as it was intended, passing a series of resolutions against Iraq's invasion of

---

[30] The U.N. High Level Panel would not agree with these suggestions, the Panel states that "there should be no change to Article 51" (the right of self-defense) and although positing a greater role for regional security organizations, it would not permit them to act without explicit authorization by the Security Council.

[31] U.N. Charter, Art. 41.                [32] U.N. Charter, Art. 42.

Kuwait in 1990 and ultimately authorizing the use of force, which permitted the United States and a broad coalition of countries to expel Iraq in the Gulf War of 1991. After that success, the U.N. Security Council authorized a purely humanitarian mission to Somalia, where people were starving and in need. After the United States abruptly withdrew from Somalia in 1993, this U.N. mission failed.

The United Nations, however, continued to function without much U.S. support, and understandably, the Security Council's performance was uneven. There were successes, such as in Haiti and Cambodia, Timor-Leste independence, the ceasefire between Ethiopia and Eritrea, the demilitarization of Croatia, and the withdrawal of Syrian troops from Lebanon. Disappointments occurred in Cyprus, where the Greek Cypriots voted down the U.N. peace plan, and in the Western Sahara, where efforts to hold a referendum have been stymied. Failures include efforts in Somalia; Bosnia; Rwanda; Kosovo; and Darfur, where there was a reluctance to intervene.

The U.N. Security Council has particularly low standing in the United States, where its failures are trumpeted and exaggerated and its successes ignored. Neo-conservatives like Richard Perle make fun of the Council, asking why in the world should the United States have to ask permission of Ghana before carrying out a military operation. A more fair-minded expert, former U.N. Ambassador Richard Holbrooke, says, however, that the United Nations "is indispensable to American national interests."

In truth, the Security Council and the United Nations have accomplished much in the face of American hostility. Throughout the 1990s, the United States withheld funds and in many cases refused support for Council peace-keeping operations. Senator Jesse Helms, an implacable U.N. foe, used his power as chair of the Senate Foreign Relations Committee to block funding and cooperation for U.N. initiatives. Nevertheless, as of 2005, there are 16 UN-led peacekeeping missions involving over 60,000 troops on three continents.

## Reforms

The U.N. High Level Panel calls for the exercise of greater responsibility on the part of the Security Council and strengthened collective security. For the Security Council to perform better, the Panel states that its actions must meet three criteria:

1. effectiveness – meeting operational goals
2. efficiency – use of time and resources

3. equity – promoting security of people all over the world without regard to location, resources, or relationship to the Great Powers

The U.N. Panel also set out important new principles to guide Security Council action. It recommends more attention to the prevention of violence and proactive involvement to this end. Preventive measures include a range of actions, such as working with regional organizations to develop frameworks of minority rights and protect elected governments from coups, preventive diplomacy, mediation and other dispute settlement programs, and, at times, preventive deployment of troops[33] to avert impending violence.

## Sanctions

The U.N. Panel also recommends more effective use of sanctions as a means of deterrence and prevention. Targeted sanctions – financial, economic, travel, aviation, and arms embargoes – are useful methods of putting pressure on leaders and groups. They may be adapted to specific situations, frequently cost less than other options, and serve the symbolic purpose of isolating violators of international standards and laws.

The Security Council has employed sanctions in many instances, sometimes with great success. Two cases stand out: U.N. sanctions played dominant roles in ending apartheid in South Africa and in inducing Libya to end its nuclear weapons and terrorism programs.

At the other extreme was the Security Council's use of sanctions against Iraq and the oil-for-food program, which operated until the U.S. invasion of 2003. A corruption scandal concerning the Iraq oil-for-food program broke in 2004, which produced a frenzy of action, including much gleeful condemnation by U.N. opponents, grandstanding by hitherto obscure members of the U.S. Congress, and self-righteous calls for the resignation of U.N. Secretary-General Kofi Annan.

Understanding what happened involves considering the origin of the Iraqi sanctions. The Security Council imposed them after the Gulf War when Saddam Hussein refused full cooperation with U.N. weapons inspectors. But the sanctions hurt ordinary Iraqis, especially children, not Saddam and his Baathist elites, who were able to avoid their effects through massive smuggling. To relieve the suffering of the Iraqi people, the oil-for-food program

---

[33] An instance of such preventive deployment – a success – was in the Former Yugoslav Republic of Macedonia in 1996.

was authorized in 1996. This handed Saddam a made-to-order opportunity for corruption, of which he took full advantage.

The U.N. officials who ran the oil-for-food program reported, not to Kofi Annan, but to the Security Council and to its sanctions oversight committee. Two major problems were readily apparent and were widely and publicly reported at the time: (1) The sanctions were ineffective because of massive smuggling, and (2) kickbacks were flowing in every direction. American officials, who were not involved in the corruption, apparently decided that blowing the whistle would endanger the entire sanctions program, which, imperfect as it was, they considered essential. A major cause of the scandal was the fact that the U.N. bureaucracy was suddenly given a $100 billion program to manage without adequate training or preparation. The Independent Inquiry Committee (headed by former U.S. Federal Reserve chairman Paul Volcker) charged with investigation the program correctly put the blame for its failings – that ranged from poor administration to outright corruption – on the entire UN, not only the bureaucracy, but the Security Council and its member states.[34]

The U.N. High Level Panel's Report is strangely silent concerning the oil-for-food program scandal, but it makes the point that in the future, when the Council imposes a sanctions regime, it must be better monitored and implemented. A senior official should be given the authority and resources to administer and police it. If there are violations, secondary sanctions should be imposed on sanctions-busting states. Above all, the report says, "The Secretary General, in consultation with the Security Council, should ensure that an appropriate auditing mechanism is in place to oversee sanctions administration." The oil-for-food scandal must never be allowed to happen again.

## Use of Force

The U.N. Panel recommends that the Security Council should rely first on prevention and peaceful resolution of international security threats through the dispatch of humanitarian, human rights, and police missions. Force should be deployed as a last resort. The Panel sets out five "criteria of legitimacy" for the Council's deployment of force under its Chapter VII enforcement powers:

---

[34] Despite its failings, the Independent Inquiry Committee's Report credits the oil-for-food program with (1) providing crucial humanitarian aid to needy Iraqis and (2) supplementing the effort to prevent Saddam from acquiring weapons of mass destruction. Out of a total of $101 billion in contracts overseen by the program, approximately $1.88 billion was illegally diverted into Saddam's coffers; and $8.4 billion in oil was sold outside the program illegally. In addition, Saddam sold approximately $2.6 billion before the program's inception in defiance of sanctions.

1. the seriousness of the threat
2. a humanitarian motive
3. the exhaustion of every nonmilitary option
4. proportional means
5. a reasonable chance of success

The U.N. Panel calls for these guidelines to be specifically endorsed by individual members of the United Nations, even those who are not members of the Security Council. The Panel's recommendations constitute an important new blueprint for the Security Council's exercise of its responsibilities.

## THE SECURITY COUNCIL AND IRAQ

The American government, politicians of both political parties, and the U.S. media are all in agreement that the U.N. Security Council failed miserably in Iraq. This is unfair because with regard to Iraq, the system has worked better than is generally believed.

After the successful Gulf War, which in 1991 expelled Iraq from Kuwait, the Security Council passed a series of resolutions requiring Iraq to pay compensation for damages caused by the war (including environmental damage) and created a Compensation Commission to adjudicate claims. The Security Council also required Iraq to dismantle its programs for weapons of mass destruction (WMD) and began its weapons inspections, which continued for several years. The U.N. inspection program, it is now known, was successful in terminating Iraq's WMD programs.

The major failures of the United Nations in Iraq occurred in the late 1990s when President Saddam Hussein, with the knowledge of the Security Council, circumvented U.N. sanctions by smuggling oil exports. The United Nations also allowed the Iraqi oil-for-food program to become corrupt. When Saddam abruptly threw out the U.N. inspection team in 1998, the United Nations acquiesced and the United States and the United Kingdom settled for a punishing four-day bombing campaign, Operation Desert Fox, but Saddam's action was allowed to stand.

The U.N. weapon inspections resumed only at the Bush administration's insistence and after the American troop build-up began in 2002. The Security Council finally returned to action on November 8, 2002, unanimously passing Resolution 1441, which declared that Iraq was "in material breach" of its obligations under previous U.N. resolutions and giving Iraq "one last opportunity to comply with its disarmament obligations." Iraq reluctantly agreed to full cooperation. But this was too late; Bush administration officials had given up on the United Nations.

The U.S./U.K. invasion of Iraq in March 2003 cut short the U.N. inspections and toppled the Iraqi government. The twin justifications for the war – Iraq's supposed weapons of mass destruction and Saddam's links with Al Qaeda – turned out to be false, the result of CIA and other intelligence failures. (George Tenet, the director of the CIA during the period before 9/11, as well as the man who told President Bush that it was a "slam dunk" that Saddam had weapons of mass destruction, was awarded America's highest civilian honor, the Presidential Medal of Freedom in December 2004; one wonders what he would have merited if he had been correct). This failure to find WMD proves the success of the U.N. inspection programs of the early 1990s, which did disarm Iraq after all. It was the United States and United Kingdom, rather than the United Nations, that misjudged the situation.

After the U.S./U.K. invasion in May 2003 the U.N. Security Council unanimously passed Resolution 1483 in order to contribute to the peacemaking effort there. This resolution neither approved nor condemned the invasion. Rather it provided for the appointment of a U.N. Special Representative with responsibilities for economic reconstruction and humanitarian assistance. Tragically, a terrorist bomb destroyed the U.N. mission to Iraq in the summer of 2003, and the U.N. Special Representative, Sergio Viera de Mello, was among the many dedicated U.N. officials killed in the blast.

Despite this setback, in June 2004 the Security Council unanimously passed a second postconflict resolution (1546) endorsing the new interim government of Iraq and putting the United Nations into a leading role to guide Iraq's political transition to democratic government. This resolution requests that U.N. member states contribute assistance both to the new Iraqi government and to the U.S.-led military force in Iraq. The Council's action, eagerly sought by the Bush administration, provided a major boost to the chances of stabilizing Iraq, mitigating part of the political (and perhaps economic) burden on the United States.

The success of the Iraqi elections in January 2005 reflects this renewed international cooperation in the effort to bring democracy to Iraq. NATO has agreed to help, particularly with the training of Iraqi police. A United Nations electoral team trained the members of the Iraq Independent Election Commission, which ran the elections, as well as many of the electoral workers in the field. U.N. help was termed "essential" by the Commission in January 2005. Twenty-three U.N. agencies are now working in Iraq to coordinate international aid in rebuilding the country. As of February 2005, forty-six projects have been approved and funded for a total of $494 million. The United Nations within the World Bank has established an International

Reconstruction Fund, and so far twenty-four donors have committed about $1 billion in aid for Iraq.

U.N. Secretary-General Kofi Annan stated in February 2005, "I am determined to make certain that the United Nations plays its full part in helping the Iraqi people achieve [democracy]." A supreme irony is the fact that the United States, after bypassing the United Nations in its decision to use force, has found the United Nations indispensable to realizing the goal of peace and democracy in Iraq.

## HUMANITARIAN INTERVENTION

### Is There Such a Thing?

There is lively debate whether, as an exception to the international rules against the use of force, manifest and large-scale abuse of human rights within a country should be met with "humanitarian intervention." Many legal experts argue that the international community cannot stand idly by in the face of atrocities committed by a government or with its acquiescence against a population within its territory. There is great appeal to this view, but skeptics and opponents of such a right argue that humanitarian intervention would, if permitted, be abused by states for their own purposes, invite stronger states to beat up on weaker ones, and contravenes fundamental concepts of law and international relations, such as respect for sovereignty and the principle of nonintervention.

Finding stellar examples of pure humanitarian intervention in history is difficult. There are, to be sure, instances of intervention that received almost universal support from the international community: Tanzania's action in 1979 that overthrew the odious regime of Idi Amin in Uganda and Vietnam's invasion of Cambodia that ended the genocidal Pol Pot government readily come to mind, but in neither case was a right of humanitarian intervention cited as justification.

The most important recent case of claimed humanitarian intervention undoubtedly is the Kosovo crisis of 1999, in which a NATO bombing campaign was conducted without U.N. authorization to stop human rights abuses against the ethnic Albanian population of that province of Yugoslavia. This was justified at the time as a limited use of force in exceptional circumstances and as a last resort to prevent a large-scale human catastrophe. Subsequent to the action, the Security Council, by a vote of 12–4, defeated a resolution of condemnation. The Council instead passed Resolution 1244, which approved the withdrawal of Yugoslav forces from Kosovo after the bombing and deployed civilian and military peacekeepers under U.N. auspices.

The use of force in Kosovo caused a split in the international community and among international lawyers as well. Those who defended humanitarian intervention argued that the NATO campaign was not directed against the territorial integrity or independence of Yugoslavia, but was an action of last resort to rescue a population in danger. Those against the action argued in favor of a strict construction of Article 2(4) of the U.N. Charter, which cannot be changed by state practice to the contrary. The full extent of the arguments is readily available elsewhere[35] and cannot be explored here, but the nub of contention is the scope allowed for customary international law. Given the fact that, under the U.N. Charter, one permanent member of the Security Council can interpose its veto against the will of the entire international community, scope must be given to international customary law to justify an action that may be illegal under treaty law alone.[36]

## Needed Safeguards

The fact that the NATO bombing campaign in Kosovo was accepted, although not approved, by the great majority of the international community provides some support for the recognition of a right of humanitarian intervention in extreme cases. Although sovereignty and nonintervention remain important principles of international order, neither principle is absolute. No state should be allowed to commit atrocities against its own citizens. The U.N. Security Council has the duty and should act in such a situation, but there may be a case when the Council is deadlocked or unable to act. The recognition of the legitimacy of humanitarian intervention may in fact both spur Security Council action and deter states and their leaders from repressive conduct so that the right will not have to be used.

Humanitarian intervention is best considered as an emerging right under state practice and customary international law.[37] Although the U.N. Charter is the principal international legal instrument governing the use of force, it is not

---

[35]  Compare, I. Bownlie and C. Apperley, "Kosovo Crisis Inquiry: Memorandum on International Law Aspects," 49 *International and Comparative Law Quarterly* 886 (2000) and C. Greenwood, "International Law and the NATO Intervention in Kosovo," 49 *International and Comparative Law Quarterly* 929 (2000).

[36]  Mary Ellen O' Connell, "The UN, NATO and International Law after Kosovo," 22 *Human Rights Quarterly* 57 (2000); Editorial Comments: NATO's Kosovo Intervention, 93 American Journal of International Law 824 (1999).

[37]  Christopher Greenwood, "International Law and the NATO Intervention in Kosovo," 49 *International and Comparative Law Quarterly* 926, 929–934 (2000). Other international lawyers argue that the U.N. Charter Article 2 (4) should be interpreted to permit humanitarian intervention. See the "Editorial Comments" in the previous note.

the exclusive basis for international law. The International Court of Justice has implied that customary law relating to the use of force continues to apply even after the adoption of the U.N. Charter.[38] Thus, humanitarian intervention can be considered a customary law exception to U.N. Charter Article 2(4).

Nevertheless, it is imperative to surround the doctrine of humanitarian intervention with criteria for its application so as to prevent its misuse. There must be clear and convincing evidence of extreme humanitarian distress on a large scale, an urgent need for relief and no practical alternative to military force. Nonviolent means to resolve the distress must have been exhausted. The use of force should be limited to what is required to alleviate the situation, be consistent with international humanitarian law, and be multilateral, preferably exercised by a regional organization, such as NATO.

Significantly, the U.N. High Level Panel gives a boost to the doctrine of humanitarian intervention. Its report states

We endorse the emerging norm that there is a collective responsibility to protect, exercisable by the Security Council authorizing military intervention as a last resort, in the event of genocide and other large-scale killing, ethnic cleansing or serious violations of international humanitarian law which sovereign governments have proved powerless or unwilling to prevent.

This is an implicit admission that the Security Council was wrong not to have acted in Kosovo. But the U.N. High Level Panel still would limit humanitarian intervention to Security Council-approved actions. This seems too restrictive and even contradictory. Regional security organizations should be recognized to have the right to intervene as a last resort if the Security Council is paralyzed and unable to act.

## Regime Change

Humanitarian intervention should be distinguished from regime change, a much-discussed topic since the 2003 invasion of Iraq. Humanitarian intervention should be handled as a limited use of force that does not necessarily attempt to replace the existing government. The exit strategy should therefore be clear. Of course, there may be cases where regime change is imperative or, as in Yugoslavia, here intervention leads to regime change. If so, this fact should be clearly considered in advance because regime change is not only

---

[38] In the Nicaragua case (*Nicaragua v. USA*), 1986 ICJ Rep. 14, the ICJ applied customary international law rather than the U.N. Charter because of a U.S. reservation in the acceptance of its jurisdiction.

extremely difficult but also involves extensive follow-up responsibilities. Under the laws of war (the Hague and Geneva Conventions), the intervening countries may find that they have the status of occupying powers with long-term responsibilities. Under the Hague Convention IV of 1907, territory is considered occupied when it comes under the authority of an army hostile to the government. The occupying power is required to "take all the measures in his power to restore and ensure, as far as possible, public order and safety, while respecting, unless absolutely prevented, the laws in force in the country."

Accordingly, regime change is usually a difficult, expensive, and long-term business, as the United States belatedly "discovered" to its chagrin in Iraq. Even regime change under the auspices of the United Nations is difficult, as proved by the terrible bombing of U.N. headquarters in Baghdad in August 2003. Regime change as part of humanitarian intervention requires additional limiting criteria: There should be significant support in the target country, an acceptable and better alternative government should be available, the costs should be manageable, an exit strategy should be devised beforehand, and the mission should be completed within a reasonable time.


## REGIONAL SECURITY ORGANIZATIONS

The U.N. High Level Panel Report advocates a greater role for regional security organizations, such as NATO and the African Union, in undertaking enforcement and peacekeeping operations. In accordance with Chapter VIII of the U.N. Charter, authorization for peacekeeping missions must be sought from the Security Council, although the Panel recognized that "in some urgent situations authorization may be sought after such operations have commenced." Regional security organizations should be reinvigorated so that they might play an enhanced part in maintaining international peace.


## CONFLICT PREVENTION, PEACEMAKING, AND PEACEKEEPING

### U.N. Charter Chapter VI and One-Half

The U.N. Charter does not explicitly authorize peacemaking and peacekeeping missions; they have come about through custom and necessity. (International relations specialists sometimes refer to this section of the U.N. chapter as "Chapter VI and one-half" because it falls between Chapters VI and VII). Not all U.N. peace missions have succeeded; in fact some have failed utterly and disastrously. The miscues and failures are well publicized, but not the successes. But there is great potential if reforms are made.

## Conflict Prevention and Peacemaking

The U.N. Department of Political Affairs operates within the Office of the Secretary-General to carry out preventive diplomacy to head off crises and to support conflict resolution and peacemaking efforts. Perhaps the most important work of this department is electoral assistance. Currently there are ten peacemaking missions in the field, including U.N. Assistance Missions in Iraq and in Afghanistan.

## Peacekeeping

U.S. policymakers underestimate the value of U.N. peacemaking missions. Since the tragedy of Somalia during which the "Blackhawk Down" incident sparked U.S. public revulsion, U.N. peacekeeping has been reviled both by politicians and many commentators. This is unfortunate. U.S. security policy is focused on the homeland, but security threats can develop anywhere in the world. U.S. security is inseparable from global security policy. Every human life is precious. One important measure of security policy progress should be the number of people worldwide who are killed each year in armed combat. Peacekeeping operations are essential to reduce this number. Peacekeeping is also an immense bargain: The total annual cost of the sixteen current U.N. missions is about $4 billion, a tiny fraction of annual U.S. military spending.

Peacekeeping may be used for various purposes and in different situations:

■ to prevent the outbreak of conflict or the spill-over of conflict across borders

■ to provide stability after a cease-fire and to create conditions so the parties to the conflict can reach a lasting peace agreement

■ to assist the implementation of a peace agreement

■ to assist a "failed" state or territory to establish a stable government based upon democratic principles

Peacekeeping operations for these purposes are planned, prepared, and managed by the U.N. Department of Peacekeeping Operations under the authority of the General Assembly and the Security Council. Peacekeeping missions traditionally have been based on the principle of "consent" – they enter by invitation extended by all concerned parties. This means that they are lightly armed and will use force only in self-defense. They are also expected to be impartial.

In recent years, however, more "robust" peacekeeping missions have been approved under Chapter VII of the U.N. Charter. Such missions are more aptly termed "peace-enforcement," rather than peacekeeping. Now it is considered appropriate for the U.N. Security Council to approve both consent-based and coercion-based missions under Chapter VII, because experience has shown, as in Somalia, that a consent-based mission can turn ugly.

Each peacekeeping operation has a specific set of mandates and tasks depending on the situation. Both military and various types of civilian personnel may be deployed. Often as a practical matter their task is not only peacekeeping but also "peace-building" and reconstruction.

Does peacekeeping work? To judge this we must move beyond the headlines, media bias, and anecdotal sensationalism. Only empirical studies can yield objective evidence. Political scientists who have studied peacekeeping operations and their effectiveness in comparison with conflicts in which there are no peacekeeping mission are virtually unanimous in concluding that peacekeeping is indeed effective. For example, Columbia University Professor Virginia Page Fortna's 2004 study[39] of peacekeeping in the aftermath of civil wars, which examined all post-World War II cases to determine empirically whether peace lasts longer when U.N. peacekeepers are present than when they are absent, concluded that "[peacekeeping] tends to make peace more likely... and to last longer." Figure 5.1 shows an unmistakable correlation between U.N. peacekeeping missions and the reduction of civil conflicts in the world.

## Peace Enforcement

In addition to the traditional type of peacekeeping, the U.N. Security Council has authorized two additional forms, both under the rubric of "peace-enforcement" missions. For example, on February 29, 2004, the Security Council adopted Resolution 1529, authorizing the deployment of a multinational force in Haiti after former Haitian President Jean-Bertrand Aristide, facing insurrection and public disorder, abruptly resigned and left the country. This peace-enforcement force was sent into a country in which offensive operations were necessary, and the mandate authorized "all necessary *measures*" to maintain peace.

A second type of U.N. peace-enforcement operation may be necessary to intervene militarily against belligerents. Ironically, this was done in 1994 in support of Aristide's restoration as the elected president of Haiti, when the Council passed Resolution 940, authorizing a multinational force to use "all necessary *means*" to restore democracy in Haiti. The same formula was used

[39] "Does Peacekeeping Keep Peace?" *International Studies Quarterly* 48 (2004): 269–92.

Figure 5.1. U.N. peacekeeping has reduced civil conflict. *Source*: U.N. Department of Public Information, 2004.

in Resolution 1528 (2004), which authorized French forces to use "all nec-essary means" to restore order in the Ivory Coast. Use of the word "means" in place of measures is meant to clearly authorize robust offensive force, and such peace-enforcement is indistinguishable from a collective security enforcement action.

## Needed Improvements

The United Nations currently has sixteen peacekeeping operations in the field: three in the Middle East (Golan Heights, Lebanon, and Israel/Palestine), three in Europe (Cyprus, Georgia, and Kosovo), one in Asia (India/Pakistan), one in the Americas (Haiti), and eight in Africa (Sudan, Burundi, Ivory Coast, Liberia, the Democratic Republic of the Congo, Ethiopia and Eritrea, Sierra Leone, and Western Sahara). The U.N. peacekeeping force in Sierra Leone concluded its work, apparently successfully, at the end of 2005. The missions in the Middle East and those in Kashmir and Cyprus have remained in place for many decades. Over a dozen peacekeeping operations have been success-fully terminated, including in Croatia, Cambodia, the Dominican Republic, Angola, Guatemala, El Salvador, Namibia, East Timor, and Mozambique. Despite well-publicized failures in Somalia and the former Yugoslavia in the 1990s and in the Congo in 2004, U.N. peacekeeping is a qualified success and an essential part of international cooperation.

Despite this success, reforms are necessary to guard against future failings.[40] Implementing them will require cooperation from key U.N. members, especially the United States. First, every peacekeeping force should have a clear, credible, and achievable mandate before it starts operations. Lightly armed, invited peacekeepers should be properly prepared for a possible worst-case scenario, and despite the need for impartiality, victims must be protected and aggressors punished if violence breaks out. More robust peacemaking units should be prepared in different fashion from traditional peacekeeping operations in accordance with the difference in their mission. In many cases, military and civilian personnel may have to be put under the same command. The details of logistics and expenditure management should be worked out in advance.

Three new types of operations would make peacekeeping more effective:

1. There is urgent need for a substantial *rapid reaction* force to be on call for possible peacekeeping or peace-making operations. In situations where lives are at risk, as happened in Rwanda in the 1990s and in Darfur in 2004, the United Nations should have the capability of dispatching a mission quickly. This peacekeeping force requires both on-call military units and civilian experts. This type of mission will also require more rapid mission planning and an upgrade in the U.N. Secretariat's capacity. Help can be provided especially by the European Union, whose Rapid Intervention Force can be placed at the disposal of the U.N. Security Council. The EU force may be deployed within ten days anywhere in the world.

2. The U.N. High Level Panel and Secretary-General Kofi Annan recommend that the Security Council establish *peace-building* missions: mixed military and civilian units whose job would be either to rehabilitate a failing state or assist in the rebuilding of a state after the end of a conflict. This has been done in the past in such cases as Namibia and Mozambique; it is time to formalize these operations and to establish a Peace-Building Commission with a support office in the U.N. Secretariat. At the 2005 World Summit the U.N. General Assembly formally accepted the recommendation.[41]

3. A new category of mission that is needed is a response force. This should be a force of both civilian experts and military personnel under a joint command whose task would be to intervene to protect civilian populations

---

[40] See the Report of the Panel on United Nations Peace Operations, 39 ILM 1432 (2000) for a comprehensive critical view.
[41] United Nations General Assembly, 2005 World Summit Outcome, A/60/L.1, 97–105 (20 September 2005).

threatened with violence. The goal would be simply to stop the violence and to establish the rule of law in order to provide an opportunity for conflict resolution and political solutions. An example of human security intervention was Operation Artemis in 2003, in which the Security Council authorized the European Union to go to Ituri in the Democratic Republic of the Congo where local vigilantes, including thousands of young children, were pillaging, looting, and raping villagers; this mission succeeded in establishing order and saved many lives.

Peacekeepers are in short supply. The United Nations must rely on and coordinate more fully with regional organizations, such as the Organization of American States, NATO, the European Union, the Arab League, and the African Union. Such regional organizations may be more politically acceptable than forces administered by individual states or the United Nations itself. The United States, as the most powerful U.N. Security Council member, should take the lead in working with the United Nations to establish more and better-trained peacekeeping units.

## TERRORISM

Acts of terrorism provoke a visceral response in all of us. We can all sympathize with the talk-radio mentality – "Get our planes up and flatten 'em" is a typical caller's advice. We long for a quick, unequivocal solution – this is why we are comforted that our president has declared a War on Terrorism.

If only it were so simple. There is undoubtedly a military component to fighting terrorism, but in emphasizing warfare, we may be failing to take advantage of existing international institutions and the established rules of international law with regard to terrorism. The "war on terrorism" cannot be won by unilateral action by the United States, nor can it be won by bilateral contacts with U.S. allies. These actions must be combined with coordinated multilateral and legal networks to ensure that there are no safe havens for terrorists and that there are coordinated international policies to prevent, suppress, and prosecute terrorism. What is needed is a comprehensive international strategy to combat terrorism.

An international legal and institutional structure to combat terrorism has been created to combat terrorism. This structure can be analyzed on four levels.

1. First, the U.N. Security Council has passed a series of resolutions condemning and combating terrorism that are binding on all states. Resolution

1368 (2001), passed just after the attacks of 9/11, condemns terrorism as a threat to international peace and security. It was followed by Resolution 1373 (2001), which requires all states to prevent and suppress terrorist acts, freeze financial assets of terrorist groups and individuals, and cooperate with other states. A permanent Counter-Terrorism Committee was established as well, and Resolution 1377 (2001) authorizes to assist and promote best practices so that all states can achieve the legal, technical, and financial ability to combat terrorism.

2. Particularly important and useful is U.N. Security Council Resolution 1617 (2005) that obliges all states to freeze the assets and impose travel bans and trade embargoes on individuals, groups, and entities associated with terrorism. Any business or individual who supplies any such entity or individual is also subject to punishment. The Security Council compiles a "consolidated list" of terrorist groups and individuals for this purpose. U.N. member states must report on their actions with respect to this obligation, and implementation guidance is available through the U.N. Financial Action Task Force. This resolution imposes a global freeze on terrorist assets and activities and cuts them off from the world of business and finance.

3. Second, the United Nations has adopted thirteen international conventions dealing with specific types of terrorist acts, including hijackings of aircraft, airport violence, illegal possession of nuclear material, shipping and port safety, use of plastic explosives and bombings, hostage taking, and financing. On April 13, 2005 the U.N. General Assembly unanimously adopted the International Convention for the Suppression of Acts of Nuclear Terrorism.[42]

4. Third, the U.N. General Assembly has adopted many resolutions condemning specific acts of terrorism, calling for the ratification of international conventions on terrorism, and requiring cooperation. Well before the attacks of 9/11, the Security Council in 1999 established an Al Qaeda/Taliban sanctions committee.

5. Fourth, regional security organizations in every area of the world have adopted programs for the prevention, suppression, and prosecution of terrorists.

This multilateral solidarity against terrorism is welcome. *The 9/11 Commission Report* in 2004 called for "Turning a National Strategy [against Terrorism] into a Coalition Strategy." It went on to say, "Practically every aspect of U.S.

---

[42]  44 *International Legal Materials* 815 (2005).

counterterrorism strategy relies on international cooperation." In other word, multilateralism is key to defeating terrorism.

One additional important item should be added to the multilateral campaign against terrorism: – a comprehensive international convention that outlaws all forms of terrorism by whatever means and for whatever purpose. Such a convention is needed to end for good the practice of being selective about what acts of terrorism to condemn and what groups or causes are "terrorist" in nature. Such a convention is proposed both by Secretary-General Kofi Annan and the U.N. High Level Panel. The key to the success of such a convention is to draft a definition of terrorism that is comprehensive and capable of gaining universal acceptance. In the words of the Secretary-General, "An action is terrorism if it is intended to cause death or serious bodily harm to civilian or non-combatants with the purpose of intimidating a population or compelling a government or international organization to do or abstain from doing any act."

The U.S. War on Terror beguiles us into thinking that our government is protecting us. This is comforting, especially considering that the U.S. government was asleep for so long. But after the successful campaign in Afghanistan to remove the Taliban and the sanctuaries and terrorist training camps, the strategy of relying primarily on conventional military force seems flawed. Only the United States is involved in a "war" on terrorism. Other nations take terrorism very seriously, but have the view that declaring a war and applying conventional military force can serve to provoke more terrorism. What is needed is precisely what the 9/11 Commission recommended: a multilateral strategy instead of a national strategy. In the near term this means the following: (1) military force that is applied very selectively and judiciously, (2) international police work, (3) intelligence and infiltration of terrorist organizations, and (4) commitments by all states and regional peace organizations to implement the U.N. antiterrorist programs as required under Security Council resolutions.

The U.N. High Level Panel Report echoes the Security Council's call in Resolution 1566 (2004) for a comprehensive global strategy against terrorism, the conclusion of a comprehensive agreement to combat terrorism to be ratified by all U.N. members, and assisting states through a U.N. Counter-Terrorism Directorate that would acquire effective legal, administrative, and police tools to prevent terrorism. The report included this telling criticism of the U.S. approach:

[T]he current "war on terrorism" has in some instances corroded the very values that terrorists target: human rights and the rule of law. . . . [A]pproaches to terror focusing wholly on military, police, and intelligence measures risk undermining efforts to promote good governance and human rights, alienate large parts of the world's population and thereby weaken the potential for collective action against terrorism. The crucial need . . . is to address not only [the] capacity but also . . . the will to fight terror. To develop that will – with States drawing support rather than opposition from their own publics – requires a broader-based approach.

This highlights the need for an additional long-term strategy against terrorism to supplement the near-term strategies now being implemented. There are two elements crucial in the longer term.

1. Of the forty-one predominantly Muslim countries in the world, not one is rated by objective measures as a democratic state that is respectful of fundamental rights and civil liberties. Virtually all Muslim countries are economically backward as well. Eradicating Islamist terrorism means combating its root causes – poverty, ignorance, and political repression. The United States, as we have seen, has organized a military theater of operations that stretches across the entire arc of the Muslim world. This military effort should be supplemented by a political and economic effort to transform the Muslim world. Achieving democracy, liberty, and an end to tyranny requires the separation of church and state in the Muslim world.

2. Ending the ongoing civil wars and regional conflicts in the Muslim world, particularly the Israeli-Palestinian conflict, should claim the highest priority.

In addition, we must seek to understand the political origin of suicide terrorism, a particularly virulent phenomenon of our times. America, having suffered the worst of such terrorism in the attacks of 9/11 and now facing it in Iraq, has a particularly great stake in ending this horror.

Professor Robert Pape of the University of Chicago has compiled a database of all reported suicide terrorist incidents between 1980 and 2003, some 315 attacks in all.[43] He reports that, contrary to widespread assumptions, suicide terrorists are not religious fundamentalists, but rather are members of organized groups motivated by a clear, secular strategic objective – to establish or maintain political self-determination. In particular, the data point to an exact correlation between suicide terror attacks and hostile military occupation. Hezbollah suicide attackers began operating only after Israel's invasion of Lebanon in 1982, the Tamil Tigers began attacks only after the Sri Lankan

---

[43] Robert A. Pape, *Dying to Win: The Strategic Logic of Suicide Terrorism* (2005).

military began moving into Tamil homelands in 1987, Palestinian attacks increased after the huge increase in Jewish settlers in the 1980s, and America was attacked after establishing bases in Saudi Arabia. And there were no documented suicide terror attacks in Iraq until after the U.S. military occupation in that country.

Therefore, the logic of how to eliminate this most virulent form of terrorism is clear: The United States in particular should project its power in more subtle ways, such as through sea power and island bases offshore. When troops are needed on the ground the United States should rely on the United Nations and regional security organizations, which are much less likely to provoke a terrorist response.

## CONTROLLING WEAPONS OF MASS DESTRUCTION

No security policy is more important than controlling weapons of mass destruction (WMD). These are nuclear, biological, and chemical weapons that could kill tens of thousands of people and cause social and economic chaos. In the post-Cold War era, not only states may seek to possess and use such weapons; they are weapons of choice for terrorists as well. We now know that for over ten years Al Qaeda sought to acquire WMD. Osama Bin Laden reportedly considers the acquisition of WMD a "religious obligation," and his associates say he intends to carry out a "Hiroshima" against the United States. Islamist terrorists will not hesitate to use WMD against innocent civilians. The U.N. High Level Panel Report states the danger of nuclear terrorism in graphic terms:

Experts estimate that terrorists with 50 kilograms of highly enriched uranium, an amount that would fit into six one-liter milk cartons, need only smuggle it across borders in order to create an improvised nuclear device that could level a medium-sized city.

The terrorist threat is associated with the more general danger of nuclear proliferation: the spread of nuclear weapons among states. About sixty states currently operate nuclear power or research reactors, and at least forty of these have the capacity to build nuclear weapons if they choose, either openly or covertly. Nuclear proliferation would produce a vastly more dangerous world.

In addition to the danger of nuclear proliferation is the grave risk posed by the existence of large stockpiles of nuclear and radiological materials. Highly enriched uranium stockpiles exist all over the world, and many are inadequately guarded. Twenty cases of nuclear material diversion and more than 200 incidents of illegal trafficking of nuclear materials have been documented in the past decade.

What is the United States doing to counteract these threats? Regretfully, the U.S. has a patchwork of policies that range from woefully inadequate to counterproductive. As the following analysis shows, the U.S. has a three-tier vision when it comes to international policies and rules designed to control WMD. First, U.S. policymakers feel the U.S. itself is free to flout any rules or controls. Rules are for other nations not for us, they say; America, after all, knows best. Second, the U.S. turns a blind eye when nations friendly to U.S. interests disregard the international rules. Third, the U.S. government demands of states it regards as rogue or "criminal" regimes to follow not only international rules, but also U.S. unilateral demands.

## The Proliferation Security Initiative

The George W. Bush administration's effort to prevent and deter WMD is the Proliferation Security Initiative (PSI), begun in May 2003. The PSI seeks to involve nations in what is termed a "willing partnership" (another coalition of the willing), bringing together their national capabilities to use military, economic, and diplomatic tools to interdict threatening shipments of WMD and missile-related technology. The PSI ignores or attempts to move beyond established multilateral arms control and nonproliferation approaches. The Pentagon defines this new strategy as the "full range of military preparations and activities to reduce, and protect against, the threat posed by nuclear, biological, and chemical weapons and their associated delivery systems." This strategy is focused on homeland defense and includes the deployment of a missile defense system. The Bush administration has also focused on the threat posed by the "axis of evil," the term coined to refer to the three rogue nations of North Korea, Iran, and Iraq. The major reason for this term of opprobrium was that all three were believed to have clandestine programs to develop WMD.

Operation Iraqi Freedom in 2003 was an early test of this policy. The major reason for the attack on Iraq in 2003 was to end the threat of WMD. Now it is believed that Iraq ended its WMD programs in the early 1990s. In any case, Iraq is no longer a threat. That leaves the two other charter members of the axis of evil – North Korea and Iran. North Korea is believed to have two or more nuclear bombs, and Iran is suspected of having a secret nuclear weapons program. The U.S. government's PSI program has been ineffective against both North Korea and Iran, in part because of significant policy differences between the United States and other concerned states. In the case of Iran, key EU nations – the United Kingdom, France, and Germany – concluded a much-criticized deal (because plutonium production is allowed) to get Iran to suspend its nuclear programs, contrary to the Bush administration's tougher line of condemnation and sanctions. Differences of opinion with major allies – South Korea and Japan – have also hampered progress in the six-party talks with North Korea.

Once again, American unilateralism has been ineffective. The erroneous intelligence claims by Secretary of State Colin Powell just prior to the Iraq War in 2003 that there were "many smoking guns" of WMD in Iraq (a statement he now says he regrets as a "blot" on his record) have hurt the American campaign for action against Iran and North Korea. How can U.S. intelligence information be taken at face-value after the fiasco in Iraq?

## North Korea and Iran

By any standard, U.S. policy dealing with North Korea and Iran has failed. U.S. "policy" – if it can ever be called such – which consists of international isolation, name calling, and vague threats to use military force, has been counterproductive, producing only defiance in both countries. As charter members of the U.S. "axis of evil" and with the example of what happened to a fellow "member," Iraq, North Korean and Iranian intransigence is perfectly comprehensible.

Odious governments run both North Korea and Iran, but both must be engaged, although in different ways, to give up their nuclear ambitions. Survival of odious regimes is a far lesser evil than nuclear proliferation. In both cases international agreements must be reached so that both countries give up the nuclear option in a verifiable manner. These agreements must involve an appropriate mixture of positive and negative incentives, including the threat of Security Council sanctions. The failure of the 1994 "Agreed Framework" agreement by the Clinton administration with North Korea is a lesson that should be learned so that this time there are iron-clad guarantees against cheating. Any new agreements should also make full use of the multilateral machinery against nonproliferation.

## Using International Law and Institutions

Multilateralism and international law present alternative means that can prevent war and create security. As always, multilateralism requires patience and effort, a reordering of priorities, and concessions that the United States has refused to make in the past. But this may be the best and only way to prevent both war and terrorism. On April 28, 2004 the U.N. Security Council adopted Resolution 1540, a strong statement against proliferation of WMD, as well as their means of delivery, that is binding upon all states. This landmark resolution compels all 191 U.N. members to draw up legislation and strengthen laws to prevent terrorists from being able to "manufacture, acquire, possess, transport or use nuclear, chemical, or biological weapons and their means of delivery." The Council also established a 1540 Committee to monitor, evaluate, and follow up on compliance with this requirement.

**Nuclear Weapons.** In the post-Cold War era, the major regime of nuclear weapons control is the Treaty on the Non-Proliferation on Nuclear Weapons, known as the Non-Proliferation Treaty or the NPT.[44] This treaty originally entered into force in 1970 and was extended indefinitely in 1995. Under the NPT, the five nuclear weapons states (the United States, United Kingdom, France, China, and Russia) agree not to transfer or assist other states to acquire nuclear weapons technology, and nonnuclear weapons states that accept the treaty agree not to acquire nuclear weapons. Only three states have not accepted the NPT – Israel, India, and Pakistan. North Korea was a party until January 10, 2003, when it announced that it was withdrawing, effective immediately. Iran is still an NPT party.

For the last thirty years the NPT has been largely effective in limiting the number of nuclear-weapons states. In 1970 when the treaty regime began there were five nuclear powers (China, France, the Soviet Union, the United States and the United Kingdom). In 2006 that number is nine, defying predictions in the early 1970s that there would be at least 25 by the year 2000. The NPT, however, assumes a modicum of good faith on the part of participating states. Nonnuclear NPT states may employ nuclear technology for peaceful purposes. They may legally carry out uranium enrichment, which produces material that is useful for peaceful uses like electric generating facilities, but may also produce bomb-grade materials.

To ensure that states keep their pledge not to acquire nuclear weapons, the International Atomic Energy Agency (IAEA) carries out inspections to verify that nuclear material and technology are not diverted into weaponry. As the U.N. High Level Panel has pointed out, the IAEA is an extraordinary bargain – its regular budget is less than $275 million per year.

The U.N. High Level Panel Report recommends several excellent multilateral initiatives to supplement the NPT:

---

[44]  729 *United Nations Treaty Series* 161; 7 *International Legal Materials* 811 (1968).

■ Develop a verifiable fissile material cut-off treaty that would end the production of bomb-grade, highly enriched uranium and plutonium by individual states. This idea is of the utmost importance because it would close the loophole that allows states like North Korea and Iran to develop a nuclear weapons program under cover of the claim they are producing enriched uranium and plutonium only for civilian uses. To combat nuclear proliferation and to prevent nuclear terrorism, countries must agree to give up the right to produce bomb-grade nuclear fuel.

■ Use Security Council Resolution 1540 to offer all states model legislation for security, tracking, criminalization, and export controls regarding nuclear fuel and the adoption of minimum standards that must be fulfilled by all states.

■ Implement the UN's Global Threat Reduction Initiative, which facilitates the conversion of existing research reactors to "proliferation-resistant" status and reduces existing highly enriched uranium stockpiles.

■ Designate the IAEA as the supplier of low-enriched and reprocessed spent fuel at market rates to guarantee a supply of fissile material to civilian reactors.

The United Nations and the NPT regime are the most appropriate forums for bringing unified international pressure against North Korea, Iran and other states that either develop nuclear weapons or engage in illegal proliferation. In 2003 nuclear weapons proliferation was traced to Pakistan. The United States should persuade Pakistan and Israel, two allies, to join the NPT. Pakistan will no doubt only agree if India also joins. Bringing these three states into the NPT should have the highest priority. Israel, which reportedly has nuclear weapons, should come onto the NPT as a nonnuclear state because nuclear weapons do not enhance Israeli security. But Israel will not give up nuclear weapons unless Iran does so as well. Thus, there are many interconnected issues, and nonproliferation is a major reason why a comprehensive and fair solution to the conflict between Israel and the Palestinians is so important.

The United States can claim the moral high ground with respect to both Iran and North Korea emphasizing the illegality of their development of nuclear weapons. Iran as a party to the NPT has a legal obligation not to develop nuclear weapons. Any breach of this legal obligation would warrant a unified multilateral response. North Korea's withdrawal from the NPT was legally deficient because withdrawal requires three months' notice. Furthermore, because North Korea apparently maintained a nuclear weapons program during the time it was an NPT party, it is guilty of a serious violation of international law. The United States should emphasize this violation in its diplomacy – multilateral solidarity is more effective than unilateral bluster. The United States should also work harder to solve the underlying regional problems that lead to nuclear proliferation. Regional security enabled such states as Brazil and South Africa to renounce nuclear weapons.

These additional specific recommendations of the U.N. High Level Panel Report should be implemented as well:

■ more stringent IAEA inspection rules as contained in a Model Additional Protocol

■ Security Council action in cases of noncompliance with nonproliferation and safeguards standards

■ delivery of a twice-yearly report to the Security Council by the IAEA on the status of nonproliferation and safeguards programs

COOPERATIVE THREAT REDUCTION. The initial program to combat a potential nuclear 9/11 was the Cooperative Threat Reduction Program begun in the 1990s under the leadership of two far-sighted U.S. Senators, Sam Nunn and Richard Lugar. This program aims to keep WMD, especially nuclear materials, out of the hands of potential terrorists. According to *The 9/11 Commission Report* of 2004, this program is "in need of expansion, improvement, and resources." The 9/11 Commission calls for a maximum effort in this regard. A major focus must be the large stockpiles of highly enriched uranium around the world. Although plutonium can also be used to make a bomb, the design of plutonium bombs is highly technical, so terrorists are much more likely to use highly enriched uranium. Controls on highly enriched uranium require multilateral cooperation. As Senator Nunn puts it, "We are in a race between cooperation and catastrophe."

THE GLOBAL THREAT REDUCTION INITIATIVE. In 2004 President Bush announced the Global Threat Reduction Program (GTRI), which is centered in the U.S. Department of Energy. The purpose of GTRI is to remove or at least secure high-risk nuclear and radiological materials and equipment throughout the world in order to prevent them from falling into the hands of terrorists or other rogue actors. The U.N. and the IAEA immediately welcomed this program. Under GTRI five actions are being taken:

1. the repatriation of all Russian-origin fresh, highly enriched uranium fuel as well as Russian-origin spent fuel

2. the repatriation of all U.S.-origin research reactor spent fuel from locations around the world

3. conversion of the cores of civilian reactors that presently use highly enriched uranium to the use of low-enriched uranium fuel

4. identification on a priority basis of nuclear and radiological materials and equipment not yet covered by threat reduction efforts

5. review of nuclear reactor facilities worldwide to assess and reduce their vulnerability to sabotage, theft, or terrorist attack

**Chemical and Biological Weapons.** The Biological and Toxin Weapons Convention, in force since 1975, comprehensively prohibits the development, production, and stockpiling of bacteriological and toxin weapons. A similar Chemical Weapons Convention, in force since 1997, bans and mandates the destruction of chemical arms. Today, there is an historic opportunity to fully eliminate these weapons. The U.N. High Level Panel recommends that chemical-weapon states should expedite the scheduled destruction of these weapons by the agreed date of 2012. Destruction of biological and toxin weapons is being held up by an impasse on negotiations for a verification regime. The U.N. High Level Panel urges the resumption of negotiations and diplomatic efforts to universalize membership in these conventions.

## WMD American Style

Why has multilateralism proved so difficult for the United States? Over the years, U.S. policy has established a double standard on WMD and arms control. We say to the world, "We know best – you do what we say and let us do as we please." The United States has implemented this arrogant stance in number of ways. In 1997, it rejected the U.N. Landmines Convention, which prohibits the deployment of landmines and mandates their destruction. Landmines kill thousands of innocent people each year, and most other countries, including virtually all American allies, regarded the Landmines Convention as absolutely essential. The United States continues to remain outside the international cooperation arena on landmines despite the fact that they clearly play no role in the ultra-sophisticated, smart-weapons U.S. military machine. The reason given for the rejection of the landmines treaty was the need to use mines to protect South Korea from invasion by the North Koreans, a highly debatable assertion.

In 1998, the U.S. Senate voted against U.S. ratification of the Comprehensive Nuclear Test Ban Treaty (1996), which prohibits nuclear weapons test explosions. Most other countries have accepted this treaty, and experts state that the United States has the capability to maintain and develop its nuclear arsenal without actual test explosions. The United States puts no pressure on Israel to join the NPT regime, which taints its hard line against Iran in the eyes of many who regard this as a double standard that is indefensible. In 2005 the United States agreed to make sophisticated nuclear technology available to India with no mention of the fact that India is an NPT scofflaw. The United States also calls for tough and intrusive international inspections for WMD in certain countries while opposing international inspections of American facilities. For example, in 2001, the United States rejected the Verification Protocol to the Biological Weapons Convention out of fear that weapons inspectors would harass U.S. government laboratories and steal industrial secrets.[45] The United States is also the world's leading exporter of small arms and has refused to accept any international restrictions on small arms trade even to nonstate actors.

U.S. initiatives against proliferation of WMD have also been hurt by the refusal of U.S. administrations to take arms control seriously since the end of the Cold War. The NPT, which is at the heart of the non-proliferation effort, is in fact a grand bargain between nuclear and nonnuclear states. In 1995 the nonnuclear states agreed to renounce nuclear weapons in return for a pledge by the nuclear-weapons states to reduce and eventually eliminate their nuclear weapons. This pledge may be unrealistic, but in 2000 the nuclear powers, including the United States, made an unequivocal undertaking to reduce their nuclear arsenals. This was a vague undertaking, however noble, but it was accompanied by a concrete plan to achieve ratification of the Comprehensive Nuclear Test Ban Treaty and to ban the future production of fissile material for nuclear devices. The U.N. High Level Panel recommends that the nuclear weapons states honor this pledge as required under Article VI of the NPT.

However, the Bush administration has disappointed and antagonized allies by ignoring this pledge and beginning efforts to develop a new generation of nuclear weapons, so-called bunker busters or mini-nukes.[46] U.S. policymakers also have abandoned past pledges of no first use of nuclear weapons. President Jimmy Carter has concluded, "The United States is the major culprit in the erosion of the NPT."[47]

---

[45]  U.S. State Dept. Daily Briefing, July 21, 2001.
[46]  U.S. Department of Defense, "Nuclear Posture Review" (Jan. 2002).This weapon is known
      by its technical name, robust near-earth penetrator (RNEP).
[47]  "Saving Nonproliferation," *International Herald Tribune*, March 29, 2005.

The NPT system is in crisis now that the May 2005 review conference has ended without agreement and no final consensus document was adopted. Such pressing issues as North Korea and Iran, as well as black markets in nuclear materials, were discussed but no recommendations were forthcoming. "It is a sobering moment, a very bad signal," said Main Committee Chair Laszlo Molnar of Hungary. Conference participants, including important U.S. allies, cited U.S. opposition to a number of proposals as key to the conference failure, especially U.S. opposition to the Comprehensive Test Ban Treaty, the U.S. objection to any mention of the nuclear-weapons states' disarmament obligations, and Bush administration talk of modernizing its nuclear arsenal. Not surprisingly, a U.S. initiative to amend the NPT to prohibit all states (except certain allies) from manufacturing nuclear fuel, because such fuel can be used to produce weapons as well, fell on deaf ears.

The United States also damaged its international standing by withdrawing from, rather than renegotiating, the 1972 Anti-Ballistic Missile (ABM) Treaty. Missile defense itself is neither technically reliable nor worth the enormous cost. As *The 9/11 Commission Report* points out, "A nuclear bomb can be built with a relatively small amount of nuclear material. A trained nuclear engineer with an amount of highly enriched uranium or plutonium about the size of a grapefruit or an orange . . . could fashion a nuclear device that would fit in a van . . . Such a bomb would level lower Manhattan." This would indicate that the principal WMD danger is not from an incoming missile. But even granting the need for missile defense, unilateral denunciation of the ABM Treaty in the face of universal opposition, even from allies, was not the best strategy. Former President Jimmy Carter has condemned ending the ABM Treaty "without a working substitute" and has recommended that the United States "curtail development of the infeasible missile defense shield which is wasting huge resources."[48]

## Weapons in Space?

In May 2005 the U.S. Air Force announced that it is seeking to put weapons in space: "We must establish and maintain space superiority. Simply put, it's the American way of fighting."[49] The U.S. effort is reportedly centered on deploying weapons in space that would be able to efficiently destroy command centers and missile bases anywhere in the world. The Air Force has

---

[48] Ibid.
[49] General Lance Lord, May 19, 2005, quoted in Richard Reeves, "Star Wars, All Over Again," *International Herald Tribune*, May 25, 2005.

spent billions of dollars on to development of a space-based laser, as well as of conventional weapons that would strike the ground at speeds of about 7,200 miles per hour with the force of a small nuclear weapon. The United States has already launched an experimental microsatellite with the technical capacity to disrupt other nations' military reconnaissance and communications satellites; it is increasingly worried that other nations could follow suit, threatening U.S. communications technology. The Pentagon is also frustrated by the failure, after spending twenty-two years and over $100 billion, to develop a reliable earth-based missile defense system; an alternative would be a space-based system, estimated to cost anywhere from $220 billion to $1 trillion.

Under international law – the 1967 Outer Space Treaty – stationing WMD in space is prohibited; otherwise the United States is free to "weaponize" space. But other nations are sure to follow suit, and it would be more sensible (and a lot less expensive) to use international law to ban space weapons altogether and to prohibit interference with unarmed satellites. Because the United States has a huge lead in space technology, it can afford to try the multilateral approach first; other states are likely to be receptive to it.

## THE U.N. MILLENNIUM DEVELOPMENT GOALS: FIGHTING POVERTY AND DISEASE

Preventable poverty and disease kill millions each year, especially children. An integral part of peace and security in the twenty-first century is to respond to human needs by alleviating poverty, disease, environmental degradation, and other ills that breed hopelessness, despair, and violence. This is the aim of the U.N. Millennium Development Goals, adopted by the U.N. General Assembly in its Millennium Declaration of 2000. This is an eight-part, fifteen-year program with these objectives:

- eradicate extreme poverty and hunger
- achieve universal primary education
- promote gender equality and empower women
- reduce child mortality
- improve maternal health
- combat HIV/AIDS, malaria, and other diseases
- improve environmental sustainability
- develop a global partnership for development

The U.N. Secretary-General has set achievement targets for all these programs and has asked for cooperation from U.N. members. The World Bank and the International Monetary Fund have also approved these goals.[50] However, the United States, which has demanded total cooperation from all regarding the War on Terrorism, has largely rejected cooperation on these matters, although they are important to the great majority of U.N. members. In 2005, a third of the way into the program, the percentage of U.S. income going to poor countries stands at 0.14 percent, near the bottom of the U.N. member list.[51] Even when the United States responds, as with President Bush's dramatic announcement in 2002 of a Millennium Challenge Account to increase U.S. foreign assistance to countries that promote free market development, there is usually a hitch. Although Bush promised $1.7 billion the first year, $3.3 billion the second, and $5 billion the third, his administration did not ask the Congress for the $1.7 billion the first year; it requested only $1.3 billion, which the Congress cut to $1 billion. The second year, the administration asked for $2.5 billion and got $1.5 billion. And worse still, none of the money was appropriated, so as of 2005, not a single dollar had been disbursed. This is from a nation that can afford to spend $450 billion a year on defense and $10 billion alone on missile defense.

As the U.N. High Level Panel emphasized, diseases, and social and economic problems are security issues because they lead to civil and international violence. In particular, HIV/AIDS is a worldwide pandemic that is out of control in many countries, especially in Africa, and has reached a tipping point in China, India, and Russia. Increasingly, women and children are being infected by HIV/AIDS. The U.N. Panel recommends immediate Security Council attention to the problem as a threat to international peace and security. There is the need to adopt a long-term strategy for diminishing the threat, as well as and a global initiative to build local and national public health systems throughout the developing world. This can be done if international policies are framed and coordinated to achieve definite outcomes.

The United States should rethink its priorities. How should it employ its great power, wealth, and influence? It could become the leader of a coalition of democratic states dedicated to the UN's Millennium Development Goals. Democracies and free societies make up almost half of U.N. members as of 2005. Secretary-General Kofi Annan proclaimed in June 2000 the dream of making the U.N. a "community of democracies." The United States could help realize this dream by working with, rather than at cross-purposes with, the United Nations. As the Harvard economist Jeffrey Sachs, who heads the

---

[50]  Global Monitoring Report (2005).
[51]  The U.N. Millennium goal is 0.7 percent of the national income.

U.N. Millennium Project, has said, "No level of military might will ensure U.S. security when hundreds of millions of people are hungry, disease-ridden and without economic hopes."[52]

Meeting basic human needs all over the world – so that having enough to eat, clean water, minimal health services, and basic education would be the birthright of every child – is a goal that is within reach in the first part of the twenty-first century. This is not just a humanitarian goal; it is vital to international peace and security. Meeting this goal will take money from the developed world, and this is an effort that should be led by the United States. No action would do more to put an end to civil violence and conflict, terrorism, and instability – the major security problems we face. The monetary investment involved would be much cheaper than fighting even a minor war, as demonstrated by the great economic cost of the Iraq War and fighting the insurgency. Success in meeting the U.N. Millennium Development Goals will take great effort and leadership. Developing countries and multilateral agencies must coordinate and focus their aid strategies. Priority should be given to those developing countries that agree to achieve good governance goals so that money is not wasted through corruption and poor policy choices. Developing countries should also be required to meet specified environmental standards and goals as a condition of assistance.

Meeting the U.N. Millennium Goals will necessitate a tripartite strategy:

1. doubling and coordinating international financial assistance

2. providing debt relief and forgiveness for developing countries

3. reforming of rules of international trade that stifle economic activity in developing countries

Jeffrey Sachs, who heads the U.N. Millennium Project, an independent advisory group, says "We are in a position to end extreme poverty within our generation. . . . If we want to . . . we can do that by 2025."[53]

## DISASTER WARNING AND HUMANITARIAN RESPONSE

On December 26, 2004 over 240,000 people died (the final toll will never be known) as a result of a tsunami in the Indian Ocean triggered by a massive

[52] Jeffrey Sachs, Africa's Future is Threatened by U.S. Neglect," *International Herald Tribune*, June 15, 2005.
[53] "UN Outlines Strategy to Fight Global Disease," *International Herald Tribune*, Jan. 18, 2005, p. 5.

earthquake. The deaths were largely preventable had a tsunami alert system been in place. In 2005, after an unprecedented international outpouring of sympathy and funding, the United Nations launched comprehensive plans for a global early warning system to reduce the loss of life from natural hazards, such as tsunamis, hurricanes, droughts, wildfires, floods, and volcanic eruptions.

The Asian tsunami disaster highlights the fact that only the United Nations is in a position to coordinate global disaster warning and relief. What is needed is a comprehensive strategy to prevent, if possible, but also to respond to global disasters. Such a program can only be worked out through an international conference and a international agreement that would establish and maintain the necessary warning systems and resolve the complex set of issues surrounding international disaster relief. International law can develop rules to facilitate and secure disaster response and relief. A start was made to establish such a program as long ago as 1927, when twenty-six countries including the United States established the International Relief Union.[54] International law concerning disasters is currently inadequate; a priority should be to enlist the United Nations, its specialized agencies, and regional agencies to formulate operational rules and plans for disaster prevention and humanitarian response.

## SUMMING UP

America occupies a unique position in the world of the twenty-first century. American military, economic, political, cultural, and technological powers have a global reach. Never in history, at least since the end of the Roman Empire, has any state exercised such influence. The question is, How should such power be wielded? American political leaders and most Americans think of the United States as a benign, good nation, "a shining city on a hill," in contrast with the evil empires that have frequently dominated world history. American leaders and Americans frequently feel misunderstood – "Why do they hate us?" is a question frequently asked about people in other countries.

Americans must realize that there is a difference between leadership and arrogant flaunting of U.S. power. Consultation is not the endorsement of a course already set. The rest of the world wants, expects, and needs American

---

[54] The functions of this body were transferred to UNESCO. See Patrick Myers, *Succession between International Organizations* (1993).

leadership. But the United States does not have a monopoly on wisdom and truth. America's great power does not exempt it from having to follow the rules like everyone else.

Rules not only bind but they also empower – they can be used to great advantage. A couple expecting a baby may wake up in the middle of the night with the woman experiencing labor pains. The hospital is far away, they are in a great hurry, and it is an emergency. What to do? They may decide to ignore the law, break the speed limit, and drive to the hospital at 90 miles per hour. Or they may call an ambulance or a police escort. In either case they may arrive successfully. The easiest and most straightforward way is to ignore the law, but following the rules and getting help are surely safer and worth the extra trouble in the end.

**FURTHER READINGS**

Adam Roberts and Benedict Kingsbury (eds.), *United Nations, Divided World: The UN's Role in International Relations* (1996).

Stanley Meisler, *The United Nations: The First Fifty Years* (1995).

Report of the U.N. High Level Panel on Threats, Challenges and Change, *A More Secure World: Our Shared Responsibility* (2004).

Report of the U.N. Secretary-General, *In Larger Freedom: Towards Development, Security, and Human Rights for All* (2005).

Christine Gray, *International Law and the Use of Force* (2000).

Joseph Nye, *The Paradox of American Power* (2002).

Richard Perle and David Frum, *An End to Evil* (2004).

John B. Judis, *The Folly of Empire* (2004).

Stephen Halper and Jonathan Clarke, *America Alone* (2004).

Zbigniew Brzezinski, *The Choice* (2004).

Phyllis Bennis, *Before and After: U.S. Foreign Policy and the September 11th Crisis* (2003).

Robert Cooper, *The Breaking of Nations: Order and Chaos in the Twenty-First Century* (2003).

Donald Kagan, *On the Origins of War and the Preservation of Peace* (1995).

William Bennett, *Why We Fight: Moral Clarity and the War on Terrorism* (2003).

Chalmers Johnson, *The Sorrows of Empire* (2004).

Yolanda Taylor, ed., *Battling HIV/AIDS* (The World Bank, 2004).

E. Agius and S. Busuattil, eds., *Future Generations and International Law* (1997).

U.N. Millennium Development Project Report, *Investing in Development: A Practical Plan to Achieve the Millennium Development Goals* (2005).

U.S. National Intelligence Council Report, *Mapping the Global Future Out to 2020* (2005).

Jeffrey D. Sachs, *The End of Poverty: Economic Possibilities for Our Time* (2005).

# 6 International Political Economy

## A MULTI-BILLION DOLLAR DILEMMA

In the spring of 2005 Masatsugu Asakawa, a top official of the Japanese Ministry of Finance, was not sleeping very well, and we can all sympathize with his plight. Mr. Asakawa is in charge of managing the portfolio of U.S. government securities held by the government of Japan – which totaled $720 billion at the end of 2004. A lot of money, you might say, but consider this: From 2002 to 2005 the value of the U.S. dollar fell 24 percent against the Japanese yen. And Mr. Asakawa's sleep problems were exacerbated by the fact that, when he goes to sleep each night, a wireless monitoring device at his bedside beeps whenever the U.S. dollar drops below a set range. "This thing wakes me up, it's terrible," he says. "Fortunately my wife is very understanding."

What should Mr. Asakawa do? Because of Japan's trade surpluses with the United States, the dollars keep rolling in, but the value of the dollar may keep falling. If Mr. Asakawa pares back his dollar holdings, it will only cause the dollar to fall even more, perhaps to a dangerously low level. So at least for the time being, he will continue to buy dollar-denominated assets, even in the face of a declining dollar.

Japan's dilemma is typical of those faced by governments and companies around the world. American economic policy changed drastically beginning in 2001. War and increased military spending coupled with huge tax cuts and easy monetary policy have combined to produce a "twin deficit" phenomenon – a huge 2004 federal budget deficit of $ 413 billion (3.7 percent of the gross domestic product [GDP]) and an even larger current-account deficit (the difference between what the United States buys and sells to the rest of the world) that reached a record $665.9 billion for all of 2004 (5.7 percent of GDP).

The unprecedented glut of dollars that these twin deficits produced meant a falling dollar on world markets. It would fall faster and further if it were not for the fact that the dollar is the world's principal reserve currency – a store of value held by central banks all over the world. Currently, central banks hold over $2.3 trillion in dollar-denominated assets. Fortunately, in the fall of 2005, the dollar gained some ground against other world currencies because of the U.S. Federal Reserve's tightening of monetary policy.

But the U.S. dollar's position is under threat, which concerned Alan Greenspan, the former chairman of the U.S. Federal Reserve. In a November, 2004 speech in Berlin, he stated, "The situation suggests that international investors will eventually adjust their accumulation of dollar assets or, alternatively seek higher dollar returns, elevating the cost of financing the U.S. current-account deficit and rendering it increasingly less tenable." He reiterated this warning in his retirement speech in November, 2005.

In plain English this means that central banks and private investors may switch from dollars to euros, pounds, yen, and other currencies, endangering the dollar as the world's principal reserve currency. If this goes far enough there will be a seismic shift in America's position in the world. The fallout may throw both the U.S. and the world economy into recession.[1] U.S. net foreign liabilities stood at $3.3 trillion (and rising), 28 percent of GDP, at the end of 2004. Never before in history has the world's main reserve currency been the biggest net debtor. As a result, central banks all over the world are reducing their holdings of dollars.[2] This was a factor leading to increased interest rates for Americans as the Federal Reserve was forced to raise rates to prop up the value of the dollar in international markets.

The best remedy for the "twin deficit" problem is to bring the U.S. budget deficit under control; economists reckon that each $100 added to the budget deficit adds $25 to the current-account deficit. But the Bush administration seems unconcerned. In fact, U.S. government borrowing is expected to increase to deal with crises in Social Security and the mess in Iraq. One eminent economist has said that the current outlook is for an "eternal" budget deficit.[3] The decline of the dollar and its future implications are causing some to question whether the United States is a declining economic power.[4]

---

[1] "The Disappearing Dollar," *The Economist*, Dec. 4, 2004.
[2] This was reported in a survey conducted by the Royal Bank of Scotland Group. See "Central Banks Spurn Dollar Assets," *Japan Times*, Jan. 25, 2005, p. 22.
[3] Robert J. Samuelson, "America's Budget Poses Eternal Deficits," *Washington Post*, Feb. 19, 2005.
[4] George Soros, *The Bubble of American Supremacy* (2004).

A second severe financial imbalance that currently threatens the welfare of the global economy is the artificially low valuation of the Chinese currency, the yuan (also known as the renminbi). The yuan was pegged to the value of the U.S. dollar for over ten years and is now allowed to float only in a narrow range against an unannounced "basket" of currencies, including the U.S. dollar. With the spectacular growth of the Chinese economy and the erosion of the value of the dollar, the artificial peg has increasingly perverse economic effects. The low value of the yuan makes China's exports artificially cheap, and its current-account surplus has soared. The expanding trade surplus and the investment flowing into China are sparking inflation in China's domestic economy. Internationally, the undervalued yuan is causing trade friction as trade deficits mount in many countries, including the United States and the members of the European Union. The combination of huge U.S. deficits and huge Chinese surpluses is particularly perverse, and economic problems are spilling over to the political sphere. The tensions also cause the bending of rules of international trade as China places export charges on textiles and the United States and European Union impose import quotas.

Multilateral coordination is particularly important to the health of the world economy. Working through established international organizations and adhering to rules, which the United States played the dominant role in creating, are key to maintaining U.S. and world prosperity. If the United States and other countries follow their own narrow interests, there may be short-run political and temporary economic benefits, but long-run disasters loom.

**POLITICAL ECONOMY**

The phrase "international political economy" refers to how politics and economics interact to mold governmental and societal attitudes toward economic and financial relations with other countries. International political economy provides insights into (1) the goals and values underlying international trade, (2) the international relations aspects of economic policy, and (3) domestic political concerns. Public choice theory posits bargaining among interest groups that influence trade policy. Trade and financial policies are shaped both by politics and economics through international negotiations, as well as domestic political forces.

For example, in 2002 President Bush imposed emergency tariffs on imported steel products in response to political and economic concerns about U.S. job losses and declines in U.S. industrial production. The Appellate Body of the WTO declared these tariffs inconsistent with U.S. commitments under the General Agreement of Tariffs and Trade (GATT). In testimony before the U.S. Senate Steel Caucus in 2004, steel industry executives urged defiance of this decision. Several U.S. senators agreed; some urged withdrawal from the WTO. The Bush administration had to choose whether to comply with international obligations or flout them for political advantage. Fortunately, the decision was made to comply with international law.

Two values interact in the formation of policy. Realists and nationalists assert that reciprocity and state interest should be the crucial determinant of international economic policy. Economic liberals traditionally promote free trade and the operation of markets without governmental interference. Both camps see the need for international institutions or regimes as the basis for international cooperation. The principal international regimes that guide international economic and financial policy were conceived at a famous conference held in Bretton Woods, New Hampshire, in the waning years of the Second World War.

## GLOBALIZATION

At the dawn of the new millennium, for the first time in human history, virtually all nations and peoples are participants in a single world economy. In socioeconomic terms, this globalization means that there is relatively free movement all over the world of goods, services and service providers, capital flows, information, and technology. Arguably this is what makes the age we live in unique; never before in human history has the world been truly undivided. This remarkable reality has both advantages and disadvantages, but it is a fact of human life in our time, not something to be for or against. What must be done is to understand and manage globalization so we can keep the good and control the problems. Understanding how we got to this point and what must be done is the subject of this chapter.

## THE UNITED STATES AND INTERNATIONAL ECONOMIC RELATIONS

In the post-World War II era, the United States has been at the center of the effort to establish and maintain the global economic "architecture" – the multilateral trading system and the international financial institutions essential to world order. The United States has played what political scientists call the role of *hegemon*, a word derived from classical Greek meaning dominant power. By and large the United States has continued to play this role, and despite its waning or at least shared hegemony in recent years, multilateralism has been maintained. International economic policy is the one area of international relations in which the United States has consistently (though not without exception) upheld law and multilateral institutions. It is no accident that international economic policy is the biggest success story of the postwar period.

The fact that the United States played this essential role is remarkable because foreign trade is not as important to the U.S. economy as it is to the rest of the world. With its huge internal market, the United States in 1945 had little need for trade. Even in the 1950s, international trade constituted only about 6 percent of U.S. economic activity. In the early twenty-first century, after decades of full participation in the international economy, U.S. exports and imports combined only amount to about 25 percent of the U.S. economy, a far lower percentage than in most other advanced nations. By contrast, for most European nations imports and exports account for more than 50 percent of the GDP.

This chapter tells the story of multilateralism in international economic affairs and whether it has paid off for the United States and the rest of the world. Critics both on the right and the left as well as "anti-globalizers" argue in favor of a change in course; they believe U.S. participation in the international economy should be curtailed. Are they correct?

The economic prosperity of the last sixty years has no parallel in world history. Yet, we take it for granted. Misconceptions abound about how it was achieved and how such economic prosperity can be maintained. Many smart people condemn the very characteristics and institutions of the world economy that we have created; globalization, free trade, foreign investment, the International Monetary Fund, the World Trade Organization, and the North American Free Trade Agreement are controversial. What is going on here? Should we reverse course? International economic policy is too important to be left to the experts. All citizens should understand and participate in the debate.

Let us start with the facts. Is there any way to measure the extent to which trade liberalization has contributed to the U.S. economy? Two recent studies using different techniques of measurement conclude that Americans have derived great benefits from trade. The Organization of Economic Cooperation and Development (OECD) in Paris, using economic models, concludes that trade accounted for 20 percent of the gain in America's GDP per person between 1950 and 2003. A second recent study, by the Institute for International Economics in Washington, using a variety of measurements, puts the benefit at about 1 trillion in GDP per year or about $9,000 of extra income for each American household.[5]

But economic success is not evenly distributed around the globe – far from it. The United States with its approximately $11.7 trillion economy leads the pack, and the EU's twenty-five member states constitute a single economic area with a GDP of over $13 trillion. Then comes Japan (GDP about $5 trillion), which is growing again after largely solving the bad debt problem plaguing its financial system. Advanced economies are also enjoyed by Canada, Switzerland, Iceland, Norway, Australia, New Zealand, and Singapore. A lower tier of advanced economies includes newly added members of the Organization of Economic Cooperation and Development (OECD) – Turkey, Mexico, and South Korea.

Emerging market and developing countries still are in the majority, but the 2005 World Economic Report of the International Monetary Fund states that economic growth is the highest in thirty years. The world economy expanded 5.1 percent in 2004 and was predicted to grow 4.3 percent in 2005 and 4.4 percent in 2006. Asia is powered by the development of China and India, which have averaged economic growth of 9 percent and 5.5 percent, respectively, for the last decade. Latin America is growing at a slower rate, led by its biggest economy, Brazil. Russia is growing economically again after a recent decline. The countries of sub-Saharan Africa and the Middle East are in the most problematic areas of the world, largely because of the noneconomic factors of disease and warfare. But even here, many growth rates are higher than 5 percent per year.

The economic growth of the last sixty years has not come about by accident. The first part of the twentieth century was largely characterized by economic chaos all over the world. In the nineteenth century, even most advanced countries had economies largely based on agriculture despite the Industrial Revolution. Only Great Britain (later imitated by Germany), of all the countries of the world, maintained an open economy based on trade, but this was based upon its status as an imperial power.

## BRETTON WOODS AND THE "TWO SISTERS"

The genesis of the post-World War II economic boom is complex and various; no simple explanation is adequate. However, critics and admirers alike

---

[5] "Trade's Bounty," *The Economist*, Dec. 4, 2004.

consider one meeting held in 1944 to be of special importance – this was the *Bretton Woods Conference*, called by the Americans and the British in order to plan the economic recovery after the war. Representatives of forty-four nations gathered at Bretton Woods, New Hampshire on the slopes of Mount Washington to talk over future policies. But the conference was dominated by two men: John Maynard Keynes, a brilliant English economist, and Harry Dexter White, President Roosevelt's trusted economic advisor. Under their guidance, the Bretton Woods Conference resolved to create two international organizations (often called the two sisters because of their common origin), as well as agreed on international rules to guide postwar international economic relations. An International Monetary Fund (IMF) would be necessary to enforce rules relating to currencies and international monetary policies. A World Bank (officially the International Bank for Reconstruction and Development) would finance postwar reconstruction and necessary development projects. These two organizations were launched in 1945.

After the war, over fifty countries participated in negotiations to create an International Trade Organization (ITO) as a multilateral forum for trade negotiations and to supervise new rules of international trade. An ITO Charter was agreed, but proved too controversial to be ratified, especially in the U.S. Congress. But a General Agreement on Tariffs and Trade was provisionally put into operation as the organization known as the GATT. It was not until 1995 that it became possible to transform the GATT into the World Trade Organization (WTO). The IMF, World Bank and WTO are still at the heart of the world economy in the twenty-first century. Their founders would probably be amazed at the notoriety and controversy surrounding them today.

## THE INTERNATIONAL MONETARY FUND

The International Monetary Fund (IMF) came into existence in 1945 when twenty-nine states signed its charter, formally known as the Articles of Agreement of the IMF. The original function of the IMF was to establish and maintain a standard (the *par value system*) for determining the value of national currencies. This was a system of fixed exchange rates based upon the value of the U.S. dollar, which was in turn pegged to gold. Currency convertibility was encouraged by a system of currency support, which allowed the IMF to provide short-term financial aid to help member states overcome balance of payment problems.

To become a member of the IMF a state has to contribute a certain sum of money – known as its *quota subscription* – expressed in the "special drawing rights" (currently a weighted average of the euro, the U.S. dollar, the Japanese yen, and the British pound). Each member's quota is based on the relative size of its economy; the quota also determines the member's voting power in the Fund. The United States accordingly has both a quota and voting power of about 17 percent, the largest share. Quota subscriptions are subject to change from time to time. A Board of Governors consisting of representatives of all member states manages the IMF. Many key powers, however, are delegated to an executive board of twenty-four and the Fund's managing director. Most decisions of the executive board are made by consensus.

Member states of the IMF must observe a Code of Conduct, but this is a largely voluntary undertaking. The Code requires states to (1) keep other members informed of arrangements for determining the value of its currency, (2) refrain from exchange restrictions, and (3) pursue orderly and constructive economic and monetary policies.

The IMF's role changed radically after the par value system collapsed in 1973, with the decision by the United States to terminate the convertibility of the dollar into gold. A new system was established in 1978 with the adoption of the Second Amendment to the IMF's Articles of Agreement, which allows members to define the value of their currency by any criteria except gold. Many countries peg their currencies to the currencies of other countries, special drawing rights, or a currency basket. Most developed countries allow their currencies to float freely, so their values change daily according to market forces. Although IMF rules prohibit manipulation of exchange rates to prevent effective balance of payment adjustment or to gain a competitive advantage, members with floating exchange rates may intervene "to prevent or moderate sharp and disruptive fluctuations from day to day and from week to week in the exchange value of its currency" (International Monetary Fund, Articles of Agreement, Article IV).

Currently the IMF has three principal duties: (1) supervising the cooperative system of currency exchange, (2) lending money to members in order to support their currencies and economies, and (3) providing auxiliary services to assist members to manage their external debt obligations and their financial policies (see "IMF Lending Faculties").

## Do We Need the IMF?

Is there any need for the IMF? Many say the IMF only makes things worse. Critics on the left say the IMF encourages moral hazard – foolish, risky loans by international banks that gamble that the IMF will bail them out at the expense of the poor in developing countries, who then must endure economic

## IMF LENDING FACILITIES

Except for the Poverty Reduction and Growth Facility, all facilities are subject to the IMF's market-related interest rate, known as the *rate of charge* and some carry an interest rate premium or surcharge. The rate of charge is based on the *SDR interest rate*, which is revised weekly to take account of changes in short-term interest rates in the major international money markets. The rate of charge was 3.39 percent as of February 28, 2005. Large loans carry a surcharge and must be repaid early if a country's external position permits.

The amount that a country can borrow from the IMF – its *access limit* – varies depending on the type of loan, but is typically a multiple of the country's IMF quota.

**Poverty Reduction and Growth Facility (PRGF):** Concessional lending arrangements to low-income countries are underpinned by comprehensive country-owned strategies, as specified in their Poverty Reduction Strategy Papers (PRSPs). In recent years, the largest number of IMF loans have been made through the PRGF. The interest rate levied on PRGF loans is only 0.5 percent, and loans are to be repaid over a period of $5\frac{1}{2}$–10 years.

**Stand-By Arrangements (SBA):** The SBA is designed to help countries address short-term balance of payments problems and is the facility that provides the greatest amount of IMF resources. The length of a SBA is typically 12–18 months, and repayment is normally expected within $2\frac{1}{4}$–4 years. Surcharges apply to high access levels.

**Extended Fund Facility (EFF):** This facility was established in 1974 to help countries address more protracted balance of payments problems requiring fundamental reforms to the structure of the economy. Arrangements under the EFF are thus longer – usually 3 years. Repayment is normally expected within $4\frac{1}{2}$–7 years. Surcharges apply to high levels of access.

**Supplemental Reserve Facility (SRF):** This facility was introduced in 1997 to meet a need for very short-term financing on a large scale. The motivation for the SRF was the sudden loss of market confidence experienced by emerging market economies in the 1990s, which led to massive outflows of capital and required financing on a much larger scale than anything the IMF had previously been asked to provide. Countries are expected to repay loans within $2$–$2\frac{1}{2}$ years, but may request an extension of up to six months. All SRF loans carry a substantial surcharge of three to five percentage points.

**Compensatory Financing Facility (CFF):** The CFF was established in 1963 to assist countries experiencing either a sudden shortfall in export earnings or an increase in the cost of cereal imports caused by fluctuating world commodity prices. The financial terms are the same as those applying to the SBA, except that CFF loans carry no surcharge.

**Emergency Assistance:** The IMF provides emergency assistance to countries that have experienced a natural disaster or are emerging from conflict. Emergency loans are subject to the basic rate of charge, although interest subsidies are available for PRGF-eligible countries, subject to availability. Loans must be repaid within 3¼–5 years.

hardship because of IMF loan conditions. Critics on the right say the market should be allowed to operate freely, and states foolish enough to get in trouble should be forced to work things out on their own.

These criticisms reached a crescendo in the late 1990s when the IMF was severely criticized for its performance with respect to the Mexican peso crisis of 1994–5, the Southeast Asian financial crisis of 1997–9, and the Russian ruble crisis of 1998. Each of these cases involved an international financial crash as foreign investors pulled out their money, and the resulting sharp reduction in the exchange rate value of the currency led to runway inflation, financial chaos, bankruptcies, unemployment, and recession. In each case investor panic was caused by the high levels of international debt accumulated by business firms and the government. For example, Mexico in 1994 had been borrowing up to 6 percent of its GDP for several years – a very high level of capital inflow from abroad. Thailand and Russia had done the same just before their financial meltdowns.

Once panic starts, the withdrawals are exacerbated by fears and ever higher orders of speculation. The fear soon becomes irrational and spreads to other countries that are presumed to be vulnerable. As the selling continues in country after country, the downward pressure on exchange rates becomes a self-fulfilling prophecy. Currencies depreciate by 40 percent or more in a few weeks. International loans, which are in dollars, euros, or yen, are suddenly hugely greater in value, and interest payments are over the top.

Enter the IMF to the rescue. But the IMF exacts a price: Its standard remedy is an austerity program, perhaps including economic and political reform. Austerity in the form of increased interest rates, reduced government spending, and the end of subsidies and monopolies simply makes things worse, causing political and economic unrest and hardship. And for what? To repay the international banks and financial institutions.

Certainly reform is needed, but the solution is not to get rid of the IMF. In addition to these high profile cases, the IMF at any one time is providing short-term monetary or technical assistance in fifty to sixty countries; this less controversial work of the IMF is essential. The IMF should certainly say no on occasion, but a bailout may be necessary from time to time, for example to dampen speculative contagion so that financial panic does not spread irrationally from country to country.

Some improvements the IMF might consider include the following:

■ The IMF should be more proactive – the IMF should have seen the financial crises of the 1990s coming and taken preventive steps months before they occurred.

■ There should be greater supervision by the IMF of financial policies and institutions. Governments typically get in trouble because of distorted economic incentives, inadequate regulatory standards, corruption and cronyism, and excessive risk taking.

■ Fiscal and monetary reforms should be mandated *in advance*, rather than during an international currency crash.

■ Greater disclosure and transparency should be encouraged.

■ The IMF should develop a Code of Minimum Financial Practices and should encourage its adoption on a global basis.

In addition, the IMF should assume a position of neutrality on the full repayment of international loans. Collective action clauses should be a feature of international debt instruments so that a write-down of the debt can be negotiated by and agreed to by a majority of the bondholders. This would give developing countries more negotiating clout with their creditors and would discourage high-risk lending.

Argentina is a case in point. When the Argentine economy collapsed in 2001, it rejected the orthodox economic medicine of draconian domestic discipline so that foreign creditors could be paid. Instead, it declared a debt default of over $100 billion and put in place fiscal and monetary policies designed to boost economic growth. As a result, in 2005, the economy is now growing at an 8 percent rate, the currency is stable, exports are increasing, and unemployment has declined. Chastened foreign investors are gradually returning as well. This was achieved without a debt settlement or the approval of the IMF.

Countries should be strongly encouraged to allow their currencies to float and not to use artificial currency pegs. Once a currency peg becomes notoriously misaligned, the imbalance causes problems. When the currency is overvalued, speculators inevitably move in, and the government will be compelled to intervene. This action will often attract additional speculators, and frequently intervention will fail and panic will ensue. There are many instances of this sequence of events occurring in the currency crises of the past. In contrast, when the pegged currency is undervalued – as is the case with China in

2005 – trade imbalances and inflationary pressures build. This is the reason the system of floating exchange rates, although it came about by historical accident, is best.

On a selective basis, IMF members should be encouraged to place controls on short-term capital outflows. The international short-term movement of capital has increased exponentially in the last twenty years, and at present almost $2 trillion is traded on currency markets each day. Money can frequently be withdrawn from a country with the click of a computer mouse. Countries should be permitted to levy a surcharge, impose a holding period, or place some other reasonable restrictions on short-term capital liquidations.

## THE WORLD BANK

The World Bank, which is funded primarily through assessments from its member governments, annually doles out over $26 billion in developmental grants and loans. Although the Bank was founded to aid the reconstruction of war-devastated Europe, its main task now is development assistance. Because voting power at the Bank is a function of each member's contribution, the United States as the largest shareholder wields the most voting power – 16.41 percent. By tradition the president of the World Bank is an American, and in June 2005 a prominent Bush administration official, Paul Wolfowitz, became the bank's tenth president.

The World Bank consists of five affiliated institutions: (1) the International Bank for Reconstruction and Development (IBRD), which provides loans and development assistance to developing countries; (2) the International Development Association (IDA), which provides grants and interest–free loans to the world's poorest countries; (3) the International Finance Corporation (IFC), which finances private sector investments and provides technical advice and assistance to business and governments; (4) the Multilateral Investment Guarantee Agency (MIGA), which encourages investment in developing countries by providing investment guarantees against loss caused by noncommercial risks; and (5) the Investment Center for Settlement of Investment Disputes (ICSID), which provides a facility for dispute settlement between investors and governments. The last two institutions serve to encourage private investment in developing countries (see "The World Bank Group").

In the past the World Bank has concentrated on poverty reduction, and that indeed remains its primary mission. For example, one of its biggest current projects is a dam being constructed on the Nam Theun River in Laos that

## THE WORLD BANK GROUP

### The International Bank for Reconstruction and Development (IBRD)

■ Established 1945

■ 184 members

■ Cumulative lending: $394 billion

■ Fiscal 2004 lending: $11 billion for 87 new operations in 33 countries

IBRD aims to reduce poverty in middle-income and credit-worthy poorer countries by promoting sustainable development through loans, guarantees, and (nonlending) analytical and advisory services. The income that IBRD has generated over the years has allowed it to fund several developmental activities and to ensure its financial strength, which enables it to borrow in capital markets at low cost and offer clients good borrowing terms. IBRD's twenty-four-member board is made up of five appointed and nineteen elected executive directors, who represent its 184 member countries.

### The International Development Association (IDA)

■ Established 1960

■ 165 Members

■ Cumulative commitments: $151 billion

■ Fiscal 2004 commitments: $9 billion for 158 new operations in 62 countries

Contributions to the IDA enable the World Bank to provide approximately $6 billion to $9 billion a year in highly concessional financing to the world's eighty-one poorest countries (home to 2.5 billion people). The IDA's interest-free credits and grants are vital because these countries have little or no capacity to borrow on market terms. In most of these countries, the great majority of people live on less than $2 a day. The IDA's resources help support country-led poverty-reduction strategies in key policy areas, including raising productivity, providing accountable governance, improving the private investment climate, and improving access to education and health care for poor people.

### The International Finance Corporation (IFC)

■ Established 1956

■ 176 members

■ Committed portfolio: $23.5 billion (includes $5.5 billion in syndicated loans)

■ Fiscal 2004 commitments: $4.8 billion for 217 projects in 65 countries

The IFC promotes economic development through the private sector. Working with business partners, it invests in sustainable private enterprises in developing countries without accepting government guarantees. It provides equity, long-term loans, structured finance and risk management products, and advisory services to its clients. IFC seeks to reach businesses in regions and countries that have limited access to capital. It provides finance in markets deemed too risky by commercial investors in the absence of IFC participation and adds value to the projects it finances through its corporate governance, environmental, and social expertise.

### The Multilateral Investment Guarantee Agency (MIGA)

■ Established 1988

■ 164 members

■ Cumulative guarantees[1] issued: $13.5 billion

■ Fiscal 2004 guarantees issued: $1.1 billion

The MIGA helps promote foreign direct investment in developing countries by providing guarantees to investors against noncommercial risks, such as expropriation, currency inconvertibility and transfer restrictions, war and civil disturbance, and breach of contract. The MIGA's capacity to serve as an objective intermediary and to influence the resolution of potential disputes enhances investors' confidence that they will be protected against these risks. In addition, the MIGA provides technical assistance and advisory services to help countries attract and retain foreign investment and to disseminate information on investment opportunities to the international business community.

### The International Center for Settlement of Investment Disputes

■ Established 1966

■ 140 members

■ Total cases registered: 159

■ Fiscal 2004 cases registered: 30

[1] Amounts include funds leveraged through the Cooperative Underwriting Program.

will generate up to 1,070 megawatts of electricity, most of which will be exported to neighboring Thailand. In the past this kind of project would raise questions about the Bank's attention to the needs to ordinary people and environmental protection. However, this time, under the watchful eyes of the Bank's International Advisory Group, villagers and even a group of Vietic-speaking hunter-gatherers are being carefully compensated and resettled. The creation of a new nature reserve is an integral part of the project, which will provide local people with jobs as gamekeepers that are funded by the dam's revenues.

In 2000 the Bank wisely adopted a new emphasis: lending to improve good government, public administration, democracy, and the rule of law. As a result, 25 percent of the Bank's lending now goes to support law and public administration, and the Bank is now the greatest source of funding for HIV/AIDS care and prevention, as well as education and health care in the world. Traditional lending for transportation and other infrastructure is still huge, but its proportion of the Bank's work has decreased. In short, the Bank has learned a hard lesson: Politics must enter into its work. No longer can roads, oil pipelines, and dams be blithely funded in states with oppressive and corrupt governments. Poverty reduction must go hand in hand with good governance.

Criticism of the World Bank is three-fold. First, the World Bank simply duplicates the money-lending function of the IMF, so the Bank should be eliminated or the two institutions should be merged. But clearly the IMF and the Bank play different roles – the IMF supplies short-term capital and financial advice to countries experiencing international financial difficulties, whereas the Bank grants longer-term loans and technical assistance to reduce poverty. The critics are correct, however, in calling for a sharper division of labor between the Fund and the Bank.

A second criticism is that most recipients of the vast amount of aid dispensed by the Bank over the last sixty years are no better off today and that, without economic and political reform, their economic performance cannot improve. Thus, the Bank is little more than an international welfare agency. This criticism does not disprove the need for the Bank; it merely states the obvious. World Bank poverty reduction efforts are necessary but not sufficient and they must be supplemented and coordinated by political and economic reform measures: (1) sound macroeconomic policies, (2) measures to promote microeconomic efficiency, (3) liberal trade and openness, and (4) social investment. The Bank's work also must be better coordinated with other U.N. agencies, including the U.N. Development Program. To be outside monitor of its performance, the Bank has created an Operations Evaluation Department (OED), whose job is to analyze and evaluate its programs and identify lessons learned from sometimes negative experiences.[6] The third major criticism of the Bank is that environmental and social costs of its development loans have been ignored. For example, the Bank has funded dams and highways that have caused social dislocations and environmental degradation. In response to this criticism the Bank has introduced a series of reforms, including carrying out environmental assessments of all its projects and funding air and water pollution controls and other environmentally protective projects. The Bank also created the World Bank Inspection Panel, a supervisory body authorized to receive and consider claims from any affected party regarding the Bank's failure to observe its own policies and procedures.

## THE WORLD TRADE ORGANIZATION

### From the GATT to the WTO

After the Bretton Woods Conference came negotiations on the touchy subject of international trade. The Depression-era U.S. Smoot-Hawley tariff had triggered protectionism and retaliatory tariffs in other countries, exacerbating global economic chaos, which contributed to the rise of fascism and militarism in the world. The Smoot-Hawley-inspired world tariff structure was still largely in place in 1945. Every one realized that tariffs should be reduced, but no country wanted to take unilateral action.

In Geneva in 1947 negotiations were successfully concluded on two matters – reciprocal tariff cuts and what was called a General Agreement on Tariffs and Trade (GATT), a code of international rules to govern trade relations among countries. The third piece of the puzzle, the creation of the International Trade Organization, was to be completed in Havana, Cuba in 1948. But President Harry S. Truman decided to bring the tariff cuts and the GATT rules into force immediately, and he signed a Protocol of Provisional Application applying the new tariffs and the GATT "on and after January 1, 1948." Later in 1948, work was completed on a charter for the new International Trade Organization (ITO). Truman duly submitted the charter to Congress, but Republicans were in control after the 1948 elections, and approval was impossible. In 1950 Truman conceded that the ITO was dead.

International cooperation on trade was very much alive, however, despite the demise of the ITO. The twenty-three countries, including the United

---

[6] For example, see the report, *Capacity Building in Africa: An OED Evaluation of World Bank Support* (2005).

**TABLE 6.1. THE GATT TRADE ROUNDS**

| Year | Place/name | Subject covered | Countries |
|------|-----------|-----------------|-----------|
| 1947 | Geneva | Tariffs | 23 |
| 1949 | Annecy | Tariffs | 13 |
| 1951 | Torquay | Tariffs | 38 |
| 1956 | Geneva | Tariffs | 26 |
| 1960–1 | Geneva (Dillon Round) | Tariffs | 26 |
| 1964–7 | Geneva (Kennedy Round) | Tariffs and anti-dumping measures | 62 |
| 1973–9 | Geneva (Tokyo Round) | Tariff, nontariff measures, 'framework' agreements | 102 |
| 1986–94 | Geneva (Uruguay Round) | Tariff, nontariff measures, rules, services, intellectual property, dispute settlement, textiles, agriculture, creation of WTO, etc. | 123 |

States, that had agreed to tariff cuts and the GATT needed a forum for international administration of the details of their agreements and a place for talks. The GATT set up offices in Geneva for these purposes. By default the GATT became an international organization – in effect, without a license – and operated this way until 1995. Between 1948 and 1995 the GATT attracted new "contracting parties" (the GATT could not have members because it lacked the formal attributes of an organization) and organized new rounds of tariff reductions and trade agreements (see Table 6.1). Every U.S. president regarded the GATT as essential to international cooperation on economic matters. In 1994, at the successful conclusion of the eight-year trade negotiation known as the Uruguay Round, there was international agreement to create a new World Trade Organization (WTO) to replace the GATT. The WTO came into existence on January 1, 1995 (see Figure 6.1).

## What the WTO Does

There is great misunderstanding about the functions and powers of the WTO. Often portrayed as an imperious international commission answerable to no one and handing down decrees from on high, the WTO is actually a very weak organization (total budget, $140 million) with about 550 employees (including receptionists, secretaries, file clerks, and messengers) headed by a

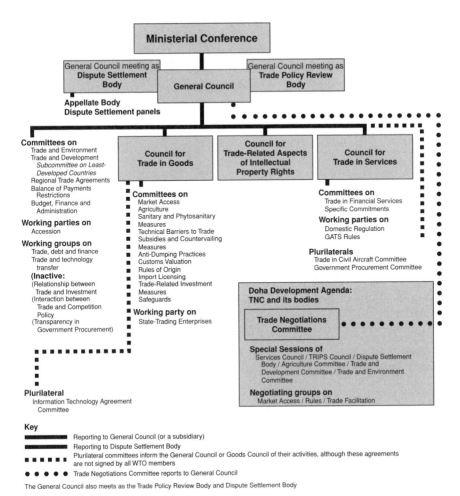

Figure 6.1. The World Trade Organization.

director-general who has no independent executive powers. Representatives of the WTO's 148 members make all the decisions in the meetings of all the WTO committees and on the WTO General Council. The only governing body able to take new policy initiatives is the WTO Ministerial Conference, which is a meeting of the trade ministers of member countries held every two years.

It is extraordinarily difficult for the WTO to take action because decision making hearkens back to the old GATT, in which informal discussions would eventually produce a consensus of opinion. Consensus, not voting, is still the usual practice in the WTO, and as it has grown now to 149 members, consensus is ever harder to achieve. In the GATT, consensus building depended primarily on agreement among the three big players – the United States, the European Community and Japan. In the WTO, developing countries, now in the majority, play an increasingly powerful role. At present, decision making in the WTO depends on shifting coalitions of countries.

What does the WTO do? First, the WTO's job is to supervise and foster the observance of the international rules that the members have approved over the years. This is done through periodic inspections and reports, a process known as the Trade Policy Review Mechanism. Second, the WTO functions as a forum for discussions, negotiations, and future agreements on trade. Third, the WTO cooperates and coordinates with its sisters, the IMF and the World Bank. Fourth, the WTO administers an extensive system of dispute settlement among its members.

## Dispute Settlement

One of the most extraordinary aspects of the WTO is dispute settlement. Since 1995 the WTO has operated what is effectively a court of international trade. Any member can bring a complaint against another member concerning a violation of the agreed rules, their avoidance, or any situation that "nullifies or impairs" a trade benefit. Unless this dispute is settled by negotiation as consultation, a Panel of legal experts hears both sides of the case and renders a written decision. The Panel's decision may then be appealed to an Appellate Body – effectively a Supreme Court of International Trade – that can affirm, overrule, or modify the ruling. The Appellate Body's decision is authoritative unless the WTO's dispute settlement body agrees by consensus not to adopt it (which has never occurred). The Appellate Body's decision (or a Panel's decision if there is no appeal) is binding on a WTO member to whom it is addressed, and compliance is mandatory within a set time period. In the event of noncompliance, the dispute settlement body may authorize onerous trade sanctions against the recalcitrant member.

In the last eleven years more than 400 cases have been filed at the WTO, making it the busiest and most interesting international tribunal in the world. Most of the cases are quite technical, but some make front-page news, such as a 2004 decision that the U.S. program granting subsidies to cotton farmers is illegal under WTO rules. This is where the WTO has its bite: The United States and 148 other WTO members have agreed among themselves on certain very complex and detailed rules to govern international trade. These rules sometimes deal with domestic programs, such as subsidies to agriculture, which affect trade. If Congress or the executive branch ignores these rules, another WTO member can challenge this, and the inconsistency must be corrected. If the United States or any other member fails to comply with a WTO final ruling, other countries can levy trade sanctions in the form of increased import duties – taxes – on that member's exports.

Actually the record of compliance with WTO decisions is quite good. Trade sanctions have been authorized only in a few cases. The United States was allowed to retaliate against the European Union when it refused to comply with a WTO ruling that a ban on imports of hormone-fed beef was contrary to WTO rules. In another case, the U.S. program allowing deferred taxation for foreign sales corporations was held to be an illegal export subsidy under WTO rules. Until the United States changed the program in 2004, WTO members were authorized to raise tariffs against U.S. products.

The remarkable characteristic of the WTO's rules and dispute settlement program is that the rule of law governs the vast majority of the economic inter-actions among states. Although power politics plays an important role, once the rules are agreed, they apply, and all members, even the most powerful, must comply or pay the penalty. Weak WTO members can challenge the non-compliance of strong members and vice versa. Although no system is perfect, the WTO provides a solid basis for multilateral cooperation in international trade. The proof of WTO success is the fact that there is a long waiting list of appleants who wish to join it. Russia, the only "big" country not a member, is expected to join in 2006 or 2007, and some 25 additional states are currently negotiating for admission. Within ten years the WTO will have a universal membership of virtually all the states of the world.

## International Economic Law

International economic law is the basis of the multilateral trading system whose obligations may be found in treaties and agreements among states. Law supplements politics as a rule-based system of governance. As Arthur Dunkel, director-general of the GATT, stated in 1992,

International economic policy commitments in the form of agreed rules have far-reaching domestic effects. . . . They form the basis on which a government can arbitrate and secure an equitable and efficient balance between diverse economic interests: producers vs. consumers export industries vs. import-competing indus-tries. . . . I am convinced that it is in the national interest of every trading nation to abide by the rules, which were accepted as valid for good times and bad, and to frame their policies accordingly. One of the major benefits of international [rules] is that they offer equal opportunities and require comparable sacrifices from all the countries involved in international competition.

## Principal WTO Obligations

What are the legal obligations that a WTO member undertakes? All WTO members must abide by the rules contained in some sixteen major agreements, as in well as in scores of additional understandings and interpretations. This body of international law began in 1947 with the GATT and was added to and updated over the years. This process continues today based on negotiations agreed to in 2001 at Doha, Qatar. The ongoing negotiations are known as the *Doha Development Agenda*. The United States and other original GATT parties participated in the creation of these rules from the beginning. New members must agree to the existing rules and can participate in creating new law.

Three overarching principles are fundamental to the WTO:

1. *Most-favored nation treatment (MFN):* This is actually a principle of nondiscrimination, not special treatment. WTO agreements specify that all WTO members must treat all other members as equal trading partners. This means no special favors to friends. If a low tariff rate is given to one, it must be given to all. MFN is a principle that applies to trade in goods, trade in services, and to intellectual property rights. All WTO members have the right to the same "best" treatment. Trade concessions therefore have a multiplier effect – they spread automatically throughout the multilateral trading system. Some significant exceptions are allowed, however. A WTO member that is also a member in a customs union or free trade area can maintain special lowered barriers within the group. Special low tariffs can apply to products from developing countries.

2. *National treatment:* This principle holds that imported and locally produced goods and services must be treated equally once they have entered the internal market. This is a principle of nondiscrimination between foreign and domestic production. National treatment applies only after a product, service, or item of intellectual property has entered the market. A tariff or charge may be levied at the border, but afterward competition between domestic and foreign goods and services should occur on a fair basis. Thus, for example, a sales tax levied on the sale of a product must not discriminate between foreign and domestic goods.

3. *Bindings and transparency:* The multilateral trading system must be predictable and knowable to all participants. Businesses and their customers in international trade need stable and clear rules, which foster investment, trade, job creation, and consumer choice. WTO members must

**TABLE 6.2. INCREASED TARIFF BINDINGS AFTER THE URUGUAY ROUND**

Percentages of tarifs bound before and after the 1986–94 talks

|                      | Before | After |
|----------------------|--------|-------|
| Developed countries  | 78     | 99    |
| Developing countries | 21     | 73    |
| Transition economies | 73     | 98    |

\* These are tariff lines, so percentages are not weighted according to trade volume or value.

therefore "bind" their commitments when they agree to reduce trade barriers and open their market to imported goods and services (see Table 6.2). A member can change its bindings, but only after negotiating with its trading partners, which may require compensating them for any loss of trade. A WTO member pledges to make trade rules clear and public through regular publication and by notifying the WTO.

## Major WTO Concerns

WTO rules cover a wide spectrum of international trade, business, and investment concerns. Here is a brief summary:

**Trade in Goods.** The principal agreement here is still the General Agreement on Tariffs and Trade (GATT), as updated, amended, and supplemented. The rules of the GATT generally prohibit quotas on imports of goods, but permit tariffs, taxes levied at the border by customs officials. Through the successive rounds of trade negotiations and the "bindings" process, tariffs of developed countries have been reduced from an average of about 40 percent in 1947 to 3.8 percent today. This has generated a tremendous growth in worldwide merchandise trade, as well as growth in world GDP (see Figure 6.2).

The GATT not only seeks to reduce formal barriers to trade but its rules also try to minimize or eliminate so-called nontariff barriers. Accordingly there are WTO agreements aimed at coordinating certain customs procedures and product, health, and safety standards.

Although the GATT unabashedly favors free trade, there are exceptions. A country may temporarily increase tariffs and even impose quotas if a domestic

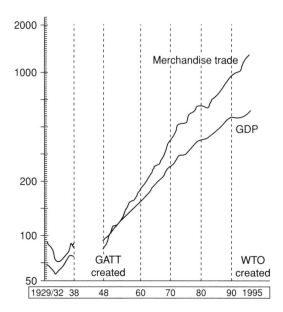

Figure 6.2. World trade and production have accelerated. Both trade and GDP fell in the late 1920s, before bottoming out in 1932. After World War II, both have risen exponentially, most of the time with trade outpacing GDP. (1950 = 100. Trade and GDP: log scale). *Source*: www.wto.org.

industry experiences serious injury caused by trade. This is a concession to political realities. This "safeguard" as it is called has proved controversial and difficult to apply in practice. For example, when President Bush imposed quotas on imported steel in 2002, just in advance of the mid-term Congressional elections, other WTO members cried "foul," and the U.S. action was later declared contrary to WTO rules by the Appellate Body. Nevertheless, the United States was able to maintain the quotas for over two years before bowing to the WTO determination.

The GATT and supplemental WTO agreements also allow WTO members to act to restrain so-called unfair trade – "dumping" (selling imports at lower prices than in the home market) and government-subsidized imports.

**Agricultural Products.** There is a special WTO Agreement on Agriculture because of the importance and unique aspects of this economic sector. Agriculture is unique because most countries extend some kind of financial support to agricultural producers. On a worldwide basis this support is estimated

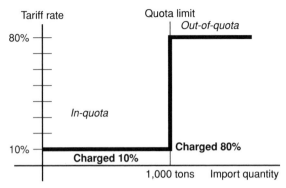

Figure 6.3. A tariff quota. Imports entering under the tariff quota (up to 1,000 tons) are generally charged 10%. Imports entering outside the tariff quota are charged 80%. Under the Uruguay Round agreement, the 1,000 tons would be based on actual imports in the base period or an agreed "minimum access" formula. Tariff quotas are also called "tariff-rate quotas." *Source*: www.wto.org.

to be about $300 billion. These subsidies distort markets and cause special trade friction. The WTO Agreement on Agriculture, which took effect in 1995, requires that all trade restrictions on the import of agricultural products must be converted to tariffs. Thus, for example, import quotas, common in many countries, had to be converted to equivalent tariffs. The effect of this requirement is to standardize agricultural trade barriers and to make them more transparent. Most WTO members now apply tariff-quotas to agricultural product imports (see Figure 6.3).

The Agreement on Agriculture also required all WTO members to cut their import tariffs and domestic agricultural subsidies to producers. Export subsidies on agricultural products also had to be decreased (see Table 6.3).

These reductions were completed for developed countries in 2000 and for developing countries at the end of 2004. A major aspect of the new WTO trade talks, the Doha Development Agenda, is whether to impose additional cuts in tariffs and subsidy programs, particularly those in developed countries that keep out or disrupt developing country exports. On July 31, 2004, WTO members reached an agreement in principle to amend the Agreement on Agriculture to make further "substantial" cuts in tariffs and domestic subsidies and to completely end export subsidies by a "certain date." These measures, if implemented, will increase agricultural trade worldwide.

**TABLE 6.3. REDUCTIONS IN AGRICULTURAL SUBSIDIES AND TRADE PROTECTIONISM AS A RESULT OF THE URUGUAY ROUND**

|  | Developed countries 6 years: 1995–2000 | Developing countries 10 years: 1995–2004 |
|---|---|---|
| Tariffs | | |
| Average cut for all agricultural products | −36% | −24% |
| Minimum cut per product | −15% | −10% |
| Domestic support | | |
| Total AMS cuts for sector (base period: 1986–8) | −20% | −13% |
| Exports | | |
| Value of subsidies | −36% | −24% |
| Subsidized quantities (base period: 1986–90) | −21% | −14% |

Least developed countries do not have to make commitments to reduce tariffs or subsidies.
The base level for tariff cuts was the bound rate before January 1, 1995, or, for unbound tariffs, the actual rate charged in September 1986 when the Uruquay Round began. The other figures were targets used to calculate countries' legally binding 'schedules' of commitments.

**Textiles and Clothing.** International trade in textiles and clothing was conducted for many years outside the rules of the GATT. Importing countries enforced a system of import quotas on textiles and clothing; exporting countries had to observe the quota limits assigned to them. The WTO Agreement on Textiles and Clothing (1995) integrated textile and clothing trade into the GATT on a phased basis completed on January 1, 2005. A Textile Monitoring Body oversees this difficult process and tries to resolve disputes.

The end of quotas has led to a restructuring of the market for clothing and textiles in the United States. The big winners are China and India – the lowest-cost producers. This has caused job losses not only in the United States and the European Union but also in many developing countries that are traditional suppliers of clothing to the U.S. and EU markets, such as Mexico and countries in the Caribbean and in Central America. The huge surge in exports from China has had to be controlled, at least temporarily, by a combination of export taxes and import quotas. Regretfully, this control undermines the free trade intent of what the WTO members agreed to in 1995.

But at that time, China was not a member, and the situation in 2005 could not be foreseen. Thus, the new quotas represent a further transitional period, due to expire in 2008, to allow markets to adjust to freer clothing and textile trade.

**Food Safety and Health Standards.** Food safety and health standards are necessary to protect public health, but they may be used arbitrarily to restrict trade. The WTO Agreement on Sanitary and Phytosanitary Measures (SPS Agreement) seeks to distinguish between genuine health and food safety standards and idiosyncratic measures adopted to restrict imports. The SPS Agreement automatically approves all food safety and health standards set by recognized international bodies. Three such organizations are particularly important: the the Food and Agriculture Organization/World Health Organization Codex Alimentarius Commission, which has adopted thousands of standards on foods; the International Animal Health Organization, which recommends food standards to safeguard animal health; and the FAO's Secretariat for the International Plant Protection Convention, which deals with plant health.

WTO members are encouraged to adopt these international standards. Members may, however, use higher national standards if they are scientifically justified based on appropriate evidence and assessment of risks. Precautionary temporary measures may be applied without scientific evidence if scientific uncertainty warrants this action. The scientific basis claimed by a WTO member is subject to review under the WTO mechanism for the settlement of disputes. A famous example is the *Hormones Case*[7] of 1998, which involved a challenge brought by the United States against an European Community (EC) import ban on beef products from hormone-fed cattle. The WTO Appellate Body ruled that there was an inadequate scientific basis for such an import ban. When the European Community refused to lift the restriction, the United States was authorized to raise compensating tariffs on imports from EC members.

**Product Standards.** Technical regulations and standards affect tens of thousands of products and are important to producers and consumers alike. However, differing standards can be an artificial barrier to trade or even be used unnecessarily to restrict trade. To minimize the protectionist impact of national product standards, the WTO has a Technical Barriers to Trade Agreement. This agreement encourages members to adopt international

7 European Communities – Measures Concerning Meat and Meat Products, WT/DS/AB/R, adopted Feb. 19, 1998.

standards where they exist and to harmonize national product standards. Members retain the right to adopt national standards they consider appropriate for human, animal, or plant life or health; for the protection of the environment; or to protect consumers. Such standards must be rationally justified, however. This justification is subject to WTO review. Thus, when the European Community adopted a standard allowing only Atlantic species of sardines to be labeled and sold as sardines, Chile and Peru, exporters of Pacific sardines, successfully challenged the standard as protectionist.[8]

**Trade in Services.** Services are now the fastest-growing sector of the world economy, accounting for 60 percent of global GDP, 30 percent of global employment, and 20 percent of international trade. International services range from banking, tourism, telecommunications, and insurance to medical, legal, engineering, and architectural services. There are four ways that services can be supplied internationally: (1) cross-border supply – from one country to another; (2) consumption abroad – consumers travel to the place of supply; (3) commercial presence – a foreign company sets up a subsidiary or branch in another country to supply services; and (4) the presence of natural persons – individuals travel from their own country to another country to supply the service.

Legal standards for trade in services are set under the WTO's General Agreement on Trade in Services (GATS). Service trade is affected internationally not by tariffs, as is the case with trade in goods, but by regulations that keep foreigners out or give preference to nationals. Under the GATS, WTO members commit to open their markets to services on a selective, reciprocal basis and agree to publish all laws and regulations that affect foreign service suppliers. International payments and transfers of capital also must be liberalized as a part of the commitment to open market access.

**Intellectual Property Rights.** The WTO's Agreement on Trade-Related Aspects of Intellectual Property Rights (TRIPS) introduces minimum requirements for the protection of intellectual property (IP) rights that must be observed by all members. These requirements affect products and services sold abroad as a result of either foreign investment or trade. The IP rights that attach to such products and services must be recognized, protected, and enforced. Minimum standards are set out for seven different types of IP: copyright, trademarks, patents, geographical indications, industrial designs, layout designs of integrated circuits, and trade secrets. IP protection is new and

---

[8] European Communities – Trade Description of Sardines, WT/DS231/AB/R, adopted Sept. 26, 2002.

controversial in many countries, such as China and India. The benefits of protection flow largely to richer countries and multinational corporations. In the future, however, IP protection may spread to developing countries in proportion to their entrepreneurial spirit.

**Investment.** Foreign direct investment (FDI) has been a defining feature of the world economy and of globalization for the past twenty years. Today some 60,000 parent companies worldwide have established over 500,000 affiliates in foreign countries with a value estimated at $4 trillion. Investment is a major reason why the production and consumption of goods and services are increasingly international. FDI flows are growing exponentially: from $200 billion in 1993 to over $1.5 trillion in 2003. FDI is growing at a faster rate than either product or service international trade.

However, there is no comprehensive international agreement on investment. A controversial effort by the OECD to negotiate a Multinational Agreement on Investment foundered in 1999. Most nations, such as the United States, that have a large stake in FDI have negotiated a broad network of bilateral investment treaties – known as BITS – to define the rights and duties of investors.

Certain WTO agreements deal with investment in the context of other concerns, notably TRIPS and GATS. The WTO's Trade-Related Investment Measures Agreement applies only to measures that affect trade in goods. This agreement requires national treatment to be applied to foreign investors and outlaws measures that require particular levels of local procurement of supplies and parts (local content requirements). It also prohibits the host country from limiting an investor's imports or setting targets for exports (trade balancing requirements).

**Government Procurement.** The WTO's Agreement on Government Procurement is optional and has been accepted by only 28 members, but these include the United States and most developed countries that are WTO members. This agreement opens government procurement to foreign competition on a limited basis. For international competitive bidding to apply, the contract must be in excess of certain defined monetary value thresholds.

## THE CASE FOR INTERNATIONAL TRADE

The secret is out: The WTO is not a neutral umpire on trade. Rather, the WTO agreements unabashedly promote international trade. Opponents of globalization are correct when they target the WTO. Yes, but the WTO is only a creature of its members; it has no power, no mind of its own. If the WTO is designed to promote trade – and it is – the reason is that its membership wants it that way. The members, not the WTO, are the culprits. And the most influential member over the years has been the United States. The WTO makes no apology for favoring international trade.

This is not the place for the technical arguments in favor of trade, which are many and persuasive. The evidence in favor of free trade is irrefutable; there is a strong statistical link among freer trade, open markets, and economic growth. Every country – even the poorest – has various assets, human capital, natural resources, industrial stock, and financial worth, which can be used both to produce for their domestic markets and for export. Principles of economics tell us that all countries benefit if these products and services are available for trade, which is not a zero-sum game (one player loses if the other wins), but one that produces winners all around. The principle of comparative advantage says that countries prosper by first taking advantage of their assets in order to concentrate on what they can produce best and then by trading these products for products that other countries produce best (see "The Principle of Comparative Advantage as Explained by the WTO").

Free trade – the unrestricted flow of goods and services – allows the benefit of competition to produce the widest variety of goods and services at the lowest prices. Because innovation is encouraged, an open market will produce the best, most advanced products at the best price. Free trade makes the pie grow larger for all. Both exporting and importing countries benefit. The gains from trade are the result of specialization and differences in what economists call *opportunity costs* involved in the production of different goods and services, (i.e., the amount of one good that must be given up in order to produce more of another good).

Important noneconomic benefits flow from trade as well. Because of economic interdependence, increased intercourse, and the mutuality of interests created by business activity, trade usually enhances peace. Trade also leads to the diffusion of knowledge and technology. It leads to greater openness to ideas and greater human freedom, democracy, and respect for human rights.

The other side of the coin is protectionism, which is an indirect subsidy for domestic producers. With protectionism there is less incentive to develop new, innovative products, and higher prices mean fewer goods for consumers. Lack of international competition leads to bloated, inefficient domestic producers. Consider the U.S. automobile industry: How good would American cars be today without the constant competition from foreign companies? Clearly, the quality has constantly improved because of international competition.

The benefits of free trade are such that most economists favor the unilateral opening of markets to trade, but that is not the approach of the GATT or the

## THE PRINCIPLE OF COMPARATIVE ADVANTAGE (AS EXPLAINED BY THE WTO)

This principle is arguably the single most powerful insight into economics.

Suppose country A is better than country B at making automobiles, and country B is better than country A at making bread. It is obvious (the academics would say "trivial") that both would benefit if A specialized in automobiles, B specialized in bread, and they traded their products. That is a case of *absolute advantage*.

But what if a country is bad at making everything? Will trade drive all producers out of business? The answer, according to the classical economist, David Ricardo, is no. The reason is the principle of *comparative advantage*.

According to this principle, countries A and B still stand to benefit from trading with each other even if A is better than B at making everything. If A is much more superior at making automobiles and only slightly superior at making bread, then A should still invest resources in what it does best – producing automobiles – and export the product to B. B should still invest in what it does best – making bread – and export that product to A, even if it is not as efficient as A. Both would still benefit from the trade. A country does not have to be the best at anything to gain from trade. That is comparative advantage.

The theory is one of the most widely accepted among economists. It is also one of the most misunderstood among noneconomists because it is confused with absolute advantage.

It is often claimed, for example, that some countries have no comparative advantage in anything. That is virtually impossible.

Think about it.

Source: www.wto.org

WTO. From the very beginning the multilateral trading system has operated on the principle that all participants must make reciprocal trade concessions. And when a new member joins, it must, as its ticket of admission, phase in market-opening measures roughly equal to what older members have done. Multilateralism involves broad principles of reciprocity and conditionality so that free trade is also fair trade.

## THE DOWNSIDES OF TRADE

Yes, there is a down side to international trade. Very few things in this world are unmixed blessings, and trade is no exception. International trade competes with domestic suppliers of goods and services, and sometimes it eats their lunch. Naturally this does not go over well with the industries and workers affected. There may be real hardships suffered by real people and their families. How should we handle these costs of trade?

Several points are relevant here. First, these hardships are why there are long, difficult negotiations over trade concessions in the multilateral trading system. The best time to consider hardships to domestic suppliers is before, not after, agreeing to reciprocal concessions. There is ample opportunity to weigh the impact of trade concessions before the fact. Second, we have to remember that multilateralism is a bargain; if the United States agrees to open its market to foreign competition in a certain economic sector, subjecting domestic industries to international competition, other countries are opening their markets to U.S. producers. After the fact, it is easy to focus on the downside but we must not forget the upside, which too often gets overlooked (who cares about good news?). Third, the WTO permits tariffs to some degree; it is always possible to retain a degree of protection for a domestic industry. Fourth, under WTO rules, the responsible agencies of the U.S. government − the Department of Commerce, the International Trade Commission, and the Office of the U.S. Trade Representative − may evaluate whether the foreign competition is unfair. If so, there are remedies in the form of anti-dumping or countervailing duties or even total exclusion from the U.S. market in the case of infringement of intellectual property rights. Even if no unfairness is found, temporary protection in the form of "safeguard" relief may be ordered by the President to give domestic industry the time to adjust to foreign competition. President Bush famously did this in 2002 when he granted safeguard relief to the steel industry. Unfortunately, he ignored the rules, this action was reversed by the WTO, and the U.S. had to remove the safeguard.

Yet we must realize that foreign trade is not a special case; it is part of the competitive market that must be allowed to function in any healthy economy. The U.S. economy is not static; it is a dynamic system that is constantly changing, creating new industries and jobs and punishing and eliminating inefficiencies and products and services no longer in demand. In the last 100 years the U.S. economy has shifted from agriculture to manufacturing to services and now to services/information technology. This dynamism must be allowed to continue in order to provide consumers the best products and services at the lowest prices. International trade is merely a part of this competitive process, and government should not artificially shield industries or workers from it. Rather, government must cushion the human costs by providing unemployment benefits, education, and training to displaced workers. All workers should be provided this safety net; there is really no distinction between workers displaced by trade and workers displaced by domestic competition.

## Employment and Wages

The most serious contemporary challenge to free trade and globalization focuses on employment and wages. Exports may be good because they create jobs and economic growth, but imports are bad because jobs and wages are transferred to foreign workers. As our politicians put it in the heat of battle: "We are shipping our good jobs overseas." This is a blanket charge that must be unpacked to be analyzed properly.

When people make this charge, they mean two things: (1) Trade means job losses and increasing unemployment, and (2) trade leads to low wages and a larger gap between the rich and poor. Do these charges withstand scrutiny?

In reality, trade both creates and destroys jobs, that is, trade changes the mix of jobs in the economy. According to the U.S. International Trade Commission, 25,100 jobs are created for every $1 billion of U.S. exports, and 23,100 jobs are created for every $1 billion of import replacements. Now it would perhaps be nice from an employment standpoint to block imports as a means of creating jobs. But trading partners would then do the same, and the result would be job losses in exporting industries. Furthermore, the import-replacement jobs created would likely be jobs with relatively low productivity that are not a source of comparative advantage for U.S. workers. The job losses would be in high-productivity labor fields. So we would be trading low-productivity jobs for higher productivity employment, which does not make sense. There is no empirical evidence of large net employment losses from trade. Trade simply means a different, more productive mix of jobs.

Does trade lead to low wages? The argument here is that U.S. workers cannot compete against all the workers in Mexico or China willing to work for a fraction of the wages of an American worker. This leads either to job losses in the United States as factories are moved abroad or to lower wages in the United States. Economists call this phenomenon *factor-price equalization* – as American workers are forced to compete with workers from developing countries, wages are depressed. Trade takes the blame for unemployment or underemployment, decreased job security, declining fringe benefits, wage stagnation, and the growing gap between rich and poor.

But this cannot possibly be true. First, international trade only competes with about 30 percent of U.S. economic activity; 70 percent is insulated from trade (when you need a plumber you are not going to call China), including entire industries, such as retail sales, health care, law, and real estate. Second, there are vast productivity differences between U.S. workers and workers in low-wage countries. Wages depend primarily on productivity, so there are reasons why even with trade American workers can continue to demand higher wages. Third, imports from low-wage countries, even with the increases of recent years, still amount to only about 4 percent of GDP. In certain industries this has an undeniable effect. For example, the number of textile and apparel jobs has dropped from about 1.2 million to 700,000 since 1999. But overall import wage competition does not depress U.S. wages to any significant degree.

It is easy to blame economic ills on foreign trade, but wage stagnation and the gap between rich and poor in American society are due primarily to other factors – the impact of technologies, social problems, and different levels of education and training. Trade plays a contributing role only for the unskilled worker. Highly skilled Americans do not face significant competition from poorer countries. The solution is not to cut off trade, but to invest more in human capital and in upgrading the skills and productivity of American workers.

## Deindustrialization

Another objection to trade is that it leads to a decline in the industrial base or to deindustrialization. The facts belie this charge. The U.S. economy has undergone a series of structural shifts – from agriculture to manufacturing to services and information technologies. Agriculture is still important, of course, but we produce more than enough food with only 2 percent of the workforce.

Manufacturing has a similar history: The percentage of the workforce engaged in manufacturing has declined in all advanced countries because of growth in the services and technology sectors. Gains in productivity in manufacturing and the development of new kinds of technologically advanced manufacturing have shifted certain manufacturing to developing countries. What is perceived by some as deindustrialization is simply a natural and healthy shift to higher economic productivity.

## Outsourcing

Outsourcing – the shift of certain information technology jobs to India and other developing countries – makes front-page news. What is going on here? Is this a worry? To a great extent the news media have blown this phenomenon out of proportion. Outsourcing, in the sense of shifting jobs from the United States to other countries, has occurred for many years. What is new is the perception that job losses to trade are worsening – hitting even the highly educated middle-class in America.

The impact of the outsourcing of information technology jobs is being exaggerated by anecdotes and media hype. What outsourcing reflects is simply trade in services, rather than the traditional trade in goods. With the GATS agreement in 1995, vast new areas of services trade were opened up all over the world – in banking, insurance, financial services, telecommunications, and many other fields. The United States with its services-dominant economy is well positioned to take advantage of this openness; in fact we have pushed hard for this very thing. It is certainly true that imports of business services are increasing: From 1997 to 2002, annual imports of business, technical, and professional services increased by an average of $6.3 billion. So there is more outsourcing. But what the headlines do not mention is the increase in U.S. exports of business services. Each year from 1997, U.S. business service exports have increased by an average of $20.5 billion per year. In 2002 alone, the United States ran a $ 27 billion trade surplus in business services. This adds up to a big plus for U.S. information technology (IT) workers.

Outsourcing of workers is minor even on an absolute scale. According to U.S. government statistics, of the 1.5 million jobs lost in 2003 in layoffs involving more than fifty workers, less than 1 percent was attributed to foreign relocations, and most of these outsourced jobs were in manufacturing, not IT. The recession and the busting of the technology bubble – not outsourcing – are the cause of IT job losses. At the present time IT hiring has resumed and is expected to grow 2 percent annually from 2004–8. IT outsourcing during this period is forecast to stay constant at about 100,000 jobs per year.

## Trade Deficits

In most countries trade statistics are collected and announced on a monthly or quarterly basis, and the focus is on trade in goods, typically reported either as a deficit or a surplus. When the media report these figures, a trade surplus is considered good news, whereas a trade deficit is worrisome.

Is this assumption correct? When a country runs a trade deficit, does this call for protectionist policies to restrain trade? Not necessarily, because the situation is more complicated than the media reports indicate.

Parenthetically, it is remarkable to compare our contemporary views concerning trade deficits with how they were viewed in the past. For example, during the period when India was a colony of Great Britain up until 1947, India ran a trade *surplus* averaging 1.5 percent of GDP. This meant, of course that India was sending more goods to Britain than it received and that 1.5 percent of its GDP was being sent as capital abroad. This trade surplus was regarded as colonial exploitation.

What is a trade deficit? It is one component of a country's balance of payments over a given period – it measures all exchanges of value between residents of the country and the rest of the world. These exchanges are typically grouped into five broad categories: (1) trade in goods, (2) service trade, (3) unilateral transfers (government aid and private gifts), (4) private capital flows, and (5) official asset flows (intergovernment transfers). An important component of the balance of payments is the *current-account balance*, net credits minus debits in the flow of goods, services, and unilateral transfers. Another important measure is the *net private capital account balance*, net credits minus debits of capital flows.

The current-account balance is a more meaningful statistical measure than the trade deficit; services trade and unilateral transfers may make up or nullify a trade deficit in whole or in part.

Furthermore, if there is a current-account deficit, it will be made up by the net private capital account balance. This is because a current-account (trade) deficit means that the country in deficit is receiving more from abroad than it is sending abroad. The deficit country is therefore borrowing from abroad to pay for what it consumes. The country in surplus is consuming less than it is transferring abroad; thus, a trade surplus represents net savings. The deficit is the same as a capital flow into the deficit country – a net foreign loan or investment of assets.

Whether a deficit is a problem depends on the circumstances. If a country with a small economy runs a chronic current-account deficit, the value of its currency will fall, foreign loans and investment will dry up and be pulled out, and an economic crisis will result. This is in fact exactly what happened during the Asian economic crisis of 1997–9.

The United States is a special case, however. The U.S. economy is huge; it can absorb a lot more foreign investment and borrowing than any other country. A deficit of a few hundred billion dollars, which would be devastating for most countries, is only a small percentage of the U.S. GDP and can be easily managed. The United States also offers an excellent investment climate from which good returns are usually made; thus, investors have a tendency to stay invested even during economic recessions. Another important factor is that most governments of the world hold U.S. dollars as official monetary reserves. This produces a chronic surplus for the United States in the "official asset flows" category of its balance of payments account. Governments hold these dollar reserves indefinitely, so the United States has the capacity to run what French economist Jacques Rueff has termed "deficits without tears."

Nevertheless, the trade deficit poses an important worry for the United States at the present time. In 2004 the United States not only ran a record trade deficit of $410 billion but its budget deficit was also $450 billion. This combination of twin deficits is dangerous even for the United States. The reason for this is that foreign savings are in effect being used to finance the U.S. government debt. Not only will the United States eventually have to repay this borrowing with interest, but foreign money invested in U.S. government bonds also is "hot" money that can be easily withdrawn, posing the danger of economic meltdown in a crisis. The present trade deficits are therefore much different from the deficits of the 1990s when the U.S. budget was in surplus. When the U.S. government is not borrowing, trade surplus capital goes into productive private investment that directly benefits the U.S. economy and creates jobs for American workers.

In any case, running a trade deficit does not mean necessarily that U.S. trading partners are more protectionist or unfair. Trade deficits reflect macroeconomic facts – whether a nation is consumption oriented, whether it has low levels of savings, and whether it is importing foreign capital. Moreover, trade surpluses or deficits with particular countries are not important unless there is a misalignment of their currency exchange rates. The cure for a trade deficit is macroeconomic policy change, not protectionism.

In the early years of the Clinton administration, there were proposals to correct trade imbalances with managed trade agreements with major trading partners under which governments would manage trade flows to achieve roughly equal exports and imports. This managed trade was directly counter to the multinational trading system, which implements reciprocal trade concessions but does not mandate any specific levels of trade. Managed trade would also require government-sanctioned cartels that would limit sales and allocate markets in violation of U.S. antitrust laws. Fortunately, this proposal was dropped. Fair trade does not mean exact reciprocity of outcomes between countries. This would be unworkable and unwise.

## Environmental Protection and Health

Protection of human health and the environment is essential, but antiglobalist groups routinely argue that the WTO and international trade damage both health and the environment. This charge is demonstrably false. There is nothing inherently unhealthy or polluting about transfers of products and services across international borders compared to such transfers within countries. So the real issue is whether the rules of the multinational trading system ignore or impede environmental protection and health measures.

The WTO has addressed environmental protection and health in two key cases. In the 2001 *EC Asbestos* case,[9] the WTO examined a challenge to a French law prohibiting the manufacture, sale, and importation of asbestos products because of their danger to health and the environment. The WTO Appellate Body upheld this measure on the grounds that, if a product entails health or environmental risk, an import ban coupled with a ban on domestic manufacture and sale is in accord with WTO rules.

The U.S. *Shrimp/Turtle* case (1998–2001)[10] involved a U.S. law prohibiting imports of shrimp from countries that failed to enact protections for endangered species of sea turtles. The U.S. law and import regulations were ultimately upheld by the WTO on the ground that a unilateral measure protecting endangered natural resources located beyond national jurisdictions is permissible as long as there are serious, ongoing good faith efforts to reach a multilateral agreement. The GATT and WTO rules make specific provision for limited trade restrictions in exceptional cases that protect natural resources and the environment.

Of course, this is not to say that the WTO can force all its members to enforce highly protective environmental measures. The WTO has no environmental mandate, so environmental concerns must be addressed in other forums. Neither can a WTO member use trade threats to require its trading partners to adopt what it considers necessary environmental standards. Such "environmental imperialism" is prohibited because every nation has a right to determine its own environmental policies and priorities. More stringent international environmental standards must be worked out by international agreement.

Advanced member nations of the WTO with strict pollution standards can require that international investors within their jurisdiction observe the same high standards with regard to international operations. Studies show, however, that transnational companies do not make foreign investment decisions to avoid environmental costs, and on the contrary, international investment usually maintains higher standards than local companies.

## Protection of Workers

Controversy surrounds the issue of labor standards and international trade. The exploitation of workers and child labor generally should be condemned,

---

[9] European Communities – Measures Affecting Asbestos and Asbestos Products, WT/DS135/AB/R, adopted April 5, 2001.
[10] United States – Import of Certain Shrimp and Shrimp Products, WT/DS58/AB/R, adopted Nov. 6, 1998 and WT/DS58/AB/RW, adopted Nov. 21, 2001.

but exact rules and standards for such matters are difficult to define and enforce. Wages, benefits, and working conditions vary enormously from country to country, and nations have different priorities and situations. Since 1919 the International Labor Organization (ILO) has addressed workers rights, labor standards, and conditions of employment. In 1998 the ILO specifically mounted an effort to inject these concerns into the new global economy and to mesh its work with the WTO. The ILO identified four "core principles" that should be observed universally: (1) freedom of association of workers and the effective recognition of their right to bargain collectively, (2) the elimination of all forms of compulsory labor, (3) the effective elimination of child labor, and (4) the elimination of discrimination in employment and choice of occupation.

The WTO issued ministerial declarations in 1996 and 1998 supporting the ILO and its core principles. The competency of the ILO in the field of labor standards was affirmed, and cooperation between the two organizations was initiated. This cooperation has been limited by the fact that the developing country members of the WTO – the vast majority of the total membership – oppose linking labor standards and trade in any way. Thus, there is more that can and should be done in this important field both by the WTO and the ILO, but for the time being further initiatives and closer cooperation between the two are politically stymied.

## DEVELOPING COUNTRIES RISING

Since the turn of the twenty-first century a new political force has burst onto the scene. Developing countries, which were long accustomed to playing only a supporting role, are newly assertive in international economic negotiations. Which countries are considered developing countries? International law permits a self-selection process for this designation, but there are objective standards: World Bank guidelines specify that a GDP per annum of less than $825 per capita qualifies a country for low-income developing country (DC) status, between $826 and $3,255 defines a lower-middle-income DC; and between $3,256 and $10,065 qualifies a country for a upper-income DC status. By these standards, the majority of nations in the world are developing countries.

Most of us in the wealthier countries have long since become accustomed to international political hand-wringing about poverty in developing countries. We accept the term "developing," but secretly regard it as a euphemism for "poor" or even "destitute." We also accept the ideas that the poor will always be with us, and God must favor the poor because He made so many of them. In short, people tend to simply accept the idea of two worlds – the haves and the have-nots, and that they are quite separate. This way of thinking is wrong. We experience donor fatigue or something worse when the topic of developing countries arises.

In fact, developing countries are on the rise economically, as well as polit- ically. For the first time in a generation, all areas of the World are experi- encing economic growth, many spectacularly. For example as of 2005, China is growing at a 9.9 percent rate each year, India at 7.6 percent, Argentina at 7.0 percent, South Korea at 5.5 percent, and Russia at 7.4 percent. The IMF forecast that even sub-Saharan Africa would grow a healthy 5.8 percent in 2005. The WTO announced in April 2005 that developing countries' share in merchandise trade has risen to a fifty-year high of 31 percent. This growth is not fortuitous, but is the result of correct policy initiatives carried out over many years by both developing nations and international institutions.

Developing countries first organized internationally in 1964 when a meeting of nonaligned, Third World nations led to the creation of a permanent body, the U.N. Conference of Trade and Development (UNCTAD), headquartered in Geneva. The main initiative of UNCTAD was a so-called *New International Economic Order* promoted in the 1970s by a U.N. General Assembly resolution entitled the Charter of Economic Rights and Duties of States. This charter called for restitution by industrialized countries for the economic and social costs of colonialism, racism, and foreign domination. As far as trade was con- cerned, the charter mandated all states to adjust the prices of exports to their imports so that all international trade flows would be in balance.

This kind of economic nonsense was not well received by the United States or any other developed country. The New International Economic Order deservedly fell by the wayside, although three programs were approved at the GATT in 1979 to benefit developing countries. One was the Generalized Sys- tem of Preferences, which allows developed countries to adopt special low or even zero tariffs to benefit developing country imports; a second, the Global System of Trade Preferences, allows developing countries to maintain trade preferences with each other on a global basis. The third initiative was to insert a variety of provisions into GATT trade agreements allowing " special and differential treatment" for developing countries. Under this program develop- ing countries are granted special privileges, such as longer deadlines, special trading opportunities, and technical and financial assistance.

Will the outcome be different this time? There is reason to believe that the coming decade could be a pivotal time for developing countries. If all countries and the WTO follow the correct policies, significant progress can be made toward a new global prosperity that will lift many developing countries and their people out of the abject poverty of the past. A real new international economic order is within our reach.

Since the end of the Cold War, many developing countries have made important economic advances. The fall of communism demonstrated the folly of central economic planning, and the example in the 1970s and 1980s of the East Asian "Tigers" – Hong Kong, Singapore, South Korea, Thailand, Malaysia, Taiwan, and Indonesia – pointed the way toward changing economic policies fostering open markets and privatization. Very quietly, developing countries have adopted responsible economic policies that are leading to solid economic growth. We know what these policies entail:

- fiscal policy stability – keeping budget deficits low and avoiding high inflation, thus creating a stable climate for business

- responsible monetary policy – avoiding the temptation to print money to fund deficits in state-run enterprises and government agencies

- building human capital through education and health care

- welcoming international investment, ideas, and technology

- decreasing or ending costly subsidy programs and privatizing public sector enterprises

- reforming and streamlining tax policies

- investing in infrastructure – seaports, transport, communications, and electric power

- encouraging high levels of savings

- opening to international markets and trade – developing countries' share of world trade is about 30 percent

The relationship between openness to trade and investment and economic growth has been the subject of intense study in recent years. A leading example is a study by Sebastian Edwards of the University of California at Los Angeles[11] that focused on total factor productivity (TFP), which measures how efficiently an economy uses both capital and labor. A country's TFP comes from two sources – domestic innovation (human capital) and imported ideas and technology. Developing countries generally have a shortage of human capital and therefore need imported innovation more than rich countries. Edwards examined this thesis by examining productivity in 93 countries and

---

[11] "Openness, Productivity, and Growth: What Do We Really Know?," *Economic Journal*, March 1998.

their openness to trade according to nine criteria for trade openness. He found that, however openness is defined, countries with a higher level of trade distortions had lower productivity growth than those with fewer trade distortions. The conclusion: Free trade is clearly good for productivity growth.

Almost unnoticed, there has been significant progress in reducing poverty in the world. Between 1980 and 2001, the proportion of people living in poverty in the developing world fell by half, from 40 percent to 21 percent, life expectancy increased by 20 years, and adult illiteracy was cut in half. Yet, there is much to do: 2.8 billion people live on less than $245 per year, one billion people lack access to clean water, over 100 million children receive no education at all, and over 40 million people in developing countries are HIV-positive with little hope for treatment.

New departures in economic policy were initiated by many states in recent years. The end of the Cold War realigned the states formerly dominated by the Soviet Union. The Eastern European former satellite states either have or soon will join the European Union. Membership in the European Union will enable them to complete the difficult transition from communist central planning to a free market economy. The nations of Eastern Europe have shown the path to robust economic growth. Russia's transition was more difficult, but after experiencing runaway inflation and depression in the 1990s, Russia and the states of the Commonwealth of Independent States have started on the path of growth. China has become an economic star, reducing subsidies and privatizing state enterprises, investing in education and infrastructure, and embracing free trade and investment. India has opened to trade as well, discarding its old policy of import substitution and economic autonomy. Japan and the East Asian Tigers are growing again after the difficult recessions of the late 1990s. Australia and New Zealand are prospering. Latin America, led by Brazil and Mexico, has embraced market economics and has mastered the killing inflation and debt crisis that retarded its development for so long. The most laggard areas of the world are sub-Saharan Africa and the Middle East. The 48 states of sub-Saharan Africa have a per capita income of less than $300 per year; their economies continue to be mismanaged, and most states have heavy international debt burdens. The Middle East is beset by continuing violence and upheaval.

New initiatives have begun in the multilateral trading system to aid developing countries. In the WTO, the 2001 Ministerial Conference announced the Doha Development Agenda, a new trade negotiation to reduce trade barriers that hamper developing country growth. A major issue is the reduction of agricultural subsidies in rich countries that compete unfairly for market share with developing country products. At the WTO Ministerial Conference in Cancun, Mexico in 2003, developing countries, led by India and Brazil, asserted their power. A deal on agricultural subsidies and other trade matters was rejected because, as Brazil put it, "a bad deal is worse than no deal" and the Conference ended without agreement.

The Cancun failure was at least partially recouped when in July 2004 an interim agreement was reached by the WTO membership to end agricultural export subsidies completely and to significantly reduce agricultural tariffs and domestic subsidies. On August 1, 2004, the WTO Council adopted a new Doha Work Program, which was confirmed at the WTO Ministerial Conference in Hong Kong in 2005, and negotiations are continuing. Meanwhile, a WTO dispute settlement panel ruled in 2004 that the U.S. cotton subsidies program was unfair to developing countries. Moreover, under the WTO Agreement on Textiles and Clothing, quotas on developing country imports in this economic sector ended December 31, 2004. In any case it is now evident that the WTO must meet developing country demands in order to move forward on the international trade agenda. Negotiations are presently on track for a successful completion of this negotiation in 2006 or 2007. If this is done, developing countries will receive great benefit.

The WTO in 2002 also adopted a work program to benefit least developing countries. This was part of an initiative by six international organizations (the International Monetary Fund, The International Trade Center, the U.N. Conference on Trade and Development, the U.N. Development Program, the World Bank, and the WTO) to formulate assistance and debt relief to least developing countries.

In the twenty-first century we must no longer accept the radical division of the world into economic haves and have-nots. The countries of the world are intimately linked; there can be no peace and stability in the world unless poverty is reduced. Developing countries must help themselves, but the rich countries can help in three fundamental ways: (1) implementing measures to enhance trade and increase developing country exports, (2) providing debt relief, especially for the world's poorest countries, and (3) offering financial and technical assistance.[12]

Developing countries must realize, however, that the path to economic growth is slow and steady, rather than quick and easy. Even with the correct economic and social policies in place and economic growth at 6–7 percent per

---

[12] The United States provides foreign aid to developing nations, but most assistance goes to the Middle East (Israel, Egypt, Jordan, Iraq, and Afghanistan). EU countries tend to provide assistance to former colonies in Africa, Asia, and the Caribbean. Japan through its Overseas Development Assistance (ODA) program donates mostly to Asian countries and is the largest contributor to the Asian Development Bank and the African Development Bank.

**THE MILLENIUM DEVELOPMENT GOALS**

Goal One: Eradicate extreme poverty and hunger: Cut in half by 2015 the proportion of people in the world who suffer from hunger or whose income is less that $1 a day.

Goal Two: Achieve universal primary education by 2015.

Goal Three: Promote gender equality and empower women: End gender disparity in access to educational facilities.

Goal Four: Reduce child mortality: Reduce by two-thirds the under-five mortality rate by 2015.

Goal Five: Improve maternal health: Reduce the maternal mortality ratio by three-quarters by 2015.

Goal Six: Combat HIV/AIDS, malaria, and other diseases: Halt the increase and reverse the spread of major diseases by 2015.

Goal Seven: Ensure environmental quality: Cut in half the proportion of people in the world without access to safe drinking water and basic sanitation facilities and reverse the loss of environmental resources.

Goal Eight: Develop a global partnership for development: Foster continued economic growth in developing countries.

year – the rate of the East Asian Tigers – attaining a modicum of prosperity will take decades. The fear is that residents of developing countries will become impatient and through revolution will seek a quick fix – in reality only a return to the failed government interventions of the past. If we can stay the course, the divide between rich and poor nations can be greatly diminished in the new century.

For the first time in their history, the three global economic organizations – the World Bank, the IMF, and the WTO, as well as the UN, are united and working together to benefit developing countries and to slash world poverty through a combination of economic and technical loans and aid, debt reduction, and increased trade. All three organizations are fully committed to working to implement the UN's Millennium Development Program, with a target deadline of 2015 (see "The Millennium Development Goals").

The Millennium Development Goals represent an unprecedented world effort to set accepted benchmarks to reduce poverty and to establish stable civil societies around the world.

This coordinated effort can bear fruit. A major step forward occurred in June 2005 when the G-8 agreed to cancel $40 billion in debt owed by eighteen of the world's poorest countries, all located in Africa. As a *quid pro quo*, the recipient countries had to meet objective criteria for democracy and good governance set up by the World Bank and the IMF. The G-8 also set out incentives for twenty additional countries, which can qualify for future debt relief if they meet the good governance standards. This debt relief package will save Africa about $1.5 billion in debt service each year. This relief, combined with increased aid for health, education, public administration, and infrastructure, can make a difference in tackling poverty in Africa

## REGIONAL ECONOMIC AGREEMENTS: THE PATH TO GROWTH

One of the dominant movements of the recent past is the spread of regionalism in trade and investment. Regional economic integration can provide an engine for economic growth and can lead to peace and stability. This is a fundamental lesson of the second half of the twentieth century. The best paradigm for this is the European Union, which has brought peace and prosperity first to Western Europe and now to Eastern Europe as well. The successful idea that the European Union put into practice is known as neofunctionalism – economic cooperation provides a foundation for social and political cooperation that makes war unthinkable. The European Union and its related international institutions have successfully overcome centuries of war and ethnic hatred in Europe.

The way to achieve regional economic integration is to negotiate international treaties that provide the necessary framework and create the institutions necessary for implementation. There are several forms such an agreement may take. The most limited model is to integrate one economic sector. This was done in Europe as a way of initiating cooperation with the European Coal and Steel Community (ECSC) formed in 1954. Another example is the US-Canada Auto Pact of 1967. This limited form of cooperation conflicts, however, with WTO rules against preferences, and both the ECSC and the Auto Pact have been folded into broader economic agreements.

A *free trade agreement* (FTA) is the most frequent form of regional economic agreement and is permitted under WTO rules. An FTA is an agreement among two or more countries to eliminate tariffs and other barriers with respect to substantially all trade in goods and services. The most important example of an FTA is the North American Free Trade Agreement (NAFTA) between the United States, Canada, and Mexico. This has established free trade within the borders of the three member countries, but all three retain complete control over imports and economic policy toward non-NAFTA nations.

A closer form of economic integration is a *customs union*, which not only abolishes restrictions on intramember trade, but also establishes common institutions and rules with respect to imports and trade with nonmembers. In a customs union, the participating nations give up control over their external trade policy to common institutions. The European Union is a customs union, but over the years it established even closer forms of economic and political cooperation. In 1986 the passage of the Single European Act created a *common market*, the removal of all barriers – physical, technical, fiscal, and legal – to intra-union trade. The Maastricht and Amsterdam treaties in the 1990s created *political and monetary union*, although not all EU members have adopted the euro as a common currency, and the U.S. invasion of Iraq in 2003 split the EU members on an important question of foreign policy. In 2004, the European Union expanded to twenty-five members, but its new proposed "constitution" (in reality an institutional agreement) appears to have failed after "no" votes in referendums in France and the Netherlands.

What is the economic impact of the European Union? The most noticeable effect is the *four freedoms*: the free movement of goods, services, capital, and persons throughout the European Union. The evidence shows that trade and investment have not only increased within the European Union, but businesses from outside have benefited as well. Non-EU firms can invest in the common market and can move factors of production freely inside the European Union. This experience shows that regional economic integration can benefit global trade.

In a similar fashion free trade areas (FTAs) can complement and enhance the multilateral trading system. FTAs create more trade and investment among participating countries, but divert trade from the rest of the world to members. This diversion will not be a problem if the FTA does not raise barriers to nonmembers. The economic prosperity fostered by the FTA will more than make up for the trade diversion, and enterprises outside the FTA will be able to benefit from the increased prosperity and to take advantage of several of the integrated market rules. There is a certain tension between FTAs and the rules of the WTO, but there is also complementarity because an FTA allows trading partners to go beyond the rules of the WTO to promote greater integration, coordination of policies, and harmonization of laws.

FTAs are proliferating. There are now about 180 FTAs in the world, and this number is increasing. In 2000 four FTAs – the European Union, NAFTA, MERCUSUR (Brazil, Chile, Argentina, Uruguay, and Paraguay), and ASEAN (ten countries in Southeast Asia) accounted for 64.5 percent of world export trade and 69.5 percent of total world import trade. The failures of the WTO ministerial conferences at Seattle (1999) and Cancun (2003) accelerated the trend toward FTAs. The United States has been particularly active in concluding FTAs. In addition to NAFTA, the United States has concluded FTAs with Israel and Jordan in the Middle East, Morocco in North Africa, Australia, as well as CAFTA (the Central American Free Trade Agreement) with six countries in Central America and the Caribbean: the Dominican Republic, Costa Rica, Honduras, Nicaragua, Guatemala, and El Salvador.

FTAs could serve as an engine of growth for developing countries by providing economies of scale for their products in a larger market and attracting outside investment. A Pan-African FTA should be considered to replace the many conflicting and overlapping trade agreements on the African continent. In the Western Hemisphere, a Free Trade Area of the Americas has been proposed that would unify NAFTA, MERCOSUR, and other blocs into a giant market extending from Alaska to Tierra del Fuego. The settlement of the multiple crises in the Middle East will ultimately require the negotiation of an FTA in that troubled area.

Perhaps the most dynamic new FTA likely in the future is an East Asian Economic Community composed of ASEAN (the ten-member Association of Southeast Asian Nations), South Korea, Japan, and China. It would also include Hong Kong (and perhaps eventually Taiwan) as part of China. Negotiations have begun to establish this entity, which could have political repercussions if it helps settle the Taiwan question. East Asian economic unification would have inevitable consequences for North Korea as well; the communist system there would become even more isolated and, like the Soviet empire confronting European unification and Western economic success, may well crumble from within.

## SUMMING UP

The international political economy during the last sixty years has benefited immensely from American participation and leadership. The global economic institutions created at the end of World War II have significantly shaped the world economy and global prosperity. They have changed greatly since their inception and will continue to evolve and improve. As a result of American participation, international economic law and institutions play a significant role in the world. This rule of law and institutions can provide the necessary framework for future economic growth and the diminution of world poverty, as well as the management of the process of globalization. We must continue on this path and guard against a return to trade and economic unilateralism.

Multilateral cooperation is the hallmark of the growing world economic prosperity. U.S. adherence to multilateralism is essential. The day is long past when the United States can ignore the rest of the world when setting fiscal and monetary policies. U.S. unilateralism in economic policy that results in large budget and current-account deficits threatens continued U.S. and world prosperity. The United States must take steps to reduce these twin deficits so as to maintain its role as the world's economic superpower.

There are two principal areas in which the United States has used unilateral trade measures as an instrument of foreign policy. Section 301 of the U.S. Trade Act allows the president to approve trade retaliation measures against alleged unfair or discriminatory foreign trade practices. In the 1980s and early 1990s, the United States acted unilaterally under this law against a number of countries, especially Japan. At the conclusion of the Uruguay Round of trade negotiations in 1994, however, the United States pledged to honor its commitment to retaliate only when authorized under WTO rules. A second area of unilateral action by the United States is the use of trade sanctions to further foreign policy goals. Some eighty countries are now under some sort of U.S. trade boycott because the United States faults some aspect of their foreign policy. Most such measures are ineffective at best and contradictory at worst – sometimes the same country is both favored and sanctioned under U.S. law. Moreover, studies show that unilateral sanctions are almost always ineffective.[13] Only multilateral sanctions, such as those decreed by the U.N. Security Council to end apartheid in South Africa, are truly effective.

Multilateral cooperation must be continued in the future for the benefit of both developing and advanced countries and to diminish the economic divide in the world. Now that developing countries are the new majority in the WTO, multilateralism must become more inclusive. Particularly important is the success of the Doha Development Work Program. The WTO has been compared to a bicycle that, if it does not keep moving, will fall over. The WTO must not be allowed to fail; otherwise the world may split into mutually antagonistic trading blocs that will do irreparable damage to the multilateral trading system. The United States must continue to play the leading role if multilateral economic cooperation is to continue.

---

[13] Gary Clyde Huffbauer, Jeffrey J. Scott, and Kimberly Ann Elliot, *Economic Sanctions Reconsidered* (2d ed. 1990).

## FURTHER READINGS

Jeffry A. Frieden and David A. Lake, eds., (3d ed. 1995).

Joseph Stiglitz, *Globalism and Its Discontents* (2002).

Amy Chua, *A World on Fire* (2003).

Manfred Steger, *Globalism* (2002).

Mitsuo Matsushita, Thomas J. Schoenbaum, and Petros Mavroidis, *The World Trade Organization: Law, Practice and Policy* (2003).

*The Future of the WTO: Addressing Institutional Challenges in the New Millennium: A Report by the Consultative Board to Director General Supachai Panachpakdi* (World Trade Organization, 2005).

Jan Aart Scholte, *Globalization: A Critical Introduction* (2000).

Andrew Hurrell and Ngaire Woods, eds., *Inequality, Globalization, and World Politics* (2000).

Jonathan Pincus and Jeffrey A. Winters, eds., *Reinventing the World Bank* (2002).

Martin Wolf, *Making Globalization Work* (2003).

Thomas L. Friedman, *The World Is Flat: A Brief History of the Twentieth Century* (2005).

Jagdish Bhagwati, *In Defense of Globalization* (2004).

Lou Dobbs, *Exporting America* (2004)

Lester Thurow, *Fortune Favors the Bold* (2004).

Shallendra D. Sharma, *The Asian Financial Crisis* (2003)

Yujiro Hayami, *Development Economics* (2001)

John Gray, *False Dawn* (1998).

Eric Neumayer, *Greening Trade and Investment* (2001).

Jeffrey D. Sachs, *The End of Poverty: Economic Possibilities for Our Time* (2005).

The target of the Millennium Development Goals is to foster continued economic growth in developing countries.

# 7 International Environmental Protection

## A PROMISING START

Beginning in 1925, a smelter that was processing copper ore in the town of Trail, British Columbia, spewed out tons of sulphur dioxide fumes, causing respiratory diseases and inflicting damage to homes and businesses across the border in the state of Washington. The U.S. government protested to Canada, but to no avail. The company was privately owned and was doing nothing illegal. Lightly populated British Columbia did not require pollution controls. The smelter was beyond the reach of U.S. law, so nothing could be done. After years of protests and worsening misery, the Canadian government agreed to submit the controversy to a Special Arbitral Tribunal. In 1941, a decision was handed down, the first case involving adjudication of an international pollution dispute. The tribunal found that, under principles of international law, "no State has the right to use or to permit the use of its territory in such a manner as to cause injury... in or to the territory of another when the case is of serious consequence and the injury is established by clear and convincing evidence." The tribunal awarded compensation to the United States and imposed measures of control upon the smelter's operations, including the maintenance of meteorological records and the specification of maximum hourly emissions of sulphur dioxide under various conditions.

The *Trail Smelter case*,[1] as this is known, is still a landmark decision of international environmental law. Regretfully, although much has happened since this decision was handed down, the world is still struggling to find solutions for international environmental problems.[2] World population has

---

[1]  3 U.N. Rep. Int. Arb. Awards 1911 (1941).
[2]  Especially discouraging is the fact that, despite the decision in the *Trail Smelter* case, conditions at the smelter did not improve. The smelter is operating in 2005, and U.S. and Canadian

more than doubled in the last sixty years, and increased prosperity has put increased pressure on the environment and the natural world. In the twenty-first century we are faced not only with local transboundary pollution problems such as the Trail Smelter but also with such global crises as climate change and the loss of biological diversity. The focus of international environmental law has shifted from reparation for environmental injury to the prevention of environmental harm and the conservation and sustainable use of natural resources and ecosystems. Unfortunately, the record so far is dismal: Very few international environmental initiatives can be judged a success, the problems are compounding, and there is a lack of political will and leadership.

## U.N. INITIATIVES

Until the 1970s, there was little in the way of international institutions or international law relating to environmental protection. Environmental degradation was regarded as a local or national problem of little concern to the international community. This changed in 1972 with the meeting in Stockholm of the U.N. Conference on the Human Environment. The U.N. General Assembly resolution convening this conference recognized "an urgent need for intensified action at national and international levels to limit and, where possible, to eliminate the impairment of the human environment."

The Stockholm Conference, as it is now called, was a grand success; four major initiatives resulted from it. First, the Stockholm Declaration of Principles was adopted – this proved to be a seminal document in the development of international environmental law. Second, the U.N. Environment Program (UNEP) was established as a permanent new international organization within the United Nations to foster protection of the global environment. The decision was taken to create a "program" and not a full-fledged organization because of the related work of many existing U.N. organizations, such as the Food and Agriculture Organization, the International Maritime Organization, and the World Health Organization. Third, the Stockholm Conference adopted an action plan for the development of environmental policy to be administered by UNEP, and fourth, an Environmental Fund was created to receive voluntary contributions.

environmental agencies report that a century of heavy-metal-laden emissions has resulted in extremely polluted soil, air, ground water, fish, and wildlife in the Columbia River watershed for miles downstream of the smelter, including beyond the international border. See www.miningwatch.org/emcbc/Publications/briefing_papers/trail.htm, visited Feb. 26, 2005.

In the years following the Stockholm Conference, discussion about international environmental protection measures became entangled with the increasing influence of developing countries and their emphasis on development and a New International Economic Order. Developing countries came to resent calls for environmental measures that would inhibit their right to develop. The stand-off remained until the World Commission on Environment and Development published a report, *Our Common Future* (called the Brundtland Report after its leader, Gro Harlem Brundtland, later Prime Minister of Norway), calling for a new approach – *sustainable development* – combining the right to develop with environmental concerns.

The Brundtland Report opened the way for the U.N. General Assembly to convene a new conference, which was held amid great fanfare in Rio de Janeiro in 1992 and attended by 176 states and 103 heads of state or government. This U.N. Conference on Environment and Development (UNCED) was a major event that built upon the Stockholm meeting, but went beyond it in scope and depth. Five important international instruments were adopted at it:

1. *The Rio Declaration on Environment and Development* – a set of twenty-seven nonbinding principles setting out the recommended contours of sustainable development;

2. *Agenda 21* – an action program containing recommended strategies to be followed by all states in order to deal with environmental issues and resources. Every conceivable environmental problem is addressed in its forty chapters, and the interconnections among economic, developmental, and environmental issues are explored in depth. The financial chapter recommends a doubling of financial aid to developing countries to assist them in carrying out the recommended goals;

3. *The U.N. Framework Convention on Climate Change* – the beginning of a new international regulatory regime to deal with the consequences of rampant use of fossil fuels for the production of energy;

4. *The U.N. Convention on Biological Diversity* – a worldwide initiative to combat the loss of biological diversity through overexploitation of natural resources; and

5. *The Non-Binding Authoritative Statement of Principles on the Management, Conservation, and Sustainable Development of All Types of Forests* – an attempt to forge a consensus leading to reduced exploitation of forests. Developing countries blocked both a legally binding treaty and a convention on tropical forests alone. Many developed countries, led by the

United States, opposed any treaty that would place any international constraints on harvesting temperate zone forests.

All these measures, as we shall see, are being ignored or are in severe difficulty. The United States not only played no role in organizing these U.N. initiatives but also consistently obstructed them.

In 2002, under a mandate from the U.N. General Assembly, the World Summit on Sustainable Development was held in Johannesburg, South Africa. At this summit there was a ten-year review of the progress made toward achieving the sustainable development goals agreed upon at Rio de Janeiro. The news was not good, and the Johannesburg Summit produced only a political declaration[3] and laments on the lack of progress and inability to agree on future actions. The United States came in for particular criticism, and the U.S. delegation led by Health and Human Services Secretary Tommy Thompson walked out and went home early.

## INTERNATIONAL ENVIRONMENTAL GOVERNANCE

A multiplicity of international regimes have responsibility for the global governance of environmental matters. All are weak, especially compared with international economic institutions. The universal rhetoric of states that the global environment is a concern has not translated into effective action. The organizational structure of environmental protection is fragmented. There is an urgent need for a *World Environment Organization* similar to the World Trade Organization that would centralize and coordinate the international regimes that deal with global environmental issues.

At present the United Nations Development Program (UNEP) plays the central role in international environmental governance, but its charter authorizes it only "to promote international cooperation in the field of the environment and to recommend, as appropriate, policies to this end" – not a very strong mandate. Fifty-eight member states are elected triennially to UNEP's Council by the General Assembly, and there is an executive director and a permanent secretariat based in Nairobi, Kenya. Despite little funding and a narrow mandate, UNEP has a solid record of accomplishment. It has served as a forum for the conclusion of important international agreements, developed new international legal principles and guidelines, and assisted developing

[3] Documents from the Johannesburg Summit are available from http://www.johannesburgsummit.org.

## THE UNITED NATIONS ENVIRONMENT PROGRAM

The United Nations Environment Program (UNEP) was established by U.N. General Assembly Resolution 2997 on December 15, 1972. UNEP has a Governing Council composed of fifty-eight members elected by the U.N. General Assembly to serve four-year terms. The day-to-day functions of UNEP are the responsibility of its Executive Director.

The functions and responsibilities of the Governing Council are as follows:

■ to promote international cooperation in the field of environment and to recommend, as appropriate, policies to this end

■ to provide general policy guidance for the direction and coordination of environmental programs within the U.N. system

■ to receive and review the periodic reports of the executive director of UNEP on the implementation of environmental programs within the U.N. system

■ to keep under review the world environmental situation in order to ensure that emerging environmental problems of wide international significance receive appropriate and adequate consideration by governments

■ to promote the contribution of the relevant international scientific and other professional communities to the acquisition, assessment, and exchange of environmental knowledge and information and, as appropriate, to the technical aspects of the formulation and implementation of environmental programs within the U.N. system

■ to maintain under continuing review the impact of national and international environmental policies and measures on developing countries

■ to review and approve the program of utilization of the Environment Fund

countries in the reform and administration of their environmental laws. In 1997 the General Assembly of the United Nations established a Global Ministerial Forum to confirm UNEP's role as the setter of the global environmental agenda, the coordinator of the UN's environmental protection efforts, and the advocate on behalf of the global environment. UNEP now has responsibility for the coordination of U.N. environmental treaties and their implementation (see "The United Nations Environment Program").

A second U.N. environmental body, the Commission on Sustainable Development (CSD), was created after the 1992 UNCED Conference to review the implementation of Agenda 21 and other Rio documents. The CSD comprises of representatives of fifty-three states elected by the U.N. Economic and Social Council for three-year terms. Meeting only annually, the CSD has confined its work to making policy recommendations, such as the Program for the Further Implementation of Agenda 21, which was adopted in 1997. Agenda 21 has languished as a result.

Many other U.N. specialized agencies are involved in some aspect of the environment or resources. For example, the Food and Agriculture Organization (FAO), which was created to improve efficiency in the production of food and agricultural produce, promotes sustainable approaches to fishing and water resource management and raises awareness of the harmful impacts of chemical pesticides and fertilizers used in agriculture. The FAO played a key role in the negotiation of regional fisheries agreements and the 1995 Agreement on Straddling and Highly Migratory Fish Stocks. The FAO also collaborated with UNEP in the negotiation of the 1998 Convention on the Prior Informed Consent Procedure for Certain Hazardous Chemicals and Pesticides in International Trade.

The International Maritime Organization (IMO) in London has responsibility for the environmental protection of the oceans. Beginning in the 1950s, the IMO convened international conferences, which led to international conventions preventing and controlling pollution from ships. As a result, oil pollution from shipping discharges and accidents has greatly decreased, although the transport of oil by water has increased. The IMO established a Marine Environmental Protection Committee after the Stockholm Conference of 1972, and there is also a legal committee. Agenda 21 called upon the IMO to address broader environmental issues; it responded with regulations protecting sensitive sea areas and the regulation of the discharge of air and ballast-water, garbage, and plastics pollution from ships. To be effective, however, these rules must be implemented by member states.

The U.N. Economic, Scientific, and Cultural Organization (UNESCO) administers the 1972 World Heritage Convention, which calls upon states to designate areas within their territory that deserve special recognition and preservation. UNESCO's Man and the Biosphere Program establishes a world-wide system of natural areas designated as "biosphere reserves." Designation is voluntary, however, and reserves remain under state sovereignty.

Additional international environmental governance is exercised by scores of treaty regimes that have been established to deal with particular environmental or resource problems – from the Amazon to wetlands and whales and everything in between. Because there is no central, coordinating environmental organization, there is great need to upgrade UNEP's status to become the operating agency or the coordinating organization for all international environmental agreements and understandings.

Nongovernmental organizations (NGOs) have played a leading role in international environmental efforts. They range from advocacy groups, such as Greenpeace International, to scientific bodies, such as the World Wide Fund for Nature, to political NGOs, such as the Water Resources Institute. Perhaps the leading NGO is the International Union for the Conservation of Nature (IUCN, also known as the World Conservation Union) in Gland, Switzerland, whose membership includes 79 states, 149 government agencies, 690 national NGOs, and 68 international NGOs. The IUCN passes resolutions and offers advice and expertise to governments and has played a key role in preparing international conventions and documents, such as the World Charter for Nature, which was adopted by the U.N. General Assembly in 1982.

Environmental governance is exercised by many international bodies, but despite their individual competence, there is no clear leadership or direction to the effort to deal with global environmental problems.

## DISTINCTIVE DOCTRINES OF INTERNATIONAL ENVIRONMENTAL LAW

### "Soft" Law and Framework Treaties

A distinctive feature of international environmental law is the development of legal doctrines and principles, which serve as policy guides for more particular, concrete standards and legal norms. These policy guides are too general to constrain conduct and so are regarded as "soft" law, which appears to be a contradiction, because law denotes social rules that are compulsory and are therefore "hard." Nevertheless, because of its novelty, international environmental law has made use of halfway, general principles that attract wide assent, avoiding details and standards that bite or reserving them for later. Soft law can thus be regarded as the essential beginning of a law-making process. Soft law may also be aspirational, preparing the way for future progress. Soft law also denotes general, commonly agreed-upon principles that provide the basis for international negotiations.

International environmental law also makes use of a distinctive method of law making known as the *framework treaty process* . Typically this process involves concluding an initial multilateral treaty at which states agree only that there is an international environmental problem that requires action. However, detailed rules are eschewed in favor of a requirement to monitor the problem and take "all practicable measures." Although such a treaty has little immediate impact, it may be very effective in providing a framework for future action. To accomplish this the treaty must establish a permanent secretariat and a conference of the parties that meets periodically. This process will result in the adoption of protocols, annexes, or action plans that set out precise measures to be taken by the parties. Environmental treaties have a dynamic character and flexibility that, if taken advantage of, enable the parties to respond to changed conditions and circumstances. An example is the 1992 Climate Change Convention, which was followed by such agreements as the Kyoto Protocol.

## Sustainable Development

Sustainable development is an overarching concept of international environmental law. The Rio Declaration and most treaties and other international understandings state sustainable development as their general goal. The origin of the idea of sustainable development is that environmental protection should not prevent economic growth, especially in the developing world. But what does this mean? Sustainable development is a complex issue containing both substantive and procedural elements. Its substantive component means that, although there is a right to development, resources should be used wisely and efficiently, pollution should be prevented or controlled, and environmental impacts should be minimized. Resources should be used so as not to endanger future needs, and recycling and reuse should be the norm. Procedurally, sustainable development means that environmental considerations will be integral to developmental decision making; there should be full disclosure of information and public participation in significant decisions. Nevertheless, there is an inherent ambiguity in the concept of sustainable development. The product of political compromise that seeks to integrate environmental protection and economic growth, sustainable development contains an undeniable tension that is difficult to resolve.

## Intergenerational Equity

The 1987 report of the World Commission on Environment and Development, *Our Common Future*, defined sustainable development as meeting the needs of the present "without compromising the ability of future generations to meet their own needs." Thus, intergenerational equity is an important concept in conservation and preservation efforts. Principle 3 of the Rio Declaration echoes this concern.

Few would argue with intergenerational equity as an abstract principle, but how is it to be realized? There is no accepted way to measure whether any action will harm any future generation, and there is no recognized advocate for future generation rights. This principle would seem to have limited utility. Intergenerational equity is, however, stated as a reason for the conclusion of many environmental treaties, such as, for example, the International Whaling Convention (1946). The Supreme Court of the Philippines has also cited this principle as a reason for allowing citizens to sue the government over excessive timber logging.[4]

## Common but Differentiated Responsibility

A fundamental but controversial principle of international environmental law is that, although all states have common responsibility for environmental amelioration, developed countries bear the greatest burden. This is based on the idea that the developed world has and continues to pollute more than developing countries. No specific differentiation of responsibility is defined by this principle, but its realization may be embedded in various ways in most environmental treaties. This principle has three aspects.

First, developing countries will not be called upon to bear the same corrective burden as developed countries. Rio Principle 11 makes this explicit, stating, "[Environmental] Standards applied by some countries may be inappropriate and of unwarranted economic and social cost to other countries, in particular developing countries."

Second, developing countries have a right to receive technical and financial help to comply with environmental obligations. This principle was partially implemented with the establishment of the Global Environmental Facility (GEF) in 1991, which provides funds for agreed-upon incremental costs of environmental measures in developing countries. Although the World Bank acts as trustee, GEF is operated by its own council; composed of thirty-two states balanced between donor and recipient countries, this council the manages GEF. Decisions require a double majority of 60 percent of all members and 60 percent (by contribution) of donors.

Third, Rio Principle 5 injects the idea of intragenerational equity, that there is an obligation to "decrease the disparities in standards of living and better meet the needs of the majority of the people of the world." This statement connects the common but differentiated responsibility idea to the right to development. Under Rio Principle 9, developed states also "should cooperate" to

[4] Minors Oposa v. Secretary of Environmant and Natural Resources, 33 ILM 173 (1994).

strengthen capacity building of developing states for sustainable development through the transfer of technology and scientific knowledge.

## Precautionary Principle

Article 15 of the Rio Declaration refers to the "precautionary approach" to protecting the global environment. This is the idea that "where there are threats of serious or irreversible damage, lack of full scientific certainty shall not be used as a reason for postponing cost-effective measures to prevent environmental degradation."

The precautionary principle is a feature of most international environmental treaties that deal with resources or environmental degradation. As a principle it is inherently flexible – it does not define the kind of threat that triggers its application, nor is it specific about measures to be taken. As a principle it can be adapted to specific treaties and particular circumstances.

All versions of the principle justify action when there is some evidence but not proof that a human practice is harming the environment. The central concept here is *causation* and the evidence necessary to establish it. First, it can justify taking action in the form of environmentally protective measures; second, it can remove a reason to avoid actions – scientific uncertainty cannot be used to avoid action – so that decisions can be made on other, clearer grounds; and third, it can justify a reversal of the burden of proof – instead of requiring proof by an environmental interest, the burden can be placed on the side that believes an environmental measure to be unnecessary.

The precautionary principle also makes possible a focus on risk and risk assessment. Scientific findings may be expressed in terms of risk either because limitations of inherent in data or because of the inability to conduct experimentation on human beings. The focus on risk makes possible a decision-making process that takes into consideration the degree and magnitude of the potential harm. The greater the risk, the greater role there is for precaution and for precautionary action. But the principle does not state what level of risk is socially acceptable or how to control any particular risk. Thus, invocation of the precautionary principle cannot be determinative.

## State Responsibility for Environmental Harm

The *Trail Smelter case* promulgated the principle that states are responsible for significant transboundary environmental harm. International law accordingly does not allow states to either conduct or permit activities within their territories that harm other states or the environment. This doctrine, called the *harm prevention principle*, is derived from the Latin maxim, *sic utere tuo, ut non laedas* – a principle of "good neighborliness" that is now a duty of customary international law. In its *Advisory Opinion on the Legality of the Threat or Use of Nuclear Weapons (1996)*,[5] the International Court of Justice affirmed that

The existence of the general obligation of states to ensure that activities within their jurisdiction and control respect the environment of other states and of areas beyond national control is now part of the corpus of international law relating to the environment.[6]

The harm prevention principle is now recognized by state practice and was restated in both the 1972 Stockholm Declaration (Principle 21) and the 1992 Rio Declaration (Principle 2). The U.N. International Law Commission has elaborated draft articles creating liability under international law for transboundary environmental damage.[7]

State responsibility under the harm prevention principle is now recognized as applying not only to transboundary harm but also to the global environment and to areas beyond the jurisdiction of all states, such as the oceans. Thus, the right to development is qualified, and integration of development and environmental protection is required.

Three aspects of the harm prevention principle are apparent: First is the duty to prevent harm, second is the duty to compensate for harm that has occurred, and third is the duty to cease or modify an activity that has caused harm.

However, uncertainty obscures many aspects of the harm principle. For example, is there state responsibility without fault?[8] What degree of damage is necessary before responsibility arises? These ambiguities make the harm prevention principle difficult to apply in particular circumstances. Thus, the development of specific international regimes through appropriate international agreements on a global, regional, and bilateral basis is essential.

## Cooperation

States are obliged to cooperate with each other and with relevant international institutions to deal with international environmental problems. This

---

[5]  1996 ICJ Rep. 226.                    [6] ICJ Rep. 226, para. 29.
[7]  Report of the ILC (2001) GAOR A/56/10.
[8]  Under the Draft Articles of the International Law Commission there is liability without fault for harm arising from hazardous activities (presumably nuclear and industrial accidents). ILC Doc. A/CN.4/L.662.

duty was first recognized in the case of shared natural resources. In the *Lac Lanoux* arbitration case (France and Spain, 1957), the tribunal posited a duty of notification and good faith negotiation with respect to a proposed diversion of water by France from a watercourse shared with Spain. Conflicting state interests must be reconciled through negotiations and mutual concessions. This duty of cooperation has been extended by state practice and treaties to include the management of transboundary risks posed by hazardous or potentially harmful activities, such as nuclear installations and factories near frontiers, continental shelf activities, and long-range transboundary pollution.

The Rio Declaration of 1992 codifies this duty of cooperation in several provisions. Principle 18 requires states to notify other states if natural disasters or other emergencies are likely to produce transboundary environmental effects. Principle 19 requires prior notification, good faith consultation, and the provision of relevant information to affected states before undertaking any activity likely to produce significant adverse transboundary environmental effects. Principle 17 requires an environmental impact assessment to be undertaken for such a proposed project. Thus, the cooperation duty can be summarized including the following components:

- prior and timely notification

- disclosure of relevant information

- consultation and good faith negotiation

- prior impact assessment

- environmental monitoring

The International Court of Justice addressed the duty of cooperation in the *Case Concerning the Gabcikovo-Nagymaros Dam (Hungary v. Slovakia)*; (1997).[9] In this case Hungary argued that environmental risks were grounds for terminating a treaty with Slovakia to build a series of dams on the River Danube. The court, although rejecting treaty termination, ruled that in implementing the treaty the parties were obliged to apply new and developing norms of environmental law relating to impact assessment and mitigation of environmental degradation. The parties were required to negotiate in good faith concerning how to adapt the project to meet new environmental requirements.

---

[9]  1997 ICJ Rep. 7.

## Common Concern

*The principle of common concern* recognizes an obligation on the part of all states to protect and restore the global environment, resources, and areas beyond the limits of national jurisdiction. The Rio Declaration (Principle 7) mandates a "global partnership" for this purpose. It constitutes an obligation to assist in the creation and maintenance of international environmental regimes to protect the global environment and areas beyond national jurisdiction.

A corollary of the principle of common concern is the concept of *equitable utilization*, an idea first developed for the law governing the use and allocation of shared resources. In the *Icelandic Fisheries* case,[10] the International Court of Justice called for the application of the principle to common property fishing stocks as well. Applied to global and common property resources, the equitable utilization principle has a dual aspect: (1) equitable allocation among all legitimate claimants and (2) equitable limitations on use to comport with the principle of sustainability. The equitable utilization principle requires a broad process of balancing of interests and consideration of all relevant circumstances.

An additional implication of the common concern principle is that all states have an interest in the enforcement of common concern rules and regimes. Under accepted principles of international law, violations of rules (so-called *erga omnes* obligations) that affect the collective interest of a group of states or the international community as a whole may be the subject of claims by any state.[11]

Should the principle of common concern be transformed into the idea that certain areas or resources are a common heritage of humankind? Two agreements, the 1979 Moon Treaty and the 1982 U.N. Convention on the Law of the Sea (UNCLOS), employ this phrase. The Moon Treaty uses the term "common heritage" to mean that the resources of the moon cannot be made subject to the sovereignty of any state. UNCLOS (Articles 136 and 137) states that the resources of the seabed and ocean floor beyond national jurisdiction are "the common heritage of mankind," which means not only are they subject to international management but also all states must share in any profits.

The United States has rejected both of these treaties primarily because of the common heritage idea. Moreover, the U.N. General Assembly rejected a proposal to designate the global climate as the common heritage of humankind

---

[10]  1974 ICJ Rep. 3.
[11]  International Law Commission, 2000 Draft Articles on State Responsibility, Articles 43 and 49, GAOR A/55/10.

in favor of the common concern formula. A case can be made that the continent of Antarctica should be designated a common heritage regime, but the Antarctic treaty system avoids the use of this term. The system of World Heritage Sites established under the 1972 World Heritage Convention does not create any independent authority for the management of these areas, and they remain under national control. Thus, the concept of the "common heritage of humankind" is controversial.

## The Polluter Pays Principle

The *polluter pays principle* is based upon the economic doctrine that the costs of pollution and environmental degradation should be borne by the party creating them and benefiting from the activity that produces the pollution. Under principles of classical economics, a market operates efficiently only if the business or firm making a product or service bears all the costs entailed by that activity. Pollution is an external cost, one not borne by the business involved. Thus, the market can be efficient only if the cost of pollution is "internalized"; that is, imposed on the business in question.

The polluter pays principle, adopted as Principle 16 of the Rio Declaration,[12] states that national authorities "should endeavor" to promote the internalization of environmental costs and that "in principle" the polluter should bear the costs of pollution. Despite this obvious flexibility, important points are involved in this principle.

First, not only states but also private companies and individuals are responsible for cleaning up and paying for environmental degradation. In the cases of pollution of the sea by oil spills and nuclear accidents, international treaties channel liability to the private operator of the facility responsible for the pollution.[13] In the future more international instruments may channel responsibility and liability directly to private actors.

Second, the polluter pays principle involves the use of economic instruments to internalize pollution costs. These instruments include the imposition of environmental taxes and charges, trading mechanisms, deposit and return fees, and recycling incentives. Such economic instruments can be used as supplements or in place of traditional command-and-control government regulation.

---

[12] The OECD in a series of recommendations in the 1970s first endorsed the polluter pays principle. OECD Recommendations C(72) 128 (1972); C(74) 223 (1974); and C(89) 88.
[13] Vienna Conventions, 1963 and 1997, impose strict liability on operators of nuclear facilities. The 1969 Civil Liability Treaty and 1992 Protocols place liability for oil pollution damage on the operator.

Third, private companies increasingly participate in voluntary codes of conduct, such as the U.N. Global Compact, a code of best practices. Most multinational companies have in place a company-wide environmental management system that goes beyond legal requirements, and most companies comply with the OECD Guidelines for Multinational Corporations.

Fourth, the polluter pays principle correlates with Principle 11 of the Rio Declaration mandating states to enact effective environmental legislation. States have an international law obligation to control pollution and environmental degradation *within* their territories and not just transboundary pollution. This obligation is appropriate because we live on one earth, and ecosystems and natural systems are interconnected without regard to political boundaries. Domestic pollution has a cumulative effect on the earth's environment.

## Public Participation

Principle 10 of the Rio Declaration requires states to provide information and encourage participation in environmental decision making by individual concerned citizens. This principle includes providing "effective access" to judicial and administrative proceedings to obtain redress if necessary.

## Implementation, Compliance, Effectiveness, and Enforcement

Principle 11 of the Rio Declaration requires states to enact effective environmental legislation to implement international treaty obligations. This is the first step toward compliance with treaty commitments. The state must also apply domestic laws and regulations in an effective manner.

If a state fails to comply with an environmental treaty, what can be done? The traditional remedies for noncompliance under international law are countermeasures and/or expulsion from the regime. Member states can also terminate their obligations toward the state in breach of the treaty. In the case of environmental treaties, however, such measures are counterproductive. Accordingly, most environmental regimes provide for compliance checks in the form of inspections, disclosure, and monitoring. Noncompliance triggers a special procedure that may involve consultations and technical and financial assistance.

There may be full compliance with a treaty, but still without effectiveness. For example, full compliance with the Kyoto Protocol will lower greenhouse gas emissions below 1990 levels only for a handful of developed countries, a beginning step but not enough to make much difference for the global climate. Effectiveness and compliance are different issues and must be separately considered.

## Dispute Settlement

Despite proposals for a specialist international environmental court, there does not seem to be any great need for such a tribunal. Environmental disputes often involve general international law questions; environmental law is not a self-contained, codified system. Indeed, there are a multiplicity of international regimes dealing with such disparate issues as climate change, chemicals in international trade, biological diversity, and other matters. There are already a wide variety of means of dispute settlement under general international law, and every environmental treaty sets out dispute settlement procedures. In 1993 the International Court of Justice created a special chamber for environmental cases, but no case has yet been brought before it. In 2003 the Permanent Court of Arbitration adopted special rules for environmental cases, but this court too has not been used.

States are very reluctant to submit environmental controversies to international dispute settlement. Environmental treaties typically provide for the settlement of disputes by negotiation or nonbinding conciliation. Binding adjudication of environmental controversies thus requires the agreement of all parties to the dispute.

## "Soft" Law – A Verdict

These "soft" principles of international environmental law developed over the past twenty-five years are still evolving. On the plus side we have made progress; on the minus side the rules are still so vague they can be easily ignored. The principles of international environmental law are still soft in the sense that either they are nonbinding recommendations or they are flexible enough to be circumvented at will. Only when translated into specific binding obligations in particular treaty regimes do they really have bite.

In the next sections of this chapter we consider the multilateral agreements that have been concluded to deal with particular environmental concerns.

### THE ATMOSPHERE

Protection of the earth's atmosphere requires both decreasing emissions from mobile (autos, trucks, and buses) and stationary sources (factories, refineries, power plants, and smelters) that directly damage humans, animals, and plants and also controlling emissions that threaten the integrity of the earth's natural systems that regulate climate and radiant energy from the sun.

## Long-Range Transboundary Pollution

When pollution emanates from a discrete source, such as a smelter near an international frontier, responsibility can be readily assigned and abatement action taken. More difficult is long-range transboundary pollution in which multiple pollution sources pollute the upper atmosphere and winds carry the contaminants long distances, sometimes thousands of miles. In this case, the contribution of each source to the problem is small and difficult to prove. Long-range transboundary air pollution is severe in many parts of the world. Two pollutants pose special problems: sulfur oxides (SOx) and nitrous oxides (NOx). Primarily coal-fired electricity-generating facilities and nonferrous ore smelters produce sulfur oxides; nitrous oxides are emitted by vehicles and by fuel combustion. Not only are these pollutants carried long distances by wind patterns but when they are aloft in the atmosphere they are also transformed into acids,[14] which then fall to earth most commonly as acid rain but also as acid fog, snow, and dust.

Despite the widespread nature of the problem, there are only two international regimes for the control of this kind of acid deposition – one in North America and one in Europe.

The North American Acid Rain Control Program was established in 1991 when the United States and Canada signed a Bilateral Air Quality Control Agreement[15] after more than ten years of arduous negotiations. This agreement commits both nations to reduce emissions of SOx and to enforce a permanent cap on such emissions. Both nations also agreed to employ technology-based controls to reduce NOx emissions. To monitor compliance, a permanent bilateral Air Quality Committee was created to operate within the International Joint Commission formed under the 1909 Boundary Waters Agreement between the two countries.

In order to comply with the mandated reductions, the Unied States operates an innovative emissions trading program that allows emitters the option of reducing emissions or purchasing excess allowances from other sources that have reduced their emissions more than necessary. This builds flexibility into

[14]  The resultant chemical formulas are: $H_2O + SO_2 = H_2SO_3$ (sulfuric acid); and $H_2O + NO_3 = H_2NO_4$ (nitric acid).
[15]  30 ILM 676 (1991).

## CAP AND TRADE – HOW IT WORKS

Cap and trade programs allow pollution reduction limits to be reached at lower cost. Consider the following example of two electric generating plants:

Plant A emits 600 tons of $CO_2$ each year while plant B emits 400 tons for an annual combined total of 1000 tons. The required cap on $CO_2$ emissions is 700 tons per year, a 30 percent reduction. Each plant is required to reduce emissions by the required 30 percent.

Under a traditional approach plant A would reduce its emissions by 180 tons and plant B would reduce its emissions to 120 tons (in both cases a reduction of 30 percent) to achieve the annual required limit of 700 tons. However, the cost of such reductions may well be different, depending on such factors as plant efficiency, the type of fuel involved, the plant's location, and whether pollution control equipment is already in use. Suppose, therefore, that this reduction would cost plant A an average of $50 per ton and plant B an average of $25 per ton.

In such a case it will be more efficient to achieve the required 30 percent reduction if plant A were to reduce emissions by 100 tons, and bargain with plant B for a purchase of 80 tons of reduction. Plant B would be willing to make such a trade if it could reduce by 200 tons and sell the extra 80 tons in excess of its reduction quota at a profit. This may be possible if, for example, the market price of pollution reduction is $30 per ton. In such a case plant B would make a profit of $400 on its trade with plant A, and plant A would realize a total savings of $1,600 over the cost of pollution controls. The total efficiency saving in such a case would be $2,000, and the required reduction of 30 percent would be met.

the program and allows reductions to be made as efficiently as possible. This cap and trade program has decreased emissions by more than 30 percent compared to 1990 levels (See "Cap and Trade – How It Works.")

The European system for the control of acid rain is the 1979 Geneva Convention on Long-Range Transboundary Air Pollution, which is accepted by over forty states and operates as an ongoing forum and framework for cooperation. The Geneva Convention has a permanent secretariat and an executive body, composed of advisors to governments of the parties, whose main task is to monitor compliance and the effectiveness of national policies. Although the original 1979 treaty contained only "soft" obligations, a series of protocols have been adopted mandating specific actions. For sulfur a first protocol signed in 1985 required a 30 percent reduction by 1993. A second protocol, signed in 1994 and in force since 1998, requires an innovative *critical loads approach*, which sets different reduction targets for different areas based upon actual mapping of sulpher oxide deposition patterns and sources. The critical loads are designed to reduce sulfur emissions to the point where human health and the environment are protected "without entailing excessive cost." A critical loads approach is also being devised for NOx. In 1991 a protocol dealing with low-level ozone was adopted that requires parties to either reduce emissions of volatile organic compounds by 30 percent or to stabilize emissions at specified levels. Two protocols adopted in 1998 mandate bans or controls on the air-borne deposition of persistent organic chemicals (pesticides and industrial chemicals) and heavy metals. As a result of these efforts, transboundary air pollution in Europe has fallen substantially according to every measure.

Although the North American program is not as advanced as that in Europe, the result has been a significant improvement in air quality. This demonstrates the benefits of international cooperation. In 2002, however, the Unied States took a unilateral decision to undermine the program's effectiveness. Under the U.S. Clean Air Act, new sources of pollution are subject to more stringent controls than existing sources. Until 2002, a significant modification of an existing source required compliance with the upgraded standards that apply to new sources. In 2002, however, the U.S. Environmental Protection Agency issued a new rule that exempts most equipment replacement from the new source standards. Canada protested this change, but to no avail.

## Ozone Depletion and Climate Change

There are two threats on a global scale to the atmosphere of the Earth – (1) depletion of stratospheric ozone that shelters us from the sun's ultraviolet radiation and (2) climate change, the greenhouse effect, that is responsible for increasing mean global temperatures. With respect to these concerns, Europeans have taken the leadership role, and the United States has been either a follower or absent altogether.

**Ozone Depletion.** A protective layer of ozone in the stratosphere (the atmospheric zone that is twelve to fifty kilometers above the earth) surrounds the earth, affording a natural shield against the harmful ultraviolet rays of the sun. A decrease or depletion of this ozone layer would mean an increase in the ultraviolet radiation that reaches earth. This would elevate the risk of skin cancer and cataracts in human beings and cause damage to plants, including crops and phytoplankton, the basis of the marine food chain.

Stratospheric ozone (chemical formula $O_3$) is formed initially when a molecule of oxygen ($O_2$) absorbs short-wave radiation and is split into two atoms of oxygen (O); each is then able to combine with other O atoms to form ozone. Photochemical reactions in the stratosphere ordinarily break down ozone at about the same rate it is formed, producing a natural balance between formation and depletion.

This natural balance is disturbed by a group of highly inert gases that were produced and used for industrial purposes in the twentieth century. The most common and destructive of these gases are chlorofluorocarbons (CFCs), particularly CFC-11 ($CFCL_3$) and CFC-12 ($CF_2CL_2$). CFCs were developed in the 1920s and came into widespread use as refrigerants, aerosol propellants, solvents, and cleaning agents. Their usefulness stemmed in part from their unique properties: They are virtually unreactive in the lower atmosphere, nontoxic, odorless, nonflammable, and noncorrosive, and they do not readily combine with other substances.

This characteristic of inertness means, however, that CFCs are extremely long lasting, and substantial quantities eventually make their way to the upper atmosphere unchanged. There they meet their match as strong ultraviolet radiation breaks them apart, liberating chlorine atoms (Cl) that destroy ozone by catalyzing its conversion into molecular oxygen. The process[16] is as follows. Step one – ultraviolet rays release stray atoms of Cl. Step two – the chlorine combines with ozone: $Cl + O_3 = ClO + O_2$. If a single atom of oxygen is further encountered, there is a subsequent reaction: $ClO + O = Cl + O_2$. This frees an additional atom of chlorine to destroy additional ozone. Because CFCs and other ozone-destroying chemicals[17] may remain in the atmosphere for 40 to 150 years, each chlorine atom may remove as many as 100,000 ozone molecules from the atmosphere during its life cycle. Thus, even a small amount of CFCs can have a devastating impact.[18]

The ozone-destroying reactions occur fastest on the surface of micro-ice crystals, so depletion is greatest in polar regions, particularly over Antarctica. Each year up to 95 percent of the stratospheric ozone is destroyed above Antarctica, ozone in the Artic is thinned about 60 percent, and there is measurable ozone loss over the entire planet except the equatorial regions.

But wonderful to relate, this crisis is being managed quite successfully by the international community. Its resolution was (and still is) far from a sure

---

[16] The role of CFCs in the destruction of the ozone layer was first exposed in a brilliant article by F. Sherwood Rowland and Mario Molina, "Stratospheric Sink for Chlorofluoromethanes: Chlorine Atoms-Catalyzed Destruction of Ozone," 239 *Nature* 810 (1974)

[17] Other ozone-destroying chemicals include: methane ($CH_4$), nitrous oxides ($N_2O$ and $NOx$), carbon monoxide (CO), carbon dioxide ($CO_2$), and certain sulfate aerosols (OCS and $CS_2$).

[18] Depletion of the ozone layer can also contribute to global warming in two ways: First, the sun's rays penetrate more deeply, changing the heat balance of the atmosphere, and second, CFCs trap radiant solar heat and are significant greenhouse gases.

thing despite the obvious seriousness of the problem, but more than twenty-five years of tortuous but skillful diplomacy is paying off. The story of how the world came to grips with ozone depletion is encouraging and hopeful.

The first step was hardly a step at all: After years of discussion and prodding by UNEP, forty-three nations (including sixteen developing countries) negotiated the Vienna Convention for the Protection of the Ozone Layer in 1985. This did no more than establish a basis for cooperation, research, and exchanges of information; however, a Conference of the Parties was established to review further developments. The latter was the key to future progress. As the consequences of ozone depletion became better understood and the public became involved, successive conferences of the parties introduced ever-stricter controls. The key first conference produced the Montreal Protocol in 1987, which mandated phased deep reductions in the production and consumption of eight different types of CFCs. There followed a series of further amendments and adjustments to the Montreal Protocol; every two years the Conference of the Parties convenes to assess progress and to decide on further steps. As a result, 176 nations are participating in this effort led by UNEP, the consumption and production of the worst ozone-destroying substances (ODS) have been banned, and virtually all others are being phased out by certain varying dates.[19]

If all parties to the Montreal Protocol continue to comply with the scheduled bans and reductions, the ozone layer will stabilize around the year 2050 and gradually restore itself thereafter. The fact that so many nations were able to agree to take action to deal with a major crisis and to phase out the use of over ninety varieties of ODS is a triumph of international diplomacy.

How was this possible? Six reasons explain this success.

1. First, the science was not in dispute: There was agreement on both the cause and effects of ozone depletion.

2. Second, the manufacture of CFCs and other ODS was concentrated in a few multinational companies. In the early 1980s powerful voices in the U.S. government and industry strongly opposed regulation on the grounds of incomplete scientific evidence. But Dupont Corporation, the largest producer, agreed to cooperate with the phase-out effort, and other companies reluctantly followed suit. Thus, there was minimal industry and interest group lobbying against the Montreal Protocol.

---

[19] The current schedule allows developing countries (so-called Article 5 countries) to continue to use hydrofluorocarbons until 2040, but this will probably be accelerated.

3. Third, substitutes were readily available for all the major uses of ODS, and the Montreal Protocol became "technology forcing," speeding their further development and manufacture.

4. Fourth, the total cost of the ODS phase-out was relatively low, estimated to be about $6 billion spread over several decades.

5. Fifth, the United States, the most important producer and consumer of ODS, overcame initial reluctance and cooperated with the phase-out. The United States ratified the Montreal Protocol in 1988 and enacted strong domestic legislation. The Europeans took the lead in calling for a speed-up of international controls.

6. Sixth, developing countries were persuaded to join both through the incentive of financial help and technology transfer and the threat of trade controls.

Nevertheless, in 2004 the United States regrettably backtracked and rejected the agreed-upon ban on the ODS, methyl bromide, which was set for total elimination in 2005. Citing concerns expressed by farm groups, the United States asked for and received a "critical use" exception that allows this chemical, which is used as a fumigant, to continue to be used in 2005 and beyond.

The Montreal Protocol regime features an innovative noncompliance procedure to enforce the commitments of the parties and to ensure that obligations are kept. An Implementation Committee consisting of ten parties elected for two-year terms heads this effort; there are procedures to ensure equitable geographical distribution of the committee members. The Implementation Committee receives reports both from parties who may have concerns about the compliance of other parties and from parties that are having trouble complying. It investigates and makes recommendations. If these are ignored, a Meeting of the Parties can take a variety of measures, including providing assistance, issuing warnings, and suspending privileges under the Protocol concerning such matters as trade, industrial rationalization, transfer of technology, and financial assistance.

**Climate Change.** In the Clinton administration, under the leadership of Vice President Al Gore, the United States in 1998 joined most of the other nations of the world in signing the Kyoto Protocol, the global pact designed to reduce the greenhouse gases emitted onto the atmosphere that contribute to the phenomenon of climate change or, more popularly, global warming. This decision was politically unpopular from the beginning: Shortly after the Kyoto Protocol was signed the U.S. Senate passed a nonbinding resolution 95–0 rejecting the pact because it placed no emission controls on developing countries, such as China and India.

In March 2001, the day before an important meeting of Environmental Ministers of the Americas was to begin in Montreal, President George W. Bush announced his rejection of the Kyoto Protocol. In an article the next day in the New York Times, David Sandalow, a Clinton administration official who helped negotiate the accord, called this rejection "a textbook case of unilateral diplomacy, which...always brings resentment." He was right, at least as far as the predicted resentment was concerned; rejection of the Kyoto Protocol ranks right behind the invasion of Iraq as a source of international resentment toward America.

Climate change refers to alterations in the earth's climate systems that may occur due to increased concentrations of greenhouse gases in the atmosphere. Certain gases – carbon dioxide, methane, and nitrous oxide – earn the name "greenhouse gases" because, like a glass greenhouse, these gases allow sunlight to pass through the atmosphere while trapping heat or infrared radiation close to the earth's surface. If all other factors remain constant (such as forests and clouds, which affect the capacity of the earth to remove these gases from the air), increases in greenhouse gases will lead to global warming and other alterations in climate.

There is now ample evidence that the climate of the earth is undergoing relatively rapid change (see Figure 7.1). As a whole the climate is warming by an indeterminate amount, although certain geographical areas such as Western Europe may experience colder temperatures because of changes in ocean currents (in this case the Gulf Stream, which provides Europe with a relatively mild climate). The exact consequences of this changing climate are difficult to predict, but there will be rapid changes in ecosystems and crop patterns and changing conditions of rainfall and drought. The levels of the oceans, already rising during the twentieth century, will rise further, perhaps forcing the evacuation of some coastal cities and low lying island areas (the Maldives and Cook Islands, in particular). The U.S. NASA (National Atmospheric and Space Administration), which tracks sea-level rise all over the world, says that the sea has risen for the last 50 years at a rate of 0.7 of an inch each year, and this rise has accelerated to an annual rate of 0.12 the past dozen years.[20]

Rapid global climate change coupled with projected increases in human populations during the twenty-first century adds up to a recipe for a global

[20] "NASA able to pinpoint changes in sea-levels," www.washingtonpost.com, visited October 8, 2005.

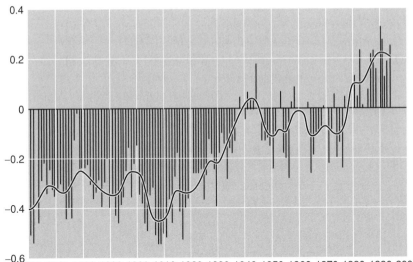

Figure 7.1. The rise in global temperature since 1860. Combined global land, air and sea surface temperatures relative to 1961–90 (anomaly in degrees C). *Source*: IPCC.

disaster of epic proportions. According to the Intergovernmental Panel on Climate Change (IPCC)[21] – a joint scientific body established by UNEP and the World Meteorological Organization in 1988 – the consequences of climate change will include the following:

- ocean and sea-level rise, alteration of ocean circulation patterns, and loss of sea ice cover

- widespread changes in coastal and marine ecosystems

- weather intensity – a more vigorous hydrological cycle

- public health impacts – certain diseases (malaria) will become more widespread

- threatened agriculture and food security in many areas

- increase in deserts and desertification

- changes in water resources

- biological diversity loss

Of course, there are natural changes in the earth's climate over time, but what is unique to our time is the rapidity of change and the fact that it is anthropogenic – caused by human activity. The changes are being caused

[21] IPPC, *The Science of Climate Change* (Third Assessment Report, 2001).

primarily by the emissions into the atmosphere of certain gases that are the product of the combustion of fossil fuels – carbon dioxide ($CO_2$), methane ($CH_4$), nitrous oxides (NOx), hydrofluorocarbons (HCFC), perfluorocarbons (PFC), sulfur hexafluoride (SF 6), and others. The emission of these gases disrupts the earth's natural carbon cycles.

The first of these carbon cycles occurs when plants break down carbon from the atmosphere and it accumulates in their biomass; this carbon is returned to the atmosphere in the form of $CO_2$ through the decay of organic matter and by animals that consume plants through their respiration and decomposition after death. The oceans also absorb and release vast quantities of $CO_2$. These processes keep the quantity of carbon in the atmosphere fairly stable over time.

A second carbon cycle takes place on the scale of geological time: Plant and animal remains are locked into sedimentary deposits where they remain for hundreds of millions of years under natural conditions. These remains are sources of our fossil fuels – coal, oil, and natural gas. The natural release of this carbon occurs only when the geological formations are exposed to weathering and erosion.

During the past century humankind has greatly accelerated this second carbon cycle by the unrestricted burning of fossil fuels. We continue to release from 6.5 to 8.5 billion tons of carbon into the atmosphere each year. Ice core samples from the Antarctic and Greenland ice caps show that atmospheric concentrations of anthropogenic greenhouse gases – carbon dioxide, methane, and nitrous oxide – have increased by about 30 percent, 145 percent, and 15 percent, respectively, in the industrial era. From 1958 to 2000 atmospheric concentrations of carbon dioxide, an especially critical greenhouse gas, have increased from about 318 parts per million to about 379 parts per million. This increase is continuing at an accelerated rate – about 2 parts per million annually. Experts[22] predict that at somewhere above the threshold of 450 parts per million, the world will be at a point of no return. In effect, an ecological time bomb is clicking.

No one can predict with certainty either the extent or timing of global warming, but there is a consensus that it is occurring. During the twentieth century the average surface temperature of the earth increased 0.5 degrees Celsius (0.8 degrees above the average world temperature in 1750, before the Industrial Revolution); computer models developed by the IPCC predict a further increase of between 1.4 to 5.8 degrees Celsius by the year 2100. Such a rapid change in climate is beyond our experience. We have no way of knowing

---

[22] "Meeting the Climate Change Challenge," Report by the U.K. Institute for Public Policy Research, the U.S. Center for American Progress, and the Australia Institute (2005).

its consequences; they are beyond our capabilities of prediction. Adaptation may be difficult but possible if changes in climate are slow and gradual. However, many scientists[23] predict abrupt changes as climate-modulating systems are pushed to extremes, and the resulting chaos would pose a challenge to world order and civilization.

What can and should be done? Obviously, worldwide cooperative action is needed. Like ozone depletion, climate change is beyond the capacity of any one or group of nations to solve. Will it be possible to duplicate the successful effort to control ozone-depleting substances in order to stabilize or reverse climate change? This is the great question we face at the beginning of the twenty-first century. So far the outlook is not good.

A first step toward a worldwide climate change regime modeled on the Vienna Convention/Montreal Protocol regime was taken at the UNCED Conference in Rio de Janeiro in 1992. All the participants – 176 nations – signed the UN Framework Convention on Climate Change, a binding treaty that recognized the problem and called for "precautionary measures to anticipate, prevent or minimize the causes of climate change and mitigation of its adverse effects." However, this Framework Convention did not mandate concrete actions to reduce greenhouse gases. The parties to the Convention were required only to limit their emissions and enhance their carbon "sinks" and reservoirs "with the aim of returning . . . to their 1990 levels of these anthropogenic emissions." But as was the case with the ozone regime, the Framework Convention created a Conference of the Parties and an ongoing process to strengthen international action against climate change.

In the decade of the 1990s the "soft law" injunction of the 1992 Framework Convention to reduce greenhouse gas emissions to 1990 levels was largely forgotten as states went back to business as usual and fossil fuel prices remained low. Finally a breakthrough was made at a meeting of the Framework Convention's Conference of the Parties in 1997 – the Kyoto Protocol was agreed to and specific reduction commitments were assigned to thirty-eight so-called Annex I parties – the relatively developed countries of the world responsible for most greenhouse gas emissions (see "Greenhouse Gas Reduction Commitments by Annex I Parties to the Kyoto Protocol").

The Kyoto Protocol, signed by 170 nations, requires Annex I parties to show "demonstrable progress" by 2005, but there is a flexible five-year deadline for

---

[23] Peter Schwartz and Doug Randall, "An Abrupt Climate Change Scenario and Its Implications for United States National Security" (2003), available at www.pentagon.gov; pentagon_climatechange.pdf.>.

**GREENHOUSE GAS REDUCTION COMMITMENTS BY ANNEX I PARTIES TO THE KYOTO PROTOCOL**

All of the Annex I parties have agreed to fulfill their commitments except the United States and Australia. Reductions as a percentage from the base year 1990:

**92:** Austria, Belgium, Bulgaria, Czech Republic, Estonia, Denmark, European Community, Finland, Germany, France, Greece, Italy, Latvia, Lithuania, Liechtenstein, Luxembourg, Monaco, Netherlands, Portugal, Romania, Slovakia, Slovenia, Spain, Sweden, Switzerland, United Kingdom
**93:** United States
**94:** Canada, Hungary, Japan, Poland
**95:** Croatia
**100:** New Zealand, Russia, Ukraine
**101:** Norway
**108:** Australia
**110:** Iceland

final compliance – from 2008 to 2012. As for the method of compliance and how to cut emissions, each party can decide for itself, but the Kyoto Protocol introduces several important flexibility provisions to make compliance easier.

First, trading of emission credits is allowed between Annex I parties. This means if one Annex I party has reduced more than its mandate, the excess can be sold or transferred to another Annex I party that is having trouble meeting its reduction target. This is a cooperative solution to make compliance easier. Many countries, such as Russia and countries of Eastern Europe, are expected to have reduction credits available for sale.

Trading of pollution allowances will also take place between individual firms that emit greenhouse gases. To comply with the Kyoto Protocol Annex I, countries are expected to assign emission caps to larger emitters of greenhouse gases. These companies will be assigned pollution allowances, and emissions in excess of allowances will be illegal. If a polluter is unable to stay within its allowance allotment, it must purchase additional allowances from companies that have cut emissions by more than their allowances mandate. This system also produces efficiency and lower costs. For example, if a utility company finds that it will cost $1 million for equipment to meet its allowance requirements, it has a choice: It can purchase the equipment or it can buy sufficient pollution allowances, whichever is less costly.

Because many firms will rely on trading allowances, international markets for trading allowances are developing. A multibillion euro market has begun in Europe as the European Union has adopted a program to comply with Kyoto. This is a whole new industry that is a direct result of the Climate Change regime.

A second flexibility mechanism allowed under the Kyoto Protocol is called Joint Implementation (JI). JI allows reduction units to be generated in an Annex I country by a specific project that reduces emissions or increases removals; these reduction units can then be sold to other Annex I countries. Thus, country A could modernize a utility-generating plant to cut emissions, and the reductions can be sold to country B. JI would also allow a private enterprise in country A to sell reduction credits to a private company in country B. Finally, JI would allow high-cost countries to benefit from purchasing reductions from countries where costs are lower.

The Clean Development Mechanism (CDM) of the Kyoto Protocol allows cooperation between Annex I countries and non-Annex I (developing) countries. Annex I parties or their private companies may fund emission reduction projects or activities in developing countries that produce emission reductions; these reductions can be counted toward the Annex I party's compliance. On the level of the private company, CDM could mean that a company in an Annex I country can fulfill its reduction duty under national law by funding a reforestation project in a developing country.

These flexibility mechanisms will have a tremendous impact on business around the world. International investors will have totally new incentives to consider. Under JI and CDM a foreign investor – either a government or a private company – can pay for reduced emissions abroad and count the reductions as its own. This may lead to a whole new style of investing. For example, a Western European company might consider modernizing Russia's leaky gas pipeline network or its polluting coal-guzzling power plants. Such an investment that would have been foolish before Kyoto may now become a sure-fire winner.

After the Kyoto Protocol was signed, a controversy among the parties arose concerning the interpretation of Article 3.3, which allows parties to meet their targets by counting the net changes in greenhouse gas emissions resulting from "human induced land use change and . . . afforestation, reforestation, and deforestation." In order to ensure that emission reductions would be the principal mechanism for compliance, the Conference of the Parties adopted the Bonn Agreement in 2001, which put a ceiling of 2 percent on the amount of credits an Annex I party can take for forest management activities. The Kyoto parties, most of all the European members, wish to avoid a business-as-usual scenario and seek to make the Kyoto obligations a prelude to greater future emission reductions.

The Bonn Conference of the Parties also adopted compliance-monitoring and enforcement provisions. A Compliance Committee has two branches: a facilitative branch to assist all parties to meet their commitments and an enforcement branch to resolve contested issues and to determine compliance. Penalties for noncompliance include the assignment of increased reduction targets and withdrawal of trading privileges.

Will the Kyoto Protocol work? Will the climate change regime save us from the adverse effects of global warming? The good news is that the Kyoto Protocol entered into force in February 2005. But even with perfect compliance, Kyoto would reduce greenhouse gas emissions by only 5.2 percent relative to 1990 levels. Yet, even this small reduction will not be achieved, if for no other reason than that the United States, responsible for over 30 percent of total greenhouse gas emssions, is not participating. President George W. Bush in 2001 formally withdrew from the Kyoto regime on the ground that it would damage the U.S. economy. The United States and Australia are the only Annex I countries that took this view; thirty-six other industrialized countries accept Kyoto and are committed to making the emission reductions by 2012.

A second major problem is that, unlike the Montreal Protocol, developing countries have no specific reduction obligations under Kyoto. At current rates of growth, China will overtake the United States as the world's leading greenhouse gas emitter in 2015, and developing countries' emissions (primarily China and India) will reach 50 percent of the total by 2040, and after that date will continue to grow unchecked.

Thus, two deep political divisions, the split between developing and industrialized countries and the divide between the United States and its major allies, particularly the nations of the European Union, stymie international progress over climate change.

**Climate Change Policy after 2012.** If progress stops with Kyoto, the climate change regime will be only an exercise in futility. Therefore it is not only urgent that Kyoto be implemented but also that the United States must be pressured to join, as well as most developing countries. The Kyoto program must be viewed only as the first step. Because additional emission cuts may not be feasible for developed countries already struggling to comply with Kyoto, the focus should now be placed on preservation of forests and reforestation. One tree sequesters about one ton of $CO_2$ per year. Future Conferences of the Parties to the Climate Change regime should combine reduction of greenhouse gases with a worldwide program of preservation of forest ecosystems, particularly in tropical countries. Forests are currently diminishing in many parts of the world. This has an adverse impact on biological diversity, as well as on climate change. Forest preservation properly should go hand in hand with emission reduction.

Climate change is a problem of global security that will be high on the international agenda for the entire century. A multifaceted strategy is needed of mandatory emission reductions combined with economic incentives and the development of new and improved energy technologies. The international community should adopt a specific target ceiling for atmospheric levels of carbon dioxide – say 450 parts per million – and all countries, whether developing or industrialized, whose emissions exceed a certain specified level should be required to participate in a long-term strategy going beyond the Kyoto requirements.

The Climate Change regime cannot succeed without U.S. participation and leadership. U.S. participation would put pressure on developing countries to join and would inject greater value into the Kyoto flexibility mechanisms of trading, JI, and CDM. The U.S. government claims that Kyoto would harm the American economy, but the opposite is probably the reality. Unless it joins, the United States will be excluded from the new multibillion-dollar market in pollution allowances, and American investors will not be able to take advantage of JI and CDM projects and profits. Phased reductions in greenhouse gas emissions would not hurt the U.S. economy. For example, the United Kingdom is cutting back to 1990 emission levels by producing more of its energy from renewable sources, mainly wind power. Britain projects a 60 percent reduction in $CO_2$ emissions by 2050 at an annual cost of only 0.01 percent of GDP.[24] Energy, particularly fossil fuels, is so cheap in the United States that there is great waste; Europe and Japan consume far less energy per capita, yet maintain standards of living as high as those in the United States. Emission reductions would improve the air, and consuming less energy would foster another necessary goal – decreasing oil imports from the unstable Middle East.

Sooner or later the United States will pay an economic price if it remains *outside* the Climate Change regime. For example, the Kyoto parties may propose an energy tax on U.S. imports that will equalize the energy tax levied

---

[24] A study by the U.S. Energy Information Administration (EIA) released on April 16, 2005 found that mandatory limits on carbon dioxide and other greenhouse gases in the United States would not significantly affect average economic growth rates through 2025. The EIA estimated that the cost per household of using a market-based approach to limit greenhouse gases would be $78 per year.

on domestic products. If this happens, American industry will not avoid energy taxes but will have to pay foreign governments, who will raise revenue from U.S. nonparticipation in Kyoto. Unilateralism may thus backfire on the United States in the end.

Another problem with current American energy policy is the growing dependence on imported energy supplies, especially imported oil. Oil imports – primarily from the Middle East – now constitute 58 percent of our oil supply and are predicted to rise to 68 percent by 2025. As Senator Richard Durbin of Illinois puts it, "As long as America's energy needs are tied to the interests and profits of [international] oil cartels, we have no control over our future."[25] Both President Bush and U.S. Congressional leaders have urgently called for action to wean the country from dependence on foreign oil, but there is no agreement about how to do so. Adherence to the Kyoto Protocol would be key because reducing greenhouse gas emissions would spur energy efficiency and reduce at least the rate of increase of oil consumption.

Political leaders and institutions have great difficulty dealing with long-range issues, such as climate change. As with the crisis in Social Security and Medicare, our political leaders mask realities and refuse to spend political capital to deal with problems that will arise only after they are safely in retirement. When President Bush stated that joining Kyoto would damage the U.S. economy, did he take into consideration the risk of future economic breakdown and chaos that we incur by not joining? Did he weigh the damage to U.S. interests caused by breaking on this important policy matter with U.S. friends and allies?

Sometime during the twenty-first century the era of cheap energy based on fossil fuel availability will end. Experts differ on the timing; some think the rise in the price of oil in 2004 presages permanent higher prices,[26] whereas others believe prices will come down as they have in the past. But two realities mean there will be rising prices at some point: (1) World-proven reserves of oil and gas are dwindling faster than new discoveries, and (2) the areas of the world where reserves are concentrated are politically unstable. The energy policy of the United States, which is almost wholly oriented to more supply, should be balanced by market-based mechanisms to reduce demand.

Rather than waiting for the chaos of climate change and higher energy prices, the world should act to reduce emissions and to stimulate energy

---

[25] Quoted by Carl Hulse, "Senators Split on Ways to Reduce Oil Imports," *International Herald Tribune*, June 17, 2005.

[26] The International Monetary Fund predicts a permanent and continuous rise in the price of oil for the next several decades. *Japan Times*, April 9, 2005, p 17.

efficiency through environmental taxes and gradual increases in the prices of fossil fuels. This would spur the development of new energy technologies, such as new solar technologies, advanced fuel cells, gas-electric hybrid engines, and advanced design wind turbines. The inevitable transition to new sources of energy will be facilitated. Kyoto is not only good environmental policy; it is good energy policy as well.

**Climate Change and U.S. Industry.** More and more companies in the United States, including large utility companies, are calling for mandatory controls on greenhouse gas emissions.[27] These calls belie the claim that such controls will harm the U.S. economy. Why is this happening? The reason is that, in this era of globalization, the world economy is so interconnected that, with virtually every industrialized country now in the process of implementing the Kyoto regime, U.S. companies are finding they must participate even if the United States does not. And they are finding that as long as the United States remains outside Kyoto, they must participate at a competitive disadvantage.

How are U.S. companies involved in the Kyoto process?

First, all U.S. companies with facilities in one or more of the thirty-six Kyoto countries must fully comply with applicable mandatory controls. For example, a U.S.-owned factory in Europe is subject to the E.U. "cap and trade" regulatory system that initially imposes individual emission limits on over 12,000 facilities and levies heavy fines for violations. This system is slated to expand in 2008. In order to comply, a company must surrender allowances to cover its emissions; these allowances can be bought and sold in the EU Emissions Trading System, which began to function in 2005.

Second, U.S. companies with facilities in developing countries can participate in the Kyoto regime though the Clean Development Mechanism, which allows emission-reduction projects to generate reduction credits that can be sold in industrialized countries.

Third, although U.S. companies cannot directly sell emission reduction credits into the Kyoto market, they can enter into joint ventures with Kyoto country companies, particularly in developing countries, and thereby generate a profit on any reduction credits.

---

[27] For example, in May 2005 Jeffrey Immelt, the chief executive of General Electric, announced that GE will double investments in energy and environmental technology to prepare for what he sees as a huge global market for products that help reduce greenhouse gas emissions. John Stowell at Cinergy, a utility based in Cincinnati, says, "We want this issue addressed sooner rather than later because we have to start building new power plants. It's tough to move into a billion dollar plus program without knowing the rules of the road." *International Herald Tribune*, June 7, 2005, p. 15.

In brief, reducing and trading greenhouse gas emissions are evolving into a multi-billion dollar global business. Within a few years a huge, worldwide trading market for carbon and greenhouse gas emissions will come into being. This is predicted to make compliance with the Kyoto Protocol much cheaper than anticipated; carbon allowances are surprisingly cheap, and the price is expected to fall as global trading expands. U.S. companies will be unable to participate fully in this global market; they may fall behind in energy-saving technological innovations because they will not face mandatory controls. Competitor companies, particularly in Europe, may lobby for an energy import tax on U.S. imports, and this may spark an international trade row. Financial service companies and U.S. banks may similarly lose out on business opportunities, particularly the financing of investments in developing countries. The United States is likely to find it impossible to remain the world leader in the development of energy-saving technology and products that reduce greenhouse gas emissions.

With the growing support for mandatory action from U.S. business, the controls enacted by several U.S. states, including California and New York, and increasing international pressure, the United States will find it difficult to maintain its present policy of encouraging only "voluntary" emission reductions.

## THE OCEANS

### Ocean Governance

On April 1, 2001, a U.S. Navy EP-3E reconnaissance plane on a routine information-gathering mission was flying over the South China Sea about eighteen nautical miles off the coast of China. Suddenly, two Chinese fighter jets appeared and began harassment maneuvers, repeatedly flying into close formation with the EP-3E. After several passes, one of the Chinese jets clipped the EP-3E's wing. As a result, the Chinese jet spiraled out of control and crashed into the ocean below. The larger EP-3E with its crew of twenty-four was damaged and unable to return to base; it made an emergency landing on the Chinese island of Hainan.

This "spy-plane incident," as the world press called it, was the first major foreign policy flap of the Bush administration. China was holding an American plane and its twenty-four crew members. The initial reaction of Bush's team was to condemn China and to demand immediate release of the EP-3E's crew. Soon it was realized that, however good this sounded to the American public, it was not going to accomplish much with the Chinese authorities. China was in the driver's seat. The United States was forced to back down and to say it was "very sorry" for the death of the Chinese pilot and the crash of the Chinese plane.

The EP-3E controversy was fundamentally a difference of opinion over the international laws governing the oceans of the world. China maintained that under the 1982 U.N. Convention on the Law of the Sea (UNCLOS), it has the right to control overflight in its exclusive economic zone (EEZ), an area of ocean extending 200 nautical miles off its coasts. This is incorrect; under both the Law of the Sea treaty and customary international law, airplanes have a right of transit over the EEZs of the world, as well as over the high seas. A coastal state can prohibit overflight only in its territorial sea, the band of ocean waters twelve nautical miles offshore.

The United States was in the right in the EP-3E controversy, but was at a disadvantage in asserting its claim on legal grounds because it is one of the only states in the world not to accept the UNCLOS. In dealing with China in the aftermath of the EP-3E incident, the United States would have received more international support and would have been in a stronger position if it had more forcefully asserted its rights under international law. The United States asserts its rights in the oceans only on the basis of customary law, but customary law is weaker than treaty law.

The oceans – covering more than two-thirds of the planet – are traditionally a common property resource open to all for navigation, fishing, mineral extraction, and disposal of wastes. In the twentieth century with the increasing use of ocean resources, a revolution in ocean governance occurred. Under the UNCLOS, binding legal rules now govern all of the ocean and its resources. There is now an international ocean regime in the classic sense as international relations scholars define the term: "a set of principles, norms, rules and decision-making procedures around which actors' expectations converge."[28]

The UNCLOS is so comprehensive that it serves as a kind of constitution of ocean governance. Although the United States applies many of the rules concerning the seas as customary international law, it is excluded from many forums, decisions, and other advantages by its failure to accept the regime.

The UNCLOS divides ocean space into zones and defines the rights of states – both coastal and noncoastal states – in each area. The territorial sea is sovereign territory of the coastal state out to twelve nautical miles subject only to the right of the innocent passage of ships. The exclusive economic

---

[28] S. D. Krasner, *International Regimes* 2 (1983).

zone (EEZ) extends 200 miles offshore from the coast to confer jurisdiction and control over living and nonliving resources (fish and minerals). The continental shelf extends at least 200 miles and may run out to 350 miles in order to give coastal states rights to mineral development. Beyond these zones are the high seas. Beneath the high seas lies the deep seabed, which is the "common heritage of humankind," administered by a special International Seabed Authority. Navigation and shipping are facilitated to be compatible with the new zones. A new International Tribunal for the Law of the Sea is functioning to resolve disputes, though states may choose among a variety of options for dispute settlement. Because the United States was not a party to UNCLOS, it was unable to challenge China and to test its claims in an international tribunal.

## Marine Pollution

An extensive system of treaties deals with pollution of the marine environment. Four categories may be distinguished: the UNCLOS, regional seas agreements, general multilateral treaties, and bilateral treaties.

The UNCLOS deals comprehensively but in general terms with marine pollution control. An important feature is the legal duty on all parties to protect the marine environment as a whole, including the high seas. Moreover, "rare and fragile ecosystems" and "the habitat of depleted, threatened, and endangered species and other forms of marine life" must be "protected and preserved."[29] This ecosystem approach goes beyond former requirements. The UNCLOS also mandates control of all sources of marine pollution: from land-based sources, the atmosphere, vessels, and seabed and national mineral development activities.[30] All states' parties must apply and enforce "international rules and standards established through competent organizations." Thus, UNCLOS is a framework for the elaboration of specific controls.

The UNCLOS breaks new ground in the enforcement of pollution control rules. "Flag" state enforcement (by the country where the ship is registered), which is traditionally weak or nonexistent because of the common practice of registering ships under "flags of convenience," such as Panama and Liberia, is supplemented by enforcement by the port state – any port of call can seize a substandard ship or otherwise require compliance with international standards. Coastal states can also apply environmental rules in their exclusive economic zones and can enforce them against ships navigating in their coastal zones.

---

[29] UNCLOS, Art. 194.          [30] Ibid., Arts. 207–212.

Some twenty regional agreements exist to protect the marine environment. UNEP inaugurated its Regional Seas Program in 1974, and the first and most developed of such programs, the Barcelona Agreement for the Protection of the Mediterranean Sea against Pollution, dates from 1976. The Barcelona Agreement is a framework treaty that was followed by protocols dealing with particular issues: specially protected areas and biological diversity, dumping, land-based pollution, seabed pollution, and hazardous waste. Additional UNEP regional seas programs exist for the Persian Gulf, the Red Sea and Gulf of Aden, the Black Sea, the East African side of the Indian Ocean, the Latin American side of the South Pacific, the West African side of the South Atlantic, and the Caribbean. In Europe there are special agreements on the North Sea and the Baltic Sea. The advantage of regional programs is that they allow integrated measures to be adopted for both marine and coastal areas, and they establish a process for continuing progress if there is sufficient political will.

Multilateral antipollution agreements are used to deal with pollution from ships. The 1973/78 MARPOL Convention is an IMO creation that enforces detailed pollution regulations and mandatory equipment standards for world merchant shipping. MARPOL prevents and regulates oil and chemical pollution as well as dumping of plastics, sewage, and garbage. Flag states have responsibility to inspect their vessels at periodic intervals and to issue pollution prevention certificates. Port states may check compliance whenever the vessel enters port. The MARPOL rules are supplemented by another IMO program, the International Convention of the Safety of Life at Sea (SOLAS, 1974). In 2002 SOLAS brought into effect the International Management Code for the Safe Operation of Ships and for Pollution Prevention (ISM Code), which focuses on the human element as a means of preventing pollution and promoting safety. The ISM Code requires the adoption of a safety and environmental protection policy, instructions and procedures for crews, and emergency response training.

The Ocean Dumping Convention (1972) regulates the dumping of wastes at sea. A protocol adopted in 1996 now prohibits the ocean disposal of radioactive and hazardous wastes. Certain categories of waste, such as sewage sludge and dredged material, can only be dumped in designated areas. The Dumping Convention adopts the precautionary principle that everything that is not specifically permitted is prohibited.

Oil pollution of the oceans, whether accidental or operational, is regulated by a series of IMO Conventions adopted beginning in 1954. The centerpiece is an Oil Pollution Liability and Compensation Scheme that imposes liability on ship operators and pays oil pollution claims, including fishermen's claims and restoration of environmental damage. In 2004 a similar scheme, the Hazardous and Noxious Substances Convention (1996), came into force to deal with the problem of hazardous chemicals.

A striking fact is that the United States has not played a leading role in any of these important initiatives and has actively sought to weaken or destroy some of these regimes. It remains outside UNCLOS and does not participate in the IMO oil or hazardous substances civil liability schemes. Despite U.S. recalcitrance, the prevention of marine pollution is an environmental success story. Both operational and accidental pollution from ships has been dramatically curtailed in the past twenty years. All claims to IMO's International Oil Pollution Compensation Fund have been paid promptly and in full, and the degree of compliance with international standards is high. The major threat to the marine environment today is from land-based sources.

## Fisheries

In March 1995, Canadian gunboats seized the *Estai*, a Spanish fishing trawler that was fishing for turbot in international waters in the North Atlantic just outside Canada's 200-mile exclusive economic zone. Spain and the European Union protested that the *Estai* was in the right and Canada had no business policing international waters. Canada claimed a moral though not a legal right to act – the *Estai* was destroying its turbot fishery that straddled the high seas. Only 2 percent of the turbot in the *Estai's* cargo hold had reached spawning age, and its net had an illegal small mesh. Canada's Fisheries Minister exhibited the net – seventeen stories tall – at the next U.N. fisheries conference that same month.

The case of the *Estai* dramatized the fact that the natural bounty of the oceans is limited. Every fishery in the world is in decline and in urgent need of conservation. Marine fish are being depleted by a double whammy of degradation of natural habitats and modern industrial fishing methods.

A fishery is a common property resource that presents inherent management difficulties. There is no limit on those who may fish; all comers are welcome. But because the fish are common property and belong to no one until they are caught, there is no incentive for even minimal conservation. So an unregulated fishery will inevitably lead to depletion.

But management is also difficult. One option is to limit the number of fish that can be caught. The most common management limit is known as *maximum sustainable yield* (MSY), the greatest quantity that can be caught over a given period without depleting the desirable size of the total stock. But even for a single stock, MSY is difficult to determine; there will be temptations to err on the side of exploitation, not on the side of caution. Moreover, different fishery stocks are often interrelated so that the MSY for a single stock is meaningless. The interrelationships are difficult to define, making determination of the MSY even more elusive.

A second problem is that the absence of any limit on the number of people who can enter a fishery will drive down the rate of return for all fishermen. In the long term, total revenue from the fishery will tend to equal the total cost of fishing. When this happens the usual solution is government subsidies. This happens on such a large scale that worldwide fishery subsidies are estimated by the World Trade Organization (WTO) to be about $300 billion. Such subsidies are economically distorting and stimulate further overfishing. The WTO has proposed decreasing fishery subsidies without success. It is no wonder that all fisheries are declining.

Not only are subsidies difficult to abandon but also the regulatory options are political poison. One method is to set a limit on the total allowable catch (TAC) of various stocks and then allocate it by some method, such as holding an auction. This is economically efficient, but favors richer fishing interests. A second regulatory technique is to set limits on fishing equipment by prescribing such elements as net size and banning drift nets and long lines, fishing lines twenty or thirty miles long with, 1000 or more baited hooks. Third, certain areas can be off-limits to protect spawning populations, or fishing can be permitted only at certain times of year. Fourth, limits can be placed on the number of vessels, their size, or the number of days they may fish.

By allocating EEZ and continental shelf rights to coastal states, the UNCLOS places most of the world's fisheries under sovereign control. In return each coastal state has the duty to manage and conserve fish stocks so they are not endangered by overexploitation. Fish stocks must be restored to "levels which can produce the maximum sustainable yield as qualified by relevant environmental and economic factors."[31] The coastal state must promote "optimum utilization" of the living resources of its EEZ.[32] The total allowable catch for each fish stock within its EEZ must be established.[33] These provisions grant coastal states broad discretion on choices of regulatory techniques and allocation of the allowable catch.

Where a fishery is shared among two or more EEZs, the UNCLOS requires the states concerned "to seek...to agree...to coordinate and ensure the conservation and development of such stocks."[34] In practice states agree on

---

[31] UNCLOS, Art. 61 (3).                [32] Ibid., Art. 62 (1).
[33] Ibid., Art. 61 (1).                  [34] Ibid., Art. 63 (1).

cooperative arrangements. For example, in the northern Pacific Ocean and the Bering Sea, the International Halibut Commission adopts regulations for halibut stocks shared by the United States and Canada.

Fishing on the high seas is open to all, but the UNCLOS also mandates conservation and management under MSY principles for high-seas fisheries.[35] In practice this management is hard to achieve except through the establishment of an international fisheries commission. Four such bodies are currently operating: the Northwest Atlantic Fisheries Organization, the Northeast Atlantic Fisheries Commission, the General Fisheries Council of the Mediterranean, and the Commission for the Conservation of Antarctic Marine Living Resources. In the South Pacific there is the Wellington Convention for the Prohibition of Fishing with Long-Driftnets (1989) and the Convention for the Conservation of Southern Bluefin Tuna (1993). However, much of the high seas area is unregulated as highlighted by the case of the *Estai*. To fill this loophole, in 1995 a U.N. conference adopted an Agreement on Straddling Fish Stocks and Highly Migratory Fish Stocks, which established a conservation regime and rules applicable to fish stocks on the high seas that range within the EEZ of one or more coastal states. This convention assures the enforcement of conservation measures on both sides of the 200-mile EEZ line and vindicates Canada's original concerns. The U.N. Food and Agriculture Organization (FAO) in 1995 also adopted a Code of Conduct for Responsible Fisheries.[36]

## Marine Mammals

The UNCLOS calls for states to cooperate for the conservation of marine mammals.[37] The international Convention for the Regulation of Whaling, (1946), created the International Whaling Commission (IWC) composed of representatives of member governments. The Commission has no enforcement power, but may encourage, recommend, study, and disseminate information about whales and whale stocks. Despite these limited powers, the IWC was successful in securing a ban on commercial whaling in 1982. In the 1990s one member, Iceland, withdrew from the Convention, and Norway and Japan resumed whaling on a limited basis, citing various exceptions and the recovery of certain stocks. Despite this resumption, the IWC has enjoyed extraordinary success, and whale stocks have vigorously recovered as a result.

[35]  Ibid., Arts 119.                              [36]  FAO Doc. 95/20/Rev. 1 (1995).
[37]  Ibid., Arts. 65 and 120.

## U.S. Ocean Policy: Missing in Action

As the predominant military and commercial nation in the world and bounded by three oceans, the United States has a greater interest in ocean policy than any other nation. Yet, the United States remains outside the comprehensive treaty regime that guarantees international maritime stability in the world, the UNCLOS. It also declines to play a leading role in ocean policy at IMO, preferring unilateral measures that lack international recognition and may conflict with the legitimate interests of other states. The United States thereby endangers its own interests by failing to take advantage of legitimate maritime rights, such as free and unimpeded passage through straits and the EEZs of other nations.

The United States has failed to exercise leadership in the restoration of ocean environments as well. Populations of fish and maritime resources have suffered drastic declines because of overfishing and environmental degradation. Rehabilitation of ocean ecosystems would not only serve environmental interests but would also increase fishery productivity. Estimates are that the United States could double its current catches if fish populations are rebuilt, adding $ 1.8 billion to the economy and tens of thousands of new jobs.[38]

## BIOLOGICAL DIVERSITY

The biological impoverishment of the earth is a defining characteristic of our time. The fragile balance of plants and animals that share the earth has developed over millions of years. Although most of the species that have ever lived are now extinct, we are living at a time of the earth's greatest biological diversity. We do not know how many species exist; biologists estimate their number to be from 10 to 100 million. Taxonomists have classified between 1.5 million to 1.75 million species, some 250,000 flowering plants, and 4500 mammals.

Biological diversity refers to the variation among living organisms and includes not only species diversity but also genetic diversity and ecosystem diversity. Ecosystem diversity is key because living things exist in natural communities where they interact. A rich variety of ecosystems exist on the Earth: many different kinds of forests, tundra, deserts, coral reefs, grasslands, lakes, coastal estuaries, and wetlands. An ecosystem map of the world reveals a tremendous diversity of ecosystems on every continent: the ice-covered Antarctic Peninsula; Andean, Amazon, and Atlantic forests in South America, wet and dry tropical forests in Central America; deserts, prairies, forests, and tundra

---

[38] U.S. Commission on Ocean Policy, Report 3 (2001).

in North America; broad-leaf and coniferous forests, deserts, grasslands, and tundra in Eurasia; rich shrub lands in the Mediterranean basin; deserts, tropical forests, mountain grasslands, and floristic shrub lands in Africa; tropical forests in Southeast Asia; and tropical forests and grasslands, shrub land forests, and deserts in Australia. All over the world are important island ecosystems as well. The flora and fauna of New Zealand have evolved in isolation for 80 million years, Madagascar harbors a rich variety of species found nowhere else, and Hawaii is the repository of unique plants and birds.

Experts agree that the destruction of habitat is causing major losses of biological diversity and the extinction of many species. For example, more than half of the world's species of plants and animals live in tropical forests. Yet in the last fifty years, over half of the tropical forests of the world have been destroyed, and cutting proceeds at a rate of 11,000 hectares per year.

Why should we care about biological diversity? There are both practical and philosophical reasons to care. A practical reason is the "ecosystem services" we take for granted – the work nature does for us in providing the wild plant varieties that we use for agriculture, pollinating our crops, mitigating floods and drought, controlling diseases and pests, providing clean air and water, nourishing the animals we use for food, providing fish and shellfish, and generating fertile soils. A great number of our important medicines are derived from animals or plants, and more are waiting to be discovered, at least if they survive our onslaught of destruction Wildlife diversity is a rich resource for the present and future benefit of humankind.

Wildlife and wild places contribute to the richness of human life by providing recreation, inspiration, beauty, and spiritual solace. Artists, poets, photographers, architects, and musicians create works inspired by and celebrating the natural world. Nature is part of our heritage, and we are its stewards. We have a responsibility to pass this on to future generations.

The preservation of biological diversity requires a multifaceted strategy.

## Habitat Preservation

The most important component of a strategy to preserve biological diversity is habitat preservation. A habitat, the physical and biological setting in which living organisms interact (such as a forest, a wetland, or a prairie), is a basic and indispensable requirement for all living things. Loss of habitat is the major factor causing the diminishing biological diversity of our planet. Protecting habitats and ecosystems is preferable to single-species preservation. The habitat/ecosystem approach is holistic; it is applied within a particular geographic framework or to a particular landscape defined by ecological boundaries as a logical unit for coordinated management. Human activities are not auto-matically excluded; they are assessed for their impacts – whether economic, cultural, social, or recreational – and decisions can then be made on how to accommodate both human needs and the maintenance of the ecological system.

The ecosystem approach is obviously not suitable for all areas, but every continents contains large areas of relatively undisturbed lands and waters: Latin America – 68 percent (mainly in the Amazon basin, which is now being cleared at a rate of 18,000 square miles per year); Australia – 65 percent; North America – 55 percent; Africa – 50 percent; Asia – 35 percent; and Europe – 18 percent. A first step would be to survey all such areas and identify particular ecosystem types. Second, values can be ascribed to different areas, and present and possible future impacts can be assessed. Third, analysis can be made of potential economic impacts of preservation, the compatibility of human uses, and mitigation strategies.

For example, the Nature Conservancy's Natural Heritage Network, which is made up of survey centers in all fifty states, has compiled a database of U.S. ecosystems and plant and animal species. The United States is extremely rich in biological diversity; it has about 10 percent of the known species on earth and ranks near the top in its variety of mammals, bees, freshwater fishes, needle-leafed evergreens, salamanders, mussels, snails and crayfishes. The United States has a wider variety of ecosystems – twenty-one of the twenty-eight types of recognized major world ecological regions – than any of the six largest countries of the world.

According to the National Biological Service of the U.S. Department of the Interior, however, many ecosystems in the United States have vanished or are imperiled. Among the largest imperiled ecosystems are the tall grass prairies and oak savannahs that covered most of the Midwest before the Europeans came to America, the original deciduous forests of the eastern United States, and the 60 million acres of long-leaf pine that originally blan-keted most of the Southeastern coastal plains. Smaller threatened ecosys-tems include the Hempstead Plains grasslands of Long Island, the wet coastal prairies of Louisiana, streams in the Mississippi alluvial plain, sedge mead-ows in Wisconsin, lake sand beaches in Vermont, and native grasslands in California.

As a matter of international strategy, three different approaches may be taken to preserving biological diversity.

The *hot spots approach* was first proposed by British ecologist Norman Myers and continued by Conservation International. A hot spot is an espe-cially rich but vulnerable ecosystem in which preservation efforts should be concentrated. Scientists have identified 21 hot spots – different areas defined by their vegetation that contain at least one-half percent of the world's 300,000 plant species as native species (see The Top 21 Hot Spots For Biological Diversity).

The advantage of concentrating on these hot spots is that doing so reduces the problem of biological diversity to manageable proportions. Scientists[39] argue that, at a cost of about $30 billion per year, areas within these hot spots could be designated as nature reserves, making a significant contribution to ecosystem preservation.

A second strategy is the Global 200 program advocated by the World Wildlife Fund (WWF). Global 200 would extend protection efforts not just to hot spots but also to diverse and representative terrestrial, fresh-water, and marine habitats, the broadest variety of the world's ecosystems from Arctic seas to coastal forests (see Top World Ecosystems According to the Global 200 Initiative of the World Wildlife Fund).

As part of this effort, in May 2005 the World Bank and the WWF announced a joint five-year program to reduce the destruction of the world's forests by 10 percent annually. Their strategy is to support new forest-protected areas, more effective management of already protected areas, and improved management of forests that are not yet protected.

A third strategy is to ask each of the states of the world to make a national assessment of biological diversity and to take appropriate actions to preserve it. This strategy takes into account the fact that states may have their own priorities and policies. This third strategy may incorporate aspects of the hot spots and Global 200 approaches.

All three of these approaches rely on the designation of conservation reserves as a primary tool of preservation. Of course, legal and administrative management schemes must be adopted to manage such areas. Such resource planning, to be successful, must involve and take onto consideration from the outset affected individuals and communities. Local residents must be persuaded to see such an area as a valuable resource. This will mean affording them substantial benefits from such activities as ecotourism, commercial uses of the area, and research and development.

### The U.N. Convention on Biological Diversity

In 1992 the U.N. Convention on Biological Diversity (CBD), accepted by 176 states, became the central international institution for promoting biological

[39] E. O. Wilson, "Hotspots: Preserving Pieces of a Fragile Biosphere," *National Geographic*, January, 2002.

**THE TOP 21 WORLD "HOT SPOTS" FOR BIOLOGICAL DIVERSITY**

1. Tropical Andes Mountains

2. Mediterranean basin

3. Madagascar/Indian Ocean islands

4. Central America

5. Caribbean and south Florida

6. Brazil's Atlantic forest

7. Indochina/Myanmar

8. Philippines

9. Polynesia/Micronesia

10. New Caledonia

11. New Zealand

12. Southwest Australia

13. California floristic area

14. Western Ghats (India) and Sri Lanka

15. Sundaland (Indonesia)

16. Wallacea (New Guinea)

17. South Central China

18. Cape of Good Hope floristic area (South Africa)

19. West African tropical forests

20. Central Chile

21. Brazil's Amazon tropical forest

diversity. The CBD requires all states to "identify components of biological diversity important for its conservation and sustainable use" and to take the following actions "as far as possible and appropriate":

U.N. Convention on Biological Diversity, Article 6

(a) Develop national strategies, plans, or program for the conservation and sustainable use of biological diversity or adapt for this purpose existing strategies,

**TOP WORLD ECOSYSTEMS ACCORDING TO THE GLOBAL 200
INITIATIVE OF THE WORLD WILDLIFE FUND**

Tropical forest

Temperate forest

Boreal forest

Tropical grassland and savannah

Temperate grassland

Mountain grassland and savannh

Mediterranean shrub

Deserts

Tundra

Estuarine and mangrove wetlands

Fresh-water wetlands

Marine ecosystems

plans, or programs which shall reflect, *inter alia*, the measures set out in this
Convention relevant to the Contracting Party concerned; and

(b) Integrate, as far as possible and as appropriate, the conservation and sustainable
use of biological diversity into relevant sectoral or cross-sectoral plans, programs,
and policies.

The program of sustainable use of designated components of biological
diversity is as follows:

U.N. Convention on Biological Diversity, Article 8

(a) Establish a system of protected areas or areas where special measures need to
be taken to conserve biological diversity;

(b) Develop, where necessary, guidelines for the selection, establishment, and
management of protected areas or areas where special measures need to be taken
to conserve biological diversity;

(c) Regulate or manage biological resources important for the conservation of
biological diversity whether within or outside protected areas, with a view to
ensuring their conservation and sustainable use;

(d) Promote the protection of ecosystems, natural habitats, and the maintenance
of viable populations of species in natural surroundings;

(e) Promote environmentally sound and sustainable development in areas
adjacent to protected areas with a view to furthering protection of these areas;

(f) Rehabilitate and restore degraded ecosystems and promote the recovery of threatened species, *inter alia*, through the development and implementation of plans or other management strategies.

Regretfully, the mandate of the CBD to designate biologically protected areas and to promote sustainable use of biological diversity is widely ignored. Yet, the establishment of protected areas on a global basis is one of the keys to preserving biological diversity. Six different categories of protected areas are recognized by the World Conservation Union; these range from a strict-protection regime to one permitting diverse types of sustainable exploitation. Establishing protected areas does not mean closing areas to human use. Protected areas can be created that are consistent with the needs of local people. They can serve human needs, especially in the world of the twenty-first century, when for the first time in human history, more than 50 percent of the world's population live in cities. For urban dwellers, protected areas offer mental health benefits and the opportunity for physical exercise. They store carbon, helping alleviate global warming; they provide many diverse ecosystem services, from clean water to buffers against floods. Protected areas can help prevent the loss of life in extreme natural catastrophes, such as the 2004 Asian tsunami.

The United States, alone among industrialized countries, has refused to sign or ratify the CBD. This is yet another instance in which the United States, which should be taking the lead internationally, has abdicated its responsibilities. Moreover, two additional international programs for the voluntary national preservation of natural areas, the U.N. Educational and Scientific and Cultural Organization's (UNESCO) World Cultural and Natural Heritage Program and Biosphere Reserve Program, are ignored by the United States.[40]

The United States refused to sign the CBD because it objected to provisions allowing developing countries to charge for access to their natural resources and "encouraging" the "equitable sharing of benefits" arising from the technology derived from such resources. Yet, Article 16 of the CBD requires "the adequate and effective protection of intellectual property rights," and there is no evidence either for the inability of companies to gain access to biological resources or the erosion of intellectual property rights under the CBD regime.

[40] The United States withdrew and did not participate in UNESCO from 1985 to 2003. The United States also ignores the Convention on Wetlands (Ramsar Convention), 11 ILM 969 (1972) under which 116 parties have designated 1,006 wetlands sites covering 72, 388,342 hectares of surface area.

## Regional Treaties

Because wildlife and ecosystems range over states' boundaries, regional conventions on biological diversity are essential. Unfortunately, the major regional conventions are well intentioned but ineffective. For example, the Treaty for Amazonian Cooperation (1978) signed by the eight countries that share the Amazon basin in South America calls for "a balance of economic growth and environmental preservation" and "rational planning of Amazon flora and fauna . . . to preserve the environmental balance of the region," but during the years the treaty has been in effect, increasing destruction of the forest cover has occurred.

Other regional agreements – the 1968 African Convention for Conservation of Nature, the 1985 ASEAN Convention, the 1940 Western Hemisphere Convention, and the 1979 Berne Convention on the Conservation of European Wildlife and Natural Habitats – fall into the category of "sleeping treaties" because they are totally ignored by the parties.

## Species Agreements

There is a need for international cooperation to protect particular species of animals and birds that are rare or endangered and that range over large areas. The major multilateral convention to protect species is the Bonn Convention on the Conservation of Migratory Species of Wild Animals (1979). It establishes mandatory protection for species listed in Appendix I – migratory species that are in danger of extinction – and protection by means of formal conservation special agreements for species listed in Appendix II, species having "unfavorable conservation status" (in plain English – rare species). In addition, parties are encouraged to conclude an agreement for any population of any other species of wildlife; the purpose is to promote agreements for all species that would benefit from international cooperation.

Over seventy states belong to this regime, but not the United States or Canada, which say their bilateral agreements suffice. This short-sighted position ignores the need for the United States to take a leading role to promote general protection for wildlife, particularly rare and endangered species. Once again the United States is abdicating its responsibility as a global leader.

A second important multilateral treaty regime is the 1973 Convention on Trade on Endangered Species (CITES). The sole aim of CITES is to control commercial trade in endangered species of wildlife and their products. To this end, trade is essentially forbidden with respect to Appendix I species – those threatened with extinction. For Appendix II species, which are endangered, trade is permitted with proper documentation from the exporting state. Appendix III lists species that are not threatened or endangered but for which cooperation is desirable. Reviews of CITES are mixed; lax enforcement, exemptions, and reservations create loopholes, but certainly imperfect enforcement is better than nothing. From time to time there are bitter controversies, as happened in 1997 when three African countries – Namibia, Zimbabwe, and Botswana – argued in favor of removing the African elephant from Appendix I because their populations had recovered and were causing damage to game reserve areas. The United States opposed lifting the ivory ban because of the danger of poaching and sending a message that elephants no longer need protection. The CITES Conference reached a compromise, allowing sales of 120 tons of ivory to one nation – Japan. Revenues from the sales must be used for conservation and community development. The hard line the United States took on elephants backfired as U.S. proposals to list big-leaf mahogany and the Green sea turtle on Appendix I failed. Politics may play a bigger role than biology in CITES.

## ANTARCTICA

Antarctica, the uninhabited ice-covered continent at the Earth's South Pole, is unique: It is a large continent of great natural beauty and abundant biological resources, but is inhospitable to humankind. All but 2 percent of the land and much of the surrounding waters are covered with a sheet of ice up to three kilometers thick. Seven nations – Argentina, Australia, Chile, France, New Zealand, Norway, and the United Kingdom – claim sovereignty over parts of Antarctica, and the British, Chilean, and Argentinean claims overlap. Conflict has been avoided, however, because since the signing of the Antarctic Treaty in 1959, all territorial claims have been indefinitely suspended. Additional interested parties (including the United States, which refuses to recognize any sovereign claims) have joined the Antarctic Treaty system, and there are now forty-three parties in all. Consultative meetings of the parties are held annually.

Because of overfishing in the 1970s, the parties in 1980 adopted the Convention on the Conservation of Antarctic Marine Living Resources (known as CCAMLR),[41] which, as we have seen, adopts the ecosystem approach to fishing in the Southern Ocean. CCAMLR's scientific advisory commission recommends quotas for fishing stocks, but adoption requires unanimous approval from the parties. This has led to controversy and disagreement regarding the size of certain stocks, most notably sea bass, which are being overfished as a result.

[41]  19 ILM 837 (1980).

In 1988 a Convention on the Regulation of Antarctic Mineral Resource Activities (known as CRAMRA) was negotiated to allow possible mining in Antarctica, especially for oil and natural gas. But environmental groups raised an outcry, and CRAMRA was rejected. Instead, in 1991 a Protocol on Environmental Protection to the Antarctic Treaty[42] was approved that establishes a comprehensive environmental regime for the Antarctic continent and surrounding waters. Five annexes to this protocol deal with specific topics: environmental impact assessment (relating especially to tourism and research activities), conservation of flora and fauna, waste disposal, marine pollution, and protected areas. This protocol also placed a fifty-year moratorium on all mineral exploration activities. There is a mandatory system for the settlement of disputes as well.

But important decisions on Antarctica have not been decided but simply deferred. What will be its ultimate legal and political fate? A Malaysian proposal that Antarctica be declared the "common heritage of humankind" seems misguided. This would resolve the sovereignty question, but would raise even more difficult issues, such as who would administer the continent and for what purposes. Would mining be allowed and by whom? Who would be in charge? The common heritage proposal would most likely mean that a rotating, multi-party commission would be in charge. This seems unwieldy and bureaucratic at best; there is no guarantee of wise administration.

A better idea would be to make Antarctica the first World Park, a natural reserve that would make the current provisional administrative regime permanent. All current uses – scientific research, tourism, and fishing – would continue, but all other exploitation would be permanently banned. The most controversial aspect of this proposal is a permanent ban on mining. Most experts agree, however, that the constant freezing temperatures, blinding blizzard conditions, and the necessity of drilling through the Antarctic ice sheet make mining impractical or impossible. Even with improvements in technology, mineral wealth would have to be found in superabundant quantities for mining to be commercially attractive.[43]

## WATER RESOURCES

International competition and conflict over water resources are sure to intensify as the world population increases and existing supplies of water diminish

[42]  30 ILM 1461 (1991).
[43]  Christopher Joyner, 83 *American Journal of International Law* 605, 622 (1994).

because of waste and pollution. Tensions exist and sometimes violence erupts among nations over water use rights and water diversion projects. Every area of the world is affected:

**MIDDLE EAST:**

■ Water is part of the conflict between Israel and its neighbors. Israel is accused of diverting too much water from the Jordan River and the Sea of Galilee and thereby depleting supplies in Jordan and the West Bank. A water agreement in the region and diverting water from Egypt to Israel could be part of a Middle East peace plan.

■ Syria's diversions from the Yarmuck River affect downstream Jordan; Turkey's diversions from the Tigris/Euphrates basin affect Iraq and Syria.

**ASIA:**

■ Violence has erupted from time to time over water in the Mekong River, which is shared by Laos, Cambodia, Thailand, and Vietnam.

■ Kazakhstan, Kyrgyzstan, Tajikistan, Turkmenistan, and Uzbekistan are dependent on the Amu Darya and Syr Darya rivers for their water resources. These two rivers account for more than 90 percent of the water in the Aral Sea Basin. There is a stalemate on water issues, and the Aral Sea is disappearing.

■ India and Pakistan have a dispute over Indus River waters; India and Bangladesh are at loggerheads over the Ganges River.

**AFRICA:**

■ The Nile Basin covers parts of nine African countries, and Egypt is particularly affected by upper basin diversions.

■ Tunisia and Libya have a dispute over the waters of the Medjerda River that they share.

■ There are fifty-four international rivers and lakes in Africa; eleven drain the territories of four or more states. Water issues are unresolved in all of these areas.

**NORTH AMERICA:**

■ Ten watersheds including the Great Lakes straddle the border between the United States and Canada. Since 1909 an International Joint Commission (IJC) has functioned to resolve disputes and to manage these areas.[44]

---

[44] *The IJC and the 21st Century* (1997).

■ Water diversion issues are intense along the U.S./Mexican border, particularly with respect to the Rio Grande and Colorado Rivers; ground-water
rights disputes also exist along most of the 2,000-mile border. There are
international water sanitation problems, particularly in the Tijuana/San
Diego and Mexicali/Calexico areas over untreated sewage from Mexico
discharging across the border into U.S. communities. The United States
and Mexico have established an International Boundary and Water Commission to deal with these problems.

LATIN AMERICA:

■ There are fifty-eight rivers and lakes in Latin America with drainage
basins shared by two or more countries. Disputes have erupted especially
over the Lauca River shared by Bolivia and Chile; the Parana River shared
by Brazil and Argentina; and the Rio de la Plata shared by Argentina, Brazil,
Uruguay, and Paraguay.

EUROPE:

■ International rivers abound in Europe. There has been litigation
between Hungary and Slovakia over the Danube,[45] as well as water diversion
and pollution disputes over many international waterways.

■ International commissions are functioning on most international waterways to deal not only with water use issues but also with water pollution.
For example, the International Commission for the Protection of the Rhine
against Pollution has improved the Rhine ecosystem to such an extent that
salmon have returned to the river.

■ The European Union has established a Comprehensive Water Policy
for its twenty-five member states.

These water conflicts and disputes can only be dealt with by the application
of international law and by the establishment and maintenance of appropriate
international institutions. Cooperative international regimes must be developed to deal with water issues. Effective commissions to deal with water are
functioning in Europe and North America. These should be studied as models
for other areas of the world.

A landmark international instrument setting out legal principles for the
management of international waterways is the 1997 U.N. Convention on
the Law of Non-Navigational Uses of International Watercourses.[46] This

---

[45]   Case Concerning the Gabcikovo-Nagymaros Dam, ICJ Rep. (1997), 7. This case was discussed
       supra, p. 356.
[46]   36 ILM 700 (1997).

agreement makes equitable utilization the cornerstone of how water rights should be allocated between states that share a waterway. Equitable utilization does not mean equal sharing; rather all states in a watercourse share sovereignty over the resource, and they must establish an ongoing process based on agreed-upon relevant factors to maximize the benefits and serve the needs of all users. Equitable utilization also implies full and regular exchanges of data, timely notification of planned measures, and the creation of an ongoing negotiation process, usually in the form of an international commission and a permanent secretariat.

The U.N. Watercourse Convention also adopts the principle of ecosystem management and the prevention, reduction, and control of pollution as a second key principle. This is a harm prevention principle that commits parties to act jointly to protect the ecosystem of a watercourse.

The integration of equitable utilization and harm prevention means that international commissions committed to comprehensive environmental and developmental goals should be established to manage every significant international watercourse in the world. The goal should be the efficient use of water resources both to satisfy human needs and to promote the preservation and restoration of ecosystems. Commissions must be authorized to employ a full range of implementation measures, including regulation, economic instruments, land use controls, voluntary methods, and information-based tools. An integrated management scheme should be used to improve the efficiency of the water delivery infrastructure and to promote recycling and reuse.

Differing principles of management are necessary for different watercourses to suit their particular characteristics, but the general management principles of efficiency, equitable utilization, and ecosystem management are common to all UNEP, the U.N. Development Program, and the Global Environment Facility[47] should be mandated to provide appropriate technical and financial assistance to international watercourse commissions in developing countries.

## SUMMING UP

Threats to the well-being of the planet and international and transboundary environmental degradation have been recognized as concerns by the international community only in the last generation. The creation of a network of international institutions and political and legal actions to come to grips

---

[47] Assistance can also be provided by the newly established World Commission on Dams, which makes policy recommendations on the construction of large dam projects. See *Report of the World Commission on Dams* (2000).

with these problems was accomplished in fits and starts over that time. Much remains to be done. Institutions are weak, legal and political regimes are "soft," and compliance and enforcement are sporadic. Yet, it is remarkable that international cooperation has proceeded to the point that most problems are being addressed, however inadequately.

Now the task is to broaden and strengthen the international regimes in operation. Progress will be difficult – the international community is a diffuse and complex structure, and developed and developing states have deeply conflicting priorities and views about environmental concerns. Collective environmental care of the planet poses a severe challenge because it calls for the creation of rules and vesting of authority in international institutions with respect to matters that are traditionally outside international concern – the use of resources and the promotion of economic activity. The underlying necessary political commitment is therefore hard to achieve.

Yet, we must realize that environmental protection is now an international security concern. Threats to peace and well-being in the twenty-first century not only come from weapons of mass destruction, terrorism, and military conflict but they also involve disruption of the natural systems of the earth; competition for resources, such as oil and water; and destruction of the earth's patrimony– the forests, waters, air, and living things upon which we depend. Resources are also increasingly a cause of international conflict. Effectively dealing with international environmental problems is an essential component of maintaining national security.

The progress of the last thirty-five years in creating international cooperation to deal with the plethora of international environmental concerns has occurred largely without the participation of the United States. The United States has either been obstructionist or passive, intent on bashing the United Nations and international cooperation. U.S. political leaders hide the dangers and problems of the international environment from the American people. This is more than unfortunate; it is tragic. As the world's sole superpower, only the United States has the political muscle and the resources to swing deals that would advance the international environmental agenda.

Gaining the cooperation of developing countries is particularly important if further international progress is to be made. Only the United States is capable of forging the kind of "grand bargain" that will obtain developing country cooperation to protect the global environment, in return for appropriate incentives, such as financial help through the Global Environmental Fund, significant debt forgiveness, and transfer of technology. The fact that the United States has ignored international environmental problems is a major reason for the lack of progress in recent years and the current state of deadlock on most problems.

## FURTHER READINGS

Brundtland World Commission on Envionment and Development, *Our Common Future* (United Nations, 1987).

Donald Anton, Jonathan I. Charney, Philippe Sands, Thomas J. Schoenbaum, and Michael Young, *International Environmental Law* (2005).

Patricia Birnie and Alan Boyle, *International Law and the Environment* (2d ed. 2002).

Philippe Sands, *Principles of International Environmental Law* (2d ed. 2003).

James Cameron, Jacob Werksman, and Peter Roderick, *Improving Compliance with International Environmental Law* (1996).

David Hunter, James Salzman, and Durwood Zaelke, *International Environmental Law and Policy* (2d ed. 2002).

David Freestone and Charlotte Streck, eds., *Legal Aspects of Implementing the Kyoto Protocol: Making Kyoto Work* (2005).

United Nations, *Millennium Ecosystem Assessment* (2005).

Daniel C. Esty, *Greening the GATT* (1994).

# 8 International Human Rights

## A SLAP IN THE FACE AT THE UNITED NATIONS

In March 2001, anger and consternation reigned among the members of the American delegation to the United Nations. In a routine election of the members of the U.N. Human Rights Commission, the main U.N. body concerned with human rights, the United States had just been replaced by Austria. This was an outrage, and the U.S. media picked up on the theme – a slap in the face for the new Bush administration at the United Nations.

Ironically, at the time, Austria was subject to intense international criticism on the grounds of its lack of attention to human rights. Austria had drawn fire from both the U.S. State Department and the European Union in late 1999 when Jorg Haider, the leader of Austria's Freedom Party, became a member of the country's governing coalition after his party received 27 percent of the vote in national elections. Haider and his party were notorious for their controversial, right-wing positions that many regarded as racist, anti-immigrant, and sympathetic to Nazism.

Regrettably, this state of affairs continues. The fifty-three members of the U.N. Human Rights Commission are studded with human rights offenders. In 2005, the members included the Sudan, a country that is accused of carrying out a campaign of mass murder, rape, and expulsion against non-Arab Muslims in the Darfur region; Cuba, the last bastion of communism in the Americas; China, where thousands are in jail for political offenses; Russia, where a cruel war without end is ongoing in Chechnya; and Zimbabwe, where the government is confiscating white farmers' lands.

The U.N. High Level Panel that reported to U.N. Secretary-General Kofi Annan in December 2004 minced no words in advocating reforms: "The Commission on Human Rights suffers from a legitimacy deficit that casts doubts on the overall reputation of the United Nations." This is too mild a denunciation; in truth, the U.N. Commission on Human Rights as it is presently constituted makes a mockery of the entire U.N. system of protection of human rights.

## THE UNITED STATES: PROTECTOR OF HUMAN FREEDOMS

International human rights is a much-discussed topic that is poorly understood. One misunderstanding is that the United States plays the leading role in ensuring the observance of human rights around the world. U.S. presidents often lecture other nations on human rights and freedoms. The U.S. State Department publishes annual country reports on human rights practices around the world – "report cards" grading countries on their performances. Like a stern parent, the United States issues warnings to those with unsatisfactory grades; sometimes these warnings are followed up by trade sanctions – the equivalent of requiring the nation to stand in a corner and contemplate how it can do better.

The reality is that the United States, after leading the world to recognize international human rights immediately after World War II, has largely abandoned the field to others – mainly the Europeans – and retreated into exceptionalism and unilateralism. In the last forty years the United States, with few exceptions, has been either an innocent bystander or has tried undermining the international system of human rights. It further lost the high ground as far as human rights is concerned because of its policies after 9/11 in Afghanistan, Iraq, and Guantanamo Bay; the U.S. Patriot Act provisions; and the revelations of torture at Abu Ghraib prison. The United States does not fully participate in multilateral efforts to protect human rights; it has not ratified the American Convention for the Protection of Human Rights (1969) that has been accepted by twenty-five members of the Organization of American States, and it largely ignores the human rights efforts at the United Nations.

## A SYSTEM THAT IS BROKE

The system that protects international human rights is bankrupt. The end of the Cold War, despite the collapse of numerous repressive regimes, did not increase respect for international human rights. On every continent there are abuses of human rights and oppressive governments. According to the 2004 survey of *Freedom in the World* conducted by Freedom House, only 88 of 191 U.N. members are rated "free," 55 are "partly free," and 49 countries are "not free" – in this last category are 35 percent of U.N. members with a total population of 2.2 billion.

The largest deficit of human freedom is in Muslim countries. Of the forty-one predominately Muslim countries in the world, not one is considered genuinely "free" or fundamentally respectful of political rights and civil liberties. Only eight, led by Turkey, are considered even "partly free." Many Muslim states are in the category of "most repressive," including Saudi Arabia, Sudan, Syria, and Turkmenistan. Nevertheless, the African-Muslim block at the United Nations, demonstrating its disdain for Western sensibilities, makes sure that Sudan retains its seat on the U.N. Human Rights Commission while in the midst of committing what has been termed "genocide" by former U.S. Secretary of State Colin Powell.

Yet, Islam is the fastest-growing religion in the world, and Muslim countries lead the way in population growth. So if one of the root causes of Islamist terrorism is deprivation of human rights in Muslim countries, the problem is going to increase unless international human rights are made a priority concern. The United States alone cannot bring democracy and civil and political rights to the Muslim world. This can only be done through multilateral solidarity – working with other states, particularly the Europeans, to rebuild and invigorate multinational institutions.

We should not overlook the many voices of concern in the Muslim world itself. Here are examples:

1. After the horrible massacre of schoolchildren in Beslan, Russia in 2004, Nazrine Azimi[1] wrote,

Where, I ask my fellow Muslims, do we turn when so many atrocities are committed under the banner of our faith? Most extremisms arise when people don't know where to turn: the gross vulgarities that pass for freedom in Western democracies may have irredeemably frightened many moderate Muslim societies into the arms of more dogmatic nonsecular movements. Still, Muslim countries must start questioning why so many of their sons and daughters go about claiming an Islamic inspiration for murderous acts. Who are those who perpetrated the Beslan tragedy in the name of Islam and where, pray, are Muslim politicians and commentators to condemn, unequivocally, their cruelty?

2. Yousiff M. Ibrahim[2] writes of fear choking the Arab world:

Fear is deeply ingrained in the Arab mind. . . . There is a fear to speak, write, read, or even hear truth. . . . How many times have you read about presidents

[1] "The Anguish of a Faithful Muslim," *International Herald Tribune*, Oct. 26, 2004.
[2] "The Fear that Chokes the Arab World," *International Herald Tribune*, Oct. 30, 2004.

who win new terms with 99 percent majorities? How many times have you read about "honor killings," . . . harrowing acts of bloody mayhem by a male who cuts the throat of his wife, sister, or distant female relatives, often on a rumor about her misbehaving or not marrying someone the family designated. . . . We say of countries where women are not allowed to vote, choose their life partners, drive, travel or run for office that they are preserving "Arab and Islamic tradition," when in fact they are committing flagrant violations of human rights for half their populations.

3. Muslim scholars are also beginning to look critically at the Qu'ran. Muhammad Shahrour[3] argues that Muslims will disentangle their faith from the violence committed in its name only if they reappraise their sacred texts. For example, he says that the ninth chapter of the Qu'ran, which advises "slay the infidels where you find them," should be relegated to its context, a failed attempt by the prophet Muhammad in the seventh century to form a state on the Arabian Peninsula.

Renewed efforts to establish international human rights in the world can counterbalance and defeat Osama Bin Laden and his followers, who began their campaign of terror 25 years ago and now have spread their message around the entire world.

## ORIGINS

This idea of human rights comes from the European Enlightenment of the seventeenth and eighteenth centuries. The English philosopher John Locke (1632–1704) formulated the idea of natural rights – life, liberty, and property – from the natural law, a code of rules whose authority rested on human reason.[4] For Locke and the French social reformer, Jean-Jacques Rousseau (1712–78), these natural rights preexisted governments, and with their consent to form states (the mythical social contract), human beings did not surrender these rights, but only ceded the right to enforce them.[5] The ideas of Locke and

---

[3] Neil MacFarquahar, "Muslims Take a Hard Look at Islam," *International Herald Tribune*, Dec. 11, 2004.

[4] By contrast, Edmund Burke (1729–97) rejected the idea that natural rights existed outside society or before history; he maintained that all rights derive from the history of the society in which they are exercised. Edmund Burke, "Reflections on the Revolution in France," in Isaac Kramnick, ed., *The Portable Edmund Burke* (1994), 416–74.

[5] The originator of this idea of natural rights was Thomas Hobbes, who transformed the idea of natural law into a theory of natural rights. Hobbes claimed that a right of nature is "the liberty each man hath to use his own power for the preservation of his own nature, that is to say . . . of doing anything which in his own judgment and reason, he shall conceive to be the aptest means thereunto." *Leviathan.* I, p. 79 (Penguin edition 1968).

Rousseau became fundamental to both the American Revolution and the French Revolution in the latter part of the eighteenth century. The natural and self-evident rights of mankind were embedded in the Declaration of Independence, the U.S. Bill of Rights, and the French Declaration of the Rights of Man and Citizen. For Thomas Jefferson, who participated in the drafting of all three documents, human beings are "endowed by their Creator with certain inalienable Rights, among them life, liberty and the pursuit of happiness."

In the twenty-first century, the concept of human rights is anchored in human dignity as well. Even those who dispute the divine or natural law origin of human rights accept the human rights tradition as obligatory. Two consequences flow from the affirmation of human rights: (1) Limits are placed upon the ability of governments and of majority decision making to encroach upon defined individual freedoms and (2) individuals and groups are recognized as having certain claims on society.


## UNIVERSALITY


The modern conception of human rights is European in origin. Despite this, are human rights universal? Some say that human rights must be subject to cultural and religious traditions. For example, certain Islamic states have made reservations to key provisions of the 1979 Convention on the Elimination of Discrimination against Women. Female genital mutilation is widely practiced in certain African states. State practice differs with respect to such matters as the imposition of the death penalty, corporal punishment, freedom of the press, and the rights of unborn children. Many developing countries stress economic development and a right to development, rather than traditional human rights, political rights, and civil liberties.

Yet, the U.N. system is committed to the universality of human rights. The 1993 Vienna World Conference on Human Rights declared, "All human rights are universal, indivisible, and interdependent." The solemn commitment of all states to fulfill their obligations to promote universal respect for human rights was reaffirmed. The promotion of human rights was termed a "priority objective" of the United Nations. Is this just rhetoric?

Oppressed peoples never make denials of the universality of human rights; it is always their oppressors who do so. Human rights are universal because the fundamental aspirations and needs of people everywhere are the same: to have food, shelter, and the security of family life; to be able to think, talk, and meet freely; to live free, creative lives; to practice a religion or to demur; to be free from arbitrary arrest and punishment; and not to suffer discrimination because of race, gender, religion, or ethnic status. States may behave differently, but people are the same. Human rights are universal in the sense that they transcend political, economic, and cultural differences.

This is not to deny that there are differences at the margin with respect to certain rights: for example, whether the death penalty should be an exception to the right to life, whether hate speech should be prohibited, or the scope of the rights of unborn children. The 1993 Vienna World Conference on Human Rights admitted, "The significance of national and regional peculiarities and various historical, cultural, and religious backgrounds must be borne in mind." So although human rights are universal, they may not be uniform. For example, some states may emphasize economic and social rights; others may place primary importance on cultural rights. But there is an undeniable core of human rights and values applicable all over the world.[6]

## AN AMERICAN BLACK EYE

The sensational photo of Pfc. Lynndie England pointing a finger of ridicule at the genitals of a hooded Iraqi prisoner at the Abu Ghraib prison in Iraq flashed all over the world in the spring of 2004. The photographs that came to light about the treatment of prisoners in Iraq told the truth and more: The Bush administration carried on systematic violations of domestic and international human rights laws after 2001. New details emerged nearly every week for the rest of the year. Not only in Iraq but also in Guantanamo, Afghanistan, and elsewhere, prisoners were subject to what can only be termed torture. In March 2005 the *New York Times* reported that at least twenty-six prisoners died while in U.S. custody in what U.S. army investigators have concluded were acts of criminal homicide. In Guantanamo "enemy combatants" were subjected to a variety of forms of physical and mental torture, including grabbing prisoners by their genitals, forcing them to masturbate, chaining them to the cold ground, depriving them of sleep, playing loud constant music, and "water-boarding," repeatedly submerging a naked, manacled prisoner in water until he begins to lose consciousness. The Pentagon also admits using a technique known as "rendition" – if particularly nasty techniques are needed, a prisoner can be turned over, in secret, to a friendly country where torture can be carried out with impunity.

---

[6] See the persuasive article by Amartya Sen, "Human Rights and Asian Values," *The New Republic*, July 14, 1997, pp. 33–40. It concludes, "The authoritarian readings of Asian values that are increasingly championed in some quarters do not survive scrutiny."

"Where has America Gone?" read a headline in English in a Japanese newspaper that was typical of the reaction around the world. Critical voices were raised in countries friendly to the United States. "Europe fears that U.S. contempt for human rights is not just confined to a few soldiers but represents the ethos of the Bush administration,"[7] wrote Ambassador Hugh Cortazzi, a former British career diplomat.

Independent investigation[8] has determined why this abuse occurred: lawyers who were both ignorant of and hostile to international law responded positively to the Office of White House Counsel's call for legal justification to subvert long-standing rules on the treatment of prisoners of war. The objections of lawyers at the State Department and the Pentagon were ignored, and senior officials in the government turned a blind eye to what was going on.

The architect of the scandal was White House Chief Counsel (now Attorney General) Alberto Gonzales, who put a team of hand-picked lawyers – people who could be trusted to come up with the right answers – to work on the standards of interrogation of prisoners taken in the War on Terrorism. Assistant Attorney General Jay S. Bybee, working closely with his deputy, John Yoo, produced a Memorandum of Law that was issued in final form on August 1, 2002.

The memorandum advised President Bush that the International Convention on Torture and U.S. law[9] only forbade "acts inflicting, and that are specifically intended to inflict, severe pain and suffering. . . . Those acts must be of an extreme nature to [violate the Convention and U.S. law]. We further conclude that certain acts may be cruel, inhuman and degrading, but still not produce pain and suffering of the requisite intensity to fall within the [legal] proscription against torture."

The memorandum went on to say that if executive branch personnel engaged even in torture out of "necessity" or in "self-defense [of the country]" they would not be subject to punishment:

Even if an interrogation method violated [the law], the statute would be unconstitutional if it impermissibly encroached on the President's constitutional power to conduct an military campaign. . . . It is well settled that the President may seize and detain enemy combatants, at least for the duration of the conflict, and the laws of war make clear that prisoners may be interrogated for information concerning the enemy, its strength and its plans.[10]

---

7  *London Observer*, June 19, 2004.
8  *The Abu Ghraib Investigation: The Official Report of the Independent Panel and the Pentagon* (2004).
9  The U.S. law forbidding torture is 18 USC secs. 2340–2340A.
10  This memorandum was withdrawn only in December 2004 when it was clear that it would become an embarrassment in Gonzales's confirmation as Attorney General.

## INTERNATIONAL HUMANITARIAN LAW

The Justice Department memorandum was a green light that neither international law nor U.S. law limits the authority of the president in any way. It ignored the fact that even in war and its aftermath there are standards under international law that must be upheld. These rules are known as the *laws of war* and *international humanitarian law*. The purpose of laws of war is to minimize cruelty and suffering even in this most extreme of human pursuits. The development of rules to minimize human suffering in war goes back to the nineteenth century and to reforms advocated by such persons as Florence Nightingale, who heroically sought to improve conditions during the Crimean War (1853–6), and Francis Lieber, who drafted a code of standards for treatment of prisoners during the U.S. Civil War. These rules became the subject of international law through a series of treaties, the most important on which are The Hague Conventions of 1899 and 1907 and the four Geneva Conventions of 1949.[11] These laws of war deal with such matters as treating the wounded, sick, and shipwrecked; minimizing civilian casualties and the destruction of civilian property; outlawing certain types of weapons (chemical and biological weapons, for example); and treating prisoners of war.

The right of all human beings to be free from torture applies both in war and in peace. There are no legal justifications for torture or exceptions to its prohibition. The U.N. Convention on Torture (1985)[12] requires that states adopt measures to prevent torture within their jurisdictions and ensure that torture is a criminal offense.

Torture is defined under the Convention as

any act by which severe pain or suffering, whether physical or mental, is intentionally inflicted on a person ... by or at the instigation of a public official or other person acting in an official capacity.

This definition has been applied by the European Commission on Human Rights to include failure to provide food, water, heating in winter, proper washing facilities, clothing, and medical and dental care to prisoners.[13] The U.N. Human Rights Committee holds that torture includes such techniques as punching, kicking, forcible standing for hours, electric shocks, hooding for prolonged periods, malnutrition, and mock executions.[14]

---

[11] For the text of these and other conventions, see A. Roberts and R. Guelf, *Documents on the Laws of War* (3d ed. 2000). In 1977 there were two additional protocols to the Geneva Conventions, but these were not accepted by the United States.

[12] 23 ILM 1027 (1985).

[13] Denmark et al v. Greece, ECHR Yearbook XII 1 (1969).

[14] The cases are summarized by Javaid Rehman, *International Human Rights Law* 415 (2004).

The United States has pledged to adhere to these rules and normally takes them seriously. After World War II, the United States and its allies conducted war crimes trials of German and Japanese officials, and several hundred were convicted and executed or imprisoned. U.S. military training normally includes extensive instruction on the laws of war.

The U.S. military has long adhered to international standards forbidding torture so the question of which interrogation techniques are proper for prisoners should never have arisen. The U.S. Army has long experience in conducting interrogations, and its techniques and training programs fully comply with international standards. Army Field Manual 34–52, the instruction book used since 1992 as the basis for U.S. Army interrogations, expressly forbids mental and physical torture as illegal, morally wrong, and counterproductive. Beatings; forcing an individual to sit, stand, or kneel in an abnormal position for prolonged periods; threats and insults; and other inhumane treatment are not allowed. Instead, the field manual outlines seventeen permissible interrogation techniques, including psychological ploys, tricks, and nonviolent ruses, to get a prisoner to talk.

The field manual makes several convincing arguments against torture. First, torture is usually unreliable because the prisoner will say almost anything he or she believes the interrogator expects or wants to hear. Second, it undermines public and foreign support for the U.S. military. Third, it increases the risk of abuse for captured U.S. military and civilian personnel, and fourth, torture violates the Geneva Convention (No. III).

The intervention of the White House and the Justice Department introduced politically motivated changes into what were settled military practices. It is not surprising that many of the people who were most disturbed when the new interrogation techniques were put into practice were uniformed personnel. As retired General Joseph P. Hoar testified to the U.S. Congress, the administration's decision to ignore the Geneva Conventions and the Convention on Torture "puts all American servicemen and women at risk that are serving in combat regions."

The Justice Department memorandum and its consequences also show a fundamental misunderstanding by government lawyers of the laws of war, particularly Geneva Convention (No. III). A prisoner who qualifies under this Convention has the rights of a prisoner of war (POW) under international law. POWs are neither criminals nor hostages and are detained solely for the purpose of preventing them from rejoining enemy forces. Their participation in hostilities is not unlawful, and they can be tried only for war crimes, not for deeds of war. POWs cannot be kept in civilian prisons, but must be detained in POW camps. Reprisals against POWs are not permitted, and they must be repatriated at the close of hostilities, not kept to extract concessions from the enemy. Although POWs are required to disclose only their name, rank, date of birth, and serial number, it is legitimate and customary to interrogate POWs. But they may not be tortured, mistreated, or subjected to public scorn or scrutiny.

A person who does not qualify as a POW, of course, cannot claim any of these Geneva Convention rights. He or she can therefore be tried merely for bearing arms, and the conduct of hostilities can be common crimes. However, a prisoner who does not qualify as a POW must still be treated humanely and cannot be subjected to torture.

Although humane treatment must be accorded to both POWs and non-POW enemy combatants, it is obviously important to make a determination of their status to see if the Geneva Convention applies. International negotiators in 1949 set the bar rather high for so-called irregular forces, such as those captured in Afghanistan: They must be a member of an organized force belonging to a party to a conflict, under responsible command, wear a distinctive emblem recognizable at a distance, carry their arms openly, and conduct their operations in accordance with the laws of war. In 1977 a protocol was adopted lowering the bar substantially – irregulars can claim POW status even if they blend into the civilian population as long as they distinguish themselves during actual combat. However, the United States rejected this protocol, saying it undermines the protection of true civilians.

But the United States adopted an erroneous policy regarding the determination of POW status. In January 2002, White House Counsel Gonzales ruled that the detainees in Guantanamo were outside the protection of the Geneva Convention. In an apparent reliance on this opinion, President Bush signed an order on February 7, 2002 stating, "I accept the legal conclusion of the Department of Justice and determine that none of the provisions of the Geneva Conventions apply to our conflict with Al Qaeda in Afghanistan or elsewhere throughout the world." This blanket ruling goes too far. The law under Geneva Convention No. III is clear: Article 5 provides that "Should any doubt arise as to whether [captured] persons [are POWs], such persons shall enjoy the protection of the present Convention until their status has been determined by a competent tribunal." The U.S. interpretation of this language was that U.S. officials had the right to determine that captured prisoners were not POWs and that the United States alone could determine whether there was any doubt as to a person's status. This is manifestly incorrect. In warfare there is a presumption of POW status; it is rebuttable, but only on an individual basis. Only in the summer of 2005, after two U.S. Supreme Court decisions, was the U.S. policy on POW status partially reversed.

In January 2005 the Justice Department formally renounced torture amid domestic and international furor: "Torture is abhorrent to both American law and values and to international norms." But in December 2004, the principal architect of the prisoner abuse policy, Alberto Gonzales, was named by the president to be Attorney General of the United States – in charge of the legal policies of the nation. One can only be deeply disturbed that someone guilty of incompetence and disregard of the law should be able to claim this role. It also casts extreme doubt on the sincerity of the administration's repudiation of its policy to condone torture. As the *Washington Post* declared in an editorial:[15]

It is indisputable that Gonzales oversaw and approved a decision to disregard the Geneva Conventions for detainees from Afghanistan, that he endorsed interrogation methods that military and FBI professionals regarded as illegal and improper, and that he supported indefinite detention of both foreigners and Americans without due process. . . . Senators who vote to ratify Gonzales nomination . . . bear the responsibility of ratifying such views as legitimate.

Clearly the pattern of abuse of prisoners was not an isolated occurrence; rather, independent investigations showed that it was widespread – in Iraq, Afghanistan, and Guantanamo, and elsewhere. It was also not caused by a few renegade soldiers who broke the rules; rather the blame lies with high-level Bush administration officials who either fashioned the policies or turned a blind eye to the abuse. The reaction of the Bush administration has also been a scandal. FBI reports document a cover-up operation by administration officials. Moreover, when the photos of the abuse forced some action to be taken, lower-level military personnel were sentenced to prison, whereas higher officials like Gonzales were promoted or given medals of appreciation.

One final important point – after September 11, President Bush declared a War on Terror on behalf of the United States. Is declaring "war" on terror a good idea? Perhaps not – declaring war may give terrorists rights they do not deserve. Declaring war may trigger the Geneva Convention, and terrorists may attempt to claim POW status. A better idea would be to maintain a distinction between war and terrorism so that terrorists may never have their "cause" dignified by international legal status. Terrorists, as opposed to those captured in the wars in Iraq and Afghanistan, should not be able to claim the privileges of the Geneva Convention, which can insulate conduct that is otherwise criminal from prosecution. Terrorists should remain subject to

---

[15]  Editorial, *Washington Post*, January 16, 2005.

the full force of national and international criminal law. The United States should not dignify domestic Islamist or other terrorist groups with the status of belligerents. Declaring a war on terror may be good politics, but it may also work to the advantage of the very terrorists who seek to disrupt American society.[16]

## ENTER THE U.S. SUPREME COURT

A remarkable feature of the U.S. political system is the key role played from time to time by the courts in foreign policy decisions. The U.S. judiciary usually steers clear of international relations, but there is a limit to this forbearance. While being careful not to intrude on foreign policy prerogatives of the President and the Congress, the U.S. Supreme Court will not hesitate to consider controversial foreign policy issues if it determines that important constitutional principles are at stake.

In connection with the U.S. "war" on terror, President George W. Bush determined that prisoners accused of terrorist-related activities, including those captured in Afghanistan and held at Guantanamo Bay, Cuba, are not entitled to prisoner of war status under the Geneva Convention and are subject to trial by special U.S. military commissions.[17] In November 2005 the Supreme Court agreed to review the constitutionality of the President's determination, setting the stage for a possible landmark ruling on the legality of the military courts and the power of the President to hold almost 500 prisoners at Guantanamo for an indefinite period. The issue arose in the case of Salim Ahmed Hamdan,[18] a Yemeni citizen and self-confessed Al Qaeda trainee who was Osama Bin Laden's personal driver and bodyguard. Hamdan was captured in Afghanistan in late November 2001. He argues that trial by a U.S. military commission is illegal on the ground that he is a prisoner of war under the Geneva Convention.

The Supreme Court has recently rendered key rulings in other foreign policy-related cases, causing U.S. Attorney General Alberto Gonzales to chide by name Justices Stephen Breyer and Anthony Kennedy for citing foreign law principles in their court opinions.

---

[16]  See Vaughn Lowe, "Clear and Present Danger: Responses to Terrorism," 54 *International and Comparative Law Quarterly* 185 (2005), arguing that terrorists should be treated as criminals and not as combatants.

[17]  Military Order of the President, November 13, 2001.

[18]  Hamdan v. Rumsfeld, Case No. 05-184 (Nov. 2005).

## Due Process for "Enemy Combatants"

Fortunately, the policy changes of the Bush administration attracted the attention of the U.S. Supreme Court. In June of 2004 the Court handed down three landmark rulings that required the government to change course.

In *Rasul v. Bush*,[19] the Court considered habeas corpus petitions filed on behalf of several of the aliens being detained as enemy combatants in Guantanamo. The Court ruled that the government could not hold people without charge, even at a military base outside the United States. Although they may be taken into custody as enemy combatants, they must be accorded an evidentiary hearing before an impartial tribunal that allows them to contest this status, and if they do so successfully, they must be released. The Court's ruling was on the basis of what is required under U.S. law, but it accords with the standards of the Geneva Convention (No. III).[20]

A second case, *Hamdi v. Rumsfeld*,[21] involved an American citizen captured in Afghanistan. No charges were filed against him, and he was not allowed any contact with outsiders. A plurality of the Supreme Court (four of the nine justices) ruled that Mr. Hamdi's indefinite detention without charge was illegal and as an American citizen he has the right to receive notice of the factual basis for being held as an enemy combatant and must be given a fair opportunity to rebut these facts before a "neutral decision maker." Four other Justices, in two different opinions held his detention to be squarely unlawful.

The third case, *Rumsfeld v. Padilla*,[22] was decided on a technicality, but four of the justices joined an opinion of Justice Stevens that particularly objected to the practice of holding prisoners incommunicado in order to extract information:

Executive detention of subversive citizens, like detention of enemy soldiers to keep them off the battlefield, may sometimes be justified to prevent persons from launching or becoming missiles of destruction. It may not, however, be justified by the naked interest in using unlawful procedures to extract information. Incommunicado detention for months on end is such a procedure. Whether the information so procured is more or less reliable than that acquired by more extreme forms of torture is of no consequence. For if this Nation is to remain true

---

[19]  124 S. Ct. 2686 (2004).
[20]  Regrettably, the Supreme Court did not say that the Geneva Conventions applied and largely ignored international law.
[21]  124 S. Ct. 2633 (2004).                              [22] 124 S. Ct. 2698 (2004).

to the ideals symbolized by its flag, it must not wield the tools of tyrants even to resist assaults by the forces of tyranny.

These three rulings of the U.S. Supreme Court forced the Bush administration to change its policy. Both Hamdi and Padilla were released, and the Guantamamo prisoners were granted evidentiary hearings on their status. Interrogation techniques were brought into line with accepted military practice.

## Prohibiting the Death Penalty for Juveniles

On March 1, 2005 the Supreme Court decided, five votes to four, that the death penalty is "cruel and unusual punishment" prohibited by the Eighth and Fourteenth Amendments to the U.S. Constitution when imposed on a person who was under the age of eighteen at the time the crime was committed.[23] International law and the opinion of the international community were the principal reasons for this decision.

Although international law is not "controlling" when it comes to the U.S. Constitution, the Court, in an opinion authored by Justice Kennedy, found that it provides a "respected and significant confirmation" of the Court's view that the juvenile death penalty is wrong and should not be permitted. The Court relied on both treaty and customary international law for this conclusion.

A basis in treaty law was provided by the U.N. Convention on the Rights of the Child, Article 37, which expressly forbids the death penalty for crimes committed by juveniles under the age of eighteen. In an oblique criticism, the Court pointed out that "every country in the world save the United States and Somalia" has ratified the Child Convention, and none had entered a reservation concerning the juvenile death penalty provision. For good measure the Court also cited similar prohibitions against the juvenile death penalty in the American Convention on Human Rights and the African Convention on the Rights and Welfare of the Child.

Turning to international customary law, the Court declared that the fact that the United States is "the only country in the world" that employs the juvenile death penalty means that it is appropriate for it to embrace the world consensus on this issue. "It is proper that we acknowledge," said the Court, "the overwhelming weight of international opinion" against the juvenile death penalty.

Thus, the Supreme Court based a landmark interpretation of the U.S. Constitution on international treaty and customary international law.

[23]  Roper v. Simmons, 125 S. Ct. 1183 (2005).

## Recovering Damages for Violations of International Law:
## The U.S. Alien Tort Statute

No one is exactly sure why, but the U.S. Founding Fathers thought it important to provide a cause of action allowing the recovery of damages for violations of international law. The U.S. Alien Tort Statute (ATS), passed in 1789 by the very first Congress, confers jurisdiction on the U.S. courts to hear any "civil action by an alien for a tort . . . committed in violation of the law of nations or a treaty of the United States." In a 1980 case, *Filartiga v. Pena-Irala*,[24] a U.S. Court of Appeals applied this law to allow a father and daughter who had been subjected to torture in Paraguay to recover damages against the perpetrator. Regrettably, the Filartigas are still trying to collect on this judgment.

Nevertheless, the Filartiga case sparked a revival of the ATS, and two kinds of cases flooded into the courts. One kind of case was similar to Filartiga in which citizens of foreign countries filed suits against their foreign oppressors when they came to the United States. For example, Radovan Karadzik, the former president of the Republic of Serpsa, was sued in 1996 over his actions during the Yugoslavian civil wars.[25] Despite their undoubted merit and publicity value, these actions have been largely unsuccessful in obtaining real redress. Foreign defendants simply avoid the United States, and judgments either cannot be rendered or are uncollectible.

The ATS has also been used by foreign plaintiffs allied with U.S. environmental and civil rights groups who sue U.S. companies[26] over their alleged destruction of the environment and violations of human rights in connection with foreign investments. None of these cases has ended with judgments against the companies concerned, but the negative publicity has generated controversy, and companies have paid damages to settle out of court.[27]

The quixotic character of the ATS moved one judge, Henry Friendly, to call the ATS a "legal Lohengrin,"[28] a reference to the Richard Wagner opera, *Lohengrin*, and its main character, a knight of the Holy Grail, who appears out of nowhere coming down a river in a boat drawn by a swan.

In 2004, the U.S. Supreme Court, in the landmark case of *Sosa v. Alvarez-Machain*,[29] reaffirmed that the ATS furnishes "jurisdiction for a relatively

---

[24] 630 F. 2d 876 (2d Cir. 1980).     [25] Kadic v. Karadzic, 70 F.3d 232 (2d Cir. 1995).
[26] For example, Freeport-McMoran Co. of Louisiana was sued for its environmental abuses, human rights violations and "cultural genocide" activities in Indonesia. Beanal v. Freeport-McMoran, Inc., 197 F. 3d 161 (5th Cir. 1999).
[27] e.g., Doe v. Unocal Corporation, 202 U.S. App. Lexis 19263 (9th Cir. 2002).
[28] IIT v. Vencap, 519 F. 2d 1001, 1015 (2d Cir. 1975).
[29] 124 S. Ct. 2739 (2004).

modest set of actions alleging violations of the law of nations, and might be applied to recover damages in cases of clear and egregious human rights violations."[30] The Supreme Court majority in the *Sosa* case reaffirmed that the United States and its judiciary are bound by international law norms, including customary international law, and that this is one of the narrow areas where federal common law continues to exist.[31]

## The Vienna Consular Convention Cases

The Vienna Convention on Consular Relations is a multilateral treaty that protects foreign nationals from arbitrary arrest. Any American who travels abroad can appreciate the idea behind this treaty; it ensures some protection against arbitrary detention by foreign governments. The Convention on Consular Relations requires that the competent authority allow an arrested foreign national to communicate with his or her government's consulate, and any arrested foreigner must be promptly informed of this right. The consular authorities have the right to visit and correspond with the person under arrest and can arrange for his or her legal representation.

Although the United States has insisted on these rights for Americans, U.S. authorities have largely ignored them with respect to foreign nationals in the United States until recently. In thousands of cases, including over 100 cases in which foreign nationals were sentenced to death, no timely notification was given. When this issue was raised by defense attorneys, the courts routinely denied relief either on the ground that it was too late to raise the matter or that the Consular Convention only grants rights to state parties and not to the individuals arrested.

In frustration various states brought cases against the United States in the International Court of Justice (ICJ) in The Hague, arguing that the United States was violating the consular conventions with impunity. In 1998 the ICJ ordered preliminary relief – that the U.S. government take all measures at its disposal to ensure that a Paraguayan national, Angel Francisco Breard, would not be executed before the ICJ could render a final decision.[32] U.S. Secretary of State Madeleine Albright requested that the governor of Virginia delay Breard's execution, but this request was ignored, and the U.S. Supreme Court rejected Breard's petition for habeas corpus relief on the ground that the question should have been raised earlier and furthermore, "any rights . . . [under]

[30] Ibid. at 2753.
[31] Ibid. at 2764.
[32] Paraguay v. United States, 1998 ICJ Rep. 248.

the Vienna Convention exist for the benefit of Paraguay, and not for [Breard] as an individual."[33]

Following *Breard* the ICJ decided two additional consular convention cases, one brought by Germany and the other by Mexico, on their merits. In the *LaGrand case*,[34] which involved two German nationals convicted of murder, the ICJ found a violation of the Convention on Consular Relations, but the U.S. Supreme Court refused to intervene and the violation was ignored. The LaGrand brothers were subsequently executed.

In 2004 the International Court of Justice again found that the United States had disregarded the consular notification requirement in the *Avena case*[35] involving fifty-one Mexican citizens who had been convicted of murder and were on death row awaiting execution. As a consequence of this failure, the ICJ found that Mexico was deprived of its right under the treaty to render assistance, and the individual defendants were deprived of their rights to communicate with their government and to arrange legal representation. This time one U.S. court had the courage to do something – the Oklahoma Court of Criminal Appeals[36] stayed the execution of one of the fifty-one prisoners, Osvaldo Torres, and required an evidentiary hearing on the remedy to be provided for the violation of international law by Oklahoma authorities. Oklahoma Governor Brad Henry subsequently commuted Torres's sentence, citing the international court's ruling.

The state of Texas, however, ignored the *Avena* judgment in the case of Jose Medellin, another one of the fifty-one Mexican nationals under sentence of death. In May 2004 the U.S. Court of Appeals for the Fifth Circuit denied Medellin's right to appeal the denial of his writ of habeas corpus, citing the legal rulings of the U.S. Supreme Court allowing disregard of the Vienna Consular Convention. But in December 2004 the Supreme Court decided to revisit the issue; the Court granted a petition to review the Court of Appeals' decision in the Medellin case.[37]

The United States placed great reliance on the Vienna Convention on Consular Relations in 1979 when Iran seized U.S. citizens and diplomats in their takeover of the U.S. Embassy in Tehran. At that time the International Court of Justice agreed with the United States, and ruled that its treaty rights had been violated by Iran. The ICJ decision was a factor in securing the release

---

[33]  Breard v. Greene, 523 U.S. 371, 118 S. Ct. 1352 (1998).
[34]  Germany v. United States, 2001 ICJ Rep. 7.
[35]  Avena and other Mexican Nationals (Mexico v. U.S.), 2004 ICJ 128, 43 ILM 581 (2004).
[36]  Osbaldo Torres v. State of Oklahoma, No. PCD-04-442 (Ct. Crim. App. May 13, 2004), summarized at 98 AJIL 581(2004).
[37]  Medellin v. Dretke, 125 S. Ct. 2088 (2005).

of the U.S. hostages in January 1980. One of Medellin's principal supporters was Ambassador Bruce Laingen, who was the charge d'affaires in the U.S. Embassy during the Iran hostage crisis.

After the Supreme Court's decision to review the *Medellin* case, the Bush administration apparently decided on a preemptive strike. Seeing the handwriting on the wall – that the U.S. Supreme Court might uphold the Consular Convention's notification requirement – President Bush on February 28, 2005 issued an executive proclamation that

The United States will discharge its international obligations under the decision of the International Court of Justice . . . by having state courts give effect to the decision in accordance with general principles of comity.

The president had decided – reluctantly – that the United States must comply with the ICJ's decision and the clear international obligations of the Consular Convention. Yet, he pointedly refrained from stating that the United States is obligated to comply under international law; he merely cited "comity," a willingness to act *voluntarily*, not under legal obligation.

A few days later,[38] in order to make crystal clear his intent, President Bush informed Secretary-General Kofi Annan that the United States "hereby withdraws" from the Optional Protocol to the Vienna Convention that allows the ICJ to decide on violations of the Convention. Although the United States itself originally proposed this protocol in 1963, the Bush administration decided to insulate the U.S. criminal law system from oversight by the ICJ. So now the United States has repudiated an international principle of human rights it once fought to achieve.[39]

The problem with this approach is that, although America does not have to worry any more about international law protecting foreigners charged with crimes in the United States, Americans arrested abroad also lose their ability to appeal to international law if their rights are denied.[40]

---

[38]  Presidential Communication, March 7, 2005.

[39]  The Bush administration action was successful in avoiding a potentially embarrassing clash with the U.S. Supreme Court. On May 23, 2005 the Supreme Court dismissed Medellin's petition for review as having been improvidently granted. Medellin v. Dretke, 125 S.Ct. 2088 (2005). The Court stated that the state court proceeding could provide Medellin with review and reconsideration of his Vienna Convention claim as required by the ICJ, and that was sufficient. However, Justice O'Connor, joined by Justices Stevens, Souter, and Breyer, filed a dissenting opinion in which she stated that she would vacate the Court of Appeals decision to deny Medellin a certificate of appealability and remand for further proceedings.

[40]  In November 2005 the Supreme Court returned to the sensitive issue of whether state courts and officials may ignore claims by foreign nationals of violation of the Vienna Consular Convention. The court agreed to hear two cases on this matter, *Sanchez-Llamas v. Oregon*,

## THE U.N. SYSTEM

### Substantive Rights

First Lady Eleanor Roosevelt – Mrs. Franklin D. Roosevelt as she was known in that "pre-liberation" time – was the chair of the U.N. Commission on Human Rights that drafted the founding document of the U.N. human rights system, the Universal Declaration of Human Rights. One can imagine how she would be pilloried today for such noble service. Her work is largely forgotten amid the acclaim currently accorded to the more war-like deeds of the "greatest generation."

One of the purposes of the United Nations is the protection of human rights,[41] and the Universal Declaration of Human rights of 1948 was adopted by the U.N. General Assembly as the embodiment of the human rights guarantees that the U.N. was founded to provide. The Universal Declaration was adopted without a dissenting vote (the Soviet bloc and Saudi Arabia abstained) and is today regarded as the Magna Charta of international human rights, binding on all the states of the world.

The content of the Universal Declaration is remarkable; Mrs. Roosevelt envisioned what we now call three "generations" of human rights for all people. The first generation comprises traditional civil and political rights – freedoms guaranteed as well by the U.S. Bill of Rights. These are restrictions and limitations placed upon states on interference with freedoms of speech, movement, property, life, and personal security. They also forbid arbitrary arrest and detention and require a fair trial for those accused of crimes.

The second generation of rights guaranteed by the Universal Declaration are economic, social, and cultural rights that have gained recognition in the twentieth century. These include rights to education, to work, and to participate in cultural life.

A third generation of rights include recognition of certain group rights, such as the right to democracy[42] and the right to development,[43] the latter dear to the developing countries of the world (see "The Universal Declaration of Human Rights").

---

(Case No. 04-10566) and *Bastillo v. Johnson* (Case No. 05-51). The court's ruling is expected in June 2006.

[41]  U.N. Charter, Articles 55–56.

[42]  The right to democracy can be derived from the Universal Declaration of Human Rights, Articles 21 and 29, as well as from the International Covenant on Civil and Political Rights, Article 25, which references representative government. The right to democracy deserves to be better and more explicitly defined.

[43]  This right was elaborated by a U.N. Declaration on the Right to Development (1986).

## THE UNIVERSAL DECLARATION OF HUMAN RIGHTS

**Article 1** Recognition of being born free and equal in dignity and rights

**Article 2** Right to equality

**Article 3** Right to life, liberty, and security of person

**Article 4** Freedom from slavery or servitude

**Article 5** Freedom from torture or cruel, inhuman, or degrading treatment or punishment

**Article 6** Right to recognition everywhere as a person before the law

**Article 7** Right to equality before the law

**Article 8** Right to an effective remedy by competent national tribunals

**Article 9** Right not to be subjected to arbitrary arrest, detention, or exile

**Article 10** Right to fair trial

**Article 11** Presumption of innocence and prohibition of retroactive criminal law

**Article 12** Prohibition of arbitrary interference with privacy, family, home, or correspondence

**Article 13** Right to freedom of movement

**Article 14** Right to seek asylum

**Article 15** Right to a nationality

**Article 16** Right to marry and found a family

**Article 17** Right to own property

**Article 18** Right to freedom of thought, conscience, and religion

**Article 19** Right to freedom of opinion and expression

**Article 20** Right to freedom of peaceful assembly

**Article 21** Right to participate in the governance of the state and the right to democracy

**Article 22** Right to social security

**Article 23** Right to work

**Article 24** Right to rest and leisure

**Article 25** Right to a decent standard of living

**Article 26** Right to education

**Article 27** Right to cultural life

**Article 28** Right to a social and international order suitable for the realization of human rights

Taking their cue from the Universal Declaration, U.N. members concluded a series of multilateral human rights treaties in the second half of the twentieth century. The 1966 International Covenant on Civil and Political Rights elaborates protection of first-generation rights. Because neither the Universal Declaration nor the Covenant forbids imposition of the death penalty, an Optional Protocol[44] was opened in 1989 to encourage Covenant states to abolish capital punishment. An International Covenant on Economic, Social, and Cultural Rights was also adopted in 1966 to clarify the obligations regarding second-generation rights. Because economic rights in particular involve cost and other undertakings that may be impractical, many economic rights, such as provision of all with a decent standard of living, are considered "aspirational" or promotional rights, designated goals to be achieved progressively according to the capability of each state.

Elaboration of third-generation group rights was also addressed in more detail by specifying a right of self-determination in both covenants and in U.N. declarations on the rights of minorities[45] and indigenous peoples.[46] Although the right to self-determination does not require separate statehood, national minorities and indigenous peoples must be granted a measure of autonomy within the states in which they reside with respect to their educational, cultural, religious, social, and linguistic institutions. The right of self-determination can be fulfilled through the democratic process and through *internal autonomy* – a people's pursuit of its political, social, and cultural development within the framework of an existing state.[47]

The U.N. has also adopted separate detailed conventions addressing three particular issues: racial discrimination,[48] the rights of women,[49] and the rights of children.[50]

This U.N. system for the international protection of human rights has had a revolutionary impact on international relations. First, the right of national sovereignty is no longer absolute; a state cannot hide behind sovereignty if it is mistreating its own citizens. Thus, the traditional prohibition against

---

[44] Second Optional Protocol to the ICCPR, 29 ILM 1464 (1990).
[45] Declaration on the Rights of Persons Belonging to National or Ethnic, Religious, and Linguistic Minorities (1992).
[46] A U.N. Sub-Commission on the Protection and Promotion of Human Rights has adopted a Draft Declaration on the Rights of Indigenous Populations (1994). See also International Labor Organization Convention 169 on Indigenous and Tribal Peoples in Independent Countries, 1989.
[47] See T. Franck, "The Emerging Right to Democratic Governance," 86 *American Society of International Law*, 46 (1992); See the opinion of the Supreme Court of Canada in the Quebec case, (1998) DLR (4th) 385, 437–438.
[48] Convention on the Elimination of All Forms of Racial Discrimination (1966).
[49] Convention on the Elimination of All Forms of Discrimination against Women (1979).
[50] Convention on the Rights of the Child (1989).

nonintervention in internal affairs of a state, which is contained in Article 2 (7) of the U.N. Charter, must now be balanced against the internationally recognized duty of a state to observe human rights. Although the principle of domestic jurisdiction over human rights matters is still valid, the international community has a clear interest in securing human rights and may intervene economically and even, in extreme cases, militarily when domestic enforcement is impossible.

Second, the U.N. system empowers individuals in a significant manner under international law, departing from the traditional idea that international relations is concerned solely with states. Individuals are now significant subjects of concern under international relations and international law.

Third, there is no right without a corresponding duty, and it is clear that under the U.N. system states have significant new duties to fulfill. Three separate duties of states with respect to their own citizens may be analyzed: (1) a negative duty to refrain from actions that may prevent the fulfillment of human rights, such as free speech, freedom of association, and privacy; (2) a positive duty to progressively improve educational systems, social welfare, and economic opportunity; and (3) a duty to ensure that private actors within their jurisdiction respect human rights (so-called horizontal enforcement).

There is an important duty as well that is owed by developed countries to developing countries of the world. Under the U.N. Covenant on Economic, Social, and Cultural Rights,[51] developed countries must provide "economic and technical assistance" to developing countries. The specific type and amount of such assistance are up to each developed country to determine for itself, but assistance and cooperation must be rendered "to the maximum of its available resources." Under the terms of the U.N. Millennium Declaration of 2000, signed with great fanfare by the United States and 188 other states, developed countries set a goal of giving 0.7 percent of their national incomes as development aid for poor countries.

These are international duties that are new to international relations in the last half-century. We are at the beginning of their realization. They hold promise for the establishment of a new international order in this century.

## U.S. (Non)Acceptance of the U.N. System

A key indicator of U.S. recalcitrance and unilateralism is the fact that the United States ratified its first U.N. human rights treaty – the International Covenant on Civil and Political Rights – only in 1992. The Convention on the Elimination of All Forms of Racial Discrimination was ratified in 1994.

---

[51] Articles 2, 11, and 23.

Only these two treaties are fully in force for the United States, and even with respect to these two treaties, the United States added a reservation that they are non-self-executing, which means they have no impact on U.S. domestic law and cannot be invoked in U.S. courts by citizens or residents.

It is not hard to imagine why the U.S. "holier than thou" rhetoric sometimes rankles other nations. Former U.N. Ambassador Charles Yost, in testimony to the U.S. Congress, succinctly summarized the adverse international reaction to the U.S. failure to participate fully in the U.N. system for the protection of human rights:

There are, in my judgment, few failures or omissions on our part which have done more to undermine American credibility internationally than this one. Whenever an American delegate at an international conference, or an American Ambassador making representations on behalf of our Government, raises a question of human rights, as we have in these times many occasions to do, the response public or private, is very likely to be this: if you attach so much importance to human rights, why have you not even ratified the United Nations' conventions and covenants on this subject?

Our refusal to join in the international implementation of the principles we so loudly and frequently proclaim cannot help but give the impression that we do not practice what we preach, that we have something to hide.... Many are therefore inclined to believe that our whole human rights policy is... merely a display of self-righteousness directed against governments we dislike.[52]

The United States could add immensely to its international standing and gain cooperation from other nations at a very cheap price simply by resolving to fully participate with other nations in the human rights structure that has been erected internationally over the last half-century.

## Implementation and Enforcement of the U.N. System

The United Nations has no authority to directly implement or enforce its system for the protection of human rights; it depends upon states to do so. Nonetheless, there are important international mechanisms to put pressure on recalcitrant states.

**The Office of the U.N. High Commissioner of Human Rights.** In 1994 the U.N. General Assembly created the office of the U.N. High Commissioner for Human Rights (HCHR) to give a single individual the principal respon-

---

[52] Senate Hearings on International Human Rights Treaties, S. Comm. For. Rel. 96th Cong., 1st Sess. (1979), Statement of Charles Yost, Former Ambassador to the United Nations.

sibility for the promotion and protection of human rights around the world. Outstanding individuals have served in this office, including Sergio Veira de Mello, who was killed tragically in the terrorist attack on U.N. Headquarters in Iraq in August 2003. The current High Commissioner is Louise Arbour, a former member of the Canadian Supreme Court.

The task of the U.N. High Commissioner is complex; it includes providing technical assistance to states to strengthen human rights institutions, to engage governments in dialogue to secure respect for human rights, to enhance international cooperation, and to call attention to human rights abuses in the world. For example, the Office of the High Commissioner in the ten years of its existence has worked with over forty states to train judges, lawyers, and police and to strengthen civil institutions with human rights responsibilities in various countries. The HCHR office is currently involved in both Afghanistan and Iraq to create a human rights culture of women's rights, justice, and human rights education.

**The U.N. Commission on Human Rights.** The U.N. Commission on Human Rights has been in operation since 1946 and is intended to be the principal U.N. body on the subject of human rights; it plays the leading role in drafting declarations and treaties. The U.N. General Assembly elects the Commission's fifty-three member states for three-year terms; decisions are debated and taken by states through their representatives. As a result, the Commission is highly political. In 2001, as noted previously, the United States was voted out of the Commission, an incident that made world headlines and sparked outrage in Washington.

The Commission's work – investigating, monitoring, and responding to violations – falls into three broad categories. First is what is termed the 1235 procedure (authorized by Resolution 1235 of the U.N. Economic and Social Council), which is a public examination of allegations of "gross violations" or a "consistent pattern" of human rights violations. This investigation is normally triggered by the complaint of a state, and a working group or a Special Rapporteur is appointed to prepare a report, which is then discussed at the Commission's annual meeting. If infringements of human rights are found, the Commission's powers are limited to persuasion, public criticism, or condemnation; no binding sanctions are possible.

A second procedure available to the Commission is known as the 1503 procedure (authorized by Resolution 1503 of the U.N. Economic and Social Council), which is used to examine in private allegations received by NGOs and individuals. Normally a subcommission of independent experts that may appoint a *rapporteur* to investigate and quietly make recommendations to the country concerned carries out this investigation.

A third procedure is to appoint a working group to investigate a particular problem or issue, rather than a country. For example, working groups have been appointed to investigate disappearances, violence against women, and religious intolerance. These working groups produce reports that serve as the basis for discussion by the Commission and call attentions to violations, frequently occurring in many states.

Unfortunately, the nature of the Commission means that politics frequently holds sway over the merits of the problems discussed. States that are the most egregious human rights offenders gain membership and then use their political influence to escape condemnation. For example, Cuba, China, the Sudan, and Zimbabwe line up their supporters to fend off tough resolutions. The Commission's usefulness and credibility would be enhanced by reforms that would allow independent experts to conduct investigations of abuses under more objective conditions.

**Human Rights Committees.** Each of the U.N. treaties on human rights is assigned a committee to monitor and secure its implementation. The most significant of these committees is the Human Rights Committee created under Article 28 of the International Covenant on Civil and Political Rights. It is made up of eighteen independent experts who are required to serve in their "personal capacity" (no instructions from governments allowed). The committee members have three principal duties. First, they examine, discuss, and offer "concluding observations" on the country reports that all parties to the treaty are required to submit periodically on their compliance and implementation of the Covenant. Second, the committee may issue General Comments on issues relating to the Covenant. For example, in a General Comment[53] in 1984, the committee expressed its concern about the administration of justice by military and special courts in many countries.

Third, the most important function of the committee is to examine and offer written "views" on individual complaints by persons alleging violations of human rights. Under an Optional Protocol signed by over 100 nations, persons who are the victims of violations can file a complaint with the committee, which then considers both the complaint's admissibility and its merits in private, considering also the explanation of the state concerned. The committee may suggest remedies and reparations to victims. Although the committee's views are not binding, many times the state will comply with them.

---

[53] Human Rights Committee (1984) Selected Decisions 673.

For example, in the case of *Pratt and Morgan v. Jamaica*,[54] the committee successfully requested a stay of execution of the death penalty. In another case, the committee successfully upheld a woman's claim that she was denied a Social Security benefit on an equal footing with men.[55] This individual complaints procedure has worked fairly well; the committee has handled over 1,000 complaints, and views have been issued in almost 300, with a finding of a violation in 75 percent of cases.

**Nongovernmental Organizations.** The U.N. institutional structure is both weak and political; its inadequacies make imperative the role of NGOs in investigating and uncovering human rights violations and publicizing them. The U.N. system is designed in fact for NGOs to have a large role. They can file reports with the U.N. High Commissioner's office, help individuals file complaints, and criticize the behavior of states and their subsequent pronouncements and cover-ups.

**The U.N. Security Council.** We tend to forget that the U.N. Security Council (SC) has special responsibility for human rights under the U.N. system. As the "principal organ" of the U.N. with "primary responsibility" to maintain international peace and security, member states are pledged to "accept and carry out" SC decisions under the U.N. Charter.

The Council can act under Chapter VI of the Charter to investigate "any dispute . . . likely to endanger . . . international peace and security." It can recommend "methods of adjustment." If this is insufficient, the Council, acting under Chapter VII, can determine the existence of a "threat to the peace" and can call on member states to apply sanctions of various kinds, including boycotts and embargoes, or even authorize military action.

These powers must be put at the service of human rights violations – even within a single state – that endanger international peace. The link between human rights violations and international peace is apparent. Severe rights violations may prompt refugee flows into neighboring states, enrage people in other states who are ethnically related to the victims, and even threaten regional stability or lead to war. The Council has an important role in addressing certain human rights violations in tandem with other U.N. organs.

The Council has failed its responsibility for human rights several times in recent years. In the case of Rwanda in 1994, its failure to act led to the

---

[54] HRC Report, GAOR, 49th Sess., Supp. 40, Vol. I, p. 70.
[55] Broeks v. The Netherlands, HRC Communication No. 172/1984, available at http://secap174.un.org/search.

death of almost one million Tutsi people; in Kosovo in 1998 the Council's failure to act in the face of manifest violations led to intervention by a NATO force.

The Council has also failed to take decisive action in Darfur, in western Sudan where, since February 2003, Sudanese-backed militia called the Janjaweed (bandits) have killed by some estimates 300,000 people and driven more than 1.8 million from their homes. After much delay the Council in 2004 and 2005 authorized an inquiry and passed sanctions. An inadequate force of peacekeepers from the African Union has not been sufficient to prevent the continuing killing, rape, and destruction. Seeking to curry favor in Africa, China long blocked stronger action in Darfur, and the United States has been wary of any resolution allowing prosecution by the International Criminal Court.

## Reforming the U.N. System

The U.N. system for the protection of human rights is badly in need of fundamental reform. It is a confusing patchwork of committees, none of which has real power and all of which are highly bureaucratic and inefficient. The U.N. High Level Panel has made some helpful recommendations to get reform started:

■ Expansion of the Commission on Human Rights to universal membership (all U.N. members): A better proposal for reform by Secretary-General Kofi Annan would replace the fifty-three-member commission with a smaller Human Rights Council, a "society of the committed" that "should undertake to abide by the highest human rights standards."

■ Requiring that heads of delegations be prominent and experienced human rights figures;

■ Appointment of an outside Advisory Council; and

■ Preparation of an annual report on the status of human rights worldwide.

But much more should be done. The United States should take the lead in forming a caucus of democracies (about half the U.N. members) within the United Nations. This caucus under American leadership should formulate and implement reforms, such as the following:

■ The U.N. Commission (or Council) on Human Rights should have objective criteria for membership that make clear that only those states with impeccable human rights records can be members. The criteria for membership should include ratification of the main human rights international conventions, completion of all reports, and compliance with all monitoring and implementation bodies. This would correct the present situation – at present the U.N. Commission on Human Rights is captive to some of the world's most abusive governments, including Sudan, Zimbabwe, Russia, Saudi Arabia, China, and Cuba. This must stop.

■ The U.N. High Commissioner on Human Rights should be given central control over all U.N. human rights bodies.

■ The work of examining the record of each country with respect to human rights compliance and the examination of individual complaints should be turned over in full to a U.N. Committee of Human Rights that functions within the Office of the U.N. High Commissioner of Human Rights.

■ One committee whose head is appointed by the U.N. High Commissioner and reports to him or her should replace the present multiplicity of U.N. human rights committees. Subcommittees can handle the work of monitoring compliance with individual treaties.

■ The U.N. High Commissioner should make regular reports and recommendations to the U.N. Security Council regarding the status of human rights violations in the world.

■ Country reports on human rights filed with the United Nations should be publicly available, and individual complaints should be made public once they are determined to be admissible.

Reform of the U.N. Human Rights system is just as important (and perhaps just as difficult) as Security Council reform. At the 2005 World Summit of Heads of State and Government in New York, it was resolved to strengthen United Nations human rights machinery by creating a new Human Rights Council to address "violations of human rights, including gross and systematic violations, and make recommendations thereon."[56] Regretfully, this tepid idea does not address the real problems: the hypocrisies of the U.N. Human Rights Commission and the inadequate authority of the U.N. Human Rights Committees.

---

[56] United Nations General Assembly Doc. A/60/L, para. 159 (Sixtieth Session, 20 September 2005).

## THE INTERNATIONAL COURT OF JUSTICE MEETS
## THE ISRAELI WALL

The focal point of Muslim anger against the West, particularly the United States, is the condition of the Palestinian people. Islamist terrorism feeds off this anger and what is perceived as a U.S. double standard, turning a blind eye to violations of Palestinian rights. Nothing would help win the "war" on terrorism more than a just settlement of the Palestinian problem. With the death of Yasser Arafat, there is renewed hope for peace in the Middle East. But the outlook for peace is clouded by a new reality – the Israeli wall.

In response to terrorist attacks and suicide bombings during the Palestinian *Intifada*, the State of Israel is constructing a wall in the West Bank Occupied Territories (see accompanying map). The wall is located well inside the "Green Line" that marks the border between Israel and the occupied West Bank, which was conquered by Israel during the 1967 Six-Day War. The wall traces a sinuous path around and through many Palestinian communities; some villages are almost completely encircled and others are divided in two. The vicinity of the wall is designated a closed area. The wall is designed so that the great majority of Israeli settlements (with 80 percent of Israeli settlers) in the Occupied Palestinian Territories and East Jerusalem are on the Israeli side. Because access to Israel proper will be through designated checkpoints operated by the Israeli army, the wall will be *de facto* the Israeli border.

In July 2004 the International Court of Justice (ICJ), the U.N.'s principal judicial organ, issued an advisory opinion[57] at the request of the U.N. General Assembly on the legality of the wall. After unanimously upholding its jurisdiction, the ICJ ruled by fourteen votes to one (American Judge Thomas Buergenthal was the sole dissenter) that the building of the wall violates several human rights obligations incumbent upon Israel, the wall must be dismantled immediately, and Israel must make reparation for any damage caused. Israel was found by the court to be violating the major U.N. human rights treaties, including both international covenants and the Convention on the Rights of the Child. In addition, Israel was in violation of the laws of war (international humanitarian law) relating to occupied territories: the Fourth Geneva Convention of 1949 and the 1907 Hague Regulations.

The starting point of the court's reasoning is the fact that the entire West Bank east of the green line (the 1948 armistice line marking the Israeli border)

---

[57] International Court of Justice, Legal Consequences of the Construction of a Wall in the Occupied Palestinian Territory, 43 ILM 1009 (3004). For scholarly comment, see Agora, *American Journal of International Law* (2005): 1–141.

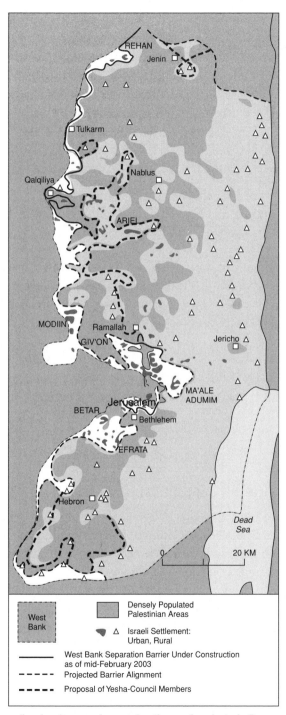

West Bank separation barrier – under construction and projected alignment.

was conquered by Israel and is therefore Palestinian Occupied Territory under international law, because it is illegal to acquire territory by force or conquest. This status of the West Bank was confirmed in Resolution 242, adopted unanimously by the U.N. Security Council after the 1967 Six-Day War, which requires Israeli withdrawal from occupied territories in exchange for ensured peace and recognition by all Arab governments.

The court did not question Israel's right to administer the Palestinian Occupied Territories, but said it must be done in accordance with international humanitarian law – the Geneva Conventions and the Hague Regulations that deal with the conduct of war and its aftermath. These require the occupying power to take all necessary measures to restore public order and civilian life within the occupied territory. Residents within occupied zones must be allowed, insofar as possible, freedom of movement, the right to work, and the right to choose where to live, as well as access to education, health care, and normal civil liberties. The Israeli wall, particularly in the way it is built – encircling, dividing, and requiring the demolition of communities – violates these norms. The creation of enclaves and the closed area seriously hampers freedom of movement and makes difficult or impossible access to health services, educational establishments, water sources, and agricultural production.

Most important, an occupying power is forbidden to compel demographic change, and the court found that the wall, by including Palestinian areas in what will now be *de facto* Israel proper, is seeking demographic change. In effect, the wall will become the new border, a *de facto* annexation, and Israel will gain substantial territory at the expense of the Palestinians. The court found that the wall's construction "severely impedes the exercise by the Palestinian people of its right to self-determination, and is therefore a breach of Israel's obligation to respect that right" as guaranteed by the two international covenants.

The court accepted the right and indeed the duty of Israel to defend itself from terrorists and suicide bombings, but found that self-defense does not justify building a wall located entirely within the Palestinian Occupied Territories.

What about the Israeli settlements within the Occupied Territories? Israel has located Jewish settlers in enclaves throughout the West Bank, and the reason for the sinuous course of the wall through Palestinian communities is to protect as many of these settlements as possible.

The unspoken assumption of the court is that these settlements are illegal under international law. The 1949 Geneva Convention (No. IV) Relative to the Protection of Civilians in Time of War prohibits actions by the occupying power to annex the occupied territory in whole or in part. This should come as no surprise because U.S. policymakers have long regarded the settlements as the single most difficult issue preventing peace in the Middle East. President Jimmy Carter has written[58]

It has been recognized that Israeli settlements in the occupied territories were a violation of international law and the primary incitement to violence among the Palestinians. Our most intense arguments at Camp David (meetings held in 1978 which led to a peace treaty between Israel and Egypt) were about their existence and potential expansion.

During the administration of President George H. W. Bush (Bush I), Secretary of State James Baker said, "I don't think there is any greater obstacle to peace than settlement activity that continues not only unabated but at an advanced pace."

Yet during the past two American administrations, the United States has largely turned a blind eye to the Israeli government's policy to lure Jewish settlers into the Occupied Territories with massive financial and political incentives, and recently the number of settlers has skyrocketed. In March 2005 the Israeli government approved the construction of 3,500 new housing units in Ma'ale Adumim, a community of about 30,000 Jews located in the West Bank ten kilometers east of Jerusalem. Although this is a clear violation of the "road map" set out by the United States for peace in the Middle East, this settlement expansion drew only a quiet rebuke from the American government.

The Israeli wall case demonstrates that the settlements issue remains at the heart of the Israeli-Palestinian dispute. As President Jimmy Carter has said: "No matter what leaders the Palestinians choose, how fervent American interest might be, or how great the hatred and bloodshed might become, there remains one basic choice, and only the Israelis can make it: *Do we want peace with all our neighbors, or do we want to retain our settlements in the Occupied Territories?*"[59]

It is a sad irony that the State of Israel, founded to provide a refuge after the Holocaust, a homeland for Jews brutally and despicably deprived of their most fundamental human rights, should itself be guilty of human rights violations. But the Israeli wall also poses an important challenge for the United States and the rest of the world. There is no more important action that can be taken to quell Islamic terrorism in the world than to broker a peace between Israel and the Palestinians.

---

[58] *Washington Post*, Sept. 27, 2003.
[59] Jimmy Carter, "The Choice," on the occasion of the 25th Anniversary of the Camp David Accords. *Washington Post*, 23 September 2003.

President Harry Truman created the State of Israel in 1948 through a unilateral action of recognition on the advice of his political operatives, who wished to improve his chances for reelection. At the time, Truman's Secretary of State, George Marshall, was conducting sensitive negotiations to partition the territory of Palestine between the Jews and the Arabs. Truman's action surprised and angered Marshall, who was not informed in advance and was in the midst of negotiations with both parties to create two states, Israel and a Palestinian state. Jerusalem was to be an international city, sacred to all – Muslims, Jews, and Christians. Because of Truman's precipitous act, instead of two states as there should have been in 1948, there has been continuing conflict.

Now after almost sixty years of bloodshed, it is possible to agree through multilateral diplomacy on the two-state solution that was on the table in 1948. As President Carter has said, the key is Israeli willingness to give up its West Bank settlements. Israel has wisely decided to relinquish its settlements in Gaza, and to implement the peace with Egypt, Israel gave up all its settlements in the Sinai; it must be willing to do the same in the Occupied Territories. All other issues between Israel and the Palestinians are soluble if the settlement issue is resolved. But without agreement on this issue, conflict will continue without end.

A final irony is that only the creation of a Palestinian state can ensure Israel's survival as a Jewish state. Within and outside Israel itself, demographic trends make it clear that it is only a matter of time before Arabs constitute a majority of the population between the Jordan River and the Mediterranean Sea.

### SUMMING UP

Human rights must be used as a weapon against Islamist terrorism. Islamic countries are among the most repressive regimes in the world. Multilateral institutions and human rights law should be enlisted in the campaign against terror.

The flouting of U.S. and international law of human rights after 9/11 has severely harmed U.S. interests and has reduced the effectiveness of the anti-terrorism effort. The official policy of the U.S. government to allow torture in the interrogation of prisoners has done great harm. By using torture, the United States has relinquished the ideological high ground – the values of democracy, freedom, and human rights – and Americans are transformed into the villains and hypocrites the terrorists proclaim them to be. Torture is a self-defeating strategy of weakness.

The extensive prisoner abuse documented in the press and in official reports did nothing to aid the War on Terror; in fact, it was counterproductive as it became a potent propaganda weapon for terrorists and Muslim extremists. Guantanamo has become the face of America for millions of Muslim people.

Americans believe their country is in the forefront of protecting human rights in the world, but the reality is somewhat different. The U.S. government's arrogance, ignorance, and unilateralism have severely compromised its ability to exercise leadership in this important area of international relations. Amnesty International in May 2005 accused the United States of condoning "atrocious" human rights violations, thereby diminishing its moral authority and setting an example of abuse for other nations.

A legitimate question is why is there such a furor over American violations of human rights standards when these pale in comparison with the terrible deprivations of human rights elsewhere – in Darfur where hundreds of thousands are driven from their homes and subjected to murder, rape, and torture; in Myanmar, where there is documented slave labor, conscription of child soldiers, systematic rape, massacres, and destruction of whole villages; and not to mention other countries such as China, and Cuba, where violations are also rife. Are human rights violations worthy of international attention only when committed by Americans?

The reason the spotlight is on the United States is that it is the most influential nation in the world, and rightly or wrongly, it sets the standards for other nations. A second reason is that the United States was founded upon the principle of human rights and has always claimed special moral authority in that area. The United States, which was the leader in creating the system of international human rights, is now compromised, and this gives comfort to other nations and leaders that may find it in their interest to violate human rights.

Since World War II, imposing structures of international human rights law and institutions have been created under the aegis of the United Nations and international regional organizations. Although this system is highly political, weak, and immature, it is a global system of standards for the protection of human rights for the first time in the history of the world. If this system can evolve in the next fifty years at the rate of the last fifty years, the twenty-first century can mark the time when the human race finally triumphs over centuries of inhumanity and discrimination. The United States by embracing multilateralism can exercise the leadership to rejuvenate this global system and realize its promise.

**FURTHER READINGS**

Javaid Rehman, *International Human Rights Law: A Practical Approach* (2003).

Henry J. Steiner and Philip Alston, *International Human Rights in Context* (1996).

Louis Henkin, Gerald L. Neuman, Diane F. Orentlicher, and David W. Leebron, *Human Rights* (1999).

David Weissbrodt, Joan Fitzpatrick, and Frank Newman, *International Human Rights* (2001).

Nigel S. Rodley, *The Treatment of Prisoners under International Law* (2d ed. 1999).

Rene Provost, *International Human Rights and Humanitarian Law* (2002).

Philip Alston, ed., *The U.N. and Human Rights* (2d ed. 2003).

Louis Henkin, *Politics and Values* (1995).

Hersch Lauterpacht, *International Law and Human Rights* (1950).

Makau Mutua, *Human Rights: A Political and Cultural Critique* (2002).

Bernard Lewis, *The Crisis of Islam* (2003).

*The Abu Ghraib Investigation: The Official Report of the Independent Panel and the Pentagon* (2004).

William A. Edmundson, *An Introduction to Rights* (2004).

Mark Danner, *Torture and Truth: America, Abu Ghraib, and the War on Terror* (2004).

Karen J. Greenberg and Joshua L. Dratel, eds., *The Torture Papers: The Road to Abu Ghraib* (2004).

# 9 International Crimes

In the summer of 2002, the International Criminal Court (ICC) began working in The Hague, Netherlands; its work was accepted by 97 nations, but not the United States. For the first time the world has in operation a permanent court that can try individuals who commit international crimes. Why is this needed? Why is the United States standing down? Could the ICC become an effective weapon in fighting the world war against terror?

## ORIGINS

The concept of international crime as distinct from national criminal activity grew out of a recognition that (1) war crimes were offenses for which the individuals who commit them should be responsible; (2) the definition and elements making up such a crime were a matter of international, not national, law; and (3) in some cases at least, the individuals accused of such crimes should be tried by an international rather than a national court or tribunal.

These three issues were confronted for the first time at the end of World War II. Many of the events of that war were considered to have far exceeded the bounds of the norms of warfare solemnly agreed to in multilateral treaties, notably the international humanitarian law rules agreed in The Hague conferences in 1899 and 1907 (see Chapter 8) and the Kellogg-Briand Pact (see Chapter 4) outlawing aggressive war. Furthermore, it was believed that the individuals who made the decisions and carried out acts of horrible brutality and consequences should not be able to hide behind the idea that their state had gone to war. States act through individuals, and when the state breaks certain rules, the individuals who actually made the decisions should be punished. This was a recognition for the first time that individuals, not merely states, have duties and responsibilities under international law.

The allied nations at the end of World War II also confronted issues of what courts should try those accused. They could not use the laws and courts of Germany and Japan, and it was considered inappropriate to choose the law and court system of one of the Allies. The solution was to create special international criminal tribunals: the Nuremberg International Military Tribunal for accused Nazis and the International Military Tribunal (Tokyo) for the Far East to deal with accused Japanese. These two courts functioned in 1945 and 1946, and German and Japanese war leaders were found guilty and either executed or imprisoned.

At the start of their work, both international tribunals adopted charters that defined the international crimes for which the accused individuals would have responsibility. Three international crimes were established and defined:[1]

1. Crimes against peace: planning and waging a war of aggression

2. War crimes: violations of the laws of war

3. Crimes against humanity: murder, extermination, and other inhuman acts against civilian populations

The International Military Tribunal at Nuremberg tried twenty-one Nazi leaders, of whom eighteen were convicted; the International Military Tribunal for the Far East tried twenty-eight Japanese leaders, and all were convicted (except for two who died during the course of the trials). In addition, special courts and military tribunals between 1946 and 1949 tried and convicted several hundred less prominent German and Japanese figures.

Some have called the Nuremberg and Tokyo trials "victors' justice"[2]; this is correct in the sense that the winners of World War II used their power to establish the tribunals and define the law and the punishment regime. Yet, the law applied by these tribunals was not invented in 1945. As the tribunals pointed out in their written judgments, there was abundant customary and treaty law relating to the use of force prior to World War II. The international law of war and the prohibition of aggressive war under the 1928 Kellogg-Briand Pact were accepted by both Germany and Japan. The individuals involved must have known that their actions contravened international law. What was new in 1945 was pinpointing individual responsibility for acts committed in warfare.

---

[1] See Agreement for the Prosecution and Punishment of the Major War Criminals of the European Axis Powers and Charter of the International Military Tribunal (1945), Article 6. A similar charter was adopted for the International Military Tribunal for the Far East in 1946.
[2] See the discussion in Richard K. Gardiner, *International Law* 285 (2003).

The charge of "victors' justice" rings true in the sense that only the losers of World War II were put on trial. It is undeniable that war crimes were committed on the allied side as well: most egregiously the fire bombing of Dresden and the killing of over 200,000 innocent civilians in the atomic bombing of Hiroshima and Nagasaki. The law of war expressly forbids such acts not only now but at that time as well. Article 25 of the Annex to the Fourth Hague Convention of 1907 forbids "the attack or bombardment, by whatever means, of towns, villages, dwellings, or buildings which are undefended." The fact of allied war crimes was put into context by the admission in 2004 by former Defense Secretary Robert S. McNamara that, as a young Army officer during World War II responsible for selecting Japanese cities as targets, he joked with colleagues that "if we lose the war, we will all be prosecuted as war criminals."

## RELATIONSHIP TO HUMAN RIGHTS

International criminal law draws its origin from two sources: international human rights laws and national criminal law. International human rights conventions provide the foundation in that certain violations of human rights guarantees were considered so reprehensible as to merit criminal prosecution. This was the case with the Nuremberg and Tokyo war crimes trials with regard to war crimes, aggression, and genocide. In 1946, the General Assembly of the United Nations resolved that it "affirms the principles of international law recognized by the Charter of the Nuremberg Tribunal and the judgment of the Tribunal."[3] In 1948, the United Nations concluded a Convention on the Prevention and Punishment of the Crimes of Genocide,[4] now with 122 contracting parties including the United States. The Genocide Convention confirms an obligation on states to prevent and punish genocide whether committed in times of peace or in times of war. The Convention prescribes a dual jurisdiction for possible prosecutions:

Article 17: Persons charged with genocide . . . shall be tried by a competent tribunal of the state in the territory of which the action was committed, or by such international penal tribunal as may have jurisdiction with respect to those Contracting Parties which shall have accepted its jurisdiction.

This provision establishes state prosecution as unequivocal, but international criminal prosecution is a recognized supplementary remedy.

[3] GA Res. 95 (I) G.A.O.R Res., 1st Sess. Part II, p. 188.
[4] 78 UNTS 277 (1951).

## CRIMES OF INTERNATIONAL CONCERN

During the Cold War the idea of creating an international criminal court became a dead letter, lost in the rivalry between East and West. Yet, events spawned a number of multilateral conventions dealing with crimes of international concern. A rash of airplane hijackings in the 1960s led to a 1970 Convention on Unlawful Seizure of Aircraft and a 1971 Convention on Unlawful Acts against the Safety of Civil Aviation.

Acts of terrorism beginning in the 1970s led to a number of international conventions calling for criminalization of various categories of terrorist activities, such as attacking athletes at international sporting events (a reaction to the terrorist killings during the 1972 Munich Olympic Games),[5] the taking of hostages,[6] attacking cruise ships[7] and people in airports,[8] and terrorist bombings.[9] These conventions did not make terrorism an international crime *per se*, but they required states to criminalize and punish various kinds of terrorist activities under their national criminal laws.

During the 1980s the international community through the United Nations also elaborated and concluded a Convention against Torture (1984), which called for the prevention and criminalization of torture under international law as a discrete offense in addition to a matter that may be punished as a war crime or a crime against humanity. The U.N. Torture Convention defines torture as "any act by which severe pain or suffering, whether physical or mental, is ... inflicted on a person ... by or at the instigation of a public official or other person acting in an official capacity." The infliction of pain or suffering must be "intentional," not merely negligent or reckless, however, to amount to torture.

## THE TRIBUNALS FOR YUGOSLAVIA AND RWANDA

After the end of the Cold War, the impetus to establish an international criminal court quickened, as international cooperation was again possible. The 1990s were marked by two bloody conflicts in which hundreds of thousands of innocent civilians suffered death, injury, and other atrocities. In response, the U.N. Security Council, acting under Chapter VII of the U.N. Charter, set up

---

[5] Convention on Crimes against Internationally Protected Persons (1974).
[6] Convention on Taking of Hostages (1979).
[7] Convention on the Safety of Maritime Navigation (1988).
[8] Convention on Unlawful Acts and Violence at Airports Serving Civil Aviation (1988).
[9] Convention on Suppression of Terrorist Bombings (1997).

two separate ad hoc criminal tribunals: the International Criminal Tribunal for the former Yugoslavia (ICTFY)[10] and the International Criminal Tribunal for Rwanda (ICTR).[11] Both courts are still at work more than ten years later. As of 2004, the ICTFY has concluded seventeen cases, but over sixty cases are still pending, including the major trial of former Yugoslav President Slobodan Milosevic. The ICTR has concluded thirteen cases, and another sixty-two are in progress.

Two obvious criticisms cannot be avoided. Both tribunals took years to get organized and to collect evidence. Only a small fraction of the guilty parties have been indicted, and many are still at large. In addition, the ICTFY has been accused of an anti-Serb bias, as few non-Serbs have been indicted despite evident atrocities committed by persons of all ethnic groups. On the other hand, the cases handled by both tribunals have brought praise for their careful and thorough procedures followed and results obtained. Perhaps the most significant precedent set was a judgment of the ICTFY on February 22, 2001[12] sentencing three Serbs to prison for operating a "rape camp" against Muslim women. The judgment established that sexual violence may amount to international crimes against humanity as well as torture.

## HYBRID INTERNATIONAL COURTS

Yet another model for international criminal prosecutions emerged in the late 1990s: hybrid international courts. By agreement between the United Nations and the states concerned, hybrid international criminal courts are now operating in Kosovo, East Timor, Sierra Leone, and Cambodia. These four courts enforce a combination of international and domestic criminal law. They are staffed by both local and international judges, prosecutors, and administrators and are based in the states in which they operate. These four courts are very new, and it is too early to judge their work. However, they appear to share the defects of the ICTFY and the ICTR: The disparate nature of the staff means there is difficulty – years of lost time and expense – getting started in any meaningful way. Their chief merit appears to be political: Their existence is a demonstration of the moral outrage of the international community. It is little noticed that most of the perpetrators of international crimes will never be brought to justice.

---

[10]  SC Res. 827 (1993).              [11]  SC Res. 955 (1994)
[12]  Cases of Kunarac, Kovac, and Vukovic, available at www.un.org/icty.

## LOCKERBIE AND PINOCHET

### Lockerbie

On December 21, 1988, 183 people were killed when Pan American Flight 103 was horribly blown apart over Lockerbie, Scotland shortly after takeoff from London's Heathrow Airport. After meticulous reconstruction of the aircraft and careful examination of physical and documentary evidence the bomb suitcase responsible for the blast was found, and clothing and a fragment of an electronic timer that were packed inside were traced to two Libyan government officials, Al Amin Fhima and Abdelbaset al-Megrahi. When Libya refused to cooperate with the investigation, the U.N. Security Council, at the request of the United States and United Kingdom, imposed stiff sanctions that isolated Libya dramatically, both politically and economically.

The sanctions cut deeply, and Libya relented finally in 1998, agreeing to turn the two wanted men over for trial in The Hague under Scottish law. After an eight- month trial before a special criminal court featuring the testimony of 235 witnesses, one of the defendants, al-Megrahi, was convicted of murder under Scottish law. The verdict on the other defendant Fhima was "not proven," a formula used under Scottish law when the court is convinced of guilt but the evidence does not rise to the level of "beyond a reasonable doubt."

The verdict in the Lockerbie case trial was much less than satisfying. Not only did the defendant Fhima who was acquitted return to Libya to receive a hero's welcome, but the court also made no findings as to the involvement of the Libyan government or, as many believe,[13] the involvement of the government of Iran in the Pan Am 103 bombing.

### Pinochet

A second celebrated international criminal case was Spain's recent attempt to extradite Augusto Pinochet from the United Kingdom. General Pinochet, the former president of Chile, was implicated by investigations conducted by the Chilean government in 2,095 extrajudicial executions and 1,102 "disappearances" of people who have never been found.[14] The Spanish government, having indicted General Pinochet for the torture and murder of several Spanish citizens, sought the extradition of Pinochet when he entered Britain for

[13]  Michael P. Scharf, "The Lockerbie Trial Verdicts," *American Society of International Law, ASIL Insights,* Feb. 2001, available at www.asil.org/insights.
[14]  *The Economist,* Nov. 28, 1998, p. 23.

medical treatment. In a landmark ruling, the judicial committee of the House of Lords, Britain's highest court, ruled 3–2 that Pinochet could be extradited.[15] The split decision, despite the despicable nature of Pinochet's alleged crimes, is explained by the fact that the Law Lords (in the majority) were clearly stretching to make their point. In fact, a straightforward application of the law would be in Pinochet's favor. First, the alleged crimes were committed while Pinochet was head of state. A head of state, like an ambassador, enjoys immunity under English law with respect to official acts, but the majority brushed this aside on the basis that an exception exists for murder, hostage taking and torture because these acts are not the normal function of a head of state. Although this decision may be welcome, it is clearly not logical. General Pinochet was clearly acting as head of state while doing his dirty work; no one believes he was simply a murderer on the side.

A second problem with the Pinochet ruling is jurisdiction. Because the murders occurred outside the United Kingdom and neither the victims nor Pinochet were U.K. citizens, there was s strong argument under English law (accepted by the two dissenting Law Lords) that the English courts were without jurisdiction. The majority found a basis for jurisdiction, however, in the 1984 Torture Convention and the 1979 Hostage-Taking Convention to which Britain was a party. This appears to be the correct decision because Spain, the requesting party, clearly had jurisdiction, as the alleged murder victims were Spanish. Despite the English court ruling, Pinochet was not extradited because the United Kingdom determined he was in ill health, and he was allowed to return to Chile. Nevertheless, Pinochet will finally have to answer for his conduct. In 2005, Chile stripped him of his immunity and ordered that he stand trial under Chilean law.

Both the Lockerbie case and the Pinochet case illustrate the difficulty of handling certain types of criminal activity under current legal conditions. In both of these cases national criminal laws were used to prosecute essentially international crimes. In both instances, responsible officials and courts experienced difficulty and less than satisfactory decisions resulted.

## NOW: SADDAM HUSSEIN

The difficulty of pursuing international crimes is illustrated by the problem of trying Saddam Hussein, who is now in custody in Iraq. Saddam's alleged

---

[15] *Ex Parte Pinochet*, [2000] 1 AC 147 (House of Lords). General Pinochet was subsequently allowed to return to his home in Chile because of ill health. He was never in fact turned over to Spain.

292    International Relations – The Path Not Taken

crimes run the gamut many times over of all the international crimes ever invented: genocide, war crimes, crimes against humanity, and aggressive war. Conviction would seem to be a cakewalk. Yet, what court should put Saddam on trial?

After much discussion, Saddam is being prosecuted by a special Iraqi court – the "Iraqi Special Tribunal for Crimes Against Humanity" – under a statute adopted by Iraq's Governing Council on December 10, 2003. This law confers jurisdiction for special crimes (tailored to Saddam's case) committed between July 16, 1968 and May 1, 2003. It remains to be seen whether this special Iraqi tribunal will be up to handling this high-profile case and whether the members of Saddam's regime will be prosecuted fairly and efficiently.

Ever since Saddam was captured hiding in his spider hole, the United States made clear that the United Nations should not be involved. Giving the United Nations a role would bring in international law and standards of justice and might lend credibility to the effort to create a viable international criminal law system. So the United States turned instead to Salem Chalabi, a London-based Iraqi commercial lawyer, who was the nephew of former Pentagon favorite, Ahmed Chalabi. As a result the U.S.-trained Iraqi Special Tribunal is handling the prosecution of Saddam and his mates, and the United Nations is watching from afar.

This U.S. strategy of shutting out the United Nations seems to be backfiring and playing into the hands of the Iraqi insurgency. The United Nations could have provided global credibility and international expertise. Without it, the prosecution of Saddam takes on the air of "victors' justice" and puts unwarranted pressure on the fledgling Iraqi government, which is having trouble establishing its credibility with Sunni Muslims who comprised Saddam's political base.

## THE INTERNATIONAL CRIMINAL COURT

The International Criminal Court (ICC) was created to take jurisdiction over the "most serious crimes of concern to the international community as a whole."[16] The ICC has handled no cases yet, so the questions are how will this court develop, and is it necessary and desirable to have a standing, permanent international criminal court?

---

[16] Rome Statute of the International Criminal Court, Preamble, available at www.un.org/law/icc/statute/romefra.htm.

## Crimes

To begin with at least, the ICC has jurisdiction over only four crimes[17]:

1. *Grave and serious breaches of the laws of war*: for example, intentional targeting of civilians, the use of illegal weapons, and attacking undefended towns that are not military objectives

2. *Crimes against humanity*: for example, murder, rape, the forcible transfer of population, torture that is part of a widespread or systematic policy or practice

3. *Genocide*: killings and other acts committed with the intent to destroy in whole or in part a national, ethnic, racial, or religious group

4. *Aggression*: but only after the parties adopt a definition of this crime by amendment of the Rome Statute

No one would deny that these four are international crimes.

Two sensitive issues immediately face the court. One is how to distinguish grave breaches of the laws of war, which are liable to prosecution, from less than grave breaches, which are not. This question can only be answered by the determination of which individual cases to bring before the court and their outcomes. This is why the immediate future, the formative period of the court, is a crucial time for the future of international criminal law.

A second question is how to define the crime of aggression. There is no doubt that aggression is an international crime; this was the most important of the charges in the Nuremberg and Tokyo war trials. Yet, there has been no international criminal proceeding for aggression since 1946 because the definition of aggression is so political. To be credible, this definition must carefully distinguish between a war that is intended and designed to take over another state or territory, which is the essence of aggression, and a war in violation of international treaties or the U.N. Charter, which is not. For example, the 1990 takeover of Kuwait by Saddam Hussein's Iraq was certainly aggression, whereas George W. Bush's 2003 Iraq War, although a violation of the U.N. Charter, was not, because there was never any intent to end the sovereignty or independence of Iraq. It is crucial that the ICC draw this distinction; otherwise, it is will deservedly lose all credibility.

---

[17] Ibid., Arts. 5–9.

## Staffing

The ICC consists of eighteen judges elected by secret ballot at a meeting of the states that are parties to the Rome Statute. Their basic term of office is nine years, and they are not subject to reelection. Judges are assigned to the pretrial, trial, or appeals division of the court.

A person with extensive practical experience, who is elected by secret ballot of the states' parties, heads the Office of Prosecutor. One or more deputy prosecutors are selected the same way from a list of nominees provided by the prosecutor. Both prosecutors are limited to nonrenewable terms of nine years.

A registrar is the principal administrative official of the court; he or she is elected by majority vote of the judges of the court and serves for a renewable term of five years (see The International Criminal Court).

## Jurisdiction

The Rome Statute for the ICC states that the court may exercise jurisdiction only in cases in which (1) the alleged crime has been committed in the territory of a party or (2) the accused is a national of a party. This means that the ICC may exercise jurisdiction over citizens of a nonparty, such as the United States, who commit alleged crimes in the territory of a party.

A key limitation to ICC jurisdiction is Article 17 of the Rome Statute, which declares that a case is inadmissible before the ICC if the matter is under investigation or is being prosecuted by a state that has jurisdiction, "unless the state is unwilling or unable genuinely to carry out the investigation or prosecution." Because this is a crucial matter, the Rome Statute defines "unwillingness" to include three situations:

1. where the investigation or prosecution is really for the purpose of shielding the person concerned

2. where there is unjustified delay

3. where the proceedings are not impartial or objective

The "unwillingness" criteria are designed to be high hurdles: the ICC's jurisdiction is expressly intended to be secondary and complementary to national criminal proceedings. Only where the national investigation is clearly a sham can the ICC intervene.

The ICC has additional safeguards against overzealous prosecution. First, the ICC Prosecutor cannot bring a case on his or her own; he or she must first obtain authorization from the seven-judge pretrial chamber of the court.

**THE INTERNATIONAL CRIMINAL COURT: ORGANS OF THE COURT**

### The Presidency

The Presidency is responsible for the proper administration of the Court, with the exception of the Office of the Prosecutor. However, the Presidency shall coordinate with and seek the concurrence of the Prosecutor on all matters of mutual concern. The judicial functions of the Court are carried out in each division by Chambers: the Appeals Chamber, the Trial Chamber, and the Pretrial Chamber.

### The Office of the Prosecutor

The Office of the Prosecutor shall act independently as a separate organ of the Court. It shall be responsible for receiving referrals and any substantiated information on crimes within the jurisdiction of the Court, for examining them, and for conducting investigations and prosecutions before the Court.

### The Registry

The Registry shall be responsible for the nonjudicial aspects of the administration and servicing of the Court, without prejudice to the functions and powers of the Prosecutor.

*Source:* Maanweg 174, 2516 AB, The Hague, The Netherlands / Post Office Box 19519, 2500 CM, The Hague, The Netherlands Tel.: +31 70 515 85 15 • Fax: +31 70 515 85 55• http://www.icc-cpi.int

Second, the Security Council may, by resolution, block the commencement or continuation of an investigation for up to 12 months.

But these limitations and safeguards were not enough to satisfy the United States, which wanted the ICC's jurisdiction to be triggered only by a Security Council referral. The U.S. position is clearly unreasonable: Making the ICC an arm of the Security Council would destroy its independence, objectivity, and credibility. It would turn the ICC into an ad hoc body similar to the ICTFY and the ICTR. The safeguards surrounding the ICC's ability to take a case seem sufficient. Not only is jurisdiction secondary to national courts but the necessity to gain the pretrial chamber's permission to proceed is also a guarantee that a prosecution will not be political and will be undertaken only where absolutely necessary. Moreover, the United States should have more confidence in its own system of justice. To avoid the ICC, the United States only has to notify the court that it has begun an investigation or criminal process. If the ICC Prosecutor decides to go ahead despite this, the ICC can block this action, or the United States can go to the court to override the ICC Prosecutor.[18]

These provisions go overboard in meeting U.S. demands for safeguards against runaway prosecutions of Americans for political reasons. What the United States demands – specific Security Council authorization for every prosecution – is unreasonable because it amounts to a demand that the United States control the ICC. U.S. control is unacceptable for an independent international court.

## International Criminal Responsibility

The ICC statute contains several provisions that define the scope of an individual's criminal responsibility under international law. A person may be criminally responsible not only for committing any of the acts defined as crimes but also for planning, instigating, ordering, or aiding and abetting such acts. This is intended to implicate people who have "command responsibility"; such persons will not be able to shield themselves from criminal prosecution if they "knew or had reason to know" that subordinates were about to commit the criminal acts and they did not try and prevent them or to punish the perpetrators. To make this point crystal clear, the statute contains an express statement that "all persons," regardless of their official capacity and even a head of state or government, may be criminally liable.

As far as lower-echelon personnel are concerned, the Rome Statute states that they are not excused per se, on grounds that they were following orders. However, "superior orders" can be a mitigating factor in their sentencing.

### TERRORISM AS AN INTERNATIONAL CRIME

One of the deficiencies of the ICC that should be remedied is that terrorism is not an international crime under the Rome Statute. Furthermore, the international conventions and U.N. resolutions condemning various forms

---

[18] In addition, steps can be taken to enhance the political accountability of the ICC Prosecutor, such as requiring prosecutorial guidelines to be made public, in order to constrain and shape prosecutorial decisions. Allison Marston Danner, "Enhancing the Legitimacy and Accountability of Prosecutorial Discretion at the International Criminal Court," 97 *American Journal of International Law* 510 (2003).

of terrorism (bombings, hostage taking, etc.) do not make terrorism in any form an international crime. Thus, terrorism is criminal, if at all, only under national laws. This is a legal loophole that should be closed. It is not even clear that there is universal jurisdiction – meaning that a state other than the one where the act was committed can prosecute – over terrorism. Thus, we are not using international law to its full potential in the international fight against terrorism.

Two reforms are essential in order to upgrade international law as a weapon against terrorism. First, a single definition of the crime of terrorism should be adopted that includes all the disparate acts terrorists may commit; this would criminalize all the forms of terrorism under international law. Such a definition can be taken from the 1999 U.N. General Assembly resolution that adopted the International Convention for the Suppression of the Financing of Terrorism.[19] Under this definition terrorism is

any . . . act intended to cause death or serious bodily injury to a civilian, or to any other person not taking an active part in the hostilities in a situation of armed conflict, when the purpose of such act, by its nature or context, is to intimidate a population, or to compel a government or an international organization to do or abstain from doing an act.

This definition is comprehensive, simple, and to the point; it succinctly summarizes all the elements of a terrorist act. It should be formally adopted by amendment to the ICC's Rome Statute in order to add terrorism to the ICC's list of crimes.

The second needed reform is to confirm that the crime of terrorism gives rise to universal jurisdiction under international law. This means that any act of terrorism can be prosecuted in every state of the world, as well as in the ICC. These two reforms would make sure terrorists can claim no sanctuary anywhere on earth.

The crime of terrorism can be added to the ICC's jurisdiction if parties to the court's Rome Statute approve it at a future review conference. Unfortunately, the United States will be unable to participate in future conferences because of its rejection of the ICC.

## THE U.S. REJECTION OF THE ICC

The refusal by the United States to adhere to the ICC is based on the lack of direct American control over its activities. This translates into an unwarranted

---

[19]  GA Res. 54/109 (9 Dec. 1999).

fear that the ICC will be hostile to the United States. President Bush plays upon this fear by castigating the ICC as "a foreign court. . . . where unaccountable judges. . . . put our troops and officials at an unacceptable risk of politically motivated prosecutions." Since deciding to withdraw its signature from the court in May 2002, the United States has waged a continuing campaign against the ICC by withdrawing aid from countries that refuse to sign a pledge shielding Americans from prosecution at the ICC. More than twenty nations have received this punishment, including Mali (a rare democracy in Africa), Ecuador (key to the war against drugs), and Croatia (a struggling democracy). The United States has also tried to bully the U.N. Security Council into granting it blanket immunity by threatening to veto U.N. peacekeeping missions. The Congress also acted, passing a law that contains what is commonly referred to as "The Hague invasion clause" because it authorizes the use of American troops "as necessary" to liberate American service personnel from the dastardly clutches of the ICC.

These tactics have backfired. The United States is not capable of destroying the ICC; most U.N. members, including all of America's allies, are participating in it,[20] and the court is now open for business. Ironically, the United States is isolated and suffering the consequences. The campaign to destroy the court has only angered other nations and strengthened their resolve. By remaining outside the court, the United States increases the chances that Americans will be subject to prosecution. If the United States were to join the ICC, it would be able to shape the direction of the court and make sure it is never used for political prosecutions.

The American campaign against the ICC has produced strange twists of events. For example, although the United States led the fight to stop the human rights abuses in the western Sudan province of Darfur, when a U.N. Commission of Inquiry in 2005 found that Sudanese government forces and militias had conducted indiscriminate attacks on civilians that amount to war crimes and crimes against humanity and recommended that the U.N. Security Council immediately refer the matter to the ICC for investigation and possible prosecution of the persons involved, the United States brandished its veto, protesting that it would not be a "party to legitimizing the ICC." The U.S. administration put its futile attempt to undermine the ICC above its interest in upholding international order and human rights. Finally, after weeks of

---

[20] Of the 139 states that have signed the Statute of the Court, 99 have ratified and become full "state parties." These include all twenty-five members of the European Union, all members of NATO (except Turkey, which is in the process of joining), Japan, South Korea, and nine of the fifteen members of the U.N. Security Council.

delay, a compromise deal was struck allowing the United States to abstain, and a U.N. Security Council resolution referring a list of war crimes suspects to the ICC was approved.[21]

The ICC has made a promising beginning despite the all-out U.S. campaign against it. In addition to opening a probe of alleged war crimes in Darfur, in October 2005 the court issued its first arrest warrants, for five members of Uganda's notoriously cruel Lord's Resistance Army, a group that is accused of abducting more than 30,000 children and forcing them to become either fighters, porters or concubines, in addition to killing thousands and forcing more than a million people to flee their homes.

## SUMMING UP

International criminal law as a facet of international relations is in a formative period. The permanent International Criminal Court, created in the 1998 after over forty years of discussions, has just begun to function. For the first time in history, individuals face a continuing, broad scope of criminal responsibility, and even heads of state are not immune.

The International Criminal Court has the capacity to act as a strong deterrent to leaders of countries who may be tempted to commit violations of human rights – punishment awaits those who commit international crimes. The U.N. High Level Panel advised in December 2004 that the U.N. Security Council should stand ready to refer cases to the ICC. In 2005, a U.N. Commission of Inquiry formally recommended that the ICC launch an investigation and possible prosecutions of war crimes and crimes against humanity in Sudan's western province of Darfur, but ironically this was opposed by the United States.

The ICC and international criminal law have great promise, but the management of this new system of law presents many difficulties. The next few years are especially crucial. The purpose of this new chapter in international relations is not only to punish criminal conduct but also to deter states, individuals, and groups from engaging in the nefarious activities that have scarred the international community in the past and continue today.

It is particularly unfortunate that the United States has passed up the opportunity to be a part of this effort to create a working system of international criminal justice. Ninety-nine states have ratified the ICC, including all the Western democracies except the United States. The system will thus proceed,

---

[21] United Nations Security Council Resolution 1593 (2005).

but without U.S. leadership, influence, and ideas. The U.S. decision not to join is counterproductive, depriving it of the opportunity to shape this important new court, which is going to become an important feature of international relations. The ICC may have flaws, but the way to fix them is to join and exercise positive leadership, not to sulk and go home.

The U.S. decision not to join is based on the idea of the lack of U.S. control, the fear that overzealous prosecution may unfairly target Americans for political reasons. Ironically, this is more likely to occur with the United States outside the ICC than in it. Being outside the ICC does not insulate a state's nationals from ICC prosecution. Americans can still be prosecuted if they commit an international crime in the territory of one of the parties to the ICC.

The United States has attempted to undermine the court and insulate Americans from ICC jurisdiction through two methods: (1) by negotiating agreements with ICC parties that Americans will not be submitted to the court without U.S. consent and (2) by pushing the U.N. Security Council to pass successive twelve-month deferrals of all prosecutions without Security Council consent.

These actions have angered many states, including close U.S. allies who support the ICC. As a result, there is great resentment against the United States, as other states see the United States now using raw power to obtain what it could not get at the negotiating table – total U.S. control over the ICC. The United States persists in its position, however, and routinely blocks U.N. peacekeeping missions without a proviso suspending ICC operations. For example, in June 2002, the United States vetoed a Security Council resolution to extend U.N. peacekeeping operations in Bosnia-Herzegovina until its got its way.

Ironically, opposition to the ICC did not stop the Bush administration from asking the United Nations for help in setting up criminal court systems in both Afghanistan and Iraq. The United Nations is helping in Afghanistan, but not yet in Iraq.

U.S. unilateralism with respect to the nascent system of international criminal law has reached the point where now the United States actively undermines the international community. In doing so, it not only rejects the values for which it has always stood but it also passes up the opportunity to use the international criminal justice system to fulfill its own interests in combating terrorism and creating a more peaceful world.

Fortunately, the U.S. government's position on the ICC does not prevent individual Americans from making a significant contribution to international criminal justice. For example, Marilyn Justman Kaman, a judge for the 4th

Judicial District of Minnesota in Minneapolis served as a volunteer international judge in Kosovo in 2002–2003 hearing cases that ranged from war crimes to trafficking in drugs and human beings. About her experience, she says, "I returned to my work as a state court judge, [but] my perspective has been permanently altered, as has my appreciation for the rule of law. It is now difficult for me to conceive of a world without the U.N. and its men and women whose mission is . . . " to save succeeding generations from the scourge of war, and to reaffirm faith in fundamental human rights . . . in the equal rights of men and women and of nations large and small, and to establish conditions under which justice and respect to the obligations arising from international law can be maintained." [Preamble of the Charter of the United Nations].[22]

## FURTHER READINGS

Philippe Sands, *From Nuremburg to The Hague* (2003).

Steven R. Ratner and James L Bischoff eds., *International War Crimes Trials: Making a Difference?* (2003).

William A. Schabas, *An Introduction to the International Criminal Court* (2d ed.) (2004).

Kurt Dormann, *Elements of War Crimes under the Rome Statute of the International Criminal Court* (2003).

Antonio Cassese, *International Criminal Law* (2003).

G. Kirk McDonald and O. Swaak-Goldman, *Substantive and Procedural Aspects of International Criminal Law* (2000).

[22] American Bar Association, *International Law News* (Summer 2005), p. 13.

# 10 Conclusions

"If America wants the rest of the world to be part of the agenda it has set, it must be part of their agenda too."
Prime Minister Tony Blair, Davos, Switzerland, January 27, 2005

In the twenty-first century we must strive for a goal that has long eluded humankind: international peace and security. To accomplish this we must invent a new kind of international society based on the rule of law. The rule of law is essential to international society just as it is to domestic order.

But the rule of law is much more difficult to achieve on the international plane. A key is the commitment of all states to international law and international institutions. There must be a realization that the problems of peace and security to a great extent are not soluble by unilateral action even by the most powerful of states. Multilateralism is therefore essential.

But law and international institutions alone cannot assure peace and security without another essential ingredient: *justice*.

Justice starts with legitimacy, which, as President George W. Bush said in his Second Inaugural Address in 2005, means democracy, liberty, and an end to tyranny everywhere in the world. Liberty means the implementation of human rights recognized in the Universal Declaration of Human Rights. Liberty also means tolerance; groups who claim to have a hold on religion or other "truth" must be tolerant of those who do not accept their ideas and beliefs.

Justice also has an economic dimension. International society must organize to fight poverty and disease. Justice also means addressing pressing international environmental problems that threaten global security and prosperity.

The overriding problem of our time is to create a *new global order*, an international order capable of dealing with the challenges and problems we face in the twenty-first century. With the end of the Cold War there was a chance for a new beginning, the establishment of new patterns of international relations. As syndicated columnist Charles Krauthammer has said, "America is no mere international citizen. It is the dominant power in the world, more dominant than any since Rome. Accordingly, America is in a position to reshape norms, alter expectations, and create new realities."[1]

Yet, almost twenty years after the end of the Cold War, U.S. and the world seem on the verge of squandering the opportunity to reshape the world order. Disappointingly, U.S. foreign policy is too often dangerously unilateral and contemptuous of multilateralism. This view should be compared to a new paradigm of international relations – a path not yet taken by the United States – created in the last half of the twentieth century. This paradigm is still incomplete and in the process of being born, but it offers new ways of state cooperation and new forums for interactions among international actors. This paradigm bases international relations on international law and international institutions, as well as on concepts of justice and human rights. This new model is espoused by a growing number of states of the world, especially by the European Union. It offers a vision of a new world public order – one that can bring prosperity, peace, and security to the world.

This new twenty-first century paradigm of international relations has several elements:

■ *Important individual state interests have converged with the collective interests of humanity.* The very concept of international interests has shifted. International problems are interconnected. The terrorist attacks of September 11, 2001 had their seeds in conflicts in the Middle East and Afghanistan. A state located in North America can no longer ignore disease, disasters, and other human suffering in Africa or Asia because it is not within its sphere of interests. That day is clearly past. Witness the Asian tsunami disaster of 2004 – all states and people all over the world were profoundly moved and wanted to help. No state could say it is not our concern. In the twenty-first century the most important problems involve all humanity – how to reduce disease, poverty, and suffering caused by disasters and how to promote peace, democracy, security, and justice in the world.

■ *The unilateral assertion of power often has very limited utility or effect.* Military power is a blunt instrument; it has its place, but it is never sufficient and not usually even the best solution to a problem. The Iraq War of 2003 is a definitive demonstration of the limitations of the world's most advanced military force. Reducing cities to rubble and killing people are never going

---

[1] *Time*, March 5, 2001, at 42.

to accomplish broader political purposes; indeed, wielding military power is often counterproductive.

■ *Collective action and the observance of international law are the keys to world public order.* No one state, no matter how rich or how powerful, can guarantee peace and security or solve international problems.

■ *International institutions have a growing (if still imperfect) capacity to exercise collective action to deal with world problems.* These institutions are, to varying degrees, still imperfect, but they have the potential of introducing new forms of international cooperation and collective action. The foremost among these is the U.N. system, which is badly out of date and in need of reform.

■ *International law has come of age.* Because of the growth of international law over the past 100 years, we have the opportunity to extend the rule of law over international human affairs for the first time in human history.

■ *International organizations, transnational companies and NGOs are important.* States are no longer the only international actors in the world. States share the international stage with influential new actors – international organizations, transnational companies, and NGOs.

■ *Important new methods of international cooperation and dispute settlement have been created since 1945.* These new forums, institutions, procedures and methods belie the realist paradigm that state cooperation is rare and difficult. An example of such new cooperation is the European Union – twenty-five sovereign states that have chosen to vest significant sovereign powers in supranational institutions.

■ *State power is most effectively exercised through collective institutions.* Powerful states, such as the United States, can accomplish their purposes through exercising influence and persuasion within international institutions and through established forms and procedures. Of course, power is still important in the world, but power can be maximized through leadership, diplomacy, and international political processes.

This is not an idealistic claim that power will or even should become irrelevant to world order. Power will always be important. But the lesson of history is that it should not be allowed to become dominant; power must be tempered by the rule of law.

Of course, it is quite easy to make the case that international institutions and law do not operate as effectively as they should. But those who argue that international law is irrelevant must present a better and more feasible alternative. That demonstration has not been done. So the only way forward is to improve on the law and the institutions we have. From the perspective of the years since 1945, great progress has been made. If we continue improving the international system, by the centennial of the United Nations in 2045, we may see a real difference in the global world order.

The attacks of September 11, 2001 caused the United States to ignore to a great extent its own ideals and the work it has labored to create throughout much of the twentieth century – the rule of law in international affairs. Ignoring international norms and institutions is not only counterproductive but also takes away the very advantage the United States possesses as the most powerful weapon against the forces of inhumanity – respect for freedom, democracy, human rights, and the rule of law.

# Index

# Index

313

state-interests theory and, 41
theories of, 44, 56–58
in WWI, 18
international society
definition of, 64, 71
international law creating, 59, 68–69,
70–71, 89
origin of, 70–71
IR. *See* international relations
Iran, 103–104, 134–135, 137–138, 140–141
Iraq 1991 war
under Bush, G. H. W., 2–3, 7
Hussein humiliated in, 1–2
multilateralism in, 9–10, 51–52
oil-for-food program and, 117–118, 119–120
outcome of, 1–2, 104–105
reasons for, 7, 293
2003 war v., 3–4, 5, 7
U.N. and, 1–2, 10, 104–105, 115–116
WMDs in, 1–2
Iraq 2003 war
Annan and, 8, 121
Bin Laden and, 7
Britain in, 4, 5–6
casualties of, 3
causes of, 5–6, 7, 33
CIA's failures in, 6, 120
coalition of the willing in, ix, 4, 89, 102,
137–138
economic burden of, 3–4
elections following, 120
France against, 4
Franks on, 3
Germany against, 4
homeland security and, xii–xiii
Hussein removed in, 1–3, 5, 8, 45, 112–113
insurgency of, 7
international institutions bypassed in, 8,
10–11
international law bypassed in, 8, 10–11,
61
Iraqi Special Tribunal of, 291–292
NATO in, ix, 45, 120
9/11 Commission Report on, x, xii–xiii
1991 war v., 3–4, 5, 7
oil-for-food program and, 117–118, 119–120
political costs of, 4
as preventative war, 112–113
Al Qaeda and, xii–xiii, 5, 7, 120

reasons for, 2–3, 7, 8, 14–15, 120, 293
reconstruction after, 3–4
regime change in, 1–2, 5, 8, 45, 112–113
Spain's withdrawal from, 4
U.N. and, ix, 4, 5–6, 7, 8, 10, 45, 52,
104–105, 111–112, 119–121
unilateralism in, 9–10
WMD and, 7, 8, 33, 120
Al Zarqawi in, 7
Islam. *See* Muslim world
Israeli-Palestinian conflict
human rights and, 279–281, 282
multilateral diplomacy in, 14–15, 282
U.N. and, 115
WMD and, 137–138

Japan, 28, 242–243
Jefferson, Thomas, 253–254
Judis, John B., 99

Kant, Immanuel, 46, 56, 66, 104
Kaplan, Robert, xi, 28
Kellogg-Briand Pact, 9, 21, 45–46, 51–52,
286–287
Kennan, George, 66–67
Keohane, Robert, 58
Korean War, 25, 115
Kyoto Protocol
industry influenced by, 227–228
legal obligation to, 79, 89, 202–203,
210–211, 221–222, 224
limits of, 70, 221–227
U.S. and, x–xii, 10–11, 70, 79, 89, 202–203,
210–211, 217–218, 221–228

Lac Lanoux case, 206–207
LaGrand case, 265–267
League of Nations, 9, 21, 45–46, 51–52
legal obligation
foundation of, 69–70, 90–92
hierarchies of, 79
jus cogens as, 80
to Kyoto Protocol, 79, 89, 202–203, 210–211,
221–222, 224
Plato on, 91
primary rules of, 78–79
secondary rules of, 78–79
soft law and, 79–80, 202–203, 211, 247–248
to WTO, 168–169
liberal democracy. *See* democracy